Coastal Cruising

Coastal cruising is probably the most severe test in sailing due to the dangerous proximity of the land, entering and leaving the many different ports, calculating and overcoming the restrictions resulting from the tidal streams and the constant threat imposed by other seaborne traffic.

The British Isles has an endless range of situations, circumstances, weather variations, sea states, sights and scenes, history, geography, people and places to be experienced by sailing. It offers wonderful adventures that were beyond our imaginations at the outset. We learned this as we went along and only came to appreciate it slowly. This was and is, the ultimate way to learn to cruise.

Practical Coastal Cruiser

Serial

Starship

Paul Constantine

Distributed Moonshine Publications

© Paul Constantine 2014 Printed by: Gipping Press Ltd.
Distributed in the UK   Moonshine Publications

©Paul Constantine 2014
Distributed in the UK by
Moonshine Publications
14/IP12 4EU

Printed. Gipping Press Ltd
1b Lion Barn Industrial Est
Needham Market
Suffolk IP6 8NZ

ISBN 978-0-9572161-2-9

British Library Cataloguing in Publication data.
A catalogue record for this book is available from the British Library.

Typeset & design & illustration. Paul Constantine
Special thanks to Alison for proofreading and advice.

Distributed. www.moonshinepublications.co.uk

Some Contents. *(Also see index)*

The journey spans a time period of four years, but the years have been omitted so as not to deflect attention from the account. There are sufficient clues for anyone wishing to discover them. The times of year (months) are of greater importance.

Serial Starship

Preliminaries
How this book came to be written.

I was a member of the Multihull Offshore Cruising and Racing Association and was appointed the MOCRA Cruising Secretary. Following this, Jack Heming the editor of Multihull International contacted me. He asked me to send him some cruising news for inclusion in his publication. Eventually, I wrote 86 monthly episodes plus other material.

How the episodes are numbered.

The first episode was in issue number 206 of Multihull International and the account ran until issue 262 when it was broken as I changed my work. The story continued in issue 278 and was eventually concluded in issue 306. Three index episodes then followed. I have retained the original issue numbers and added chronological chapter numbers to make access and referencing as easy as possible.

Illustrations, Diagrams, Text.

Early stages of the journey were covered by my hand-drawn diagrams and sketch maps with hand lettering. As the journey continued I became more proficient and computer technology advanced rapidly. Initially I typed each episode on a portable typewriter. I progressed to an Amstrad word processor, and then moved to an Apple/Mac SE30 Pagemaker system. This has resulted in variations of the book text, because although it has all been translated into the same font, it sometimes appears differently. I have retained the diagrams as they were originally, because they partly indicate the gradual improvement in the quality of production throughout the span of time covered by the sailing. Many illustrations are scanned from the original magazine pages and printing on the reverse sometimes bleeds through. I hope this will not detract too heavily from what they show.

The Boat. *Starship*.

I made *Starship* in my back garden, working in my spare time. I built her singlehanded, because I wanted to know and understand every component part of her so that if anything failed I would know how to mend it. She measured 35 feet by 22 feet and was made of glassfibre and 'Airex' foam sandwich. She was based on an extremely successful design by Derek Kelsall called *'Three Legs of Mann'*. I also used the broader cross sections from another larger Kelsall cruising trimaran called *Inkwasi* on my shorter overall length.

Serial Starship

She was almost exactly the same size as the garden.

Starship cruised fairly extensively in European waters, having visited Netherlands, Norway, Sweden, and Denmark. As she now sails Round Britain Slowly, you can come too.

News report of Starship's visit to Norway.

This Round Britain journey was made without the use of modern electronic navigational aids except a rudimentary echo sounder. Initially there was no VHF radio.

Reading the story of the journey, without delay.

The original account had much fuller preliminary details about the boat in <u>the first three chapters</u>. These have been moved from this point to be recorded in the **Appendix** along with other details of the boat, at the end of the book for reference if needed.

Serial Starship

MI Issue 209. Episode 4.

First Leg, First steps.

The days leading up to sailing were very busy but finally we assembled just before Easter at 11.30 on Thursday April 4 for the fateful moment when I turned the ignition key to begin (as they say in the introduction to Star Trek) what could be ...

A five year mission, to explore new worlds, to seek out new life and new civilisations, to boldly go where no trimaran had gone before...

Nothing happened! There was a click from the engine and then silence. It had started first time, every time, right through the winter and had been running the previous day. It was a poor battery connection which was soon sorted out then actually it was one of the crew Ray, who started the motor to get us away.

Ray Weston was ex-merchant navy, ex-lightship crewman, who started his working life as a deckhand aboard Thames barges operating UNDER SAIL from the London River, despite his still youthful age of 'fortyish'. The other two crewmembers beside myself were Gill and Jerry. Gill had never sailed before but insisted on this adventurous opportunity, because she needed a bit of experience before going on a beginners sailing course the following week. Jerry Stebbing was a young chap who was building himself a Brown Searunner 31, and was (like me) a trimaran fanatic of the worst kind, constantly talking about comparative float volumes and parachute anchoring systems. Jerry is an excellent photographer.

We were leaving our home port of Woodbridge on the tiny River Deben which is on the England's East Coast just to the north of the Thames Estuary and our first target was to pass through the Dover Strait and reach Brighton Marina to change the crew, then go on again to find a stopover place in the Solent near the Isle of Wight.

We motored down the Deben because the wind was adverse. The ebb tide took us out of the river, still empty of yachts as we were at the beginning of the season. Once at sea, we hoisted sail at about two o'clock and came close hauled on the port tack to make a comfortable course of 160°m. This might have taken us too close to the Cork Sands but the spring ebb was setting us to the north. It was a bright day but patches of mist obscured the land from time to time and the heavy commercial traffic using Harwich and Felixstowe needed careful watching. Wind strength was about force three and after an hour I was pleased to find that we were doing about 5½ knots over the ground.

1. ***Book explanations*** *are in italics.*
2. *Throughout the journey account, compass directions will be given in magnetic, as that is what we used. It is simple and straightforward with little chance of calculating error.*

We passed the rusting anti-aircraft fort at Roughs Tower with its starkly silhouetted gun and then went on to pass south of the Sunk lightship at about 15.30. Holding the same course we reached the Long Sands Head cardinal mark, the outer tip of the hidden estuary sands, where the wind piped up a bit as we turned to go south, averaging 8 knots past the North East Knock buoy with a brief period of 10½ knots. It was nice to be *really* sailing again, but of course it was too good to last and no sooner had I made the calculation that at this rate we would reach Brighton Marina in time for breakfast, than it all began to crumble.

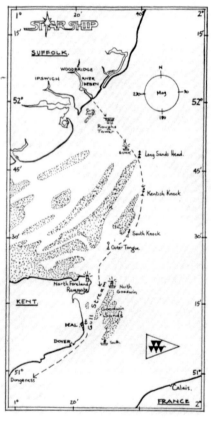

After the South Knock buoy we were crossing the Thames itself and within five minutes the wind moved from east to south to head us, forcing us either to sail into the river or out to sea. The tide was tumbling out of the Estuary, so despite us sailing 240°m into the river we still managed a fairly southerly track over the ground as far as the Outer Tongue at 16.30 when there was a significant increase in wind force to about force five with stronger gusts. Two crew were below in bunks, but Ray thanks to his immunity from sea sickness was busily peeling potatoes ready for a bit of cordon-bleu juggling. He came up to assist me whilst I reefed the boat down to improve the motion. It was a wild evening and coming dark prematurely, but the powerful lights on the North Foreland, and the North Goodwin were flashing clearly, so position fixing was secure. It was cold now and wind from the south west. I was wrestling with the decision whether to go outside the Goodwin Sands, or down through the inside passage, the Gull Stream. I dislike the Gull Stream in the dark, because the lights are tricky to pick out against shore lights and sometimes nearer smaller lights can be confused with more distant stronger ones. The rough weather convinced me to stay within the wind shadow of the land and this kept open another option, which was to stop either at Ramsgate or somewhere near Deal.

It became a dead beat with inexperienced hands on the wheel for I had to keep myself free for the tasks of sheeting in the genoa and the tricky navigating. At 21.30 just south of Ramsgate the wind began to moderate and ten minutes later we were back under full sail. At 22.30 just north of Deal the tide was about to change against us; the wind was dying and I was absolutely exhausted with this 'extended daysailing'. I rolled the genoa and motored in to anchor just off the beach at Deal near Walmer. This was the famous Downs anchorage where huge fleets of sailing craft used to gather to wait for a wind favourable to take them 'Down Channel'. It was here (for lovers of the stories) that Hornblower first joined his ship. We anchored alone and at the first attempt our small anchor dragged, so we set the bigger 35lb CQR with full scope at about midnight. I listened to the shipping forecast which gave gales everywhere except the south coast, which had S-W. 5-6 occasionally 7. Not good. I fell into bed with a heavy heart. The tide would turn favourable at about 05.30 when the battle strategy decision would have to be made.

Friday April 5.
I woke up a couple of times, because we were never still and I listened to the hum of the wind in the rigging, wondering what I should do if it was bad. Return to Ramsgate? Push around the corner to Dover? How could I communicate with the new crew who would be joining us in Brighton, (*we had no VHF radio at that time and mobiles had not been invented*.) At 04.00 the wind eased, and at 04.15 the boat began to swing, which indicated a south-going stream, so somewhere my calculations must have been amiss. The wind was down a great deal and if we were going to use the tide we had better make a move. I scrambled into my clothes and went through to grab something to eat, only to be faced with the greasy

remnants of last evening's washing up strewn everywhere in the galley, abandoned as the crew collapsed one by one. I set to and cleaned it up as Ray emerged to lend a hand and join an early bowl of cornflakes. By 04.45 we were ready to get under way again, but on the foredeck Ray was complaining that the anchor warp was stuck. Sinking heart again. I motored backwards and forwards, but with the warp lying underneath the boat I was uneasy about a fouled propeller, so I switched off. The warp felt quite solid and trapped somewhere near the stern, but the boat has no major obstructions other than rudder and propeller, yet she was lying stern to the tide across the anchor rode.

We had to do lots of pulling with extra ropes and luckily we were able to go out onto the floats to get better leverage. Eventually we worked the warp clear of the mainhull and as we cleared the rudder she came free and rotated around to face the right way. She had simply been lying across her warp, held in a balance of forces by the tidal stream. I was thankful that for once my worst fears had not been confirmed, that my £100 anchor was fouling my £250 prop and that something was going to have to be cut and lost.

We'd lost half an hour and expended our energy for the day before we got going in a wind of less than force two, which meant motoring with the main hoisted as the Dover Strait is hardly the place to be drifting around in. I expected the Force 5-7 to be arriving with the coming daylight and I wanted to at least claw around Dungeness before the tide went foul again.

At 07.00 we were dodging ferries and gazing at the Dover's western breakwater wall trying to imagine the size and force of waves which had recently crashed one of the huge Hovercrafts into its granite strength. The day was sunny and surprisingly mild, it was really quite pleasant. Everybody was in the cockpit for a second breakfast, as we headed towards the low shingle projection of Dungeness, which might have been almost invisible from afar had it not been for the monolithic mass of its nuclear power station apparently floating on the sea. Rounding beneath the shadow of the station at 10.10 we held a one-sided debate on the nature of nuclear power, the problems of nuclear waste and generally set the world to right with our cockpit discussion.

Crossing Rye Bay, one of the crew who does not wish to be identified had her first attempts at steering a compass course, which was great fun for everyone. 'New' numbers were discovered on the compass heading and Dungeness (behind us) passed the bow on a couple of the more exaggerated loops. Not to be outdone by such antics the power station provided some fireworks of its own by suddenly and explosively venting off such a huge volume of steam that it looked for all the world like a mini atom bomb and sounded only slightly quieter despite us being well to windward of it.

At mid-morning we sighted a powerful (military looking) hydrofoil passing us to seaward heading west, then at midday, a fast moving craft well inshore moving east. This second craft deflected its course and swept around towards us just as we were serving our lunch. It approach bows on from behind so that we could see no marking or detail of the craft, only its menacing bulk rearing above us. Two men stood at the bow. They wore no uniform, just anonymous blue clothes. They did not identify themselves in any way, but simply called questions across at us. 'Last port of call? Destination? Was this our boat?' We shouted our replies as we continued chugging along at four knots and soon they dropped back. When well clear they opened up their powerful engines to execute a quick turn and roar away across a flat sea. Only a small name plate *Seeker* gave a clue as to their identity. We immediately set the world to rights on the topics of piracy, smuggling and the question of firearms aboard boats.

13.10 found us off a misty headland just to the east of Hastings, still under motor on an even, glassy sea. Was it like this when William the Conqueror brought his invasion fleet in 1066? The shipping forecast gave us south-easterly force 4, which was the exact reverse direction from what we were experiencing. I used a fair chunk of the afternoon catching up on missed sleep as the others followed the scenic route about 1½ miles offshore, dodging lobster pots and inshore fishing boats.

At Beachy Head about 16.30 the tide swept us through the rougher stuff as rain descended onto the cockpit canopy.
Suddenly we emerged from the waves into a changed air mass. The mild warmth had gone and we were in clearer colder conditions. Darker clouds began to build in the south west and the quality of the white chalk cliffs, grey clouds and hazy pale sun gave us a strange feeling of having entered a faded new world.

We tried to count the Seven Sisters cliffs, but one of them appeared to have been indiscrete as we always arrived at eight for their total. Newhaven was strangely silent and appeared uninhabited as we passed the entrance. To the south a black and heavy cloud now extended right across the horizon whilst the sun overhead made a brave attempt to hang on just a little longer. The cloud advanced as we neared the marina entrance and the rain descended in a mighty deluge when we had about 100 metres to go. We grimly soldiered on with each crew member having a job to do and unable to escape the downpour. Rounding the corner we found a convenient berth just inside the first pontoon where a couple of friendly people took our lines at 19.00 exactly to conclude the first step of our journey.

Ray in Brighton Marina.   *Pic. Jerry Stebbing.*

Next morning when our bodies had recovered and we'd indulged in those luxuries of civilisation, the morning paper, fresh bread and milk, one of the crew read out the horoscope:

'You find the zestful energy to turn travel plans into trips to Paradise.'

Could this be Brighton Marina?

MI Issue 210. Episode 4.

Brighton Marina - Solent.
Easter on the English south coast that year was characterised by southerly gales which forced everyone to run for cover. Once inside the marina at Brighton there was no way out. The breakwater walls

could be as high as a house at low water, but when water was being driven over the top of them, there was a natural reluctance to leave, even if it had been possible to get out of the entrance.

We were stuck in port long after we were scheduled to leave and I was forced to resort to my most powerful magic trick for calming seas when in harbour. I paid a week's fees in advance. Then if the gale held out I would benefit from the discount on the weekly rate. IF the gale dropped I'd be free to leave (but would *LOSE* all the money for the extra payment ....Ouch!)

It was a desperate measure, but it worked ... and I lost my money.

On this short leg I had Jerry the photographer and trimaran builder who'd stayed on. Neal a computer student, who had no previous experience and my two sons, aged 13 and 10.

Tuesday 9 April.

From midnight onwards I was aware that the wind had dropped and that I should really be getting everybody out of bed at two o'clock in the morning to get going whilst the conditions were right. I didn't of course. Better to get the sleep, but I kept waking up to listen to the silence and fret that I was stuck in the harbour. I consoled myself by thinking that the sea was going down and I'd be able to get the latest shipping forecast, because for once I'd set my alarm. I missed it. The powers that be had moved it from one impossible time to an even more impossible one, 05.55... Madness!

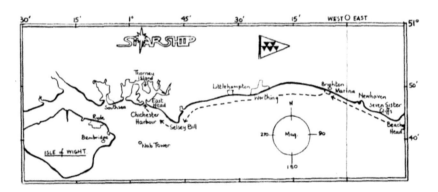

It made no difference, I'd decided to go. At 8.15 we motored out into a south-westerly Force 2 on a bright and sunny sea. All went well for a couple of hours whilst the tide was helpful. Then the tide went foul, the wind headed us and we found ourselves going either to Worthing (north), or Cherbourg (south). Between 10.00 and 11.00 we went through our worst patch as the wind shifted to head whichever direction we chose and we only made 3 miles directly towards Selsey Bill during that time. We finally decided on the inshore tack, so that at least we could have something to look at and the wind progressively freed to the South so that by 12.15 we were at last beginning to leave Worthing gasholder (conspic.) behind us.

At 13.15 we were off Littlehampton passing through the lee of a smelly dredger, admiring the rain clouds building into a storm ahead. An hour later great squalls of wind and rain forced us onto the southerly tack and under main alone we were creaming along at 6½ knots for a short while looking for East Borough Head buoy, which marks the dangerous banks off Selsey Bill. It is a treacherous place and whenever I pass, I always recall the loss of the former Prime Minister Ted Heath's ocean racer *Morning Cloud* there, overwhelmed by weight of seas. The wind had dropped again and we were beating under main and motor to maximise our tacks and give total control among the many shoals that we were entering.

After passing the buoy I continued sailing onwards into the narrow gap between the East Borough Head Shoal to starboard, and the Shoal of Lead to port. The course we sailed was like a valley between two mountains because we held the smooth water, yet witnessed the tumbling overfalls and standing waves of the tidal flow crashing with primitive force over the barriers just beneath the surface on either side. The gap grew smaller and our boat began to rise and fall on the reflected waves. We pressed ahead taking constant cross bearings on the cardinal marks, then turned at the optimum moment to be swept into the maelstrom of West Head. We were a leaf in a torrent, crashing through waves, driving ahead with cascades of water streaming from our decks. The wind was beginning to increase as we came to the tip of the Bill. We emerged from our ducking near to the Middle Owers, sailing faster and looking for the lateral marks which fixed the narrow exit from the Looe passage through which we were now moving.

On our port side the seas tumbled over the submerged Pullar Bank, like ocean waves onto an atoll, and occasionally one would detach itself from the turmoil to toss us casually with its mighty strength. The wind was momentarily up to force five and our tight course was freed. We gave her full sail and she leapt ahead. Her power was unleashed and she smoothly accelerated away, released, swift as an arrow. Up to eight knots she was aiming for the tight exit between the buoys and the only slick of level water.

Beyond it, ahead of us and right across our path lay a wall of water, foaming and tumbling like a stream over a precipice. We had no alternative. The helmsman asked for a chart check, but there was no escape, this was the correct course. Straight through and hold tight. We braced ourselves for the impact as she went faster and faster, accelerating towards the barrier of water. She hit the first wave and went straight through, knifing smoothly, hardly rising, and the next wave, and the next, we were into the thick of it, slicing, cutting, shrugging water aside, throwing it this way and that. The speed made all the difference. At East Borough Head just a little earlier we had laboured on a tight windward course without the wind power. We had crashed as a raft into steep wave fronts, or slid bumping into troughs down rough wave backs, but here, we had the power to defend ourselves and the speed deflected the worst blows of the sea. Spray went everywhere

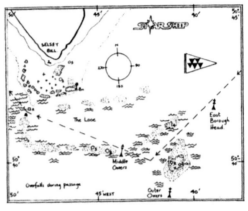

but we emerged exhilarated from a curtain of foam into the smoother seas of the Solent itself.

Visibility was good across to the south of the Isle of Wight where the pale grey, high land grew sharp edged out of rain clouds sweeping across behind the dark silhouette of Bembridge and Ryde. We aimed for Chichester on 320°m, baffled by a sudden drop of the wind now that we had cleared the Bill. The breeze shifted to north-west and fell to force two. This weather was determined to make us struggle for every inch of progress and we were forced to use the engine again.

We chugged along, alone in the biting cold wind. There was no commercial traffic to be seen and the Nab Tower stood a lonely grey smudge distantly behind us to port. The rain blotted out the tower blocks at Southsea and blustery showers peppered the deck.

The stronger gusts were suddenly sustained once more and going back westerly as we neared the land at Chichester Bar where we found the water tumbling out of the harbour. Black flurries now raced across the water towards our quarter and the boat swayed as they hit the sail. Engine off as we entered the rough water and the first wave broke under our stern pushing us along so that she tried to surf. Off she went with the helmsman struggling to try to get a grip as she finally picked up the surf. The speed was up to 10 or 12 and jets of water shot like rocket flames away from the back of the floats. A great water ski ride of speed and spray ensued, broad reaching on a stable platform into the entrance against the outward flowing river. The stream came at us at four knots looking like six, but it made no difference, we just skimmed over it as if it was a millpond and it was really good to be sailing a multihull.

We ran goosewinged through a deserted East Head, came on the wind as we entered the Thorney Channel where we close reached up through the moorings effortlessly against the tide in the rapidly shallowing creek.

A lone yachtsman greeted us from the cockpit of his polished clinker craft with a tender bobbing astern. The sun had emerged again and there was the prospect of a lovely still evening. We tacked and pirouetted as we manoeuvred for a mooring, putting on a show for our single audience. We were pleased with the exciting sail at the culmination of a day which had contained a fair proportion of slogging into adverse conditions. We were pleased with the beauty of this rural creek and pleased to have made it.

We had a lovely sunset; cooked sausages, bacon and eggs to celebrate then entertained our new-found friend who rowed over to welcome us and hear our story. The first step was concluded.

MI Issue 211. Episode 5.

East Solent holiday weekend cruise.   Early May.
Brian Hammond had hardly ever sailed a boat before. His previous experience amounted to the last twenty minutes since he had first taken the wheel and yet he found himself straining to hear the shouted commands above the thunderous noise of the flogging genoa, the deafening roar of the waves and the crash of the gear being thrown about inside the boat. "Go Left. Go Left." came the voice as he gazed blindly at the cascades of water streaming from the perspex doghouse windows only inches from his face. Another mighty thump shuddered through the hull as the boat plunged bodily into the next wave.

Behind him in the cockpit two men fought to tame a wild and dangerous jib sheet which beat with venom against the protective canopy. One blow could stun into senselessness. Muscle power and the machine gun rattle of the winch joined in the struggle for supremacy. "Spin the wheel, Right." Words torn against the wind. "Right. Right. Right!" The tension in body and structure as the sheet came tight. Crash! and the boat bodily buried so that for a moment only the reefed sails projected from the white foaming water channelling power down to drive the boat through the wave. Tacking hard, clawing to windward. Pressed on by the mighty tidal flow rushing out over the Bar on an exceptional spring tide. "Go about. Go about.... NOW!" came the command and Brian wondered desperately which way to turn the wheel. He saw nothing but water below him, around him; heard nothing but the overpowering sound of the breaking sea ... and if he could have thought, he might fleetingly have questioned, why was he here?

A couple of hours before we had left the boatyard at the head of the Thorney Channel in Chichester Harbour. Our departure had not been one of practiced smooth efficiency, purring away under diesel power. We rarely seem to start like that. We made our usual start. Engine inexplicably failing to fire; tide about to drop; one crewman missing ashore; the boat facing the wrong way and blocking everyone else's access to the river. Finally we limped away thanks to the 'belt and braces' arrangement of keeping the outboard for our inflatable tender in storage on a bracket on our transom. When the inboard refused to start at the vital moment, down went that tiny outboard and away went our 35ft trimaran with the missing crewman hanging onto the pulpit following a last minute desperate dive from the deck of an adjacent craft.

We crept out into the creek where the water was deeper, and hung onto a mooring for the crew to make a midday meal whilst the engine room mechanic (sometimes Captain) disappeared with his tool kit into the depths of the aft cabin.

The crew for this short weekend sail in the East Solent were Mavis and Brian (*actual name Bright, changed in this account to make it easier to understand*) coming along to discover what 'cruising' was all about. Gill and Paul B, some experience but keen to learn and my young son Roland, now such an experienced sailor that he usually stays below with the real excitement of comic books and Action Man. We were hoping to sail across the East Solent to look at Bembridge on the Isle of Wight and perhaps see other multihulls at a rally that was being held close by.

When our meal was completed and the fuel system bled, we turned our attention to the elements. Our course from Chichester to Bembridge was about 230 degrees which is about south-west. The wind was from the south-west and a solid force four with broken cloud and rather cold. On this particular weekend the sun and moon were so much in opposition that the earth's shadow eclipsed the moon, the net result of this heavenly situation was tides of a height and flow which would not be equalled again until close to the end of the year.

Not many people were beating their way out of Chichester Harbour on that afternoon. Glancing around the sides of the doghouse Brian could see only a lone dinghy entering, blown in beneath the broken wing of its shattered mast, the helmsman sitting disconsolate at the transom.

Once free of the impressive overfalls on the Bar, *Starship* settled to beat across to the Isle of Wight, to arrive near low water and unable to enter the shallow harbour of Bembridge. We picked up a mooring just north of the lifeboat slipway and scanned the proposed entry route across the sand flats through binoculars. We could see people walking in search of a seafood supper where soon we would be sailing. Very distantly, two men working on a beached yellow trimaran. The wind died with the onset of evening and as soon as the tide returned we began creeping in with everybody all around the deck edges giving a running commentary about what they could see on the bottom as we skimmed lightly across the flats with little more depth of water than is found in the average family bath on bath nights. The crux of the entry was buoy No 6, because we knew that from that point inwards the harbour had been dredged and safe passage was assured within the channel. Just as we approached the buoy we touched the bottom and stuck for a while, but soon we were off and past the vital mark. Once inside the harbour we had intended to pick up a mooring and have a good look around before proceeding further, but as we approached a chosen buoy we ran aground again and we were just beginning to get into a bit of a tangle when the Harbour Master's launch arrived to extract us from our difficulties.

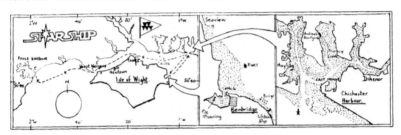

He had a perfect spot he said for a customer of our dimensions and led us up the harbour under tow in the gathering gloom, to a single pile where he attached our bow, then came around to the stern to lay out an anchor for us so that we would remain correctly aligned in the tiny area that was dredged around the post. He was most helpful and said we'd stay afloat providing our draught did not exceed two metres, but then added thoughtfully that after watching us 'tiptoeing through the tulips' to get in, there was little fear of that.

It was really quite dark when we got down to the really serious side of cruising, opening a bottle of wine and tucking into a four course meal with Mavis's sweet and sour pork chops and orange garnish as the main attraction. It was after midnight when we'd finished our first day's cruise.

The next day had warnings of gales, so we departed after breakfast to return to Chichester Harbour. On the way we spotted some of the multihulls racing in the rally. We noted an Iroquois 30 cat, a Telstar 26' trimaran, a 22' Hirondelle cat and that yellow Trailer-Tri from yesterday, but our eyes were taken with a 'no-compromise' Newick trimaran racer fast disappearing over the horizon under impeccably tailored canvas.

We zoomed back to Chichester Harbour in much clearer weather than on the previous day and had another hair-raising entrance in heavy running conditions with slower cruisers as obstacles on the course. We anchored off the sand dunes at East Head where Roland directed Paul B (a building site manager) in the building of a mighty sand castle. I watched the local racers from the comfort of the beach, especially the unfortunate crew of a racing keel boat who had cut things a bit fine, so they spent about four hours standing on a sand bank because their craft laid right over on its beam ends as the water receded.

That night it blew a gale from the south-west and we were pleased to be securely in harbour. Next morning the gale abated and a most glorious day ensued. We had a long breakfast and watched the world go by, then hoisted sufficient sail for the river and sailed gently around from Hayling to Itchenor overtaking everybody just to prove to ourselves that we were hotshot racers. Just after twelve o'clock we dropped our mainsail and drifted in idyllic conditions back up to the boatyard. We were sad to have to stop sailing, but it was a lovely conclusion to our holiday weekend cruise.

The fun had not quite ended yet. We returned as we had departed - in turmoil. Our approach to the jetty was a trifle too rapid. We checked the way off our boat a little too solidly and one of the crew, standing as rigid as a toy soldier toppled straight off the forward crossbeam into the river, to emerge feet first, still solidly 'to attention', and eventually still smiling. When we did eventually tie up we had sufficient wet clothing on deck to open a stall at a church fete. Casual observers would have thought that we'd rounded Cape Horn, at least.

MI issue 212. Episode 6.

Chichester Harbour,
Strange beginnings. 25 May.
It was all going to be quite simple. We had to start from Chichester Harbour and sail westwards through the Solent then leisurely cruise along the coast calling in to explore harbours along the way, aiming eventually to arrive in Plymouth. Our first target would be Poole Harbour. All quite simple. This time things would run smoothly; perhaps we could avoid incidents like the one where the crew fell overboard, as happened last time.

Serial Starship

<u>Very early Saturday morning</u>.
Our motto seems to be _'Don't do things easily if you can find a more difficult way'_ and so it was that we found ourselves driving towards our Chichester rendezvous at one o'clock in darkness and icy sheeting rain. The tide was at three o'clock in the morning and we had arranged to have the manager of the boatyard move _Starship_ out from the yard into Thorney Creek in readiness for our arrival. To have waited for the afternoon tide to take us out of the shallow creek would have meant us sailing most of our passage up the Solent in the late evening or maybe at night and we preferred enjoying the scenery during the day if possible.

We eventually stood on the edge of the shore casting fading torch beams out across the mudflats vainly trying to guess where our craft might be moored. Even the headlights of the car could only discover the nearer ghostly images of the heeled hulls of craft moored inshore, but mainly the beams illuminated the fine misty rain obscuring everything like a fog. We had an hour to wait whilst the tide rose, so we unloaded our fibreglass dinghy from the car roof rack and discussed our plan of action.

There were four of us and the idea was to divide the tasks between us to affect the most efficient departure. Little did we know that we were about to experience one of the most bizarre starts to any voyage.

Paul B was our 'car' man. After a long day at work he'd just driven us the 200 miles so that we could arrive reasonably fresh. He was very tired now and was to remain onshore to unload equipment. Gill was going out to the boat on the first dinghy trip to sort out the domestic details of stowing the gear on board. John was also going on the first trip. He was a very experienced sailor who had handled every kind of sailing craft in all waters since the 1930's. Experienced enough to take up any task aboard, he was like a second skipper, yet oddly it was this depth of experience which led to an extraordinary situation developing.

Gill, John and I set off in the little fibreglass tender as soon as possible and drifted over the mudflats with the wind behind us, casting light beams this way and that, gently rowing from one craft to another seeking _Starship_. We found her perfectly placed at the edge of the narrow fairway only about five minutes from our starting point. Gill and I clambered aboard and she went below to start sorting things out. My task had two parts. First I had to get out the inflatable tender and prepare it; next I had to prepare all the deck gear on the vessel. Recommissioning the boat from a laid-up state can take me up to about two hours when I am working alone, but we had barely that amount of time before we must leave the little creek to avoid taking the ground. John set off on his task which was to return the little fibreglass dinghy ashore to make a second run bringing out food and more gear.

I wrestled the inflatable up out of the fore hatch and onto the foredeck, still in its bag, but I was mentally wrestling with another problem. Should I take the fibreglass tender with us on the sea journey? There were a number of factors 'For' and 'Against'. Standing on the cold deck in the pitch dark I finally decided that I would take it along. The major immediate advantage of this decision was that I would no longer have to spend half an hour blowing up the inflatable, fitting it with all its gear including humping its outboard motor up from below. It would be so much easier just to do a couple more runs with the G.R.P. tender, and then hoist that dinghy aboard and sail away. It would save me a lot of work and allowed me to concentrate on other tasks. I was waiting for John to return. I expected him to be about 15 minutes. Time passed.

In the middle of a job I found myself thinking 'they're taking a long time...' I looked at my watch to see that almost three quarters of an hour had already gone. Where were they? I flashed a torch shorewards but there was no reply. I carried on working, they'd come soon. I began to wonder as I worked if they might have changed their plans as I had done. Maybe they thought; if he blows up the inflatable and comes back under power, then we won't have to do any rowing. We can load the G.R.P. tender back onto the car and lash it down, then stack all the gear at the water's edge ready to leave immediately the inflatable arrives, thus saving time.

BUT ... the inflatable still lay in its bag and if I started inflating it now it would be almost too late, for the torch beam cast down onto the water showed that the ebb was beginning to run quite quickly. I felt that they were bound to turn up soon, because they could come to me in less than five minutes, but it would take me almost half an hour of concentrated effort to get to them. I went below on another job.

"Nothing could have happened to John could it?" asked Gill. Suddenly I got a sinking feeling inside. John was so experienced, nothing could have gone wrong. I went up on deck again with the torch and stood looking upwind towards the shore. The first misty streaks of dawn were beginning to illuminate the gloom. The wind was slightly stronger now. I deployed the dinghy on the deck and started pumping. I was thinking that as soon as I had finished expending all my energy on it, they would turn up and it would all have been a waste of time.

I managed to get it launched and went through the whole balancing act of fitting it with the motor, but still there was no sign of them. I went back on the foredeck for another look shorewards. There was now sufficient grey light to discern detail. I strained my eyes looking, but could see nothing, then, just as I was about to return to the dinghy I realised that the shore was NOT ahead where I had thought it to be, but on the starboard beam. The wind had imperceptibly shifted through 45 degrees and all the boats in our immediate vicinity had remained wind rode against the effect of the ebb. I'd never been quite so fooled before by such a subtle shift. It gave me a moment's thought and then it was gone.

Into the inflatable, I started the motor and headed for the yard. As I approached I saw a light flash and headed for the little gully where Paul waited. The propeller was beginning to touch the mud. Paul was looking most concerned and as I landed he began to explain.... 'I just sat down for a minute ... to wait in the car ... next thing I knew I was waking up ... just closed my eyes ... dreadfully sorry...' I almost didn't hear him. I had just one question hammering inside my head. "Where's John?" He looked blankly at me. "Where's John?" I repeated.
"He came with you in the dinghy, didn't he?"
"Didn't he come back?"
"No, I haven't seen him." That sinking feeling inside my stomach just crashed and my brain went into overdrive. My crewman was lost. The heavy gear was still to be loaded. The water was ebbing so that within a few more minutes *Starship* would be aground. The crew aboard didn't know of the emergency. What should I do? What should I do? I had to choose either to remain in the yard, or to search on the water, it was now a matter of seconds before the tide receded to a point where it would no longer be possible to get onto the water across the mudflats. Gill was on the boat. Paul was on the shore. I was in a tangle and felt that I should be ringing the Police, the Coastguard, where was the phone box? and ... and yet somehow I had confidence that John was still OK. Perhaps he'd lost an oar and was clinging to a mooring? It was almost light now. We would surely find him providing that I could be on the water. In a trice we threw most of the heavy gear into the inflatable and I pushed off. I could search the river. Paul could search the shore.

Serial Starship

As I clambered back on *Starship* I could hear Paul calling from the river wall. I scanned all around. No sign. I started *Starship*'s main engine and Gill and I began to move her downstream, just another few hundred metres to try to keep her afloat to prolong her usefulness as a base from which to work. As we moved along, Gill suddenly pointed astern where steadily rowing out of the misty distance came a lone figure. Such a relief! We picked up a mooring and I returned in the inflatable to escort him.

There was still a great deal of work to be done. It was another hour before we got everybody and everything on board *Starship* and even then we were in a desperate hurry to escape the creek. When we cast off the mooring to motor out, we went aground, but by immediately reversing we slipped into the tiny channel and managed to escape by the skin of our teeth. Not many 35 footers come down Thorney Creek more than three hours after high water. I guarantee it.

We made it down to East Head where there was always water, chucked in the anchor and all collapsed into our bunks exhausted. It was useless to proceed further until we had all recovered from the separate ordeals of what was to have been our 'simple' departure.

The mistake that I had made was to take John to a strange place in the black of night. Rowed him out into a strange creek and then expected that he could retrace our steps. It appeared straightforward to me, because I had seen it in daylight and I had the geography of the place inside my head.

When John rowed back he hadn't arrived at the place we'd just departed from, but on a bare muddy shore (downstream). He didn't know whether he was to the left or to the right of the yard and so he took a guess. He might statistically have had a fifty/fifty chance, but graduates of Sod's Law will know that he had little chance of guessing correctly. Visibility was down to virtually nil in the darkness and driving drizzle. Realising his mistake, he attempted to return. He lost contact with the shore and followed a line of boats. Next, he did what any sailor would do, he aligned his course with the wind, not realising that there had been that subtle shift which had fooled me so comprehensively too. His short trip turned into a waterborne tour of the area and it wasn't until the rain ceased and the first rays of light came that he was able to make sense of his surroundings. He reappeared, still rowing, non-stop after two hours, undaunted and a little mystified.

I learned a great deal from this strange episode, which demonstrated the need in darkness for a small compass in the boat, or some agreed signalling system, or maybe C.B. or V.H.F. link, or maybe a combination of several of these when tired people are making even short journeys in poor visibility in strange places. Worth thinking about?

Chichester to Poole Harbour.

09.00-11.00 Sleeping at East Head to recover from our departure. During this time the wind fell to force 2-3 from the south-west and the sun appeared, changing a most awful day into an acceptably pleasant one.

12.00 Having restored body and soul we prepared to sail and departed the entrance at 13.00 under motor against the wind and a neap tide. Once clear of the Beacon we had a nice sail directly for Cowes under all plain canvas.

14.00 Passing No Man's Land fort.

15.00 A westerly wind shift off Cowes forced us to start a dead beat along with many other craft under sail and for another hour and a half we made westwards crossing tacks with all manner of different craft drifting to windward in ever lighter conditions. Off Newtown it became so calm and shifty that progress was a lottery and reluctantly we started the motor, passing at 17.00 into the disturbed waters of the Hurst Narrows. Ten minutes later the Class 1 monohull fleet including all the top and famous names came past in the opposite direction under power as they returned from some kind of contest out in the bay. They were quite interesting craft to observe; quite different from most monohulls in that they were packed with innovative ideas. Their crews responded to our unusual craft in a welcoming positive way and somehow we felt that we had a great deal in common.

19.30 Arrived at Poole Harbour entrance. Once inside we turned immediately to port to go round the scenic South Channel where at 20.00 we'd tucked ourselves so far up the creek that we gently ran aground on the edge of the fairway.

A big meal and at 22.45 we crept back to bed again for the second time in what had been quite a long day.

MI issue 213. Episode 7.

<u>26 May Sunday. Poole Harbour.</u>
When I think of the scenic attractions of Britain my thoughts are immediately triggered by the well-known beauty spots such as the Lake District, the Hills of Snowdonia, the Hebrides or maybe the Peak District, but Poole Harbour somehow doesn't enter into the reckoning and I really don't know why not. My pilot book said that its nautical perimeter is a hundred miles in length. There's plenty of (mainly shallow) water backed by beautiful hills to the west and studded with lovely islands with clean landings on pleasant beaches. Looking across to the range of hills, misty in the low sun, John was reminded of the way that the Hebridean islands stand behind one another, each as a paler backdrop than the last one. Clambering up through the rhododendrons into the coniferous forest on the northern end of Brownsea Island admiring the view of the water framed by pine trees, Gill was reminded of the Mediterranean.

But there's more than just scenery to provide interest. It's a nautical challenge for the aspiring pilot. The channels twist and turn. Round the back of the islands buoyage systems which you've been following with ease, suddenly reverse as you start to go against the flood into a new channel. Cardinal marks abound. Some channels are so tightly marked that to stray a metre the wrong side of a pole will put you aground; others can be left 100 metres on the wrong side. Watersheds have to be plumbed before crossing and the tides are always up to something really rather strange; staying <u>up</u> longer than they should and sometimes ebbing in the same way as the flood when on the wrong side of an island.

Yet there was a jarring contrast with the green beauty of the islands, a contrast called 'civilisation' at Poole Quay on a Bank Holiday weekend. We had to visit the quay twice on this day; once to re-provision at the busiest time and then later, after nightfall when I went in to pick up a new crew Andrew who was replacing Gill for the rest of the journey on to Plymouth.

At the Quay in the midst of the day there were many tripper boats and fishing craft ferrying and collecting fishing parties. Yachts were coming in for stores or circling, along with commercial fishing boats and passing pleasure craft waiting for the lifting bridge to open. The shores were packed with people and the water was decidedly rough, through being cut up with the wash of so many craft. We immediately decided that it was unsafe being alongside the quay and went a short distance out to pick up a mooring. Even on the mooring it was a death-defying act climbing into the inflatable in such lumpy conditions. It was so dangerous when we crossed to the quay that we went on the outside of a big traditionally built 40 foot cruiser to escape the perils of the steel piling. Within minutes there was a grinding crash and to our horror we saw that the rolling boat had hooked its guard rail stanchions under the overhanging concrete lip of the quay and wrenched them bodily from the splintered teak bulwark rail all along the inside gunwhale. There were some harassed faces on board and we were relieved on completion of our shopping to escape to a quiet anchorage on Brownsea Island.

After darkness I had to set off on a lengthy ride in the inflatable to collect my new crewman. I donned my boots and bulky floating suit and carried a powerful torch as I was making the passage in the night. It was mild and velvet and the steady drone of the outboard engine was almost hypnotic driving me like a true starship traveller through black space towards a distant group of stars. The points of light became strings of pearls which expanded to envelop me in the same way that light and sound issues from a fairground. Suddenly I stepped into the bright arena where massive powerboats with architectural saloons and upholstered bridges were moored six deep alongside. Literally thousands of people dressed in lightweight lemon, white and pink summer wear strolled slowly along the quay admiring the chromium craft and even posed before them with hands on rails to be photographed by the light of popping flashbulbs in the night. Music blared, groups of young men sang alcoholic songs; all was reflected back from tall floodlit buildings and the now unruffled, mirrored water.

With the throttle cut back to a tick over I gently slid towards the ferry steps and after securing the boat scaled their slippery treads to stand on the quay. In full sailing safety gear, carrying my robust torch I fitted in like an astronaut at a children's party.

The moving tide of revellers had been attracted to this place by its nautical flavour. They flowed along peeping down into the plush staterooms and cockpits where complete families swelled by visiting relations and friends sat awkwardly cradling full glasses in their laps - there to be admired and envied. On large gleaming flush-decked racers the gin party and cravats had moved on deck, to be watched and to stare back at the fascinating colourful pageant of people just above them. It was somehow incongruous that the only person recognised as being improperly dressed for this parade was clad in full foul-weather sailing gear.

I glimpsed through the passing throng, in the shadowed doorway of a chandler's shop a lone figure sitting on his rucksack. His head was bowed for he was engrossed in a paperback book that he was studying by the light of the decorative illuminations and the endless moving string of cars headlights. Another odd man out; my missing crewman waiting patiently. Such a pleasant meeting; and then we were away into the silent world of the water with the circus lights dwindling again to an insignificant single star in our wake.

Poole to Portland.

The following morning in a fine drizzle with no wind, we crossed the shallow mudflats at low water towards Poole Quay, sounding the depth with a boathook pole from the tip of a float. With a maximum charted depth of 0.4m the pole was hardly getting wet. A couple of times it apparently showed shallower than we can float in, but with our rudder slightly retracted we passed slowly along and never felt the bottom.

There is much talk about multihull speed, but having the ability to pass a 35 footer over a charted 18 inches of water can sometimes be much more useful. They're great all-rounders.

We put Gill ashore, did our final shopping and then departed at about midday to move westwards. With a lengthy journey in prospect we tried the sails, but twenty minutes later in nil conditions having moved exactly twenty metres sideways due to the wash of passing traffic it was back to our old friend, the diesel.

12.45 We cleared the entrance at Sandbanks and in increasingly poor visibility we headed for Handfast Point and the pierced chalk stacks of the Old Harry Rocks, which for me is one of the most picturesque sights on this coast. We motored on and saw nothing of Swanage in the murk which was getting thicker and thicker. By the time that we approached Durleston Head and Anvil Point it was almost as though we had passed backwards through a time warp into the magical medieval era of dark legend. The only sign of life was the occasional prehistoric black shape of cormorants diving into the bewitched swirling waters below our keels. Above us the headland stood impressively threatening with castellated sombre silhouette and fortress-like jagged cliffs. 'It would be nice to see it in Summer.' (*end of May IS Summer*) quipped one of the crew to lift the oppression of the place, as we shivered, chilled to the marrow with an aching rheumatic dampness in our bones. We slid furtively beneath the damp forbidding walls, engine and hearts throbbing as we anxiously watched the lazy cross swell spending itself into foam against the remote dripping rocks.

14.55 Rounding St. Alban's Head we moved on across the next bay with no sight of land. None of us had passed this way before, so we knew nothing of its nature, whether the land was high or low, yet we now began to feel that there was something strange about the clouds which surrounded us. At St. Alban's the high cliffs had materialised like a theatre backdrop from the mist giving the sense of some drama about to be unveiled. As we motored along the elements started to play astonishing visual tricks.

Whilst we were closely shrouded in the misty greyness we didn't realise that it was the land itself that was creating the cloud. We noticed that the visibility to seaward improved as the faintest of breezes came in, whereas to our right the cloud became harder and whiter than before and was slowly resolving itself into a stronger more distinctive shape, almost like an endless ice cliff materialising alongside, then hardening as it progressed ahead of us. We cruised alongside this glacial form in clearing conditions beginning to realise that maybe the land was trapped somewhere inside it. Far ahead at the distant extreme and very high up, the greyer form of land appeared projecting from the top of the ice like a mountain peak. Closer, to our immediate right a similar peak emerged way above us, yet at the base of the white cloud wall the grey sea blended perfectly with misty imperception into the cloud, so that the impression gained was of the carpet of mist upon which we floated gradually solidified into land itself by rising to a great altitude, where now the snaking line of the upper fringe of darker colour was extending forward to link up with the peaks first seen ahead.

The sight evolved continuously as with measured slowness the cloud became thinner, seeming to be absorbed into the land like water disappearing into sand. A long horizontal white line of breakers could next be distinguished at the true junction of the land and sea. Then the curtain was lifted as the clouds suddenly evaporated and colour sharply flooded into our senses which had become so jaded by the monochrome world in which we had travelled for several hours. The drama revealed was no longer a sombre threatening 'tragedy', but the attractive delights of beautiful soft-lined hills, smoothly draped in shades of purest green. Man's hand was so insignificant in scale that it did not intrude upon the impressive majesty of nature's handiwork and the coast gave the impression of being an uninhabited virgin land on first discovery. We didn't know it at the time, but the weather had taken a permanent turn towards improving and gradually over the next day or so it became sunnier, with clearer visibility. The water was about to turn blue and to be dressed overall with a sparkle. At this moment however, our eyes were riveted by the beauty of the rolling hills which at the shore had been abruptly cut through as in a sectioned geography model. We saw the land on top and the strata beneath, folded and twisting like compressed paper sheets. At 16.45 we passed the strongest evidence of man at Lulworth Cove, but we decided not to enter the tiny bay as it looked so crowded and a swell was sweeping across the entrance.

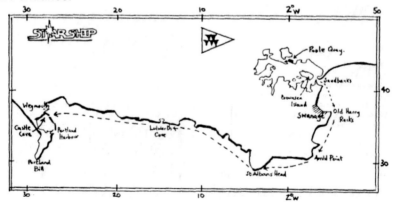

Following a brief rain shower the air cleared and once more the clouds began to produce some amazingly solid white bands to contrast with the hill tops above the cliffs which continued to show every variety of formation and textured pattern. The complete section from Poole to Weymouth proved to be a most wonderful sight, even in the poor weather that we experienced.

17.00 Looking ahead and out to sea we began to see the odd details of big harbour installations appearing from another cloud bank. We headed for the northern entrance of Portland Harbour and at 18.15 we entered and found a mooring off the Castle Cove.

This is a Naval Base. A frigate manoeuvred around the harbour and a helicopter made numerous noisy passes overhead. A police boat went by with a cheery wave, but otherwise we saw no one. We celebrated with our usual big meal and crawled into bed late with the prospect of another four o'clock start in the morning when we would attempt our most notorious headland to date, Portland Bill.

MI Issue 214. Episode 8.

Tuesday May 28. Portland Bill to Plymouth.
We'd had a quiet night on our mooring in Portland Harbour but at 04.15 we were up and about, in accordance with the instructions in all our guide books which said that we had to pass around the Bill within a couple of hours after H.W. Dover. In the darkness the lights of the harbour installations twinkled and the sky reddened as the bright disc of the sun rose clearly defined from behind the land to the east, illuminating the warships which had come in to anchor during the night.

05.30 The wind was from the north-west so under plain sail we headed for the open eastern entrance inside the harbour. We were having a good close look at a frigate and a destroyer and not quite concentrating until somebody suggested that maybe we were heading for the blocked southern entrance and a hasty dogleg in our wake showed where we turned sharp left to exit correctly.

Once outside, we reached off towards the south with a fresh breeze following a big ketch and being pursued by a big gaff cruiser coming down from Weymouth. Observing their behaviour in approaching the tip of the Bill assisted us. The boat ahead, particularly, seemed familiar with the correct approach for he stayed well out when passing through the wind shadow of the high land, but then got so close to the rocky shore that we felt that he'd made a mistake, only to find ourselves approaching rough water which gave us a bit of a shaking before we managed to motor inshore, to no more than a few boat lengths off the rocks where the water was smoother. We didn't really have time to admire the overhanging rock walls topped with their cranes, apparently for lifting or lowering boats and goods straight up out of the sea, because we found ourselves being swept along in a swift flowing river dotted with hazardous fishing floats waiting to snag our propeller.

The tip of the Bill was a wild place for the wind was funnelled against us and lumpy waves drove hard against the threatening rocks. Further out the water looked even rougher, so with our engine pounding its heart out, we turned northwards following the line of the Bill and although hurled this way and that, crept slowly out towards the safer water with the beckoning fangs of the lee shore receding far too slowly behind us.

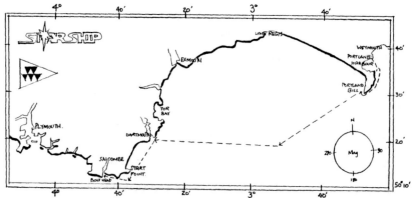

It wasn't pleasant, but on the other hand, it was a valuable experience that we wouldn't have missed. It was just wild enough and rough enough to make us appreciate what it might be like in bad weather and we counted ourselves lucky to have made it unscathed around our very own little Cape Horn.

06.30 Once clear of the immediate danger we went onto the westward tack for the long crossing of Lyme Bay. We set the sails and for a couple of hours at least made good progress closehauled out into the bay at about six knots. Gradually the wind began to fail and indifferent speeds of about three knots for another couple of hours began to make our average look a bit thin. Luckily for us it was a beautiful day with the sun on the water and a sparkling blue sea. We used engine from about midday following a course towards the distant coastline. At no time did we lose visual contact with the land to the north which was well defined by cloud banks forming over it, whilst we at sea enjoyed an unbroken blue sky throughout the day.

Our progress at sea was slowed by the lumpy conditions, but with a combination of sail and power we arrived off Dartmouth at 16.45 and might have entered, but the tide which we had stemmed

30

for most of the day was about to turn favourable again and the wind strengthened enough to dispense with the motor, so we went onto the southerly tack and sailed for Start Point. Nearing the headland it was the same old story once more. The wind headed, the course fell off, the sea got rougher, the breeze got lighter and we were back to motor boating, grimly determined to make Salcombe.

As a haven from the discomforts of the sea Salcombe comes close to being perfect. Its deeply wooded valley is dotted with white houses of the most solid and secure kind. It is lush and green, has sandy shores and is orderly and reassuring. On this evening it was quiet with most of the craft already on moorings or snugly anchored for the night. A Harbour dory came alongside to guide us to a mooring just above the town which we picked up at 20.30.

We'd watched the sun come up and we watched it go down. Our extra effort in coming up from Dartmouth would allow us a more restful morning the following day.

29 May Wednesday.

We just had to visit the town. Bathed in sunshine with the gentle hum of leisurely activity it was a joy to absorb the calm atmosphere as I sat in the small town square called Whitestrand, which was also the main landing place. Holidaymakers with buckets and spades were arriving to be ferried across to the sandy beaches on the opposite shore. Small boys were watching as dad rigged their little dinghy and there were endless antics from the inflatables arriving from the yachts out on the river. This was 'cruising' and I could have remained there all day.

At 12.00 with new butter and milk aboard and pasties and scones still hot from the bakers scenting our galley, we hoisted plain sail in the most glorious weather imaginable and ran gently down towards the sea. The river was all a-bustle in contrast to the quietness of the previous evening. Everywhere we looked we saw bright colours flashing as people really got down to the serious business of 'messing about in boats'. Most noticeable was a colourful inflatable Catapult catamaran which sped backwards and forwards like a kingfisher in flight.

Once clear of Bolt Head for the first time on the journey the wind came behind the beam and our boat was released. A force 3-4 east-south-east filled our modest spinnaker/reacher, musty from lying buried for years in the forepeak and away we went averaging six knots against the tide, looking for Plymouth. All discomfort was forgotten as we suddenly remembered why we had come sailing. Sun, speed, sparkle, and stability. Miles and miles reeling off our transoms in a long continuous ribbon. Fresh salads and soft drinks appearing from below and all other boats were simply standing still in the water.

The navy fired a mighty ten gun salute over our heads from the shore battery down the firing range as we arrived. We thought it excessively extravagant to welcome us in this way, but we appreciated the gesture nevertheless. We went up the Tamar and picked up a sheltered mooring at Mashford's Yard at Cremyll opposite Plymouth at 16.00 to complete a superb sail. The plan was to leave the boat at a yard in the shallow muddy creek of Millbrook, so that evening I explored its intricacies in the inflatable, discovering a couple of tricky bends. I felt fairly confident that I could bring *Starship* in without the string of disasters usually experienced at the beginning and end of each of our trips.

<u>30 May Thursday</u>.
Going in just before high water, a niggling problem with our gear box pitched us right into our regular finale performance. In the narrowest part of the channel with a cross wind, the crew on the foredeck keeping watch ahead suddenly started jumping up and down and waving their arms about. A floating line right across our path was just disappearing under the bows. I pushed the engine into neutral and sprang onto the aft cabin roof to raise the rudder. The line passed, but she failed to engage forward gear again, despite our best efforts. The anchor went in almost immediately, but space was too restricted and on too short a scope to hold, we found ourselves lodged sideways on a rocky piece of lee-shore Cornwall. Fortunately, the boatyard people had a rowing dinghy attending to us and they took our anchor out, but to reduce weight aboard we put our inflatable over the side and stood two crew in it. This floated *Starship* immediately and we pulled up to the anchor. We finally managed to engage forward gear, but failed to break out the anchor as we went over it. The choice was to disengage forward gear with the prospect of not being able to get back into it again, or to charge round and round in ever decreasing circles, trying to catch mooring buoys as they passed. Somebody's fingers got trapped in the mayhem. A mooring was grabbed as it went by at speed, engine disengaged, mooring dropped and grabbed again. For a moment we had one crew holding the mooring and another chap gripping him by the ankles and everybody shouting 'Don't let go!' At this juncture the

wind got under the nose of the inflatable (still alongside) flipping it up vertically to give our outboard motor a dunking.

We finished with seaweedy warps strewn everywhere, with wounded, stretched and exhausted crew slumped all over the decks and with the captain hoarse from an excess of mostly useless commands. It was a modest performance by our standards, but half of Cornwall knew that we had arrived.

Episode 9.
(*The additional 86th episode*)
Starship's Daysail. The Round Britain Race start.

How far can you travel just to daysail your boat? 50 miles? 100 miles? We *Starship* travellers journeyed the 600 miles from our homes on a round trip to Plymouth in order to watch the start of the Round Britain Race. Was this dedication of the highest order? You might think so, but ... well this isn't just any race is it? It's an especially demanding form of race and for my money it comes closest to testing the racing boats in the real way that we weekend sailors use our craft.

There is a major divide between sailors, for there are those that RACE and there are others who CRUISE, there are a few who span the divide and there are a few who are neither, but still there is a general distinction visible between the two groups. Many cruising yacht-persons will find little to interest them in racing or racing boats, but they are behaving like ostriches with buried heads if they don't recognise that the materials being used and the gear development to be found on racers can often be transferred to cruisers to make their lives more easy. This assumes that the racers are taking part in activities which somehow relate to cruising. A race like the Route du Rhum involving over 4,000 miles of ocean sailing, will probably not develop quick tacking hull forms, or more efficient ground tackle, but the Round Britain is different, because it does encompass many of the operations which occupy cruising sailors.

In our kind of cruising we sail near to the shore, in the area of maximum danger, contending with currents and a vast array of obstructions to be avoided. We have both long range and short term decisions to make about tricky pilotage with entrances and exits. We sail in close proximity to many craft and must constantly respect their rights of way. The Round Britain demands this kind of sailing. Boats which do well in flat out ocean races may not have the manoeuvrability, or flexibility for this particular race which has five legs divided by four stopover points where the competitors must wait for 48 hours before resuming the race again. The shortest leg is the first, at 230 miles. There are three legs of roughly 450 miles each concluding with a leg of about 300 miles. It could rightly claim to be a 'Cup Final' for cruisers. Early races could be called 'racing cruises' and even now, there is a heavy percentage of 'ordinary' cruisers taking part, because each craft will find its own competitor of similar ability and their struggle is as much against the adversity of the elements as against each other. The Round Britain Race breeds camaraderie not animosity and it was this quality that first led me to think of sailing my own boat on a greatly extended 'weekend cruise', Round Britain day-sailing Slowly.

Six of us had travelled overnight on clear roads to arrive in Plymouth's Millbay Dock at about four o'clock in the morning. It was floodlit and very quiet at that time, so there was ample opportunity to closely examine details on each of the boats without other spectators getting in the way. One just had to remember to speak in whispers because most of the smaller boats had their crews on board and sleeping figures could sometimes be seen through open companionway hatches. Even the big boats occasionally had support crews on board in sleeping bags on the trampolines and netting, or lying on piles of bagged sails on the dockside. Many boats were strewn with gear of all sorts, silently waiting for the frenzied activity of the preparation in the few hours immediately before the start. As the sun rose in a clear morning sky we were able to take our photographs and then reluctantly leave, to go on board our own craft, for the dock was still sleeping and the most interesting time was about to begin when the boats would be made ready to meet the sea.

Our boat was waiting at Millbrook where the yard had sorted out the problem with our gearbox which had given us such difficulties when we had arrived. We had high hopes that we wouldn't disgrace ourselves in our customary fashion when arriving and leaving. As luck would have it the wind was favourable for us to sail off the mooring and slip away silently down the creek, which I always find particularly satisfying. One moment stationary and then in one single circle-sweeping transition we were under way with the banks sliding by around us.

In the most wonderful sunny weather we joined a procession of boats going down the Tamar, out through the narrow passage to the west of Drake's Island and then close reaching towards the open sea staying well over on the Cornish side to give the racers space. The bustle and excitement was not quite as frantic as for a Trans-Atlantic Race but the electricity was there for those involved. Some contenders keen to justify their sponsor's contributions detached themselves from the melee in the start area to sail closer to the spectator craft to be photographed and to wave to well-wishers. We took the opportunity to sandwich ourselves between the immense platform of a celebrated 60 foot catamaran and a diminutive 25 foot monohull when they returned to the start area. Being a multihull we escaped being noticed by the guard boats. This allowed us to get a closer-than-legal look at the starters and to exchange a few words of encouragement with our particular heroes who would carry our colours in the coming contest.

Eventually we began to sail out to sea towards the Eddystone lighthouse which was the first turning mark on the course. Conditions could not have been better for us as we jogged slowly forwards in force 2-3 with reefed sails so that the racers would easily identify us and overtake us. The sun was strong and the motion pleasant as we listened to the radio commentary for the actual start.

Behind us at a distance of two to three miles the sails amassed, aligned and the race commenced. Within minutes we could clearly see certain larger sails becoming detached from the pack and

although we continued to potter along at three or four knots it was only a matter of ten minutes before we were being overhauled by the immediate leaders. The first one to reach us was a bright yellow trimaran with steeply arched beams which came smoothly cutting through the water with her crew relaxed at the helm. Her motion was a joy to behold, so flat and steady. Power boats racing to stay abreast of her leaped and crashed over and through waves, standing on their tails, throwing water everywhere and soaking their occupants, but the trimaran continued her sedate progress. Just down to leeward came another pale orange/pink trimaran slipping along with equal speed and then came the others; the familiar shapes of last year's models, but with newer names. As a group they passed in advance of the more formidable monohulls. Two were long and lean, carrying the colours of others countries and another was gaudy, beamy and seeming to be quite tender for she sailed at an acute angle of heel even in those light conditions with her crew clinging to the windward rail high in the air.

When all the smaller multis had passed we turned for home to sail back through a seemingly endless stream of monohulls extending right back into the harbour.

By the time that we'd reached Cawsand's Bay some of them had only progressed a couple of miles, whilst the fleet leaders were well round Eddystone and had already disappeared over the horizon. We had a little stroke of luck in picking up a floating fender which always gives an impromptu 'man overboard' exercise, but then we returned to find a handy mooring in the shelter of the river for it was now early afternoon and we'd not slept all night except for the odd disturbed snatches here and there.

We selected a nice big mooring buoy and hoisted the looped tail on board which I was in the process of securing when the rope apparently snapped leaving us heading for a nearby lee shore. How pleased I was that I'd left the engine ticking over and that our gearbox trouble had been cured. When we'd re-secured to the mooring we discovered that the eye splice around the metal thimble onto the buoy had been done with insufficient tucks and it had simply come unravelled. One can never be too careful. What might have happened if it had waited until the middle of the night before parting, with us poor unfortunates asleep below decks?

For two or three hours we slept and then awoke for a meal and a pleasant stroll along the leafy cliff-edge path to Mashford's Yard and the pub. Mashford's at Cremyll must be one of the quaintest sights of the nautical world. Tucked into a tiny rock cove with its buildings plastered onto the cliff-like walls, it is isolated yet totally self-contained. The house lights in the cove twinkled with warm security in the darkness.

The next day Sunday we replaced *Starship* on her mooring in Millbrook with the morning tide. We ate breakfast on deck in the warm sunshine whilst watching deer emerging from the forest edge to browse in the fields close by. The weather was so good and there was still time to be afloat on the tide, so we entertained ourselves in trying to thread a V.H.F. aerial cable down the inside of our mast. We seemed to have more people up the mast than on the deck, but eventually we did the deed, which demanded more drinks and sunbathing to restore us after our efforts.

It is hard to depart your boat when the sun is beating down and the water calls, but we had a long drive ahead of us and after all it had only been … just a daytrip.

MI issue 215. Episode 10.

In Plymouth.
July 28 - August 4. Summer Holiday.
When I was a youngster all the best story books always started with, 'It was the first day of the summer holidays.' Ah! What excitement that sentence generated. What visions of long hot sunny days.

Well Sunday July 28 was the first day of the holidays, but before you get carried away, the rain was falling, a misty blanket obscured distance and trapped our gaze inside the dripping windows of our little over-ladened car as we, my boys and Gill Smith, endured the 300 mile journey to Plymouth.

Our ambition was to explore the West Country cruising ground, hopefully extending our adventure out to the Scilly Isles and we had a month in which to make the journey. On such a grand trip as this we were bound (as regular readers will appreciate) to get off to an awful start and of course I committed the classic error. I had left my tide tables on the boat. I had resorted to a very tenuous calculation about the time of high water. I didn't fully trust my computations, but I reasoned that if I arrived sometime in the afternoon the tide would surely allow us to get aboard the boat at some time either in the afternoon or evening. Reasonable supposition one would think.

As we wended our way down onto the quay. Horrors! The tide had only just receded, which meant that we couldn't reach the boat until about two or three in the morning. Gill and my two boys were with me and I knew that any attempt to cross the mud would end with us all looking like the tar baby in the old Brer Rabbit story. (I'd crossed that mud before.) I had to admit defeat (an essential cruising strategy) and adopt the true cruising attitude of putting off until tomorrow what is difficult to do today. If **time** will put things right, then let time take its course. We took accommodation in the nearest village and started to explore our surroundings.

Seeking an evening snack we went to the combined villages of Cawsand and Kingsand, where the waters of Plymouth Sound lap right up to the front door. We heard that in times 'historical' the villagers of these remote hamlets had warred with each other, but how they decided where the division lay between the two places, remains a mystery, so tightly are the tiny houses crowded together. The road through the village was *incredibly* narrow. The warning sign said that cars wider than seven feet couldn't get through and they weren't kidding. We only just made it around some corners and it took careful judgement to do it. We'd been directed to a small bar down in a cellar. The doorway was so low that a small yellow plastic **duck** was suspended from the top of the doorframe to act as a warning. The bar was just big enough for two people to be behind it providing they were standing on each other's toes. The food order was written longhand on a tiny scrap of paper, casually folded and then apparently mislaid amongst the rush of orders for liquid refreshment. Looking around I saw that odd corners and crannies were filled with rudders, sailbags and outboard motors, for the place doubled as a sailing club during the day. It was being exploited to its fullest potential.

The following day dawned brighter and as we were unable to get out to our craft until the afternoon we took the opportunity to explore further. We followed the coast road along the cliff top at Whitsand Bay admiring superb views out beyond Eddystone and along the bay towards Looe. We were inexorably drawn towards the isolated promontory at Rame Head where on a bare windswept headland stands St. Michael's chapel. Motor vehicles cannot reach the ruined building. As I scrambled up the steep rocky pathway I marvelled at the tenacity and obstinacy of the ancient monks who must have laboured to erect this chapel like a hermit's cell in so remote a spot. Yet I appreciated their choice. To stand on that projecting headland apparently totally surrounded by the sea, hearing only the sound of the wind and looking down on the endless lines of approaching waves far below, you may experience intense personal isolation and maybe the fantasy of being a gull in flight. No land remained visible, only sea and sky, horizon and sound, there was a sensation of floating disembodied.

We returned to follow the narrow Cornish lane back to the little church at Rame. We went inside and were struck by the fact that electricity had never reached the place. It was equipped throughout to be illuminated by candles which alone must create a singularly supernatural atmosphere. Outside, our main interest was in the closely packed tombstones that told all manner of seafaring stories. Many of the women here had ages well over 70; many of the children didn't make it until the age of 3. Most of the men had met untimely deaths associated with the sea.

'Drowned whilst assisting others ...'
'Killed when his ship foundered ...'
'... when his ship exploded ...'
'Died in the Straits of Magellan' or 'River Tagus'
'Wrecked on Penlee Point ...' and
'shot from a besieged Spanish fortress.'

There were pilots and gunners and even a man named after Horatio Nelson. There were voices echoing down the grey tunnel of time. It was a fascinating maritime experience.

Our intention was not to immediately sail away from Plymouth but to stay in the vicinity and catch up on a bit of maintenance during the first week. Back on the boat at last, we loaded our gear and then dropped downstream to a point where we would stay afloat through the tidal sequence. I judged that the most convenient place to meet all our needs was in Millbay Dock over in Plymouth, the gathering point for all the famous racers in the Transatlantic and Round Britain Races. The next day we went for a little cruise up the Tamar to Saltash and then returned to wait for the dock to open.

As we were early on the tide we had to pick up one of the fore-and-aft moorings outside the gates to wait for opening time. I secured the bow, but I had to pass a loop through another buoy to hold my stern to avoid drifting into a boat on the next mooring. I opted to do this by dinghy and got into the tender leaving my young crew aboard *Starship*. I passed the line through the buoy and doubled back towards the boat. Of course it was two feet too short, because *Starship* had drifted just tantalisingly out of reach. The crew aboard, responding to my semaphore, put the boat into forward gear and tried to steer back towards me, but they were going dangerously close to our moored neighbour. I was signalling, Go this way ... Go that way, In gear ... Out of gear, and we commenced a delicate ballet for trimaran and tethered orange inflatable. Our arcs of circle would cross from time to time, but we were fated never to coincide. In the end I secured to the buoy with a single line and made it back aboard. The entertainment value of the performance could be gauged by the reaction of the numerous fishermen lining the nearby quay above us. They gave me a spontaneous round of applause and I must admit to taking just a small bow.

We had only ever seen the dock jam-packed with competitors making ready for a big race, so having it virtually to ourselves for a week was quite an experience. It made an ideal place for the boys to learn to row and for me to climb the mast, whilst on still water, to complete the fitting of my VHF Radio which was switched on to find ... it worked! Being a real novice I decided to be a listening station only until I had picked up courage. We were supposed to do some external painting, but although we prepared the boat, the weather during the week and indeed the whole holiday, never allowed us to apply the top coat. Instead, we contented ourselves with cleaning the interior, stocking up for the journey and visiting the nearby Royal Western Yacht Club.

Finally, we had to take on drinking water for the trip, so being unable to find a tap to fill my container I went around to the harbour office with my request. The man looked with resignation at the rain pouring down the windows, then pulled on his big coat. He had a big trolley outside with a huge shiny standpipe, a fire hose, a nozzle (almost too big to lift) and a special key like water board officials carry. He trundled all this the half mile back to the boat and wrestled with the equipment to lift a big metal grating in the road on the quay. He connected up the standpipe then turned on the water, to check that it was running freely and clean by flushing a couple of hundred gallons through the system, cascading like a waterfall into the dock. Next he unrolled the pipe, connected it and locked the nozzle onto the other end. He shot a power jet of water astern of the boat about halfway across the dock. When completely satisfied that he could deliver 'x' thousand gallons per. minute he turned to me and said 'Right, where's your tanks?' I scrambled down the wall, clambered aboard, and re-emerged with my plastic five gallon water container, which caused his face to drop somewhat. I also proudly carried my plastic funnel with its half inch diameter spout. He could see that this was not going to be one of his bigger jobs, so he slowed the water down as much as possible, until it resembled a torrent capable of holding a canoe slalom event on it, then he trudged off in the rain to leave me to it. Fortunately the other boat in the dock with me also wanted a drop, so his efforts weren't totally in vain.

On Saturday August 3 we changed crews as my boys left and a 'sea' crew came aboard, consisting of Mavis, Richard, and Andrew. We arranged to quit the dock on the morning tide of the following day and I awoke to catch the early shipping forecast at 05.30. There was hardly a breath of air outside and the usual vertical drizzle was falling when our holiday cruising weather was announced:

Serial Starship

Westerly, Storm Force 10.
Great Prospects!

(A reminder that the occasional different appearance of text results from extracting the material from different original magazines.)

MI issue 216. Episode 11.
<u>Moorings. August 4-6</u>

All prepared to leave Millbay Dock in Plymouth, but with a Storm Force 10 forecast. What should we do? At about 8 o'clock in the morning I climbed into full oilies, and splashed my way round in vertical rain to the harbour office to see what their opinion would be. They seemed as mystified by the forecast as I was. It just didn't feel as though something as extreme as a Force 10 was on its way. If it should materialise I might take quite a bouncing where I was presently moored, because waves could easily develop with a fetch as long as the empty dock. I should have been positioned at the far end tucked underneath the wall. As I'd have to move anyway, I decided to have a change of scenery. I was conscious of the Cruising Itch, the feeling of having been in one place for too long; a frustrating sense of not making sufficient progress and a strengthening determination to *do* something, even though conditions were not perfect. So when the gates were opened at high water we motored, still in the gloomy torrential rain, around into the Tamar and headed upstream past Torpoint, seeking a stout-looking mooring sheltered by the left hand bank. Just below the mouth of the Lynher tributary we found a nice selection and secured ourselves to wait out the storm.

We passed the time in reading or writing letters and postcards which perhaps told in lurid terms about the epic trip that we'd just made and how we were sheltering from a Force 10. About dinner time I was wondering how we might post these messages, when a shout of *'Starship!'* from outside called me on deck. A chap in a biggish blue boat was circling in the rain. He shouted *'Will you MOVE OFF!'* in an unmistakeable tone of annoyance. So I started the engine, released the mooring and set off up-river. (It's nice to have a covered cockpit in such circumstances, oilies aren't needed.) Once I was disturbed I thought that we might try to get our letters posted by going up to Saltash. However, as we crossed the mouth of the Lynher the wind began to increase. White caps flurried the water and everything went grey. The boat started sailing on hull windage alone. The wind grew stronger funnelled by the banks and the boats ahead were twisting this way and that in the heavy wind against tide conditions. We were shooting along and I began to fear that we would not be able to return against the wind as it was getting quite rough all within the space of just a few minutes. The moorings ahead were all occupied and the weather was rapidly getting worse. I turned, using full engine power and headed for the shelter of the river bank out of the rough stuff in midstream. We slowly crept up and as we did so the conditions seemed to ease off a bit. Eventually we regained the lee that we'd just left and picked up another mooring close in. Phew! It was rougher than we'd thought out there. Within the shelter of the land it was so calm that there was no impression that the weather was doing anything out of the ordinary.

We stayed where we were overnight and went shopping in Saltash the following afternoon. I like provisioning there, because all of the cruising requirements in the way of shops and services are to be found close together and it's a short downhill (precipitous) walk back to the boat moored in the shadow of the impressive bridges. Any sailor with an interest in structural stresses or forces would find much to ponder upon, in the clever use of materials in Isambard Kingdom Brunel's railway bridge still in use today. As a designer, I guess he went to the very edge of the known technology and I'll bet that if he was designing today he'd be building multihulls, because you could see from his work that he enjoyed a challenge.

The new crew hadn't yet had the opportunity to sail the boat, so when all the stores were aboard we put up the full main and maybe a quarter of genoa and set off for the sea. We were a bit under-canvassed at first because the wind was about Force 4 in the lower river, but past Drake's Island it was 5 and gusting, steady 6 off Cawsand. There were few other boats about; we saw only a big French racer incoming under just a Solent jib. We were doing a steady 8 knots over the ground against the tide sailing full-and-by. Although it was early evening the sun was shining brightly and everyone was taking turns at steering to see what it felt like and generally to get the hang of it. We pulled tighter onto the wind and managed to point about 260-270°m into an increasingly rougher sea. We cleared Rame Head to be faced with an endless number of hills to climb a mighty army of waves marching towards us. The boat proved she could handle it and I was tempted to keep sailing. We could see the Looe and Fowey headlands, but even my most optimistic calculations made us arrive after darkness and I judged it safer with all things considered, to leave the journey until the following day. At 17.45 we turned to run back and began to average about 10 knots running with difficult quartering seas. Richard who had only a few minutes of previous steering experience, did a superb job on the wheel as we rushed back in an exhilarating swooping speedboat ride around Rame and across Cawsand Bay. We started our motor passing Drake's Island and entered Barn Pool Bay just below Mashford's to anchor as the outermost boat just inside the north-eastern tip of the land.

The little bay had two permanent moorings which were both occupied by powerboat cruisers with people line-fishing over their transoms. Further inshore the best anchoring places were already taken by three cruising yachts. I wanted to secure to one of the mooring buoys for overnight peace of mind, so, when at dusk one of the powerboats went home we attempted to move across. I say 'attempted' because the anchor wouldn't come up. I went forward and tried it myself, but it had that distinctive feeling of being fouled under a heavy cable of some kind. Oh dear, feelings of gloom.

Now if there's one thing that I've got experience of, it's fouled anchors. In fact my record in this area is so extensive that I have a 'Golden Rule of Anchoring'. Unless the anchor is going to be accessible at low water *always* use a tripping line. I apply my golden rule about four or five times after I have had my anchor fouled and then all the problems with the tripping line deployment and recovery begin to make me feel just a little bit lazy... and then I weaken ... and then I forget my golden rule ... and then I get my anchor stuck once more. So here I was again, feeling tired after the exertions of the day, darkness about to fall, a lavish meal coming to the point of presentation down in the cabin, (and we were expected to turn up on time) and the !*******! anchor obviously hooked under a weighty obstruction.

Fortunately for me the bunglings of my early cruising years came to my rescue for the brightest jewel in my sailing knowledge is a method for recovering anchors from just this apparently irretrievable situation. I learned it long ago as a novice cruiser in Brightlingsea Creek when sailing my first tiny plywood trimaran *'Mistral'* (where is she now?). I picked up the hefty Lightship Cable used for mooring the fishing fleet and had to be rescued. I've employed the technique I learned on several occasions since and it's so effective that I now believe that it could be a contributing reason towards my lax attitude towards tripping lines.

The story of how I learned this lesson is a proper little cruising yarn which editors tell me is too lengthy to publish. However the knowledge therein has stood me in good stead over the years. It's not a deep dark secret, in fact it's probably the standard procedure, but it has to be learned the hard way by each generation of sailors. If you don't know how to get your anchor back from a situation like this then you ought to, before you drop it over the bow again. Ground tackle is expensive, don't lose it.

(The method is to catch the obstruction with a grappling anchor with tripping line attached. Take the load on this anchor. Drop the fouled anchor and using the dinghy go ahead to pull the fouled anchor out. Return on board. Start engine. Trip the grapple anchor and retrieve it.)

This particular anchor was in very deep water but with the help of Richard and Andrew, all my gear was eventually returned on board and it was a really nice feeling to see it come up and break the surface. We feasted on the ratatouille, I can tell you, and slept soundly knowing that we were securely attached to the big yellow buoy with such heavy mooring chains. It had been exciting sailing; the weather calmed down overnight and there was a moderate forecast for the coming day. Things were looking up at last.

MI issue 217. Episode 12.

August 6th – 8th

We awoke at Barn Pool just opposite Plymouth to sunshine and we were away with a cautious sailplan at 08.45 sailing out onto a sparkling sea.

We went directly out following the route of the previous day. The wind was much lighter and half way towards the breakwater we hoisted full sail. We saw a number of other craft, but we overhauled them all before Penlee Point. The wind was quite fluky and the tide strongly adverse. We pointed about 270°m but only progressed slowly over the ground until about 10.45 when well clear of Rame Head about six miles out into Whitsand Bay the wind began to rise again. The water was uncomfortable and lumpy so we tacked northwards for an hour sailing faster in progressively smoother water. We went right in to the cliffs and then tacked to pass about one mile south of Looe Island. At 12.30 I had to reduce the genoa to two-thirds and then off Pencarrow Head I had to reduce the main as the wind was genuine force 5. We sailed reasonably free courses with roughly three mile legs on each tack and made good progress. It was hard work and

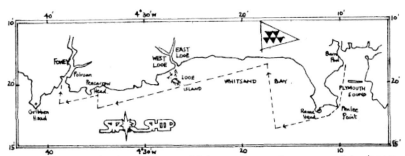

had we been in harbour we'd have been happy not to have been sailing, but as we were already out there, faces windburned by bright light reflected from a hard-edged sea, it developed into an exhilarating experience. The visibility was good and even without reference to the chart it was possible to guess the position of the harbour thanks to the very conspicuous daymark on Gribben Head. The land was green and pleasant with a patchwork of pale green pastures interspersed with woods and small villages such as Polperro where little white houses seemed to cling to precipitous green slopes.

Just before four in the afternoon we tacked into the entrance at Fowey to find the calm enfolding us after the continuous noise of the sea. It was easy and straightforward and we were able to take in sail and motor up, to look for a mooring at our leisure. The yachts were all moored on the Polruan side and the mooring spacing in the main group looked a bit close for our comfort. However, a yacht was just in the process of vacating the only mooring with adequate swinging room for us, so we rushed in to capitalise on this fortunate chance.

The sheltered strength of the sun soon had us relaxing on deck looking around at the various sights to be seen. Fowey was a little bit like Salcombe and Dartmouth combined and we were to find it a most welcoming place. In fact Fowey turned out to be so exceptional that we decided to return later and so the full story of what happened there will have to wait for other Fowey episodes to come later.

On August 7th we were awoken by a driving gale even in the harbour. There was grey mist and heavy rain and we tugged at our mooring with considerable force. Interestingly the shipping forecast was the first for many days which did not include a gale for us, but they had one for the next day when we were going to attempt to get down to Falmouth. We stayed where we were.

To take full advantage of the more settled conditions during the night and the favourable tide which was running between four and ten o'clock, we decided on an early departure and made preparations to start in the early hours.

At 03.30 the boat was abuzz because night sailing was a new experience to the crew who were all looking forward to it, except the captain who looked like a zombie. It was pitch black outside so imagine my dismay when I switched on the navigation lights and discovered that the masthead lantern wasn't working. A quick check showed that the fault lay at the masthead and it appeared that we were trapped in the harbour, because to start manoeuvring whilst improperly lit in such a restricted place was asking for trouble of the worst kind.

Not deterred we searched the boat for the necessary equipment and came up with three torches, a red sailbag and a green polythene bag from Marks and Spencer. By wrapping up two of the torches in the bags we produced the red port and green starboard lights to be held by the crew on either side of the cockpit and the third torch was lodged under the doghouse canopy directed astern with its normal white beam. Fortunately the steaming light at the spreaders was in working order so technically we were just about legal. I gathered the crew and explained how to aim the torches to cover the correct arc of visibility and when everybody was in the correct position and ready, we cast off. I reversed away from the mooring and then went ahead. Once clear I turned towards the main stream, but when I came to straighten up, the boat refused to answer the helm. It continued to circle back into the mass of moorings with yachts close around on all sides. I suddenly realised why my boat was running amuck in the dark. I'd been so concentrating on the navigation lights problem that I'd completely forgotten to drop down my daggerboard rudder. Things now began to happen with amazing speed. We missed one yacht by a whisker as I shot across the aft cabin roof and started jumping on the rudder blade. One of the 'navigation light's' hands spun the wheel the instant that the rudder blade touched the water and we avoided the most almighty collision with the next yacht, but headed for the one behind it. The port navigation light was saying 'Right hand down. Right hand down!' as I tumbled back into the cockpit and we somehow managed to squeeze through a last-minute gap which had appeared and looked about two feet too narrow for my overall beam. I then regained spaces large enough to slip the boat through. Slowly the panic subsided as I managed to work her outwards into the harbour fairway and I had a considerable sense of relief that there was absolutely no-one else about to see this string of near misses.

Phew! What a relief. We were now heading out for the open sea through the restricted harbour entrance when the port navigation light politely and apologetically asked why the light on that side was Green? Shouldn't it be in the Red sailbag? What a mess. A total shambles. Stupid! The crew privately thought of other adjectives to apply to the captain... Mess! The captain replied that we had the lights this way around for a special reason. The captain was an idiot. Of course the 'Navigation Lights' swapped torches and I (being an idiot) wished that I could have been in a boat coming in the opposite direction just to have seen the effect. Fortunately nobody was.

It was calm as we left but a lumpy swell was rolling in which caused us to bump about a bit. Slowly the day dawned and the 'Navigation Lights' were relieved of their duty to do other things such as photographing the angry red dawn which was signalling the 'sailor's warning'. We motored along with the land resolving as the light improved until it was daylight and instead of the focus of our attention being only the orange glow of the distant streetlights of St. Austell, we could now see the solid form of hills and valley. The immense open-cast workings of china clay in this area dominate the skyline where giant's hands have wrenched away half mountains and left behind pyramids of spoil which would dwarf those of the pharaohs. Once we had cleared Dodman Point we had two small bays to cross Veryan Bay and Gerrans Bay before reaching the entrance to Falmouth Harbour. Both were picturesque, but of no great note to us at the time. Later, as you will see, we were to have reason to notice Gerrans Bay and its little village of Porthscatho when it briefly became the centre of the sailing world.

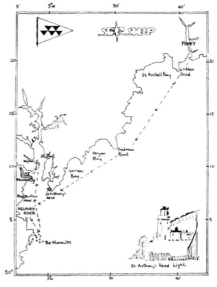

Just as we arrived off St. Anthony's head at 08.30 the breeze began to blow at a steady 2-3 on flat sheltered sunny water. There was a further one and a half hours of tide favourable to us, so we hoisted sail and with a couple of tacks of lovely smooth fast sailing across Falmouth Bay, we headed for the Helford River. As soon as we entered we immediately understood why the pilot book begins with the description *The Helford River is very beautiful.* They are the only words which apply. Near to the entrance the shores were broken woodland with sandy coves which appeared only to be accessible from the water. A little further in there was the main anchorage where the white yachts were clustered like a flock of shining white seagulls with their wings folded. We joined them on the moorings and almost immediately the weather clouded over; misty drizzle filled the air and obscured the entrance. We'd just made it with the tide and we were well pleased that our sailing day was finishing at ten in the morning. We'd seen the best of the day.

August 8
At 10.30 in the morning, although we had been on the go for six hours sailing down from Fowey, some of us still had the energy and the urge to explore Helford, even in the rain, before we called it a day and relaxed on board. We kitted up in oilies and went in to the ferry landing place. There was a small shop with tourist items, but little else, so we walked up into the village in the drizzle looking at the houses. It was quite a picture postcard with thatched houses and a ford crossing a narrow creek with clear water tumbling down through gardens across a stream. It gave the impression of being somewhere in the Lake District in the sense that everyone that we passed in the street wore stout walking boots below bare legs protruding from beneath assorted cycle capes and cagoules which were draped over bodies hunched with backpacks. There were young chaps with straggling beards who referred to dripping maps that emerged from the shelter of waterproofs from time to time. A typical schoolmarm with gull-winged spectacles secured by elastic and carrying a clipboard underneath her arm, stridently organised her party of middle-aged ladies huddled in a group below the dripping branches of a tree. They were not disheartened were they? They were rising above adversity weren't they? And then, onwards and upwards they bravely marched towards the next target on their itinery.

We rounded off our day snoozing, eating and reading as well as overhauling the electrics to try to improve the working lights situation.

August 9

For once the sun was shining, but a cold westerly wind was blowing down the river. We set off after breakfast to explore a little further upstream. The river was clear of yachts because of restrictions with oyster beds and suchlike. This gave open water and untouched, unspoiled banks. The mature oak forest was a mass of green, thick and unbroken on either hand and it was such a beautiful sight that we just gently motored at tick-over speed admiring and absorbing the beauty as we progressed on the silver pathway through that leafy wood. When we were at the safe limit of navigation we turned and hoisted only a quarter genoa to return downstream on a dead run. The nearer to the sea that we came, the windier, until we found ourselves out on the waves staying close to the shore working our way southwards, down towards the Manacles. We only used a half genoa but we were speeding along in bright and sunny conditions. The land had lots of quarries and industrial-type buildings. The sea had sharp rocks, so we turned to retrace our steps. We sailed back to Rosemullion Head and then crossed to enter Falmouth Harbour. By the time that we were entering the harbour the wind was a good force 5 and we were close reaching at 6 – 8 knots with just our half genoa. The catamaran Iroquois 150 came in at about the same time as us with half genoa and a third main and we sped up the harbour together making quite a sight. By the time we reached the moorings at Mylor the wind had been moderated by the land so we picked up a mooring to have a real meal and discuss our next move.

It was Friday and we intended a crew change on the following day so we opted to sail beck to Falmouth to ease land transport problems. As soon as we arrived we were accosted by a Customs launch, met by the Harbour Commissioner's launch and almost run down by a ferry simultaneously, another of our famous arrivals. The Harbour Commissioner gave superb service. He led us to a buoy, attached us and gave us written and verbal instructions about landings, services, water, fuel, rubbish disposal, yacht club, shops and anything else that we wanted to know about, all very impressive.

Whilst shopping ashore I noticed a trimaran of similar dimensions to mine out on the moorings, which at first looked like *Three Legs of Mann I,* so later I popped round in my inflatable to investigate. It turned out to be *Jake the Peg* originally built as *Mary Jane Louise,* but formerly known as *Livery Dole* when she had belonged to Peter Phillips. Her present owner, Rod Nichols and crew were showing me round when the Harbour Commissioners launch came by to say that Joe Harris, our next crewman had arrived asking for us, so they had ferried him out, put him on my boat with the rest of our crew and had then come over to see if I wanted transport across. What can one say about such service? We were certainly made to feel welcome.

August 10th

With all crew on board after early morning shopping we decided to go sailing, as a number of Falmouth workboats were preparing to sail and it was clear that a race was on. We dropped down through the entrance into the Carrick Roads just as the race was about to begin. There were roughly ten boats all gaff-cutter rigged and due to the wind force they only had main and a Yankee jib set to the end of their bowsprits. Some set an inner staysail but this was too heavily canvassed for the conditions. They went out to a mark inside St. Anthony's Head then reached up to a mark off St. Just, before tacking back up into Falmouth Harbour. They made a superb and exciting sight and they were incredibly closely matched in an interesting kind of way. Some were faster off the wind, some naturally excelled going to windward, whilst others had better helmsmen or tacticians aboard which made up for any lack of boatspeed. Nobody appeared to easily outgun the opposition in every department, so the result was a constantly changing situation, rather than the procession which is often seen in racing. At close quarters they were very exciting to watch because they definitely were fast on all points and in particular they went to windward well. A multihull was needed to keep pace with them under sail and it had to be good to windward to stay with them. Crossing tacks was spectacular because with their long bowsprits they resembled charging knights with angled lances, and as they had the experience to have total trust in each other, they were able to allow the finest shaving of distance between bowsprit and rudder as they passed. The whole scene looked choreographed as they crossed and recrossed each other at constant speeds and angles. The most astonishing point to note was that in order to participate in such races they had to be actual working boats. To conserve the oysters in the estuary the local laws only allow them to be worked under sail by these boats which drudged those oysters.

In the evening we went across to the yacht club to spend some time with Rod Nichols and his crew. They were very experienced in these waters and as they were based at Bristol they knew how to tackle rounding Land's End. They gave me the most useful tip about using Newlyn instead of Penzance harbour because the latter has tidal restrictions. John Nicholls drew me a sketch map of the newly dredged shape of Newlyn harbour and we also discussed the Scillies and where the best holding ground would be. This kind of discussion is a feature of travelling slowly. As we approached a new area we were always able, through fortunate meetings such as this, to discuss tactics with other cruisers who had experience of the perils that we were about to face. It made for genuine discourse rather than social chit-chat and forged warm bonds with firm friendships. It is one of the most valuable cruising qualities.

August 11th
During the night the rain was torrential and driving hard down onto the cabin roof. In the morning it was a heavy gale, really blowing. We were chasing and snatching backwards and forwards on the mooring so that leaving the boat was impossible for Mavis, Richard and Andrew who were due to leave, but by 10.30 the worst excesses of the gale had abated although as we loaded the inflatable it was still attempting to become airborne.

Eventually when they had all been ferried ashore and I had returned with the Sunday papers and fresh milk after saying farewells, we settled down to have a quiet lazy day aboard. We'd written off the idea of sailing and we were content to have one lazy day when absolutely nothing happened. How <u>wrong</u> can you be?

MI issue 219. Episode 14.
Capsize!
August 11 – 12

We'd just spent an exhausting morning changing crews in very windy conditions and began to pass our time lazily recovering whilst enjoying the safety of our relatively sheltered mooring in Falmouth Harbour.

Having snugged the boat down and fixed the cockpit canopy I sat for a moment looking out of my doghouse windows enjoying the warmth of the sunshine now that the wind was excluded. Across the harbour from us on another mooring was a French Louisiane catamaran with central pod and float accommodation rather than a proper bridgedeck. There was a French family on board.

Whilst intently studying its design I happened to glance seawards and noticed, well down the harbour, a huge mast. Not double, not triple, but quadruple spreader rig. It was on top of a narrow racing hull and I could just make out a great orange group of oily-clad crew gathered in the cockpit. It was moored to a big ship buoy and was being visited by harbour launches. I grabbed my binoculars but due to the movement I could only deduce that it was a maxi racer. I pondered what boat it might be and what they were doing here. As it turned slightly I caught the name *Lion* on its side. It could only be *Lion New Zealand* which at this time ought to have been participating in the Fastnet Race, which I think had started the previous day. With eyes drilling into the lenses of my binoculars I could see the crew was not wrestling with a big cockpit canopy as I first thought, but they were actually struggling with the mainsail which had been removed from the mast and was still attached to the boom.

I flicked the V.H.F. radio onto Channel 16 and slowly through the remainder of the day a most exciting story began to unfold as a series of exchanges. It was like a radio play that could be made real by looking out of the window where the events were taking place. The events will now be well known, having been recorded in the racing yachting press, but this is how it developed for us.

Lion had damaged her mainsail, an immensely expensive Kevlar sail which they had thought to be bulletproof. They planned to use that sail for the Atlantic leg of the Whitbread Round the World Race. Due to the damage that it had sustained they had decided to retire from the Fastnet Race in order to be totally prepared for the Whitbread Race, because that was the really important one for them. In concluding his radio exchanges the operator made a call to another yacht called *Drum*. He tried to make contact but there was no reply. He went off the air.

Just after three o'clock in the afternoon we heard the Coastguard taking a position from a yacht. We were unable to receive the yacht and could only hear the Coastguard's replies. It seemed that the yacht had seen another yacht capsize. The effect of hearing this was quite electrifying. We heard the order for the maroons to be fired to signify the launching of the lifeboat and shortly afterwards a might explosion apparently right overhead sent thousands of startled seagulls mewing into the sky all around us. Even before the maroons went up we could hear sirens and horns blaring in the town as the crew dashed to respond to what was happening. The position of the yacht, which we thought might be a multihull as it seemed to have remained capsized, was described by the yacht as being, Porthscatho bearing 150° and about three mile east of St. Anthony's Head. I immediately took out the chart and plotted the given position. It was just around the corner from us, almost within the range of visibility had not the land interposed. I was now glued to the set.

After about an hour *Lion* came back on the air asking for clarification of a 'rumour' that they had just heard that *Drum* had capsized. It wasn't confirmed at this time, but it was said that all persons had been accounted for by using the helicopter and lifeboat. Only now did I begin to recall that *Drum* was in fact a 78ft monohull originally designed for Skip Novac, which was currently owned by the British pop star Simon Le Bon from the group Duran Duran. We wondered if the owner had been aboard.

Position fixing.
At about five in the afternoon a boat came on the air attempting to discover the exact whereabouts of the wreck because he wanted to take a press photographer out to it. The Coastguard mentioned that the most accurate position would probably come from the Satellite Tracking Alarm which had been triggered. Almost immediately he gave the position 50°10'N, 04°55'W and he repeated it for clarity. After a brief silence the 'photographer' fishing boat came back on the air again, to mention rather sheepishly that although he had the coordinates of the wreck, he still didn't know where it was, because he didn't have a chart on board.

It was at about this time that we heard confirmation for the first time that the capsized craft was indeed *Drum* which had carried a crew of 24 people. Its keel had fallen off and it had capsized.

At 17.30 a modified position was supplied by a yacht and this was passed on to another fishing vessel, which was heading for the wreck to try to take it in tow. As with the last fishing vessel there was a kind of puzzled silence when the coordinates were given. He came back and

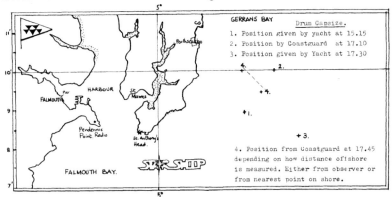

GERRANS BAY

Drum Capsize.
1. Position given by yacht at 15.15
2. Position by Coastguard at 17.10
3. Position given by Yacht at 17.30

4. Position from Coastguard at 17.45 depending on how distance offshore is measured. Either from observer or from nearest point on shore.

tentatively asked for the rough distance offshore. The Coastguard was unable to give this distance, simply saying that *HMS Yarmouth* was standing by (acting as guard ship for the Fastnet Race), so it would be easy to find.

This inability to fix the precise position of the wreck or to convey it from one craft to another was one of the most surprising aspects of the whole operation to me. The people who came nearest to accuracy were the yachtsmen. The fishing boats without charts could only find positions by reference to 'known marks'. When a skipper pleaded "OK, OK, but WHERE is it?" The Coastguard relented and gave "The Falmouth side of Gull Rock." the reply was a relieved "Thanks chief. We're on our way."

The next position given was from an observer ashore at Porthscatho (probably the charted Coastguard Station?) This was 130° True, one and a half to two miles offshore. Plotting this onto the chart with all the others showed that the direction agreed precisely with the previously given 'yacht' position, but that the distance offshore was probably greatly under-estimated. It was still communicated over the airwaves as the latest position and I wondered if it had been checked against the chart before sending it out.

Later that same evening as a dusky calm descended we went across to Falmouth to stretch our legs. The ferry pier seemed almost deserted and silent except for about four other people in attitudes of waiting. One was seated at the pier end enjoying the harbour reflections, another casually consulted the times of the ferry sailings across to St. Mawes. A man kicked a ball for a dog to fetch and another strolled gently back and forth consuming a meat pie with some relish. Odd, but as I walked around I couldn't help noticing that everyone on the pier was eating large meat pies. I was just putting two and two together when the seated man stood up. 'Launch coming in.' he said with an unmistakeable New Zealand accent. As they came together I was suddenly aware of their great bulky size and windburned faces. They descended and departed.

A couple of days later we listened whilst *Drum* was being towed into port. The sailing master was enthusiastic about designing a new keel, but the shore party were more anxious to find the old one to recover the lead. (I can't think what they'd need lead for on a boat, it sounded dreadfully heavy to me.) At three o'clock on the 14th August we watched the upturned hull enter, to be secured to a mooring just off the ferry pier in Falmouth where they extracted sails and equipment, before righting it.

Apparently it was weld failure that caused the keel to drop off. I've had almost the same problem with model aeroplane wings which use a similar construction to the top section of the keel. The skin is stretched over formers composed of shaped ribs. On model aeroplane wings the end ribs at the root of each wing are glued together to make the wing a single unit. I found that failure at this point did not neatly break off one whole wing as a complete piece; instead, it wrenched the rib-structure of the wing away from the end rib which remained firmly attached to the root of the opposite wing.

The aluminium skin of the keel was welded to this end plate and under the extreme conditions of stress reversal each time the boat tacked, gradually fatigued then parted company, fortunately within easy reach of the rescue facilities. Nobody was seriously hurt and the boat was repaired to subsequently enter the Whitbread Round the World Race. Simon Le Bon was inside the boat as it capsized.

MI Issue 220 Episode 15
August 12
It was fine and sunny but still very windy, being steady at about force 5 or 6 from the west or south. We put up a little sail and set off from Falmouth town with the vague idea of perhaps seeing the wreck of *Drum* if it was possible for it had not been towed in and then sailing up the river to explore. At the entrance to the harbour the waves were crashing in making it lumpy and uncomfortable, so needing no reminders that we were cruising we turned and ran upstream to discover what sights were hidden around the corners.

The main harbour narrowed rapidly and the stream turned a sharp corner from sea to river. In this narrow reach came our first surprise for it was filled with huge ships laid-up in pairs leaving only a narrow channel down either side. There was a ferry with a most picturesque land approach on the Trellisick side and then more ships laid-up, one of which was the former cruise ship Uganda rusting away through its formerly white paintwork with its additional helicopter pad mutely telling the story of a South Atlantic cruise (Falkland Conflict. There was a move to rescue and restore the ship). We passed by on the run as the wind was funnelled up the river valley and it was only around right angled bends that we momentarily lost the breeze.

We worked our way up to the area of Malpas where from pontoons moored in midstream we could see that the idea was to fasten up the yacht and proceed by dinghy. We furled our sails but continued in *Starship* going up slowly under motor at about two and a half hours before high water. The channel immediately narrowed and we found ourselves in a position where we couldn't turn round because the channel was a gulley completely spanned by our boat with mudflats on either side. We could only be carried on up by the tide. At a slightly broader spot a Westerly Centaur was aground in the channel and with hair standing on end, I passed as close as I dared down his port side, passing pleasantries with their crew which attempted to obscure the remarkable fact that our very wide, ocean-going tennis court was sailing by on water hardly deep enough to cover his bilge keels. We were most apologetic.

Just below the town of Truro we came alongside quays and fastened to a launch moored there. At last, we had escaped the relentless cold wind and it was now quite sunny and warm. Adjacent to the quay was an old Piver Lodestar 35 so we immediately went over to investigate. It was all chocked up and had been carefully stripped down for repairs to be done to its glass sheathing. It was a really solid job and had that distinctive classic look with its upright doghouse and overhanging roof. I must admit that I love the design of these craft and *Starship* owes something of her shape to the Lodestar. We'd just completed our illicit scramble aboard when we were caught by the arrival of her owner Richard Parr who'd spotted our arrival and had come over to talk to us. Whilst we ate lunch, we talked about multihulls and learned a bit more about Richard's boat. All that he knew was that it had been built by Texas Trimarans in the United States. It had lain neglected in this country for some time and then had been used as a daytrip boat in Torbay where it was called *Captain Jack*. Later whilst in Falmouth Harbour it had sat on a rock and sunk, but it was patched, brought upriver then hoisted out for repair and restoration.

The tide reached its height and we were obliged to leave, though we'd have liked to have visited the town. We made a mental note to return one day, before dropping downriver under motor to a place that we'd selected on our way up as being a possible mooring spot. We'd chosen well because on our arrival the previously deserted spot was occupied by four other craft, the most notable of which was *Saecwen* a famed Royal Cruising Club yacht which we'd seen frequently about the harbour. We finally settled for an alternative place a little further downstream where one crewmember tried to prove it really was summer by having a swim. After only a few minutes, cramp and hypothermia necessitated a rescue confirming our suspicions that summer had not yet arrived

We'd been cooped up too long, so in the evening we went walking ashore in the gathering gloom to find a little bay that we'd seen earlier in the day. Rather like the Helford River the shores were thickly clothed with forest. Out of sight of other craft, when progressing upstream alone, there was a distinct feeling of exploring the Amazon with the impenetrable foliage on either hand. This tiny clearing at the head of a muddy bay was the only sign of human life that we had encountered on this stretch of the river. During the afternoon there had been a couple of men working on a decrepit looking fishing boat and the presence of maybe a couple more was sensed somewhere in the forest fringe. Wood smoke drifted from a fire still smouldering on the narrow shingle beach. Lines and nets were draped over poles and branches in the undergrowth.

In the evening gloom we approached this now deserted clearing in an aromatic leafy tunnel through oak and gorse. Everything lay quiet as we emerged from the trees. In one corner stood a random pile of split oak logs, the strong scent of the newly cut wood mingled with the smell of the smouldering embers from the fire now just an indistinct pile of grey ash, yet still hot enough to feel the effect at a distance of several metres. The fishing boat had been moved out onto a mooring with the tide, but an assortment of old rowing boats filled with junk and copiously patched still remained on the tide line. Half buried in the beach were assorted pieces of defunct engine, a rusty starter motor and batteries with broken terminals. Wood, with roughly curling peels of paint, or smoothly sun-bleached worn, littered odd corners together with crab pots fabricated from discards at the edge of our society. Steel mesh cages from concrete reinforcing, cushioned in car tyre strips fashioned death traps for the unwary crustaceans that entered through the innocent opening formed from a child's plastic bucket.

In the dark stillness this place smelled of primeval life. Imagination saw smugglers dividing spoils, or pirates about to depart from their secret lair on yet another raid. A leap of the mind and a buckskin-clad woodsman might have stepped into the clearing at any moment, armed with long rifle and the skins of trapped animals slung across his back. It was eerie and atmospheric, a strange yet wonderful place.

When we returned through the woods onto our landing beach we found that a man and a boy who had come from

59

one of the neighbouring yachts had lit a small wood-branch fire. It was one of those cruising moments when we simply sat alongside them, needing no introductions and chatted for a while illuminated by the flickering flames. They had come from Lowestoft and were heading for the Scillies, but like us and many others they had become gale bound. We talked of yachts and the recent Round Britain Race.

August 13th
We had a fairly disturbed night as the wind went south and blew straight up the reach. By the time we were awoken by the usual sound of rain drumming on the roof and the boat snatching at her anchor, all the other yachts had departed for more settled berths. We stayed put during the morning and had another good go at our lighting system, which had me up the mast again. We could only conclude that damage had been done to the wiring when the VHF aerial had been fitted and the mast had been drilled for fixings, because everything else checked out.

At 1300 we set off again to explore the tributary River Fal. Once more the deserted feeling of total isolation was quite strong, with no human intrusion into the natural woodland setting. The most interesting sight was that of the herons roosting in the trees. They are so tall that they just don't seem safe balancing ungainly on tree branches. Someone should tell herons that they don't really fit in trees.

Further down, mainstream again, we left the shelter of the narrow river for what felt like the sea in the broader expanse of the harbour, heading for the romantically named Restronguet Creek. The entrance was choked with a mass of moorings and the creek appeared to shallow rapidly, so we turned and departed, picking up great streamers of weed around our prop, which had us momentarily drifting in neutral amongst the thickest moorings. We extricated ourselves and once out in clear water set a reefed main and genoa to beat down towards the harbour entrance. No sooner were we sailing than the wind began to die and gradually faded away so that we had to struggle to tack down to St. Mawes. This weather defeats me.

We asked about picking up moorings at St. Mawes from the occupants of other yachts there, but nobody seemed able to advise us, so we settled for a big one and secured.

In the evening we popped over to The Victory, a pub with a nautical flavour in a windswept and wintery St. Mawes.

August 14th
This time it was more than wind, rain and waves that woke us. At 06.30 I was roused from my slumbers by an insistent rapping on the hull. I lifted the cockpit canopy to find an elderly chap most accurately described as a Corinthian yachtsman in a small dinghy being rowed by a youth. He shouted over the wind. I was on his mooring. 'They'd just come in... it was 'dusting up' out there ...' He nodded towards the entrance. He'd have to get a motor launch to help him across as he'd picked up another mooring. Could we warp back onto another mooring? This was most understanding of him.

The conditions were atrocious. Near gale conditions were blowing cold rain upriver. We all dressed and moved further upriver under motor in a bit of a lull, but it was clear that we wouldn't be moving again. It was soon up to force 8 in our sheltered creek. Some of the racing keel boats put up scraps of canvas and beat out, but they were back again in half an hour. It was impossible even to go on deck in comfort so we spent the time watching returning cruisers and racers tangling with their moorings. We had another *Drum* programme on the VHF, for this was the day that she was towed into the harbour at three in the afternoon. It was a cruising day of eating, cooking and sleeping, but sailing was out of the question. How long could this go on for? Would we ever escape? Surely things would improve soon? What might tomorrow bring?

MI Issue. 221. Episode 16.

Progress at last.
The night was disturbed by the rain and the violent howling of the wind as we swung to our mooring in the river at St. Mawes opposite Falmouth.

One redeeming feature is that the tides seem to run quite gently in these rivers. I put this down to the general shape of the estuaries. They are broad at the entrance and then they gradually taper away as they go inland. At the mouth the sea is quite deep. The tidal rise and fall is significant, but the flow hardly seems to approach that generally experienced on the East Coast, where the narrow mouths are often constricted by sand bars. East Coast rivers often lead to broad expanses of shallow lakes and saltings inland, causing a great reservoir of water to rush in and out of the narrow lower reaches. I know that in the extreme wind against tide conditions that we were experiencing on this morning, there would have been tremendous waves generated on the East Coast rivers and the movement of the boat would have been more notable.

After breakfast we were determined to move, so we left St. Mawes into a force 5-6 on the nose. It was the limit that we could push into under motor, so as soon as we had cleared the entrance sufficiently to lay the course I unrolled just a little genoa to enable us to reach across towards Falmouth. There was insufficient sail for the beam seas coming in and the movement was uncomfortable so I set more sail and as we took off and moved faster the motion eased. When we reached Falmouth the inverted hull of *Drum* was secured to a mooring just off the ferry pier whilst sails and gear were being taken out of her, so we were able to circle around her a couple of times to have a closer look at the damage.

We spent the rest of the day stocking up on stores and visiting the yacht club where they were holding a pig-roast barbecue. Personally, I was feeling pretty dejected at our lack of progress for I had set my heart on seeing the Scillies and as time passed that ambition seemed to be draining away. Whilst shopping in the town I looked in the travel agent's window. There was a trip to the Scillies the following morning, cost £15. The temptation was strong. I was reminded of one of my favourite books *The Strange Voyage of Donald Crowhurst*. Perhaps my Log is a fabrication from this point onwards ...

I was determined to have a go the following day whatever happened. On the radio they said that Chay Blyth had just sunk off the Scillies so I thought better of my resolution. Everybody in our respective families would probably be wondering how we were surviving.

August 16th

It was quiet, calm and still when we awoke. Unbelievable conditions. Although there was no wind in the harbour there would be enough outside. We needed no second bidding. We knew what to do. We were going. We picked up a weather forecast from Channel 62 at 0900 as recommended by Rod Nichols, south-westerly 4-5 moderating later and possibly some sunshine. Some ... what?

We cleared the harbour at about 09.45 so that we'd have a roughly favourable tide for the duration of the journey. We had all plain sail up across Falmouth Bay and the wind came in opposite Helford. We were close reaching at seven knots as we approached the cardinal mark off the Manacles where we came close hauled on about 200-210°m. We were going slowly out to sea, so at 11.15 we took a tack into the bay to the east of the Lizard to see some scenery. There was the classic lifeboat shed squeezed into a tiny cove with a steep pathway down the cliff to it and an even steeper launching ramp so that one could imagine the chocks being driven away and the boat careering down the ramp towards an explosive meeting with the sea. We hoped that we wouldn't be the next customer.

The water inshore was smooth, but once off the Lizard (the most southerly spot on the mainland) it was very rough indeed and we settled into the usual routine of battling for every millimetre of headway westwards. At 12.45 we tacked onto 300°m and fought out into Mount's Bay taking bearings on the Lizard and a distinctive line of radar dishes at Goonhilly Down. Once we were well into the bay the motion eased somewhat and our course freed about 20°. The western end of the bay is dominated by St. Michael's Mount which is a very impressive sight. The building appears to grow out of the very rocks of the pinnacle, and it looks for all the world like a medieval fortress.

We arrived off Newlyn harbour entrance at about four in the afternoon in bright sunshine and made our way inside to find it well filled with fishing boats. John Nichols had drawn us a map so we knew roughly where to head for. There was a new quay projecting into the harbour and yachts should go down the left hand side to secure alongside a fishing boat. The tidal range was considerable and it was one of those places where you were left to your own devices. If you chose to moor on the edge of the dredged trench or placed yourself where you'd go aground on the horrendous boulder ramp at the end of the harbour, then that was your concern. The safest procedure was to secure to the fishing boats to stay afloat at all states, but run the risk of getting involved with the morning catch when it came to be unloaded at 05.00. Those who did were compensated by the dull thud of a weighty fish landing in the cockpit. We spent a little time ashore exploring, but our most significant discovery was the proximity of the super smelly fish market. We finally cured our navigation light problem ready for the Scillies sail which, come hell or high water we were going to go for the following morning. Nothing would stop us. We <u>were</u> going.

Saturday, August 17th
Woken by the sound of a large foghorn on the breakwater and sure enough we were thwarted in our wish to complete the last lap of our westward journey by a thick fog. We'd decided on the inevitable lie-in when the sound of clumsy footsteps on deck said that there was a stranger on board. The shouting from up above made it clear that the harbour master was directing a couple of boats in alongside us, so I had to get up and assist. When the manoeuvring was complete, I asked him how long the fog was likely to last. His reply, "We'll put you on the housing list." told us that he was quite a character. Last time, he said, it had lasted eleven days. I replied with some irony that he was really cheering me up. So he completed the job by asking with a broad grin for my harbour dues. When I winced at the price, he said that "There was only one thing meaner than a tight-fisted Scotsman - and that was a generous Cornishman!" Quite a character indeed.

As we were going to have a day of almost continuous rain we caught one of the frequent buses into Penzance to do some shopping and have a look around. The harbour there dries out and to stay afloat a yacht would have to lock into the inner harbour, which restricts times of leaving, that's why we were in Newlyn which was quite close by.

Once back in Newlyn we had to assist other yachts coming in to tag onto our moored line. Our three immediate neighbours of about the same length as *Starship* had crossed from France, where they had been attempting to have 'summer' cruises. They were so friendly with each other that at first we thought that they were cruising 'in company'. Later we discovered that they were all sailing their own individual cruises. Like many other British craft they had been bottled up in France by the bad weather and they had recognised a brief weather window between gales to get back. They all set sail individually, but as they approached our coast they were caught in the fog. One of them had a black-box navigator and knew where he was. The others had gradually made V.H.F. radio contact with him, one at a time and had come close enough for him to guide them. Eventually he entered harbour with a whole string of yachts following, all vowing to purchase their own black boxes (*GPS*) as soon as they reached safety.

These neighbouring yachts were all based in North Wales harbours, so I took my opportunity to discuss the hazards of the route ahead. This led us all to squeeze into the cabin of the boat next to us for what turned out to be one of those golden cruising experiences, where wine is being poured down throats and the sailing tales get taller and taller. Our host told a story of how in some foreign land he had fouled a rope around his propeller, which he was unable to release. He went to the locals who called a village meeting to listen to his pleas. With much gesticulating and words scraped together from every foreign language that he'd heard, he gave them an impassioned address pleading assistance, but they just listened impassively. He was on the point of desperation, when one swarthy character with curly locks and hairy chest, slowly got to his feet. There was silence. He chewed on the cheroot that he was smoking, and in the best Spaghetti Western drawl announced 'I dive!'. To a great chorus of 'Olés' from the rest of the village. Everyone assembled to watch the event as he was ceremoniously kitted up and he actually entered the water still smoking a cheroot, only removing it at the very last minute to symbolically hand it to his eldest son as he disappeared beneath the waves.

The final endless tale of the night that had us sliding off our seats with laughter, concerned the way that one yacht had been stormbound in a French port and after a few days of inactivity they decided to explore upstream. They wriggled further and further inland and eventually they had to use the tides to reach parts that yachts do not normally reach. Together with the crews of a couple of other boats that were doing the same thing, they arrived at a little village and decided to eat ashore. Whilst dining, they noticed at another table, the local mayor and other civic dignitaries who raised their glasses from across the room and sent over a bottle of their special wine. Soon the Entente Cordial was in full flow and speeches were being made. They were all invited back to the mayor's house where dancing and drinking continued until the small hours when they were taken back to their boats and all the dignitaries packed aboard. No sooner was it daylight than they all set off again to a celebratory meal in another restaurant followed by more dancing and speeches. From one speech they hazily gathered that they'd arrived for some anniversary celebrations and the official in charge of publicity was claiming that they had sailed all the way from Britain to mark the event at his specific invitation. They were too drunk and tired at this stage to argue. Following the second complete night of further celebrations they gathered that the neighbouring village across the stream was also about to celebrate its special anniversary and they were determined not to be outdone. They too needed foreign visitors who had travelled far and our friends were in the front line. Dancing by this time consisted of being supported by matronly, well corseted, black-dressed ladies to avoid slumping in an undignified heap under the tables, but between drinks and banquets as they passed each other, they planned an escape. In true Hornblower style, dragging the bodies of their incapacitated crews aboard, dropping downstream with muffled oars on the ebb in the first grey light of dawn they managed after three days of continuous celebration to escape to the lesser perils of facing the gales at sea.

Would that all cruising was as eventful as this.

Sunday, August 18th.

Woke to the rain again and very restricted visibility. Another ghastly day in prospect. The forecast was south/west 5/6. It was already blowing and grey, but I decided that if I didn't give it a go we'd never do it. We prepared to sail.

MI issue 222. Episode 17.

<u>Into the Atlantic</u>.
It had taken us more than a fortnight to sail from Plymouth to Newlyn due to the terrible weather and Sunday August 18th held no particular promise for sailing to the Scillies, our chosen destination for our summer cruise. Rain was falling and the visibility was restricted; the forecast was SW 5-6, but the boat next to us, *Branwen,* was going to try to reach Milford Haven or even go directly home to Fishguard in Wales. She was leaving at 11 o'clock, so at 10.45 we were ready and standing waiting in the rain. As we had to move the rest of the boats in our line to let her out, we opted to extract ourselves too and without a great deal of enthusiasm we waved goodbye. The entrance to the harbour is blind and we had to circle to avoid an incoming fishing boat, but at 11.30 we motored out to sea hoisting our main to try to steady us in the rough and bumpy chop. I held with motor and main for half an hour as we headed south to clear the headland at Tater Du, then I put on half the genoa, turned westwards and finished with the engine. I could hold a course roughly parallel with the coast and perhaps a couple of miles out, but even so the land appeared and disappeared in the grey misty rain.

By 13.00 after seven miles of bronco riding we were south of Gwennap Head and at 13.20 I momentarily saw a vague image of the Longships light. It was bearing 005° so it gave me a very nice feeling to have actually sailed out into the Atlantic beyond the mainland of England. I had been hoping to navigate using the Wolf Rock and Longships, but this wasn't possible as they were very difficult to see in the murk. We held a course of 260°m tight on the wind and sailed on for several hours.

I sat high in the cockpit scanning the horizon ahead all around the front of the boat but saw nothing. When the islands did appear, materializing out of rain clouds, they were well above the horizon and the first impression was stunning. To sail to an isolated group of islands, quite clearly individual, rising from the sea was a most exciting experience for a coastal sailor. Most island groups in these parts are simply extensions of the mainland and too close to be viewed as a separate entity. The angular shapes and different tones from near and far islands caught the imagination. They could have been anywhere in the world and we might have crossed an ocean to find them.

It was tricky knowing exactly where we were in relation to the group, but as we neared we could see a distinctive daymark on a larger island which was easy to place on the chart as being on the end of St. Martin's. A steep rocky island outcrop just ahead we identified as having the exotic name of Hanjagne and by taking cross bearings we were able to position ourselves easily. Having now sailed amongst the islands I think that position fixing would always be relatively easy because of the distinctive features, providing visibility was good.

We were heading for the main island of St. Mary's so we had to beat a couple of tacks to our left to get around the Eastern Islands, but once we had managed to get into the Sound to the north of St. Mary's the water was smoother and we sailed in admiring the striking beauty of the islands all around us. We passed the bar at Crow Rock on the north west corner and came close on the wind again which was being funnelled by the land, so we rolled the genoa and went the remaining distance into Hugh Town harbour motor sailing.

The little harbour was packed with boats at anchor and we motored around looking for a space. Boats generally move around more when at anchor so clearance distances had to be proportionally greater, and it became clear that there was no available space except down to leeward of the fleet. This meant anchoring reasonably close to the lee shore, with no breathing space in case the anchor should begin to drag and as it was now evening I didn't relish the thought of what might happen in the night. There was a tempting little bay just to the east of the lifeboat slip with a catamaran at anchor. We enquired and they said that they would go aground on the falling tide. We tried to anchor where we gauged that we might just stay afloat at the outer edge of the bay, but the holding did not seem good for my smaller anchor and eventually I set my 35 lb CQR and snugged down for the night.

We were to find that there is always a fair bit of movement with the reflected swell entering the harbour and this was a new experience to a river and harbour sailor. One becomes accustomed to it in time, but as this was our first night I wasn't sleeping too soundly.

At about one o'clock in the morning I was awoken to hear a crunching sound beneath the boat and I knew that we were going aground. Initially I wasn't too worried because I knew that we were near low water in a relatively sheltered bay and on a sandy bottom, but the noise and movement rapidly increased. We began to thump and shudder as each little wave came in, but worse, an awful grinding said that it wasn't a completely sandy bottom. It sounded like rocks or at least pebbles, which seemed to crunch and tear at the hull as we rolled back and forth with each incoming swell. I grabbed the tide tables and started calculating. There was another half an hour to low water and then, of course, a similar time would be needed for the rise again. I wondered if my nerves could take the punishment. I was praying that for once the tables were precise and exactly accurate, or at least that the turn might come early. I knew that I would be unable to sleep, so I sat on deck a bit, furthest away from the point at which the rocks sounded as though they were about to make an entrance. I know from experience that the contact with the ground sounds much worse than actually it is, but it was difficult to convince myself of that fact as I sat trying not to listen to the noise.

In the end the tide turned about 20 minutes later than the calculations, subjecting me to a further forty minutes of torture. The worst moments came towards the end when she lifted and then crashed back onto the ground with a juddering force that rattled everything aboard. Eventually a wave passed without her touching and we were bobbing free instead of thumping and rolling with each wave. It had been a lesson re-learned. Cruisers should not be allowed to take the ground where waves, swell, or surge can lift and drop the hull by even the smallest amount. Actually, to put things in perspective, it should be noted that the rest of the crew slept soundly through the whole process.

.

Monday 19th August

For once the sun was shining. It came streaming warm and welcoming through the windows when we awoke. There was quite a breeze blowing, but it was a summer's day, the first that we had seen. We had three things to do. First, we must move the boat so that we didn't get a repeat of the previous night's horrors. Next, we needed more Calor gas, as the previous evening's lamb joint had only just been cooked when the cylinder ran out, so - no morning tea. Finally another crew member Ray Weston would be arriving on the morning ferry.

Before going shopping we took our first priority of moving the boat. We raised the anchor and motored out a little, but the tripping line that we'd been using was in a bit of a tangle and I motored backwards and forwards whilst this was done. In the end the ground tackle was properly prepared and we approached the new anchoring position which was tightly situated between other craft. It was quite close to a permanent mooring for a harbour launch. If there was a ground chain I might foul it and my own tripping line had been removed. I decided to make just one last circle to position my boat perfectly, but as I motored between the anchored boats there was a horrible thumping sound from the stern and the boat was stopped in her tracks with the waves hitting her stern. I'd fouled a very heavy tripping line from an anchored fishing boat, which was wrapped tightly around our propeller. I thought that we might lie alongside her rusty hull, but we came to rest about twenty feet from the stern. It had a special gantry rigged astern which extended out towards us so that as we moved with the waves we were in danger of it striking our pushpit or backstay.

There were two men on board the fishing boat; an older bearded character busy welding some device together on the deck and a younger chap to assist him. The old man pushed up his welding mask and in tones of annoyance shouted across, 'That's my fifteen fathom tripping line that you just cut there, and it'll give me a hard time to get my anchor back.' I said that I was terribly sorry, but I'd not seen the line. This seemed to pacify him, for he stood looking at us for a moment and then said, 'I like your boat.' He'd once had an Ocean Bird (trimaran) he said, then he turned and went off back to his welding job on the deck and we were left wondering what to do.

Whatever option I thought of pursuing, lashing us alongside the fishing boat, anchoring, sailing, (difficult in the crowded harbour) I always came back to the same problem. The warp had to be freed from the propeller and (once again) I knew from experience that it would take considerable strength applied underwater because it would be wrapped so tightly. When it came to that job there were only two real options. Either beach the boat or dive with proper equipment.

The assistant was watching our predicament so I shouted across, "Are there any divers based here?" He went off to speak to the old man, who soon came back and pointed to a medium sized power boat only 100 metres away. "See that boat. They've got divers on board."

I launched our inflatable and went across. A young chap was sunbathing on deck and when I explained what had happened he was most helpful. "I'll put on a tank for you." he said, and started climbing into his equipment. I ferried him across. He checked his gear and then fell out of the inflatable to have a look at our problem. We passed a line back to the fishing boat and looped it around the gantry to take the strain when the tangled warp was released, then signalled to the diver to proceed. He disappeared under the boat and in a couple of minutes the line came free and was pulled back into the fishing boat. The old man had quite forgotten that we had chopped his line up. He was leaning over the back of his boat waxing lyrical about trimarans. "Sailed a boat called *TAO,*" he was saying, "Try Anything Once." whilst I was trying to converse with the diver who was swishing around in the water astern. "Is that a fully balanced rudder?" shouted the old man, "mine would steer with one finger at 16 knots ..." The diver had finished and was passing me his air tank into the inflatable. It weighed a ton and nearly dragged me overboard. "Made from foam sandwich is she?" called the old man, busy reliving his multihull experiences. I'd fortunately chosen the right chap to get all tangled up with. I returned the diver to his boat and settled up, then went back to *Starship* to cast off and wave goodbye to the misty-eyed old man, who stood motionless, watching our progress right across the harbour until we were securely anchored in a safer spot that had become available.

We had to go into the town to buy the gas. The sun was hot and the bottle heavy. The shops were closing at 12.30 because the ferry was arriving. It was one of the quaint features of the place. The shelves in the shops were getting bare because the next consignment of goods was arriving on the *Scillonian.* It was better to shop in the afternoon when the new stock was in. We rushed up to meet Ray getting off the ship and related our adventures when transporting him out to *Starship,*

One way or another it had been a pretty hectic time in the harbour. It was cramped due to so many yachts waiting for favourable weather to make passages, it was uncomfortable due to the prevailing wind and it was expensive; 'dues to the Duchy of Cornwall, the owners. It's to buy Princess Di a new dress', they explained. We pulled up the anchor set half a genoa and sailed around to Water Mill Cove on the other side of the island. It was completely empty and we dropped anchor in deep water. It was blowing quite a bit but we were relatively sheltered. We went for a walk ashore in the evening and stayed admiring the scenery and sunset until darkness.

MI issue 223 Episode 18.

Scillies.
August 20
Guess what? We awoke to grey rain and powerful gusts of wind running down the valley into Watermill Cove, twitching the boat this way and that. It must have been force seven round on the opposite south western side of the island of Saint Mary's.

We'd decided to make for New Grimsby Harbour if we could get there, but we knew that once out of the lee up by the Crow Beacon, it would be very rough. When I attempted to start the engine it gave all the signs of a flat battery, which was odd because we'd been doing plenty of motoring. The radio too was on the blink and lack of power was the prime suspect. The situation was worrying. However, the tide was right to cross the flats, so we set off. As soon as we cleared the shelter at Crow Sands

Bar the wind was howling and great waves were cresting across the bay. At heavy revs, we were only just inching forwards and after a few minutes I decided that it just wasn't worth it, so we returned to Watermill Cove.

Gill and Ray went ashore to explore whilst Joe and I tackled the electrical system to give it a much needed overhaul and to cure our problems. After lunch when the other two had returned from going right across the island the weather improved and we decided to have another go at getting to New Grimsby Harbour.

We raised sail to take us up to the top end of the island again, but now we were sailing at low water and soon we could see it shallowing. I went onto engine to go directly past the end of the Crow Sand Bar, up to the Crow Rock Beacon. We could easily see every detail of the bottom and at times it looked only a few inches deep. We held our

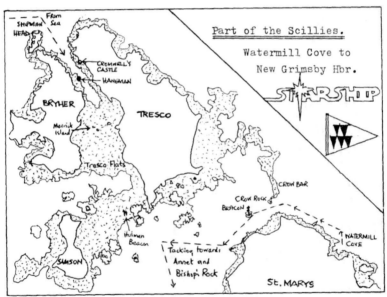

Part of the Scillies.

Watermill Cove to New Grimsby Hbr.

breath, which helped a lot and we soon passed over into the deeper water of St. Mary's Roads where we were able to start tacking in lovely sunshine, yet with still a moderate breeze.

To port, the water was smoother on the St. Agnes side in the lee of the land and as we approached it the Island of Annet was a superb sight, being an extremely picturesque series of jagged stacks and rocks tearing through smoking seas and looking like every sailors idea of hell. The Atlantic swell was cresting in to explode on those enduring rock pillars and each of us was wondering what chance we'd have if we were shipwrecked there on a dark night. It was a fearsome sight.

As we ventured further out into the unsheltered sea the swell beneath the waves grew larger until we began to feel the incoming rollers making our boat lift and soar on the crests, then swoop down into the troughs behind them. Our north-westwards tack took us clear of the off-lying rocks through the North Channel. Our view seawards showed only the tall finger of the Bishop's Rock lighthouse between us and three thousand miles of ocean. The sight landwards revealed no immediate sign of man, only the jagged sand coloured rocks washed smooth and sculptured by the waves. Sea and swell crashed and foamed, sparkling white in the clear sunshine. Everything was sharp and clean. Sea and sky were summer blue and we were enjoying a wonderful bit of sailing.

New Grimsby Sound is a narrow gap between the islands of Bryher and Trescoe. The exposed rock buttresses which face the prevailing weather give no hint that the islands could be anything except hostile. Our boat was being carried along with that distinctive motion produced by running before a big swell. Her stern would rise and we'd be facing downhill; we'd surge forward and the crest would pass beneath us to raise our bows and leave us looking at the sky. To turn across the swell at a sharp angle gave us a distinctly uncomfortable corkscrew motion as the water lifted the quarter first. The tendency was to keep her square before the rollers, yet we had to work her gently across the swell towards the headland at Shipman Head. The water was crashing into the land throwing spray and foam high into the air and the nearer we approached the steeper the waves became. Was this the correct pile of rocks to turn in behind? There was an insistent doubt in my mind because we'd already passed similar islands and seen only boiling seas and instant destruction on sharp teeth waiting in their lee, but now we were committed to being carried in by the wind and waves. Ahead and around the corner we'd either find a safe haven, or the maelstrom. We raced down a wave and glimpsed behind the spray a long narrow inlet with a cluster of yachts tucked well inside swinging at anchor in calm water. There was a sense of relief on board. We sailed into one of the most impressive entrances that I have ever seen, its grandeur enhanced by the anxiety immediately prior to our arrival. Once inside, we were

blanketed from the westerly wind, although there was a constant gentle surge from the reflected swell. To our left, on a promontory commanding the Sound stood the solitary round-towered fortress of Cromwell's Castle, growing from the rocks. Opposite to the castle the Sound was restricted by a high rocky island projecting steeply above us as we passed. On its very pinnacle stood a gibbet or gallows for executions. A frayed rope end floated lazily in the wind. It had a chilling effect. The place belonged in the legends of King Arthur.

A little further in, the steep rock sides suddenly lowered and on Bryher, to our right, gave way to a warm and welcoming sandy beach with green vegetation all around. We turned back towards the deeper water and anchored for the night.

Later, Joe and I took the dinghy and went across to see Cromwell's Castle. It looked fairly ordinary from a distance, but once inside it was very impressive. The rough granite-like walls were massively thick and the internal gloom below the vaulted roof set the atmosphere. The way that centuries of dripping water had deposited calcified stripes down walls and supporting columns, was especially evocative. The original floors had gone leaving fireplaces high on the walls and the entrance steps similarly suspended. Tiny windows admitted only the most meagre illumination. From the battlements it was obvious that the strategic siting was well chosen. It dominated the entrance to the anchorage; yet being placed on a narrow neck of land projecting into the water it was defensible from both land and sea.

Up on the hill-top above lay another building, which stood in obvious ruin. It was Charles' Castle. After we'd left Cromwell's we scaled the hill to walk through its broken arches. It had a totally different feel from the dank darkness that we had just left behind. It was light and airy (having no roof), but also warm and somehow welcoming. The views all around were excellent and the scenery uplifting. Strange, that centuries after the Civil War conflict the differences between the protagonists may somehow still be sensed.

That night the wind went slightly to the north and the anchorage became bumpy. In the darkness a big fishing boat entered using an incredibly powerful searchlight which he used to pick his way through the anchored yachts to a mooring buoy. He stayed most of the night processing his catch on deck with deck lights on and generators running, so restful sleep was elusive. In the morning he was gone.

Issue 224. Episode 19.

<u>August 21 - 22.</u>
We needed more supplies so we had to cross to St. Mary's. The tide was high during the morning and we set off to go through the channel at Tresco Flats from our anchorage in New Grimsby Sound. I detoured up to the quay at Bryher where there were a couple of Bennet catamarans. As I left and headed back for the channel I saw the tip of Merrick Island protruding awash from the water only at the very last minute and narrowly missed ignominiously sticking myself onto it. I went back into the channel immediately and followed it carefully until we were past the Hulman Beacon.

We motored over to Hugh Town and as it was close to high water we went alongside the main pier to take on water and more food. For a brief while it was gloriously sunny. *Starship* looked at her best from up on the quay and lots of people stopped to gaze and wonder. On leaving we motored over to Crow Point a landing place on Tresco so that Gill and Ray could go and look around the tropical gardens there. Joe and I worked on the boat again until just after lunch when one of the launches carrying trippers to Tresco detoured in our direction. Ray and Gill had hitched a lift back out to us, much to the delight of the many passengers. We pretended not to want them back and made as if to repel them, much to everyone's amusement. The water where we were anchored was crystal clear; it was like floating over an extensive rock garden with sandy patches and endless varieties of foliage represented by seaweeds of many textures and shapes. Whilst we were there one of the Bennett catamarans came sailing by. It surely rated maximum points in the rare-breed section of the Catamaran Spotter's Handbook.

Having got ourselves sorted out we decided to head for the linked Islands of St. Agnes and Hugh but the weather had deteriorated incredibly and was now overcast and drizzling with only a faint breeze. We were in no particular hurry so we only hoisted the genoa and started ghosting along tacking towards St. Agnes. We managed to sail into the 'roads' at Perconger Ledge before having to use the motor to get into Porth Conger a small anchorage between the two islands, which are joined by a high sand bar at low water. There were already several yachts there taking the best positions, but we were able to go inside them due to our shallow draught. We anchored in five to six feet of water on a sandy bottom at dead low water. Across on St. Agnes queues of trippers waited on the sloping ramp to be ferried back to the main island. It had suddenly become bitterly cold and then the skies opened and an almighty deluge descended so fiercely that it made us feel snug and secure to hear it drumming on the canopy and roof.

In the evening it brightened again and we went ashore to leave Ray in the Turk's Head whilst Gill and I explored the island. I thought that we might wander in peace and quiet around this remote corner of the world, but it was not to be. Each house had a diesel generator thumping away in a little shed somewhere at the bottom of the garden. The rate of stroke of each engine was erratically different from the next, so that the unsynchronised thumps and bumps emitted from sound-amplifying holes in walls produced a permanent 'traffic jam' effect which totally ruined the idyllic simplicity of the place. We walked slowly over the island on the road which had been constructed by the inhabitants. On the way we read the voters list posted in the village. There were 59 names. To the far west we looked out to sea at the lovely red sunset and the lonely finger of the lighthouse on Bishop's Rock. We returned in darkness to pick up Ray and go back aboard the boat.

Once again the wind went around to the north during the night and there was a gentle swell entering the harbour making it unsettled. At high water the strip of land linking the two islands was completely submerged so that it appeared to be a single Sound all the way through. At low water at three o'clock in the morning there was that ominous swish again which told me that we were taking the ground once more. I got out onto the foredeck to see if I could pull her forwards into the deeper water, but it was to no avail. We'd fallen foul of the wind shift. When we'd anchored the wind had been (by land deflection) from the south, a slight shift and it was deflected to the north during the night. The length of our mooring warp allowed the boat to describe a considerable circle and the distance across that circle was sufficient to put us on the sandy bottom for an hour, even though we were moving towards neaps and the tide had a smaller range than the previous one. Fortunately we faced the ripples and on the softer bottom only bobbed lightly, so that once again the crew were not disturbed.

August 22nd

The red sky on the previous night was accurate in its forecast because we woke to welcome sunshine and almost calm. We made a prompt start because the tidal sequence commenced at eight o'clock for us on our journey back to the mainland.

We left through St. Mary's Sound under motor on a course of 95°m so that the north-going stream would take us up towards the land. We gazed enthralled at the coves and caves, houses and rocks on the southern shore of St. Mary's, unfolding like an intricate model railway layout with interest around every corner. The conditions were beautiful and the air was clear. Looking just to the left of our course we were surprised how easily we could see the blue line which marked the English mainland.

We must have motored for about half an hour when a gentle breeze sprang up, so we hoisted the main but kept the motor going for there was little strength in the wind as yet. We were all lounging around on deck and in the cockpit when I noticed what I took to be a rougher patch of water surrounding us and sure enough a breeze filled in, but at the same moment Ray who was steering shouted "Dolphins, Dolphins!" and jumped up out of the helmsman's seat. Immediately the water was being cut by their fins *as* they gambolled about us and we were pointing in all directions and shouting, "There's one, there's another. See that? Over there." The water was beautifully clear and we could see them speeding through it just over a metre down and occasionally rising to the surface. Standing at the bow I'd see a pair go off to one side and then race back towards us passing just ahead or just below the boat, then they'd make a quick turn and cut back to pass us again. They came at all angles and although we were all in different parts of the boat, we each had an individual show to marvel at. We'd cut the engine and we were moving gently ahead under sail. I tried to photograph them but contact with dolphins (actually the Common Porpoise) in our waters is so precious that I couldn't help agreeing with Gill when she said (camera in hand), 'I'm not going to bother with this, I'm just going to watch and enjoy them'.

After perhaps four or five minutes the last pair of dolphins departed and it was impossible to determine whether they would return. When they had gone there was a sense of silence even though they hadn't made any noise. There was just the sun, the sound of the sea and the lolloping motion of the boat and we wished very hard that they would come back. We generally agreed that the porpoises we had seen were about four or five feet in length and we guessed that there were about ten or twelve of them and they had departed in a south-westerly direction. Contact with them was an unforgettable experience.

After such an exciting event and with big smiles on our faces we unrolled the genoa and made good progress for a while, passing about two miles north of the Wolf Rock at midday. When we were level with Land's End at 12.30, the wind dropped and the motor ran until with little warning, it coughed and died, leaving us drifting. The captain, I am sorry to say, was still thinking of dolphins and had neglected to check the fuel level in the tank, leading to the cardinal sin of emptying the fuel pipes into the engine. I paid the price for this omission by having to bleed the new fuel through the system with my head poked through an access hatch into the claustrophobic confines of the engine compartment with a lumpy, bumpy boat motion. It serves me right. I'll be more careful in future. When finally the motor was restored to health a very smart breeze suddenly arrived from the south west and we set off at a lick across Mount's Bay. The breeze seemed inclined to depart so we dug out our drifter and also our 'cardboard' storm jib which had last surfaced one desperate night in the Skagerrak. We even hung our washing out to dry and managed two precious hours at over six knots to bring us up to the Lizard where we had to combat two knots of foul tide on a dead run. We only made progress by using our width, goosewinging our genoa on one side and our spinnaker on the other, leading their sheets through snatch blocks on the shrouds.

By early evening we had managed to reach the Manacle Rock but we were being progressively blanketed by the land, so we motored the last leg into Falmouth to pick up a mooring at about eight o'clock having covered 62 miles over the ground in the twelve hours. We'd done it mainly under sail, in very light conditions with one complete run of foul tide, so for a fully loaded cruiser we were quite pleased. Ray and Joe went over to the yacht club for a shower, but most of the liquid they encountered went inside them rather than outside.

MI issue 225. Episode 20.

To Fowey.
August 23 - August 24
We'd had a fairly calm night on our mooring in Falmouth and we awoke to indifferent overcast weather but we switched our VHF to scan the working channels, i.e. 16. 67 (Coastguard) and 62 (Pendennis Radio) and listened in. We soon got the information that we needed, because several people were asking for forecasts. The usual gale was on its way and supposed to arrive about dinner time.

It's worth a short digression here to just look at this topic of weather on the VHF, because it can be a little tricky. We noted when we listened in that there were a number of different approaches. In general there were three different basic forecast methods. The Shipping Forecast, The Inshore Waters Forecast and extra weather bulletins such as 'strong wind warnings' for small craft. People calling up would ask fairly vaguely for a 'weather forecast', but the shore station might then enquire, 'What do you want, Shipping or Inshore Waters?' If one of these was chosen (on this particular morning it was 'Shipping') then the enquirer was likely to receive only that information. For this day the general shipping forecast which had been drawn up at five o'clock spoke of moderate winds with the slight possibility of some increase later. We had been tuned to channel 16 at about eight o'clock when there was a special message from the Met Office giving a strong wind warning. This was a much tougher forecast than the shipping forecast. It stated that winds over gale force were imminent. Only a few minutes had passed following this message when some fellow who had obviously only just switched on called up to ask what the weather was going to be like. Being experienced, he asked directly for the shipping forecast, and that is exactly what he received. At the end of the forecast the operator casually added that there was a strong wind warning out also, but it appeared that the significance of this was not appreciated because the enquirer simply signed off without asking for any further elaboration. The information was exactly what he'd requested, but it gave a totally false impression of what was about to occur with the weather. I think that there might be a case for not being too specific about the forecast. Perhaps we should ask for the 'latest weather information', meaning that we require information from all types of forecast, whichever is most relevant to our situation. Or at least we should understand the importance of special warnings and ask if there are any in force at the time. I'm sure that the coastal operators would add that we should try to tune in to forecasts for ourselves, or perhaps do what we were doing, which was to listen in at appropriate times to overhear the information being given to others, rather than going onto the air directly.

We had a favourable wind from the south west for our trip from Falmouth to Fowey which was of sufficient strength for me not to consider using the spinnaker. We did it with ordinary sails leaving at about eight o'clock on an easterly course, which with leeway and tide still gave us plenty of clearance on Dodman Point. Later we freed off onto a dead run. We had a storm building in the sky behind us and we went scudding along before the wind looking back from time to time to see how the black clouds were progressing. For the last couple of miles we had one or two little surfs as the waves took hold of us and we ran on. Smiles all round again. The misty rain which was the forerunner of worse to come finally caught us just as we reached Gribben Head at the entrance to Fowey and it was

West Country sailing.

blowing force five as we shot into the harbour and rounded up at 10.30 having sailed 22 miles in the two and a half hours.

It was obvious that there was some kind of event in progress from the number of craft racing in the harbour. It turned out to be Regatta week which was soon to assume significance for us. We went directly to pick up a visitor's mooring but the approach was difficult in the strong wind and it took us three attempts before we managed to secure. The mooring astern of us was so close that we were able to fasten fore and aft. The man in the Harbour launch said that he'd not noticed it and charged us the standard fee of £3 for two days with the third day free. Quite a bargain and in keeping with the way that one is encouraged to <u>stay</u> in Fowey. The reason that we had returned to Fowey was find somewhere to leave *Starship* for the coming winter. When I had departed from my home port at the beginning of the year I had no idea of where I might eventually leave my boat. I was not too badly concerned about this.

Most sailors want to lay up their boats near to home so that they can keep an eye on the craft and carry out maintenance. This is the most satisfactory solution, but I knew that if I was going to venture up to Scotland I would at some stage have to either engage in long return sails to the East Coast or come to terms with the idea of leaving the boat wherever she reached at the end of each sailing season. I had already left her several times as I progressed along the south coast and now I had to prepare to leave her a little longer. If I had been based locally I would have worked out the best arrangement for my boat and would have happily left her for extended periods throughout the winter. This is what all sailors do wherever they are based, in the Solent, in Plymouth, or in Fowey. I knew that I would have to turn myself into a local and use the same systems that they had evolved for their particular geographical situation.

I had been especially well treated in Millbrook at Foss Quay and originally I had a mind to return there, but when we first passed through Fowey we received such a generous welcome that I thought that it was well worth returning to see what might be arranged.

During the afternoon I struggled to repair a broken recoil starter spring in my outboard. Oh what super fun that was. It's a bit like one of those medical operations that you see on the television if you are not too squeamish. The main surgeon is firmly pressing down a coiled mainspring with oily fingers onto the galley draining board, coolly giving commands like 'Pliers', 'Screwdriver', to assistants who are working beneath his elbows on either side. Slowly each assistant is also drawn into holding some vital component securely in the correct place and the surgeon is reduced to indicating where the bits should be by stabbing down through the massed hands with the tip of his nose. We had to admit defeat in the end and take the bits ashore for help. Having no outboard we took the Water Taxi which we called up on the radio. The service was most convenient, but the vehicle was a wonder to behold. It was a little diesel launch with high top hamper and so self-willed that it was almost impossible to steer. Bringing it alongside anything needed dexterity in both the arms and feet of the helmsman who had to constantly spin the tiny steering wheel whilst engaging gear, fending off and throttling back simultaneously. We used it again in the evening when we took Ray ashore to return home, but this time we were forced to use it, because it was blowing top force seven or maybe eight. The driver made it clear that he'd have to stop operating the taxi at 21.30 because the weather was now force eight inside the harbour and in fact the lifeboat was called out (complete with three maroons) to rescue a couple of board sailors in the harbour mouth. Getting aboard the taxi was hard enough to go ashore, but when it came time to return the driven rain and waves made it difficult to see in the darkness. It was almost 'survival' out there with the taxi being thrown around all over the place and the driver operating a squeegee on the outside of the windscreen as well as steering and performing the intricate tap dance on gear lever, all at the same time.

We were thankful to get on board and that night we had the roughest passage of the whole trip. It felt like we were beating to windward in a choppy sea whereas in fact we were securely moored inside a very sheltered harbour.

<u>August 24</u>
Things had quietened down considerably in the morning and the sun was actually shining, but it turned out to be a very changeable day. We went over to the town to do our shopping and then we went onto the veranda at the Royal Fowey Yacht Club to eat our lunch, bask in the sun and watch the general to-ing and fro-ing of tenders, launches and people coming ashore or going afloat.

Fowey has two yacht clubs. The one already mentioned is more or less what one would expect from its title 'Royal'. It is superbly positioned in a commanding site on the cliff side just inside the harbour entrance. There is a bar and a restaurant, the atmosphere is traditional in every respect and one is allowed to take advantage of its excellent facilities in most civilised surroundings. There is a second club which is much more difficult to find at the opposite end of the town down a little alley near to the Post Office. This is the Fowey Gallants Yacht Club and we found it to be a truly remarkable experience each time that we set a foot in the place.

It had all started when we had first visited Fowey earlier in the month on our way out to the Scillies. We'd had a rough beat up from Plymouth and had just picked up a mooring to relax in the sheltered sun of the harbour when I noticed a man in a little launch circling us and showing interest in the boat. We got into conversation and we were immediately invited to go to the Fowey Gallants. From the moment that we walked in we were totally accepted by everyone as full social members of the group. We were always included into the discussions of any group of people that we found ourselves near to. We didn't need introductions, we didn't have to offer explanations, we were just part of the club and the club had the most active social programme that one could imagine.

Serial Starship

Starship had almost finished travelling for the year, but her adventures were to continue right through the winter in or near to Fowey, a place which we found to be most unusual.

MI issue 226. Episode 21.

Regatta/Carnival. <u>August 24</u>

Hoping to find a winter berth for *Starship* we went along at lunchtime to the bar at the Fowey Gallants Yacht Club to meet friends that we'd made on our previous visit. It was the last Saturday in Regatta week and the whole place was thronging with people. Almost immediately that we'd entered we were invited to crew in the afternoon's race in a 'Troy' class boat, which is the local three-man, one design, keel boat. I jumped at the chance, so Joe, my crew and I made our way down to the water to be ferried across to the moored craft. One of Fowey's most famous former residents was the writer known as 'Q', Sir Arthur Quiller Couch. In his writings he referred to Fowey as 'Troytown' and this was the derivation of the class name of the half-decker that we were approaching. Our helmsman had borrowed the boat for the race. He was a young chap in his early twenties and probably didn't want to boss two old timers around, for he had very little to say.

We hoisted sails and tensioned luffs. The jib was set flying and the luff sagged off quite a bit. Its sheeting arrangement was quite novel. The sheet was continuous and after coming in through the fairleads it went as a loop onto a single small winch at the front of the cockpit coaming and then off to a jamb cleat. The headsail area was small and could easily be pulled in by hand. The main was very large and really too big. When sailing there was a constant sense of being over-powered in the gusts. The whole rig had great flexibility and everything was twisting off at the top. Mast bend, rigging stretch, boom, bow and hull twist, gave the sensation of sailing a piece of elastic.

The one thing that we beginners weren't very sure about was the correct sequence for setting the spinnaker, but our helmsman wasn't very communicative on this topic. I suggested that it would be nice to try one hoist just to see what happened, but he said that there wasn't time as there were only five minutes to go to the beginning of the race. We manoeuvred around sailing a circular procession at the starboard end of the line and made an excellent start. Taking everything into consideration we were probably in the lead. One other boat was slightly ahead, but to leeward and the two of us broke well clear of the rest. We beat towards the harbour mouth with the windward mark in the centre of the entrance. The chap ahead was more close-winded and our advantage slipped away until we were following his transom. Rounding the top mark we immediately got into a tangle with the spinnaker gear. In the kerfuffle a blast of wind hit us and torrential rain started to pour. We had as much wind as we needed and went shooting along like a speedboat. I took the jib sheet to keep it filled and we forgot about the spinnaker for the relatively short run back up the harbour. The leading boat had gained very little as we rounded the leeward mark and started to tack up again. Unfortunately a loud blast on a hooter spoiled our next efforts. A huge ship was coming up the harbour and whilst we could have crossed his bow, we would have given everybody a fright. The lead boat was already across, but we had to tack back into a mass of small boat moorings on the Fowey side, losing contact with the leader and he gained another 50 metres.

I was doing very little work sitting up to windward except hold my weight in the right place and give an occasional twist to the bilge pump to try to keep the boat dry. Having assisted with the jib when going about, I was busy watching the behaviour of the keel cutting through the clear water as I hung over the starboard side, when all of a sudden there was an almighty bang followed by the flogging of the sails, and I looked ahead to see that we'd speared a Mirror dinghy on the end of our bowsprit. Our helmsman was shouting "Why the bloody hell don't you watch where you're going?" at the two young Mirror crew who were looking very surprised and confused. They'd pushed us through onto port tack and their forestay was entangled in our bowsprit. I shot across our foredeck, freed them and invited their helmsman to steer away from us. Their jib was torn. It was a straightforward port/starboard incident and they were in the wrong. I don't think that any of us saw any of them prior to the collision due to the huge mainsail obstructing our vision when we were heavily heeled.

As we gybed round to come back on the wind the next Troy sailed past and just as we were beginning to move ahead another one overtook us, thus we lost two places immediately. As we closed the windward mark it became clear that a third boat which had gone well inshore on the Polruan side had also caught up and gone ahead. We rounded the mark and got into the most almighty tangle with the spinnaker.

I had managed to extract the 12 feet long wooden pole from beneath the side deck and positioned it to be pushed forwards. On our first attempt at a hoist Joe gave a cry that the pole was in the water. It was such an unwieldy thing that as it was pushed forwards and swung out ahead of the shroud the sail which was clipped to its end trailed and scooped in a terrific quantity of water, causing the pole to bend alarmingly. Reaching overboard I grabbed the sail and supported it out of the water whilst sliding the pole back inboard. Once the water was drained from the sail, it became lighter and more manageable.

We tried again. Joe supported the pole and was working it outboard. I started the hoist and the sail went up about three metres. There was quite a lot of it and we were moving at speed. Joe was cursing. How the hell are you supposed to hold the end of a bloody pole like this? He stood up and the billowing sail wrapped itself around him. He disappeared inside its folds. It was pouring with rain and the wet sailcloth was sticking to him. "Hold on a minute. Hold on!" he shouted. I stopped hoisting and reached forward to start pulling the sail off Joe when he gave a sudden shout. The pole hit the water again, bent around like a banana and shattered into three or four pieces. There was an awful silence as I pulled as many pieces back into the boat as I could find. We sailed on just using the jib in very subdued mood, rounding the course again, thankfully without incident this time and then we returned to our mooring. On reflection we decided that perhaps I should have taken the steering downwind to free the experienced man who was familiar with the hoisting sequence. Our boat (with a different helm and crew) had apparently run down and written off a dinghy only the day before, so our helmsman went off looking rather dejected to plead insanity (ours) with the owner.

Back on the deck of *Starship* in the afternoon we could hear above the town sounds, the beautiful mellow tones of a brass band coming drifting across the water. All the usual favourites including The Floral Dance, which goes so well with a Cornish setting were played. Between songs there was sometimes a prolonged silence whilst the band rested. On occasion, this calm was broken by a loud explosion followed by frantic drumming interspersed with shouts, more bangs and the most awful bugle playing ever heard. It was difficult to reconcile this racket with the gentle expertise of the band when it was tune playing, so we were slightly mystified. In fact we were later to discover that the sounds came from two quite different sources.

We crossed over to the Fowey Gallants in the early evening and as we neared it, down the narrow streets we heard the now familiar patterns of noise. A sudden loud report followed by frantic drumming as though someone was about to be beheaded which then resolved itself into a steady marching beat with occasional shouts, more shots and all punctuated by the tremendous thump of a huge base drum.

As we rounded a corner an incredible rag-bag of assorted characters came marching along and into the club with us. Their dress was unbelievable. Although completely mixed together we could make out three basic costumes. There were 'Mexican Revolutionaries' with blankets as ponchos, big straw hats, all draped around with cartridge belts. There were 'Australian Boy Scouts', olive green uniforms with shorts, hairy knees and hats with one brim turned up at the side. Most striking of all were the 'French Foreign Legionnaires' straight from the pages of Beau Geste, except that they must have been most valiant, because most of them had a chest full of medals. Their General had the most lavish uniform. His tall cap alone had more braid than some of the private's complete uniforms. Some waved swords, one even carried a huge ramrod and they dragged a life-sized cannon which they parked outside before going inside to order pints of ale.

You can well imagine the effect of the entry of this band of characters. They more than brightened the place up, especially when they began to sing. Just the snatch of a tune from here and there to begin with, but then as the beer flowed so they sang more and they sang well, and they knew all the words to all the traditional songs. They were infectious and soon everybody in the building was well into the songs. When everything was in full flow the 'General' stepped up and gave a faultless recitation of 'The Wreck of the Hesperus' illustrated with actions. He got such an ovation that he went straight into 'Gunner Joe' another long and intricate poem, this time about a young chap who was fighting for Nelson and in the midst of the battle he was shot from the ship with a cannon ball under each arm.

We were all in stitches at this and giving him a hearty cheer prior to launching into the next song when in came a smashing young lady in a Bunny Girl outfit, all black leotard, black stockings with gold trimmings. She was the forerunner of a large group of such ladies who eventually turned up and started singing too. Everyone was singing, dancing and drinking. The ladies brought a chap along with them whose job it was to carry their money and pay their rather substantial bar bills.

All this first class entertainment was part of the Fowey Regatta/Carnival week. There were numbers of such fancy dress groups formed from the ordinary townspeople. Each group was based on a public house and they each dressed up to celebrate Carnival, which had been scheduled for the previous Wednesday, but on that day a torrential downpour had washed out the celebration. Feeling cheated of their fun evening they decided to celebrate instead on the Saturday. Not everyone in the original teams was available, so this had meant that the remnants of the separate groups had joined together instead of performing with their individual bands. The ladies in black were mainly the wives and girlfriends of the Mexicans, Aussies and Legionnaires. Collectively they were called the Cornish Express. When we were almost exhausted in the Gallants everybody decided to go to *The Lugger*, a pub at the far end of town which seemed to have extended hours. Everybody was invited along, but only the fittest could make it. Coming back from *The Lugger* late that night in the middle of the main high street we joined a group of bemused tourists standing in a circle around three young ladies doing an intricate song and dance act in full costume, accompanied only by their own voices to *Singing in the Rain*. Upon completion they took a bow from the crowd and then disappeared into the nearest hotel bar.

The total experience of Fowey was amusing, entertaining and memorable. The atmosphere of the town was unique. Everyone was friendly and helpful and people went out of their way to make us feel part of their group. None of us had ever experienced that degree of welcome wherever we had been. We went back aboard after a day that we will never forget, humming, *Singing in the Rain*.

MI issue 227. Episode 22.

<u>August 25 Sunday - August 27 1985.</u>
On a coast hopping journey such as ours one of the major problems is land transport. We depart from one location and complete our journey at another. The logistics of meeting the crew, linking with vehicles and supplying the ship, dominates the whole journey. This has been one of the major reasons for embarking upon this particular sail. We have done similar exercises in other countries where there has been the added difficulty of foreign currency, language and Customs clearance. Nevertheless, even on the present journey we were still faced with quite large problems which required strenuous

efforts to overcome. One can feel overwhelmed by such difficulties or accept them as a natural part of cruising. I usually find that my struggle against the elements does not cease when I step ashore, my battle with adversity continues, as will be seen.

Our cars were in Millbrook opposite to Plymouth and the journey from Fowey on public transport looked lengthy and expensive, with potentially a long walk at the end of it as the Bank Holiday meant curtailed services. Looking at the map I could see that if I crossed to Polruan on the opposite bank from Fowey, I could follow a coast road using our ship's bicycle for a 'horizontal' distance of about 25 miles. So, being prepared, I landed on a slipway, lifted my cycle over a spiked fence and started off about midday. The initial half mile of the route was vertical, straight up the main street in blazing sunshine, causing me to keep stopping to take more layers of clothes off. At the very top, already exhausted, I rested to be refreshed by the view across the bay towards Dodman Point which was magnificent. A great carpet of blue with tiny white specks of yachts leaving rippling furrows behind them. I could have wasted hours, but there was no time for that. I pressed on. It was a day of instant weather changes with torrential thunderstorms broken by tropical sun.

No sooner had I started downhill than it began to rain, and I had to keep stopping to put on my oilies. My first target village was nine miles away according to the first signpost. After flogging along for about a mile and a half I came to another sign which said that it was now ten miles. A further one and a half miles of hill climbing brought me to a third sign which said that it was still nine miles to go. The lanes in which I travelled were quite narrow and cars meeting each other frequently had to stop for one of them to reverse in order to pass one another. I, on the other hand could go unhindered and it began to develop into a very enjoyable ride of exploration only marred by the weather. Each time that I started a long ascent the sun would appear and burn fiercely on my back. As soon as I commenced a lengthy descent the rain would catch me on the steepest section when I was flying along down a gradient almost too steep to stop on. The road passed through coastal villages at sea level and then climbed, climbed, climbed to reach a kind of undulating plateau. Each time that I descended to the sea in a matter of minutes I knew that I would have to regain the height by pushing the bike up another tortuous hill.

The climb out of Looe was a killer. The weather had saved its party piece for this one. It was a narrow winding main road without footpaths. Cars coming down could only just pass cars going up when I was added to the width restriction. I was attempting to eat my soggy lunch as I walked facing cars appearing blindly from around sharp corners as I slogged upwards in full oilies. Torrents streamed down the road and the raindrops were so big that there was a constant ringing of my cycle bell caused by them hitting it. In conditions of ultimate misery I read the slogan on the top of my fizzy drinks can as I pulled the opener ring 'Cool it', it said. Obviously not designed for an English summer's day.

Eventually, after about 30 miles when all the ups and downs were taken into consideration I wearily cycled into Millbrook at about four o'clock. Now came the 64,000 dollar question. Would my old car start after more than a month of inactive neglect? Unlock, inside, turn the key, a cough and away she went. Terrific! All troubles over. Pack the bike. Take off oilies ready to drive back. Start up again, try to move away. She's stuck fast. Try again and again, but it was no good. She had been left with the hand brake on and the brakes were seized solid. I now found myself in a typical cruising situation where the unexpected failure of a minor component begins to compound itself and obstinate inanimate objects gather themselves to build a wall of adversity. Due to the holiday no help was at hand. I was too remote for the motoring organisations, the telephone was a distance away and I only had limited coins. There was a minimum of petrol in the car and any garages were about to close. I couldn't get a message back to the boat and if I arrived back too late I would be unable to get across to the boat on the mooring. A familiar picture I am sure. I won't bore you with all the details, but I made it out of this cruising situation. It took strenuous efforts, to the limits of my physical and monetary resources and a further four and a half hours to extract myself from the predicament and it was a relief to arrive back in Fowey just in time to catch the last water taxi out to the boat, arriving heavy with fatigue and ravenously hungry.

<u>August 26 Monday</u>
We took a tourist's day off and drove Joe, our departing crew to Millbrook to collect his car, returning by way of the Bodinnick Ferry just above Fowey. This was quite an experience for the car was driven onto a small pontoon which had a fishing launch lashed alongside to power it across the river at a point where the tidal flow was considerable. The whole lash-up gave me a very precarious feeling especially as the loading ramp wasn't raised high enough and the water was scooped up, until my front wheels were getting wet. I

was busy releasing my seat belt and wishing that I had a lifejacket on the crossing. I was pleased to get back aboard *Starship.*

We moved the boat into Pont Creek opposite Fowey looking for a mooring which it had been suggested that we might borrow. There was too little space around the mooring when we found it and we had to come out to the entrance of the creek to pick up one of the public moorings overnight. We had a quiet evening packing and wondering where we were going to leave the boat for we still did not know. We'd had lots of offers which had never really quite materialised. We took off the sails and the safety netting, feeling quite sad and insecure not knowing what tomorrow might bring. The harbour felt empty as this was the last recognised day of holiday and most people were heading for home. The season was coming to a close.

<u>August 27 Tuesday</u>
We were woken at about eight o'clock by the sound of powerful engines outside. A big working launch was using a crane to lift the moorings to clear the creek ready for dredging operations to begin. They asked us to move, so we went out into the main harbour where I left *Starship* moored whilst I went to see the Assistant Harbour Master to seek advice about leaving the boat. I had already met him previously and he was aware of my wish to stay. We discussed possibilities and we followed his advice.

Upstream from Fowey there is a village called Golant and on the opposite side of the river a shallow creek called Penpoll. All the craft in this area were in the care of two boatmen at Golant and we went to see one of them who told us that many craft would be laid up on the north bank of the creek and we were free to join them, providing we respected certain established positions. We were told how to lay out two anchors from the stern, with the largest one upstream to guard against easterly gales. We then had to take ropes ashore and secure to trees growing on the steep bank. In practice, I managed to lay the anchors remarkably well, because it was quite a complex affair with ropes completely covering the deck of the boat. Unfortunately as the lines were paid out and I headed for the shore one of them went out tangled and it stopped me short with just a couple of metres to go. I tried to quickly extend the line by tying another onto it, but in manoeuvring to run in again the inevitable happened and I picked up the downstream warp on the prop. The tide was now falling and the boat was drifting out into the stream. I linked a couple of ropes leapt into the dinghy and struck out for the shore to find that I was about half a metre short of the nearest securing point. I tied on the dinghy painter as well and just reached a branch which was in the water, this then allowed me to get out and pull her in. I took lines up to the trees which although they were mature oaks were in danger of falling, due to the cliff-like bank subsiding. Half the bank fell away along with rotten tree stumps as I tried to descend and I arrived back at the beach in an avalanche. The boat was now well settled high up the shale beach and I could see the rope fouling the prop through the clear water. I managed to unwind it to the last turn which was nipped. We ate, packed, and completed the stripping of the boat. Finally at about eight o'clock in the evening I was able to free the rope.

Everything had been loaded and we motored away with just enough depth of water for the inflatable feeling very sad to leave her. We crossed to Golant and managed to get all the kit into the car in the darkness, Feeling very grubby and tired we set off to drive back home, there to catch up on domestic life, do the washing, sleep, and recover from this our first year of our journey. We did not know it at the time but it had been a gentle introduction and more testing times lay ahead.

Note. Racing monohull keel failure. The Vendée Globe race captured the sailing public's imagination in 1996/7 with the dramatic rescues of Thierry Dubois, Tony Bullimore and Raphael Dinelli following keel failures. A further 17 keel failures (until January 2013) in this race probably indicates a lack of cutting-edge experience by designers. This does not mean that all monohulls with fin keels are dangerous. It is a similar story with multihulls that might be broken or inverted when racing at, or beyond, the absolute limit. Failures have often been the result of pushing technical understandings beyond known limits in the search for increased performance.

Year Two.

(Serious adventures begin)

Over winter

Repairs

Bristol Channel Force 10

Village square mooring

Fishguard officials

Cardigan solitude

North Wales

Caernarvon

Engine

Working the Weather

Making an Entrance

Scotland. Stranraer. Ailsa Craig. Arran

Rothesay & Millport Piers

Pic: *Starship* leaves the garden

Serial Starship

MI issue 228. Episode 23.

<u>Beginning the Season.</u>
I can't say that I enjoyed leaving *Starship* tied to a tree many miles from home at the conclusion of the first season on our slow sail around Britain. Just after Christmas I decided that I must return to Fowey to check that she was OK. With my good friend Paul Brown we raced across England to arrive one crisp morning at Golant where I was reassured to find that the boat was more or less as we'd left her, except that instead of standing in isolation, the whole of the northern shore of Penpol was lined with laid-up craft, forming a cat's cradle of warps to ensure that it would be impossible for any individual craft to come adrift. We cleaned up a bit inside, but essentially the boat was alright.

We could not visit Fowey without popping into the amazing Fowey Gallants club. No sooner had we stepped through the door than a chap I'd never met before asked, 'Are you coming to Jim and Jayne's party tonight? We've got a coach coming to pick us up, so we can drink as much as we like. You really must come.' Regretfully we had to decline as we were already exhausted and had booked into a local pub in the town. It was fortunate that we didn't go, as a blanket of snow fell overnight, an unusual event in maritime Cornwall. Next morning, half of the townsfolk were gently meandering the Christmas-card streets looking in wonder; most could only recall one previous snowfall.

Our plan had been to drive over to Padstow on the northern side of the Cornish peninsula to get an idea of the geography of the place. It is perhaps only fifteen to twenty miles from Fowey as the crow flies but to reach it under sail means over a hundred miles of hazardous headland hopping around the Lizard and Land's End. I was beginning to form a strategy for the coming season and I'd become aware of the fact that crossing from Land's End to South Wales entailed a long and exposed sail in open Atlantic seas. One of the best potential stopover places was Padstow, but I had no idea of the quality of the entrance and wanted to look at it from the land if possible. With snow blocking the roads over Bodmin Moor we had to rethink the Padstow plan. In fact we were fortunate to escape from Fowey at all, for the only two roads involved long hill climbs, one impossibly steep and the other blocked by cars stranded at all angles. Anyone attempting to climb the hill eventually crashed into someone else already stuck as they slithered out of control on the compacted snow. They were all very cheerful about it and all on first name terms with each other in true Fowey fashion - what a wonderful place. We escaped that bout of weather and returned home knowing that our next visit would be at Easter, when we hoped for an improvement in conditions. It was a vain hope.

The horrendous weather of our first season continued unabated into this year with more snow than at any time since 1947 and a couple of days before the early Easter break the British Isles were experiencing winds up to 153 mph. I have never seen so many trees uprooted. All around my home the streets were filled with broken branches mixed with woodchips from the chainsaws used to clear the debris. My garden shed moved ½ metre sideways and my fence blew down. Like everyone else we told ourselves that it must soon blow itself out and then turn fine for the holidays, but on the morning of departure when I put out my milk bottles for collection (*as we did in those days*) they were blown over and broken within minutes. I added the shattered glass to my list of indicators of wind strength on the Beaufort scale.

<u>March 28 Good Friday</u>.
We had a strong team of five adults packed into two cars. Our tentative plan would be to refurbish the boat, using the long weekend and then if conditions allowed, sail the boat to South Wales via Padstow and/or Lundy Island during the rest of the week, for which we'd arranged time off work. We had an elaborate plan for retrieving the cars, which was a very complex logistical problem. Heading for the West Country involved joining a 350 mile traffic jam as everybody else went the same way. After crossing the Tamar Bridge three of the crew celebrated in the pub whilst the other two stayed sober to drive the rest of the way. It was that kind of occasion, everybody going on holiday, but in the certain knowledge that being outdoors was going to be distinctly uncomfortable and for those *determined* to have a good time a bit of inner warmth was necessary. Arriving with time to spare before the tide we went into Fowey to potter about then returned to Golant at about 16.30 to commence the huge job of

ferrying gear across. As we boarded *Starship* a young chap came down the creek in an inflatable marked with the name *Slithy Tove* (a radical monohull with RBR experience), so I greeted him with some enthusiasm. He was Paul Weychan son of the designer of the same name who was responsible for the 54' Trimaran *Quest/Tele-7-Jours/Coco de Mer.* We chatted for a while and then he departed for Fowey.

The boat appeared to be just as we had left her, which was pleasing. I loosened her shore lines and pulled her a little further out into the stream to make her stay afloat a little longer, because I knew that she would heel over fairly steeply when aground, making her port side bunks difficult to sleep in. I noticed that she favoured her starboard float very strongly (i.e. she heeled that way when afloat) and I wondered briefly if I should re-trim her (take gear stored in the float across to the other one) because the port float was clean (never having been in the water all winter). I guessed that the fouling on the bottom of the starboard float was absorbing water which made it heavy; by re-trimming weight across the boat I could lift it clear of the water to dry it out and kill the weed growth. We were all pretty tired though and I had a more pressing priority which was to get the engine running whilst we were still afloat with cooling water available. I chased the fuel through the system and worked on a valve which seemed a bit sticky, then tried it. It fired and ran, to great celebrations from the rest of the crew who had been cautious with the use of electric lights until this point. I was impressed with my batteries. They had remained untouched since installation and uncharged for a full seven months, yet they responded perfectly. The crew used this success to hit the bottle again and celebrations were complete when further work succeeded in recommissioning the outlet seacock on the marine toilet which immediately became fully functioning again. By nine thirty we'd clambered exhausted to bed, as the boat took the ground. I vaguely heard the watery sounds from outside as I fell asleep - strange, I thought the water had already receded.

March 29 Saturday.
The morning had pleasant sunshine, but it was cold, windy, and dark clouds were massing. No sooner had we finished breakfast and popped out to look at the job in hand than the heavens opened and rain started bouncing off the deck. We retired below to wait. During a break in the deluge we sallied forth and around under the port side as the tide was out, to start cleaning the fouling off the main hull in

readiness for applying the antifouling paint. During this operation whilst looking for a scrubbing brush Ray opened the starboard float hatch and began to remove the odd lengths of wood stored in there. He took out a spare oar and from my vantage point on the main bow I could see that it appeared to be covered in a thin film of mud. Each piece of wet wood which emerged was the same. Slightly concerned, I went across and looked into the float and was horrified to see a thick layer of mud coating the inside of the bottom of the float, indicating a clear water level, yet there was no water there. Very worrying and a bit of a puzzle. There was obviously a hull leak somewhere. Peering more carefully into the depths I noticed between 'slabs' of mud a tiny pin prick of light, which further investigation showed to be the first evidence of two sizeable holes punched through the solid glass skin of the inside face of the float. All around the boat on the beach were logs and root clusters from dead trees which had fallen down the eroded bank onto the shore. The nearest deadhead had many jagged projections tipped with the tell-tale blue antifouling, which showed where the damage had originated. At each tide the float had filled until its sealed buoyancy had lifted it and then it had drained at low water in a trickle that I had heard before sleep the previous night. A more thorough examination revealed a third hole on the outside of the float roughly amidships, halfway between keel and gunwhale.

It was a sickening discovery and the first sensations of helplessness, self-pity and a hopeless feeling of, What shall I do now? washed over me in the usual way. Sailors have to be resourceful, so perhaps you can join me in making the decisions because at times such as these the crew will usually gather around, look at the damage then look to you for inspiration. For most of the time you are all a big bunch of friends, all equal, but now you suddenly find that you're the owner, the captain and apparently - the problem-solving genius with total responsibility. It's all up to you. Now, get out of that. If you want to be a cruising sailor you've got to learn to deal with this kind of thing. So what would **you** do?

We were tucked up a rural creek opposite the village of Golant, far distant from the technology that I wanted to restore my float and the immediate difficulties of getting everything that was required together seemed insurmountable. I wasn't seeking a temporary repair to get me home. I had to make a permanent repair so that the journey could continue. I had all the things that I needed back in Suffolk, but could I drive back, load up and return? I costed it in terms of petrol and time. Even then my troubles would not be over. I needed shore power for the grinder for cutting back the glass. I considered taking the float off and towing it at high water over to Golant behind the inflatable. This is feasible with *Starship* but securing her mast might become a problem, and inherent difficulties with towing the thirty foot hull as well as repositioning it for fixing afterwards were not to be underestimated. Whilst I pondered this, the weather was plunging us alternately from blizzard to hurricane. How could I glassfibre in such conditions? I needed a shed. How could I get the boat into one? And then there was the question which sent a chill down my spine. How much was all this going to cost? What a miserable prospect was in store for this holiday.

The problem, in total, simply seized up the mind. Complex problems have to be broken down. I started to think more logically. What did I actually *need* to get the job done? Item by Item and how could I go about getting each of them? Resin. Glass, Brushes, Solvent, Grinder, Power, Filler, Shelter, Warmth.

Now I began to make progress.

MI issue 229. Episode 24.

29 March - 1 April
Starship had a holed float, far from facilities on the rural shores of a little creek and the weather was doing its utmost to make life even more miserable. How could we affect a repair to the glassfibre under such adverse conditions? We needed glassing materials, but most of all we needed warmth and shelter to set the repair and we had to have electric power for a grinderette to cut back the glass. These last two requirements were the most difficult - sheltered warmth and power. I thought back through my experiences in building *Starship* for inspiration and realised that I had been in a similar situation once before when I had arranged for her to be hauled out at a boatyard one winter for the fitting of her new inboard diesel.

The crated engine had arrived at the yard and had been placed in the corner of a shed. I had asked the manager how much it would cost for moving the motor to the boat and then lifting it up into the cockpit for me to commence lowering it into place for fitting. With a sideways glance from the corner of his eye towards one of his workmen he began to run over the job. Well, unfortunately we can't get the crane alongside you unless we move two other boats, then there'll be the lift, and then ... and then ... etc. Well it begins to look like three men for six hours on the moving ... and another worker ... etc. I think ... maybe we could fit it in next week ... (he studied my face wondering what figure I might be stretched to). £xxx might get it up there and then maybe we could discuss helping you get it in. I was ready for him and didn't give him any sign. 'I'll just give it a little thought.' I said and wandered to the door of the shed. Outside, the snow was four inches deep and occasional flakes still fell from the overcast sky. *Starship* was on the big slipway and costing a heavy daily rate. In removing the old propulsion unit I had made a small hole in the bottom, so I could not re-launch her. Waiting for the weather to warm up was going to bankrupt me ... come to think of it, moving the engine aboard was going to bankrupt me. I saw an old railway sack barrow in the shed and a plan began to formulate. I asked if I could borrow it and with puzzled glances they agreed. They watched me struggle, but realised that even if I did manage to move the engine out to the boat I could never lift it up into the cockpit. An hour later the engine was underneath the back of the boat and I was breaking the crate away. One man leaned inside the doorway of the shed smoking a cigarette watching me through the falling snow. With a cutting wheel on my grinderette, running off a small E300 generator I cut a large hole in the hull from the bottom of the aft cabin, big enough to pass the engine through. I then clambered up and rigged the main sheet to pass from the supported centre of the boom, through the cabin door, down through the hole and onto the engine. An hour of heaving, chocking, climbing, pushing, sweating and the engine was inside and slid forwards out of the way of the hole. I was able to return the barrow with thanks. A new piece of foam was sprung into place to fill the hole and I was ready to glass the interior. I had now created a closed environment inside the boat with the weather excluded. I rigged a small heater which immediately produced tropical temperatures in the tiny cabin and the glassfibre work proceeded rapidly. Whilst I was engaged in this I realised that if I could produce that amount of warmth over the relatively small area of the repair on the outside then I might surmount the final hurdle. By taping a polythene skirt to the hull around the working area I deflected the dribbles of water which ran down the hull. By warming the resin, the glass, the area being repaired and covering only a very small piece at a time before applying direct heat I managed to complete the job, even though lying on my back in the snow.

In building my boats I have become accustomed to G.R.P. construction and I have learned that it is what happens in the first half an hour after lay-up that really counts. The resin *must* go off within an hour or so and it is dry heat that does the trick - polyester resin just loves heat, providing it doesn't exceed flash point.

Calling upon this previous experience I saw that it was possible to do the present repair in situ, but solutions would not be found in this little creek, so Paul B and I went ashore to spend a day finding the vital things that we needed. We checked a few shops in Fowey and then headed for the larger town of St. Austell. From an autospares shop, a cycle dealer, a DIY Supermarket, a wet fish shop and a tool hire firm we gathered all that was needed. Some things were easy, Polyester resin, body filler and glassfibre are used for car body repairs. Other, more unusual items such as the 1½kv portable petrol generator and grinder, together with a portable butane heater came from a hire shop where we had to wait until 4.30 in the afternoon before collection. This allowed us to retain the gear for the three day holiday whilst only paying for two days. The enforced wait allowed us to explore the town which had several interesting buildings especially the covered market.

Returning to the boat with all the equipment we found that the others had spent a lazy day as constant rain had stopped them from even antifouling the boat. I cleaned out the damaged float and to keep it clear of the water we made her lay over onto the other float. Our real concern on this Saturday evening was to return to Fowey for a disco at the Fowey Gallants. We had a good wash and brush up and then joined in the fun. They had been working hard on an old boat store beneath the club which when we had last seen it was just a rough and draughty hole with an earth floor. Now it was warm and cosy, quite tastefully converted and it included a full-sized billiard table for members use. After a couple of dances in the disco we collapsed from fatigue so by 10.30 we had to leave to be certain of catching our tide back to the boat.

30 March Sunday.
Adjectives to describe the weather begin to fail me. Just the *noise* of what was happening outside the boat was quite frightening. At first it looked as though we'd be unable to do any work at all, but then after a long breakfast the rain ceased, which left the wind strong enough to rapidly dry the boat ready for antifouling, so we rushed out during the short dry spell.

We began to tackle the repairs, which were cleaned up inside and out. Paul used bodyfiller, Mick prepared pieces of glass and Ray had the heater. I wielded the tools and the resin brush. We formed a little procession moving from one repair to the next. Ray ensured that there was no water trapped in the broken strands of glass and put a *lot* of heat into the structure around the repair. I painted on the resin,

Mick applied the patch, Ray came in with the heat, on went another layer of resin, a layer of glass and more heat. We'd rigged a crude polythene shelter over us weighted with heavy stones from the beach so that the splatter of driven sleet did not reach the work. With filler, the external repairs were effected in less than half an hour. This might sound incredible, but with small areas and a *great deal of heat,* it *was* possible. There was still a lot of work to do in smoothing, cleaning and painting, but at least the hulls were watertight again. Gill had been plugging away at the antifouling and later we also had a go at the cockpit floorboards and the rudder, which were inside the boat. I applied some paint and varnish after everyone had retired to bed in the hope that it might set overnight, but it was in vain.

During the day we'd missed every shipping forecast and weather report of course. Why the broadcasters can't come up with a simple convenient system, I just do not know. Why can't all the local stations add the forecast for their area onto the end of their news items 'courtesy of the BBC or the Met Office'? The system where the forecast 'belongs' to one organisation that only send it out infrequently and at obscure and inconvenient times effectively 'denies' the knowledge to those who need it most. Anyway, we eventually got all prepared, checking that we were listening on the right wavelength, taking into account the Sunday difference for a report at 17.50. We tuned in twenty minutes early, set the alarms on our watches and kept one another awake through the most awful drivel until the appointed moment - and past it. Yes! We'd missed it again. We'd been cut off so effectively from the world that we'd not adjusted our watches for British Summer Time and we'd been living all day in the wrong time zone. What a load of bunglers. You have to laugh.

31 March Monday.
The forecast was for gale force winds, but it exceeded that where we were. We noticed that the river valley narrowed just where our boat was tied and this created a marked increase in the wind speed. Out in the main river it could be relatively calm when the wind was westerly, but whatever the direction out there, anything from south through west to north became a strong westerly in the creek, by deflection and funnelling. On this particular day it was impossible to work outside, initially due to the power of wind and rain, but when the rain ceased I was able to get across and into the float to do the interior glassfibre. Here, I was able to work relatively easily, preparing well, glassing downhill, applying controlled heat, protecting

from the weather and ensuring a first class job to provide the strength required. Paul came out to do some antifouling, but the wind was blowing the paint off the brush and even sucking it up out of the tin.

I had now completed the float repairs, but I wanted to change the stem head roller which meant drilling through a thick stainless steel plate at the bow for a number of bolt holes. Having the generator allowed me to use a power drill, but it was still a slow task as I had to go through the plates a shaving at a time. Mick Harrison had to stay with me throughout this lengthy procedure to hold certain tools and pass them when required, because objects placed on deck unsecured (including hammers) were in danger of being blown away.

Finally we'd finished our work for the day and we indulged in some huge delicious chops which Ray had brought back after a trip ashore earlier and which he cooked to perfection as a reward for our labours. A calculation showed that we might have difficulty getting all the hire tools back to the shop at the appointed time on the following morning so we decided to take them over to load into the car on the evening tide. It was clear that some of the crew were intending to make a detour to the local pub. Eventually the inflatable was loaded almost to sinking point and then three hefty chaps balanced themselves on top of the pile. I watched as the captain of this brave little craft started the outboard, but then neglected to open the throttle. The crew had cast off and the first mate was busy fiddling with the choke control. It stalled, refused to start and they rapidly went the opposite way to the pub. The inflatable's captain took to strenuous exertions with the outboard cord and as he had done in his previous trip in charge of the engine, managed to separate the starter cord from the motor. With lots of thrashing uncoordinated strokes of the paddles they eventually made it back, unloaded the outboard and one crewman. They then departed towards the siren smell of alcohol in Golant, stroking not unlike those chaps in 'Sanders of the River', or a speeded-up film of Dragon boat racing.

On board we spent the whole evening replacing the cord in the recoil starter. It was a complex operation and we doubted if we'd remember how to do it, but our experience of last time stood us in good stead and everything went smoothly. This time I wrote down the order for next time, because the trick was to note carefully how things were arranged when dismantling, but this is easier said than done, as without experience it isn't possible to know what significant points to note at any particular time. I now have the instructions.

Serial Starship

<u>1 April Tuesday</u>.
Up at seven. The weather had calmed down. It was cold with sharp, clear sunlight. We took back the hire equipment and although I'd been involved in security deposits totalling over £100 the eventual cost of gear was only £36.43, a very light payment to escape from what I had originally seen as being such a major disaster. The propane heater which made the whole exercise possible in such atrocious conditions had used only 75p worth of gas; it was the bargain of the month.

I'd weighed up all the options, even sorting them out on paper and my decision was clear. We packed up and headed for home, leaving me with a great sense of failure and wasted effort. It had been a tremendous struggle apparently to no avail, but on the other hand it was a good job that we had caught and cured the damage when we did, otherwise it might have become very much worse. The boat was now in good condition again.

We crossed to Padstow to view the harbour in superb sunny weather with the tide ebbing to reveal the sand flats. It is a lovely place. I'd heard so much discussion about the quality of the entrance that I expected a pokey little place with a tight entrance, rather like a glorified Southwold. Instead of which, we found a huge harbour with big ships and ferries plying across to Rock on the opposite side. The channel had 2 metres depth on exceptional low water and was so inviting that I would not hesitate to call in there. After a pleasant walk we felt a little restored and able to head for home to make plans for a second assault at this exposed part of our Round Britain passage.

MI issue 230. Episode 25.

<u>Spring Bank Holiday 24 - 27 May</u>
Upon my return home from the abortive Easter attempt to sail *Starship* from Cornwall to South Wales there was a letter waiting for me from Vincent de Bode in the Netherlands, enquiring whether as a Multihull International reader he could come with us for in a sail in *Starship*? We were only too delighted to have him join us on our next effort for we needed a strong team and he was well qualified by way of experience. This journey was to turn out to be a little more than we expected and the crew members were important.

Vincent, myself and Paul Brown travelled down to Golant in Paul's car loaded with the tons of gear needed for a week's sailing. Jerry Stebbing (photographer and trimaran builder) went from Lincolnshire to Fowey by bus, to meet up with John Morton (last met in Episode 7. No.212) who was using similar transport in order to reduce the number of vehicles that we would leave littered behind needing recovery once we'd sailed away. We were a strong crew, all experienced and at least four of us with the ability to captain the craft. When we arrived in Cornwall after an overnight drive, Vincent and I stayed at Golant to ferry equipment across to the boat whilst Paul drove into Fowey to pick up John and Jerry so that the team came together for the first time.

The tide must have been a pretty big spring because the water virtually disappeared completely at low water leaving us to porter the fuel, food and gear, across the river bed. It was rather like a relief map of the Sahara after a very heavy rain and we were even obliged to carry the inflatable over endless escarpments of quicksand. It felt a bit like toiling with Scott to the South Pole trying to get everything across. In the midst of this labour, the SUN actually came out and started blazing down, so to counter that move by the weather we produced paint and attacked the main beams of *Starship* which were looking very neglected. My maintenance policy is to find a secluded beach half way through my summer cruise, put the boat ashore and in the heat of the sun prepare and paint in double quick time. Modern paints dry very rapidly when conditions are right and several layers can be applied in quick succession. The flaw in this plan had been exposed the previous season when there had never been a day dry enough to pursue it. This was the first time in almost two seasons when conditions were good enough to operate. By the time that the tide began to return in the afternoon we had a much smarter craft and we prepared to move her to a place where she would stay afloat longer. We untied from the shore, retrieved our anchors from midstream in a terrific tangle of muddy warps all over the deck then motored slowly down through the moorings to leave Golant behind. Just opposite the china clay loading quays above Fowey the river passes through its narrowest constriction at Wiseman Point and Wiseman's Reach just upstream, is filled with moorings. The weather had reverted to being cold and dull with the wind getting gusty, so we picked up a mooring to stay overnight.

25 May Sunday.
The weather continued poor, cold and mistily wet, with the wind 4 - 6 SW. We spent the day in working on the boat which was still in a stripped condition following the winter lay-up. We each had jobs to do, rigging, safety webbing, carpet cleaning, reviving the echo sounder, checking the floats, tightening bolts, freeing hatches and

generally making the place fit to live in. We moved across to an even more sheltered mooring against the eastern shore at the end of the morning because we'd heard from a passing craft that the one that we were on was going to be used. In the afternoon the Snowgoose *Ladybird* came in and picked up a mooring. Once we were shipshape we spent some time cooking and yarning about sailing topics. The old chestnut about the difficult timing of shipping forecasts came up. Jerry had problems with moles under the boat he was building and Vincent was teaching us some Dutch phrases, the best one being Break my Clogs! (applied to a most surprising and totally unexpected event, for clogs are so tough they do not usually break).

26 May Monday.
I was woken by the rain and the time was 05.53, incredible coincidence, just in time for one of those impossible shipping forecasts I sprinted from my fore cabin back to the aft cabin where Jerry had the radio, and I actually heard a forecast (delivered at breakneck speed by the announcer.) It was SW 4 - 6 for us and 8 for the Irish Sea, This made the score 5-1 to the forecast planners. (Every time we say 'We've just *missed* the forecast.' they score one. Our theory was that they had a Research dept. working on the problem. If too many yachtsmen started catching the forecast, because it is too easy or reasonable a time to remember, like 06.25, then they'd move it to 05.55, or maybe next time to 04.17).

We needed to do some more shopping, but the tide was favourable (i.e. west-going) during the morning. I decided that we should pop out of the harbour and sail around a bit to test all systems and if things looked good perhaps think about trying to make Falmouth. Alternatively, if we found that we needed to adjust things, or that it was just too uncomfortable, then we could always return here to do our shopping in the afternoon. We breakfasted and departed under motor, dropping the mooring at 09.30 and heading for the sea. There was a great bustle of small boats being prepared for racing in the harbour and we could see our Fowey friends waving from their windows as we passed, hoisting sail as we began to feel the first lift of the waves running in through the entrance. We had a tangle with a halliard which delayed us and forced us to motor round in circles in the lumpy conditions which we found at sea, but once we'd got it sorted out we went closehauled towards Dodman point in company with several other cruisers which had left Fowey at the same time as ourselves.

Serial Starship

The wind was actually quite light and we formed a tight group of boats where competitive sailing was inevitable. We each studiously looked away from one-another, pretending that there was no contest, but there was a fair bit of silent tweaking going on and I think that it was our presence that was causing the conflict. I have sailed on *Starship* long enough to know what she will do and I don't mind if some monohull gets past me under certain unequal or changeable circumstances. Conditions were very light so that each craft showed to advantage when it was slightly favoured by a gust and this did create a tension amongst my crew who felt that we should stop messing about and put those other boats in their place. Eventually we were all becalmed momentarily and began to drift together by mutual attraction, so I decided to break away onto the port tack into Mevagissey Bay and once we were clear we all relaxed again. It is always a mistake to sail too close to monohulls when cruising. I find that their sailing characteristics are so different that it spoils our performance to try to sail as they do, especially to windward.

Vincent on the genoa sheet, John steers.   Pic. Jerry Stebbing.

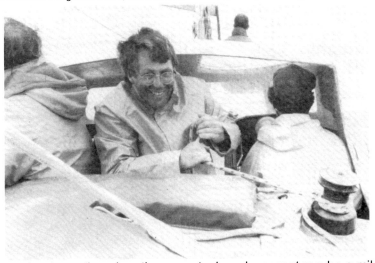

These boats continued on the same tack and we went maybe a mile and a half to windward before falling back onto starboard. Our relaxed helmsman now no longer bothered whether we were aiming as high as them, but just pointed the boat to get the right 'sound' and 'feel' of water against the hull. We picked up a little speed, maybe the wind came up a little. The sun came out and soon the other craft were dropping behind and we were making steady progress.

Serial Starship

Off Dodman Point the fluky wind and overfalls forced us to go further out sea, but once we were clear we set off again on a perfect reach with deep blue sea beneath us and puffy white clouds above, whilst ahead of us the sea was scattered with many white sails of yachts out from Falmouth enjoying the lovely conditions. It was all too good to be true and at 13.30 the wind quite suddenly died, forcing us to start the engine to bring us up to Falmouth as the tide was just going foul and we still had some shopping to do. There was a minor problem when the diesel suddenly stopped and we rigged the outboard to continue progress. After a few checks I tried the engine again and it ran OK. An odd circumstance that was soon forgotten. (*Until three months later, on August 4.*) We entered Falmouth at 14.30 and picked up a mooring.

The sun was now very hot. Vincent, John, and I went ashore at the town marina to stock up with fresh food whilst Paul B. and Jerry stayed afloat with Paul taking the opportunity to get some more paint onto the decks and doghouse. It was exhausting in the town which was crammed with holiday makers who had descended on the food shelves like locusts, making our task very difficult as we rushed from store to store looking for bread etc. Back on board and very tired we caught the forecast again (Score 6 - 2). The forecast for the day that we had just experienced was SW 4 - 6 and we had actually had force 1 in lovely sunshine. As we sat on the mooring there was no wind. The forecast now was force 6 going west, perhaps force 8. This implied another weather system on its way and probably further delays in progress unless we grasped the chance to push on a little further immediately in the calm which now prevailed. If we could reach Newlyn we would be within striking distance of rounding Land's End for the northward leg of the journey towards Wales. A south-westerly was favourable once around the corner, but it would cause a struggle to reach that corner if it was too strong. Getting around the Manacles and the Lizard would make the whole exercise much more viable and so at 20.00 we dropped the mooring and departed Falmouth under motor with plain sail set, intending to either go all the way or to go into Newlyn if conditions became too bad. It was a beautiful evening and we set the watch system so that each experienced crewman did two hours in rotation, except myself. I was to be 'second man' and navigator throughout.

Our course made good was about 180°m and at about 22.00 we were roughly four miles to the east of Black Head working our way towards the Lizard under sail by tacking against the last of the foul tide. The wind came in very gently at first and then gradually increased. At 23.30 it had become strong enough to stop the motor which gave us relief from the noise and the relatively slow progress. Under sail she began to get along much better.

<u>27 May Tuesday</u>.
At about quarter past midnight with the tide just going favourable the Lizard was due north and we were really beginning to make progress to windward on a course of 290°m using the lights on Tater-Du and the Lizard for cross reference. We were making a steady six knots, and the wind was progressively increasing so that I first reefed the genoa and then the main until we had a very modest sail plan set and we were going well, into the night, if a little bumpy.

Due to our rapid progress the plan to enter Newlyn was never really considered. We were well out to sea, well up wind and we were well able to round that tricky corner at Land's End which stood as such a major obstacle on our course. To have deflected into Newlyn would have meant missing our opportunity and then perhaps being unable to make another attempt for a further two or three days, which my experiences down in this corner of England had instructed me could mean washing out the whole trip again. The general weather forecast had said that it would be blustery until about

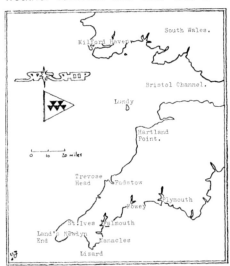

Thursday. Well it was blustery now and we were making six knots with the prospect of easing the course slightly and getting the wind behind the beam. This was our chance and we were taking it. We expected strongish winds maybe, probably about 4 - 6, but *favourable* winds to carry us along.

At 03.00 when we freed to 330°m we were midway between Wolf Rock and Gwennap Head, which is the actual corner that has to be cleared in order to turn north in order to pass the lesser obstacles of Land's End and Cape Cornwall. Visibility wasn't too good and though I would have liked to have seen these landmarks I had to content myself with the light of the Longships to signify that we were finally round and committed to crossing to Wales. I altered course again to about 010°m and cross checked to find that we had covered eleven miles in the hour up to four o'clock; what price those monohulls now?

I had been looking forward to this crossing, because I had planned to follow the coast within visible distance to see the cliffs and beaches which I knew would be so interesting from the sea. There are few natural harbours. St. Ives is just a little way up from Land's End, Padstow is about half way along and then there's Bideford right at the far end. My intention was to have a good look at the Padstow entrance behind Trevose Head, but then to leave the coast at Hartland Point to cross to Lundy Island eleven miles out in the Bristol Channel before crossing to the Welsh coast to head out towards Milford Haven.

Already I was being disappointed. The gathering light showed only a misty driving rain descending from low cloud scudding across a bleak and grey-waved waste. The wind was rising and the visibility was now right down. I checked the chart. 040°m would take us clear of the coast. 060°m meant that we would make contact with rocks at some stage. We began to take the divergent course just to be certain of safety. The motion was getting pretty bad and two of the crew had reached the comatose stage of seasickness where they were best left in continuous sleep. I had been covering for them and had had no sleep since we'd started. The wind seemed even stronger now blowing powerfully from the south-west so that there could be no going back. We forged ahead in the rough water and John went down to get the shipping forecast at 05.55. A few minutes later he returned looking most concerned. He quietly said, "Severe gale *Nine* given for Lundy, What are you going to do?"

MI issue 231. Episode 26.

<u>Bristol Channel</u>
<u>27 May Tuesday</u>.
Break my Clogs! Force Nine. There are times when you hear a forecast and you just know that the weather is never going to get that bad, but this time it was a certainty. The wind was already beginning to touch on gale force, visibility was poor, but more than that, we had slipped imperceptibly into a totally vulnerable position, we had stepped unknowingly over an invisible line into an area from which there was no retreat and Sod's Law dictated that in such a position

the gale would be bound to reach the predicted force. Severe gale Nine. The words were numbing. They just went around my head. Severe gale Nine, Severe gale Nine and no solution offered itself. 'How can it be?' I thought, 'perhaps they are wrong again, they usually are'. But my eyes and ears told me that they'd got it right, only it was too late for it to be of any use to us. We were well round the headland and travelling at high speed, there could be no going back. Beating into the south-westerly to re-round Land's End would have taken as much effort as continuing. I'd been trying to minimise the wind strength, so as not to exaggerate the situation, but now I had to acknowledge the reality of it.

We were on a very broad reach, almost a run, with the waves coming under the quarter and she was beginning to pick up and surge along like a speedboat, but trying to broach to port. Now she suddenly accelerated and we were heading down into a steep valley where the pointed bows plunged like blades into the water. I thanked our lucky stars that the undersides of the beam shelves on either side of the hull were ski shaped and designed to lift the bows to stop them from burying. They did just that. I caught a quick glimpse from the helmsman and knew that he didn't want to repeat that manoeuvre. Running and reaching courses were not the most comfortable under the circumstances and it was time to reassess the situation in the light of the deteriorating weather.

A clear line (north-west to south-east) appeared in the sky behind us where the fast moving clouds ended, to be followed by a cloudless, steel blue void from which the wind now began to howl. The waves though still confused began to throw up the odd sequence of three big ones, some of which were bigger than I have ever seen before. The fear finally got to me and unable to resist any I joined the seasick squad. Made a bit of a mess on the side of oat, but by now the occasional wave was catching us and thro en water onto the topsides, so it didn't matter too much.

 a more northerly course at about 07.30 to take up a better e waves. Most sailors will have read of severe conditi may have formed some kind of opinion about how they w ith the situation. To some extent we had little option. I had decide preferred an active rather than a passive defence, but in this se there was virtually no passive option because I had limited sea room between myself and some of the nastiest cliffs to be found. Heaving to, or lying to a sea anchor would have meant running out of space pretty soon. Running for cover hardly entered my head. We were passing St. Ives but the sea was running in from the west and the wind was forecast to go west and then north-west. My only option was Padstow, but I was unfamiliar with it from the sea. Seen from offshore the indentations of a coast are difficult to discern and problems with appreciating the scale size of unknown bays and headlands would mean the strong possibility of us ending up sailing into a blind bay from which there would be little chance of escape. My surfing days in Newquay now somewhere to leeward, had taught me that the waves got steeper as they approached the shore. Going near enough to even see the shore would take us over another of those invisible lines in this game of nautical snakes and ladders. Once near to the shore, only snakes lay sleeping. Certain disaster awaited us down there. I looked down that way because the sight to windward was getting too awful to contemplate, yet we must face it.

We sheeted in our tiny scraps of sail and headed steadily outwards into the waves, climbing diagonally up across their faces, popping through their tops and sliding down their backs. At times we'd spot one coming that instinct told us was going to get us. Some inner feeling separated those waves with malevolent intent even when they were distant and semi obscured by intervening crests; something just told us *that* one was the one to watch out for. As we were moving forward at what I guessed to be about four or five knots we had the ability to steer and each one of the helmsmen became proficient at spinning the boat into the worst waves so that the force of their punch was only a glancing blow mainly towards our stern, which helped us to point even more towards their oncoming power. Our forward motion reduced our contact time with each wave and I was contented that we were taking the correct action for survival at that time. My general plan was to continue in this way going further out to sea and if necessary pass through St. Georges Channel into the Irish Sea until I began to find a lee from the Irish landmass. I hoped that this would not be needed and that I would manage to work us into a lee on the South Wales coast, with the weather moderating.

By this time I was well-nigh exhausted. During the previous night the others had been working watches, but I had been navigating and then changing down sails. I had also stood the watches for the two sick men to give the others rest. I started to try to work out when I had last slept and began to realise that my brain would not do the calculations required. I'd been shopping. Where had I been before that? Was it yesterday or the day before? I'd sailed from Fowey. I'd got up early. How many hours had I been working?

Everything was hazy. What were the mistakes that I had made to get us into this?

The mistakes were classics, all so easy to see in retrospect. Hindsight is such a wonderful thing, if only we could obtain it in advance. Sailing is like chess, but like playing chess against the Gods. Each move is so subtle, so small, security is so warm, so surrounding. Then suddenly 'CHECK!' and you're hanging by a thread, fighting to survive. You think of all the moves that you might have made, but they'll avail you nothing in the situation that you find yourself. The chips are down and you have to climb out of the hole that you've dug for yourself, without recourse to 'If only I'd done this or that.'

We had all been very sick by this time. We had all been exhausted, but the three of us who were left seemed to have rotated our respective duties well, for we were each accustomed to running our own boats and instinctively we knew that we could only rest when the other two were well able to carry the load of responsibility. I could see in Vincent's face that he was worried about me. He was asking me questions about our position and I wasn't answering. I wanted to, but I was now a separate person looking out from inside a body that would no longer respond. Energy had ended. I had discovered my limit was about twenty eight hours of constant work and responsibility. Time for him and John to take over.

I slid down below to survey the mess in the main cabin. Everything that would move had moved. The main object was a body lying face down in a plastic bowl. The body and the rest of the floor was deeply covered in a scattered pile of pan lids, soap powder, tools, tinned food, sweets and broken biscuits. I just laid down as I was across this uncomfortable conglomeration and tried to sleep but I was shivering in an uncontrolled way through lack of food energy, so I crept forward and grabbed a sleeping bag to pull over me. Despite my full foul weather gear and floating suit, I still shivered myself to sleep, trusting in John and Vincent to keep us safe.

Sleep was elusive under these conditions. The shock of the waves hitting us; the suspended motion as we fell from waves; the crashing and the splattering of water on deck constantly drew me back to reality. I dreamed a strange dream, not of identifiable substance, but of emotional abstractions. Instead of suffering an awful nightmare from which at the critical moment I suddenly escaped to discover that all was well, I experienced exactly the reverse. I dreamed of pleasantness surrounded by menace. Whatever the threat was, it was just beyond reach, not quite discernible, sensed, around the fringes on all sides, just beyond the boundaries of my perception. Any increase in noise or motion would bring it flooding in to collapse the pleasant centre of my dream and I would have to strive to re-establish the secure area of sunny warmth and normality by pushing out the perimeter on all sides. Suddenly a lurching crash would make it instantly collapse in upon me and I would be rudely awakened into the living nightmare that I was actually in and it wouldn't go away.

Following such a crash, I found myself listening. I could hear an aeroplane. I struggled to regain my feet and clambered up into the cockpit. It was the unmistakeable roar of a heavy jet, rumbling, deafening. I expected the other two to be excited as the plane was so near, but they were just lolling like rag dolls looking ahead, their faces grey with fatigue, eyes half closed. I searched all around us. We were sailing on a great flat plain of level water covered in foam flecks. The confused sea had momentarily gone. The steady roar of the jet was a more distant rumble. There was no aeroplane. The sound that I had heard was made by the oncoming wave building higher and higher into a moving wall of water. Now, above the shrieking of the wind came the low rumble of the next one advancing across the watery plain. It came on steadily, lifting almost in slow motion, rumbling like the rolling stock of a railway or a heavy lorry on a cobbled road. How could a wave make such a noise? My mind was too tired to wrestle with the reasons. It didn't matter. I just looked and felt sick.

We were riding a series of these huge ocean waves and as we climbed their faces each one looked impossible. Their passing crests were the danger spots because the power to strike us was in the foaming top. If they just happened to become steep enough to start crashing down at the moment that our path coincided with theirs then we would be like a matchstick in their giant hands. Each one carried with it the ultimate threat; there was no doubt about that. As we watched their progress towards us, we could do nothing except hope that chance would allow us to survive each one in turn. Once they had passed they left behind a great flat trough of water, for they absorbed all smaller waves into themselves in their progress, but the momentary respite that this provided served only to emphasise the might and power of the next wave rising and moving inexorably towards us.

The howling wind in the rigging caused me to look aloft and I saw that the radar reflector which had been bolted to its stainless steel support at the masthead had disappeared, torn bodily away by the force of the movement up there. Our ensign was in tatters and water was streaming off the deck in torrents to turn to fine spray and smoke-off downwind as a mist over the water surface. We hit waves, we punched them, pierced them, rolled them, climbed and slid and all the time the battering went on. I felt physically very lethargic. The warmth of the sun hardly penetrated the soddened clothing that we wore and we all shivered. I began to think of the intense cold that we would have to endure in the night to come and whether we could survive. I felt that the weather would moderate, because it had come up so quickly, but I couldn't be certain. Our crew was decimated and the boat was enduring an unprecedented beating. I was amazed that the structure could stand up to the punishment that it was taking, but surely this could not go on indefinitely. We were experiencing the equivalent of a minor car crash three or four times every minute for hours on end, something would have to give at some stage.

A special crash from the bow and I saw the lid of the anchor well being ripped from beneath its rope lashings which still remained tied in place. The lid hit the pulpit and then the port float and drifted astern in the seas. There was no chance of recovering it without an unacceptable risk to the boat and the crew. With regret I just had to let it go. Moments later a mighty wave finally caught up with us and did what most waves had been threatening to do. John was steering and I was standing behind him, crouching just below the level of the top of the doghouse. I heard the crunch of the water and threw myself forwards so that my face was pressed right up to the perspex window. I hung on grimly as the wave descended. We were tipping further and further. Water was roaring everywhere. We were totally engulfed. I could only see dark green water through the window. I thought, 'This is it. She can't get back from this angle.'

MI issue 232. Episode 27.

27 May Tuesday.
Bristol Channel.
Starship is no cockleshell. At thirty-five feet long and twenty-two feet wide she is quite a big structure, but at this moment she was completely underwater, thrown onto her beam ends by a mighty Atlantic roller whipped up by the severe gale that we were experiencing half way between Land's End and South Wales. For a split second I thought she might not come up, when suddenly she popped out of the back of the wave with a rapid flip onto an even

keel and she was sailing to windward again immediately. We had the extra buoyancy of the inflatable dinghy lashed upside down just forward of the aft crossbeam on the starboard side. I had watched whilst Jerry triple lashed it before our departure and had casually thought that he was making too good a job of it. If we needed it in a hurry for any reason we would have a long delay whilst we untied it. Something had diverted my attention at the time and it had remained secured to the netting, in, as it turned out, the optimum position for assisting us in our moment of greatest need. I was more than happy now with that triple lashing of the dinghy. Without such powerful ties we might have lost it, or it might have sustained damage. Having already lost the anchor-well hatch cover and the radar reflector from the masthead in this gale I could ill afford losing something as vital as the inflatable.

The boat was behaving magnificently and we were coming through, but I knew that the failure of even the smallest vital component in the rig or rudder would put us in desperate trouble. I looked around the boat at my crew mates. The helmsman pale with fatigue, the others weak from sickness, myself shivering with cold. What would happen if the mast fell down? How long could we survive if we flipped? I looked below at the V.H.F. radio and agonised about what I should do. I did not want to put in motion some great rescue effort, when in fact we were as yet, alright. But I knew that we were balancing on the edge of a precipice and the slightest wobble might send us tumbling over the edge.

In sailing you find yourself in tricky situations because of your previous mistakes. The decisions that you make seem inconsequential at the time and it is only later that you can look back and see where you went wrong. I had already done this exercise for the current situation, so now I was doubly aware of the way that our futures might hinge on doing the right thing at this point. Assuming that we came to grief and by some stroke of fortune I managed to survive but others did not, how would I answer my critics when they started to ask the obvious questions (with the benefit of being warm and well rested, with rational brains, on firm dry land). 'Did you call for assistance on the radio?' 'No.'
'Why not?'
'Because at the time we were not in immediate danger.'
'As some of your crew were lost it would appear that you *were* in some danger.'
'After the incident there was no longer an aerial and the water short-circuited the electrics.'

'Why did you not call earlier?' Why? Why?
Why did I hesitate? Last season when we had been in the Scilly Isles
I'd returned to *Starship* to find a man in a launch waiting for me. He
gave me a scribbled message instructing me to contact the
Coastguard. We were just ready to leave, but I told the crew to hold
everything and I returned ashore. After lengthy problems with
telephones I eventually spoke to the Coastguard. In fact he was
really seeking someone else, a friend who was overdue in a yacht.
As our conversation developed it became clear to me that the search
was like a complex piece of detective work. They were leaving no
stone unturned and had delved into almost every contact that my
friend had ever had in the sailing world. The fact that they were in
Great Yarmouth and had found me in a tiny, remote harbour on the
other side of the country was an indication of the thoroughness of
their search. Long after the season closed I was meeting people who
had been involved in some way in tracing my friend. I did not want to
unnecessarily cause any concern, because despite everything, we
were still alright.

These thoughts took but a moment. They were not clearly
ordered, but mixed with the lurch of the boat, the blue of the sky, the
majesty of the elements in full force, bracing myself for the next wave
and the overwhelming sound of it all. I watched the boat, getting a
feel for her speed, how accurately we held the compass course,
roughly how much leeway we were making and in amongst it came a
picture of the humour of the T.V. comedian Tony Hancock in his
famous programme about the 'Radio Ham' who picked up a faint
Mayday signal from a poor chap in the Indian Ocean or somewhere
similar. I could see the look on his face when he said with a mixture
of astonishment and glee 'I've GOT one!' Isn't it every radio
operator's dream to 'Get one?' I resolved that whatever I said, it
must NOT contain the words Mayday or Pan, but it was now my
DUTY to at least let somebody know that we were out here and not
enjoying it. I had to cover all eventualities. I thought long and hard
about it, planned what I was going to say and then thought about it
some more.

My hand was working independently from the rest of my body
as I watched it reaching out to unhook the microphone. I pressed the
transmit button and saw the warm glow of the little red light which
told me that whatever I said would now travel to a place outside this
bucking, crashing, watery world.

I called All Stations a couple of times but heard no reply. Oddly
I somehow felt better; relieved that nobody had heard me and that I

hadn't made a fool of myself. There was nobody out there anyway. The range of these sets is strictly limited - line of sight or something similar, my instructor had said at night classes. Any ship would have to be quite close. I tried again, expecting nothing, when to my amazement I heard a faint voice saying that Falmouth Harbour Control was receiving me. I was completely surprised, because they were on the wrong side of Cornwall to receive me and I had not thought that it was possible to transmit that distance. I simply wanted to express my concern to a ship and tell of our whereabouts. I had chosen my words carefully. I did not want to make a distress call. I wanted no lifeboats launched or lives risked. The crux of what I said was that we were 'experiencing some difficulties in heavy seas' and gave our estimated position as being fifteen miles west of Padstow. I stressed that it was an estimate. I pressed my ear to the set to hear him saying that transmission was difficult to receive and to go onto Channel 62. I went over, but I could hardly hear his transmission at all. Only the occasional word came through. I repeated the information sticking rigidly to my prepared wording and giving our estimated position again. I could only tell that his reply was about two sentences in length and the final word was 'Out'. This meant that the exchange was completed and I hung up the microphone knowing that at least someone now knew that we were out here. The helmsman looked across with the smallest flicker of a smile and nodded his head. It was the right thing to do at the time. It was about midday.

I tried to consider our situation from the point of view of navigation. The conventional sitting at a table with ruler and dividers was totally impossible. The smallest glance at a chart brought on overwhelming retching and further exhaustion. Even the less conventional methods of just laying objects across the chart to get a rough idea of direction were only slightly feasible at times, but very difficult to execute. There was a mass of mental calculations, all very simple of course when you are sitting at home or in the classroom, but it was a major mental effort to calculate how many hours from 7.30 to 2.45pm and then multiply by knots to find out how far we had travelled. Were we doing four knots or six? It made an incredible difference. Exactly how far was our journey? It spanned three different charts with different scales. The lethargy of total exhaustion made such calculations seem like Mastermind questions. Outwardly I appeared to be almost in a coma but inwardly I wrestled to keep our track. I did not have the energy for conversation but John helped by double checking for me. I'd mumble 'How far is Land's End to

Padstow?' as he scanned the chart and ten minutes later as we passed each other he'd give me a figure. He'd wearily ask 'What do you think about speed?' and ten minutes later I'd give him my estimate. Together in this way we reached a consensus of position in our own minds. I forced myself to study, be sick, study, be sick, ignoring the discomfort until I had sorted out a confirmation based on our agreed figures. In a case such as this it wasn't possible to have pinpoint accuracy, but it was possible to have an outline strategy and I was feeling generally satisfied with our progress, because despite of everything, I felt that we were falling within the best course of action given our difficult starting point and the extreme discomfort that we were undergoing.

Our course had been determined by the safest approach to the wave faces. We had sailed west of north, but I believed that due to the tiny scrap of sail that we had set we were probably making as much leeway as forward motion. I thought that in effect we were ferry gliding on a northerly course and that the tide through the day would have helped us stay to the east of north. I decided that I wanted to fall within the shelter of the South Welsh coast, because the occasional gust was now beginning to come from the north-west, as forecast. The tide would now be taking us westwards and we needed to counteract this if we were not to miss Wales altogether. In mid-afternoon I asked for a course of 030°m and we managed to hold this slightly more reaching course without extreme danger in the wave pattern.

At about four in the afternoon Jerry suddenly recovered from being laid low and I finally managed to make a little food stay inside me. I had been sucking sweets slowly, which usually effects a cure as the sugar gives me energy, but on this occasion it just didn't seem to work. I noticed John trying cheese crackers and fortunately it did the trick for me also. It was quite remarkable what effect just four crackers had. Almost immediately I stopped feeling quite so cold and started to feel much more positive. Jerry too coming fresher to the scene seemed positive and optimistic. At first Jerry was sure that he could hear an aeroplane, but I had learned the answer to that little mystery earlier in the day. Next he noticed that there were seabirds about and this was a significant observation. Since leaving the land behind us we had seen only those isolated seabirds which seemingly soar right under the falling wave crests, storm birds gliding, banking and feeding right into the jaws of hell, but the birds that we saw now were different. Dressed in their black and white suits and moving in flocks, they belonged to the diver family and probably came from the bird sanctuaries on the rugged islands of Skomer and Skokholm somewhere ahead.

When Jerry had relieved us of the burden of steering, John had given him an ETA with the coast, which I felt was a tiny bit optimistic. I never like to be too hopeful, because in that way I can avoid disappointment. Before too long Jerry was sure that the land was in sight ahead. I didn't rush to look, but when he was still pretty sure ten minutes later, I clambered up from my comfort on the cockpit floor to have a look and it was absolutely certain.

MI issue 233. Episode 28.

The Haven.
27 May Early Evening.

The land was well above the horizon, but partially obscured in a mist of blown spume; even so it looked like a clear headland and with the naked eye I could distinguish a solitary white building. We kept coming in on 030°m until the nature of the land became more certain. I wanted to have a good look before night fell just in case the misty conditions thickened further. The building evolved into a lighthouse and I was just beginning to make out other features when it suddenly flashed red giving positive confirmation that it was Skokholm Island enabling us to turn further to starboard to run down to St. Anne's Head which was the headland marking the entrance to Milford Haven. In navigational terms we'd hit the bulls eye. The wind was down to force six or seven as we entered and whilst I was still visible to them, I called the Coastguard to inform them of our safe arrival. I requested that they should pass the message on to Falmouth Harbour Coastguard, explaining that I had radioed earlier expressing concern.

By 21.00 in failing light we were into the Haven and turning right to follow it up. After a couple of miles a bay opened up to starboard with moored yachts just inside. Almost in darkness we picked up a mooring in the welcome shelter of the land, took in the sail and revelled in the stillness, the peaceful quiet, the tangible calm. We were totally, totally exhausted and quite content to just sit wherever we had fallen, gazing ahead. An aching hand would reach out and pick up a pan lid to place it on a draining board just to see it remain there. The silence was precious after the tumult that we had just experienced. Slowly, we forced ourselves to clear sufficient debris from the floor to move about and John prepared us a meal which we ate in weary silence punctuated only by the sound of one of our toughest crew being seasick for the last time. We slept as we were in full kit.

28 May. Wednesday.
Needless to say we were not in a hurry to get up in the morning. Paul B thought his boots were pinching him and in removing them noticed that they had John's name in them. John said he had been wondering why his boots felt odd; he thought that there was something inside one of them. When he took them off, the obstruction turned out to be Jerry' socks. So Jerry took his boots off and gave them back to Paul B. That's how bad the gale had been. We made our way at leisure through a full English breakfast during the rest of the morning.

The wind was still quite blustery, but in the shelter of the harbour we hardly noticed. Leaving to sail up a strange river with the tide under us I set full main and a little genoa even though we were running. This would mean that I could manoeuvre easily and spin right around to go to windward immediately if it was suddenly needed; it also kept visibility ahead clear.

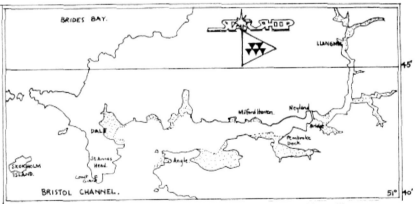

The lower reaches of the Haven were very wide with rolling green hills on either side. There were few trees so that the general impression was a little bleak. The water itself was scarred by some of the ugliest structures that an oil industry could devise, despoiling the natural beauty in a way which surely could only be tolerated far from the seat of government in the name of employment. As most facilities seemed unused I wondered if they justified their existence. At the very least they could have been more sympathetically arranged.

Serial Starship

We began to meet other sailing craft, mostly reefed right down, and gradually we came to the most populated area around Pembroke with Neyland facing it on the north shore linked by a large bridge high over our heads carrying cars which could stop for their occupants to watch us as we sailed beneath them. Past the bridge the estuary became a river, narrowing rapidly but remaining very deep in the channel with over 50 feet quite commonplace and even 25 feet out of the channel. The banks were thickly wooded and as the river twisted and turned, so the wind died and the strength of the sun could be felt. Gradually we found ourselves on an idyllic cruise with a river to explore with new sights around every corner; our only guide - some sketch maps from a loaned copy of the Bristol Channel Yachting Conference Handbook. This is the kind of sailing that I love and it is such a pity that we have to put up with the discomforts of the sea between such marvellous moments.

My journey is as much about the trials of the land as about the tribulations of the sea. Each leg takes me to a 'foreign land' where I have no contacts and no secure knowledge of where I might leave my boat. This was a constant challenge for me, yet my ignorance was the very mechanism which allowed me to make contact with the people and the places at which I arrived. I was forced to ask local people for their advice, forced to negotiate, forced to place my trust in strangers and to become more integrated into the area than if I had arrived in any other way. I had one great ally in my search for assistance and that was the boat. In almost every case, nobody had seen anything like her and she was very difficult to ignore. We stepped ashore as Martians descending from a smoking, shining saucer and public curiosity in our craft broke down the first barriers of reserve. On this occasion we were once again seeking a resting place which gave additional impetus to our search along the river banks. Every inlet (called a 'pill' in this part of the world) was a potential stopping place, every group of moorings a possible contact. Each journey's end was a search such as this one.

We came to a small inlet on the eastern bank where there was a little yacht harbour with commercial moorings, so we picked up a buoy in the mainstream and Paul and I went across in the dinghy. As soon as we landed at the combined chandlery/workshop/boatpark we were struck by the number of luxurious expensive cars and the alarm bells began to ring in our heads. Surrounding a central hotel were holiday chalets and caravans and it was clearly a total operation. We eventually made contact with the owner who arranged to meet us in the chandlery, so we went there to wait. "What do you think?" I asked Paul. "I think it's going to be expensive." was his reply and I agreed. If money was no object, my sailing would be very easy. I could sail into a place like this, leave the boat and pay upon my return, but I'm afraid money is everything to a wage slave on a fixed salary. I told Paul that I thought that I could afford about £50-60 for a two month stay, so that would be our target figure.

We met as arranged and the owner was very pleasant. When he heard of our adventures on the previous day he was surprised that we had survived, because they had recorded force 10 gusts *in the harbour*. He also said that the Coastguards had been looking for us to come on board, not, he said, looking for drugs, but to make sure that we were not injured. In the midst of this conversation he casually put a form in front of me and in a very encouraging way said 'Just fill in the details.' I mentioned an indication of price and he got out a leaflet to look it up. £3.62 a day and he'd call two months only 56 days. My mental arithmetic wasn't too good, but I guessed that would exceed my target (*with VAT it's over £230*). I explained as I always have to do in these cases, that we only wanted somewhere to <u>leave</u> the boat. We didn't need access, didn't need facilities, just a flat bit of mud normally quite useless. He offered me a twenty per cent discount, but it still came to three times my target, so I said that I'd have to discuss it with the rest of the crew and off we went, now well aware of the price to get under.

Back on board I called the Coastguard twice without reply. A chap from the local gunnery range came on and offered to relay my call, because he said everyone had been looking for us. I thought this odd, but I gave him our position and said that we'd be going further upstream. He confirmed the message.

It was lovely and sunny and the scenery was beautiful with woodland right to the edge of the water. There were odd boats fishing, a bit of water skiing and the occasional sailing boat. We motored, because the wind was lightly against us due to the meanderings of the river. We asked some people about the moorings that we were just leaving and they explained that in this area all moorings are owned by individuals, but grouped into cooperatives. This was a new system to us, so we motored slowly upstream puzzling about how the system might work. Round a couple more bends we came to another mooring group strung out before a little village. The owner of a small Wharram cat was just packing up his boat so we asked his advice. He gave us the address of the man who controlled the moorings for this cooperative and we went to find him. On shore we found ourselves to be in a very rural part of Wales and the people were some of the most helpful and kind that we had yet come across here. When we asked directions, they would stop whatever they were doing and escort us until they were sure that we were on the right track. When I arrived at the house the man was out, but his wife said that I would have to put my request in writing. It would go before the committee next Tuesday evening and I would be responsible for laying the ground tackle myself. I said that I'd come back later.

We were slowly coming to appreciate that we had sailed into a very unique situation. All my past experience had taught me that towards the head of a river beyond the point where boats could always stay afloat, there would be small boatyards sustained by storage and repairs where yachts would usually go for winter hibernation. Their facility, as quiet cheap places to leave a boat was exactly what I wanted, but on this river we were told they did not exist. Something had changed this natural system. The whole area surrounding the upper reaches was controlled by what they called The Nature Conservancy and in order to protect the river they had arranged that sailors should form committees to take up an allocated number of moorings in a particular area. Each group had a secretary to communicate with the Board and owners were responsible for their own tackle. Registration fees were very low. They told a lovely story about a 'South Coast Man' who when asked for his fee of 'One fifty' had sent them a cheque for One Hundred and Fifty Pounds and a note saying that it was cheap at the price. They sent the cheque back with their note asking for him to change it to One Pound and Fifty pence, please. There was also an annual fee which would have amounted to about £12 for my boat. This was fine for the locals but for me it was of little use, because of a vital condition which went with the cheap rates. Moorings could not be sublet, only loaned free for a maximum period of a fortnight. My devious mind could see loopholes through which I might slip my boat and financially I was prepared to pay a four year fee just for a two month stay, but I was faced with the disarming honesty of the local people who would not, could not, contemplate anything which wasn't within the true spirit of their agreement. I knew that to suggest 'rule bending' would make them unhappy, so I was faced with the looming prospect of returning to the commercial place with its avaricious demands, or like a latter day Flying Dutchman sail forever the glistening stream.

MI issue 234. Episode 29.
The village mooring.
28 May Wednesday.
How difficult can it be to find a place to leave the boat for a couple of months in an unfamiliar area? We were finding out on the upper reaches of Milford Haven where the only commercial operation was beyond my financial means and we'd discovered that local moorings could not be sublet by their owners due to their agreement with The Conservancy, the body which controlled the area.

I was fast running out of options when fortunately in the evening, I went to see the secretary of a group of mooring owners at Llangwm (pronounced Langum), a tiny village surrounding a small inlet (called a 'pill') on the western shore. The secretary was a big man with sandy Celtic colouring who spoke with a soft Welsh accent, almost singing his words. I arrived at seven-thirty and we talked for some time about my difficulty but seemed to be making no progress. I was beginning to think that this last chance was slipping away when perhaps he saw my disappointment for he suddenly said "You could always bring her onto the mud. I don't know why more people don't bring their boats in." I immediately understood the implication. As an East Coast sailor I actually preferred this solution to her lying afloat on a mooring.

Leaving a boat on the shore can be dangerous, because it makes it vulnerable to theft and, earlier in the day when we had visited a commercial haven the owner had stressed to us that pilfering was becoming quite a problem for him, but here things were a little different. I had noticed that dinghies were left ashore with rowlocks and oars aboard and a beached derelict boat, neglected for years, still had all its fittings in place. These small signs, spoke to a cruising sailor of the honesty of the people, but another fact was even more important. The village had formerly been a fishing community and the houses had been built in such a way that they nestled close to the pill which became almost like a village square. People conversed with each other across it from their gardens and the shore path around its edge was the most convenient link from one part of the village to another. I was being invited to bring my boat right into the heart of the village and to place it where it would be overlooked by the whole community. We stood in his garden discussing wind directions, anchors and how soft the mud might be and finally we settled on an agreement. When I returned aboard *Starship* I was in a much happier mood and we moved up to take a mooring close in, ready for an early start next morning.

.
We had to retrieve our vehicles and so John and Paul departed on the 08.10 bus on their long journey. John had left his car close to the railway station in Bristol and they took a series of buses to get there, then they drove right down to Golant in Cornwall arriving at 19.30 to pick up Paul's car so that he could return to Wales whilst John stopped over in Cornwall to do some sightseeing. This was all part of the logistics of our voyage which often gets overlooked.

High water in the Pill was roughly 10.30 so at about 09.15 I went into the winding gulleys in the inflatable to explore and pick a route for *Starship* which was motored in, only going aground once very briefly. We secured a line to a handy rock and laid out two anchors, which meant lots of line, chain, weight and coordination to get right then all that we could do was to settle down and wait to discover what lay beneath us as the tide receded. Of course, I could not have chosen a worse spot in the whole pill, for the boat lay steeply angled on the edge of a deeply indented gully, just where it joined the main channel of a little stream which meandered down the pill. Our bows pointed to the skies and we balanced on the rear tip of the starboard float, marooned by a sea of soft mud. We had to wait out the whole tide until nine in the evening when we began to come upright.

We spent the day in various tasks, with Jerry sewing the numbers back onto the mainsail following the gale damage and I catching up on a bit of sleep. Vincent provided the highlight of the day by attempting to reset the anchors to improve our position on the next tide, which he knew would come in the darkness of the night. He had to cross the quagmire so he got all kitted up like an astronaut in boots, oilies, leggings, etc. and started following the beds of the gullies, working his way over towards an anchor. In places the water was too deep for his boots so he returned for the inflatable and pushed or dragged it upstream which was hot work in the strong sun. Whilst in full sweat with all his protective gear hampering this mammoth effort through mud and water, cheered on by us aboard, what should happen, but along came a man, walking his dog in the most casual fashion, down the very same gulley. The newcomer, knowing the place well had a totally different approach. He wore shorts and an old pair of sandals and effortlessly strode along, paddling occasionally until he met our struggling crewman clad in all his heavy gear. For a moment they stood gazing at each other in amazement.

Our visitor Dougal, had a boat a little further up the creek and had dropped in for a friendly chat. Apparently the whole village was a-buzz with our activities and discussing our present antics of parking at an angle, blocking the main channel, making expeditions in the mud etc. Some came and watched from their gardens, some pulled up a chair to their living room windows whilst others sat with their binoculars at the very edge of the pill, intent on not missing a moment of the entertainment. It was a long time since anything as dramatic as this had occurred and everybody was taking an interest in what was happening.

Vincent succeeded in getting our stern anchor and resetting it, then as the water returned he used the inflatable to reposition the bow anchor so that as darkness fell we inched onto a large flat piece of mud which we'd selected further down the pill where she would only float right on top of the tide. This would mean that in the event of strong winds, whilst we were away, she would only be affected for a short time-span of about a couple of hours on either side of high water meaning that access to her by boat would be similarly restricted.

At eleven o'clock the flashing headlights ashore told us that Paul was back, exhausted from his long drive. We retrieved him and spent a night more comfortable than the day with the boat settled level.

<u>30 May. Friday</u>.
It was sunny and warm as we unloaded and we met several more of the local people who were very friendly and helpful. They offered to dispose of our rubbish and store our dinghy until we returned, making us feel most welcome.

We drove all day travelling hundreds of miles as we crossed the country. Jerry and Vincent were to stay at my house overnight and Paul went home, but a short time later he returned accompanied by his wife in quite a flustered state and the story began to unfold.

That radio-telephone call that we had made during the gale in the Bristol Channel had set in motion a mighty gathering of information process about which we had known nothing. The police had been around interviewing friends and relations, who had gathered a strong impression that we were lost at sea. Later it came out that my neighbour had been 'encouraged' to enter my house to find files relating to the journey. Our position at sea had not come through, so initially they had been searching between Plymouth and Falmouth and it wasn't until later that the search had moved to the

Bristol Channel. The newspapers, needing some indication that there had been bad weather, had reported that five people had been rescued in the Bristol Channel and a similar report was given on the national television evening news as part of the general weather picture. Many people close to us had been told that we were in trouble, but the same emphasis had not been placed on telling them afterwards that we were safe. We, in our involvement with finding a place to leave the boat and in the time-consuming tasks of travelling, recovering cars and making mooring arrangements had neglected to make solid contact once we had reported to the Coastguard upon our safe arrival at Milford Haven, followed by the message that we'd relayed to them on the next day.

After Paul and his wife had gone, Jerry, Vincent and I went to the house of a close friend to check that we were not presumed dead there. As we rang the doorbell we noted a refined dinner party going on within. The guests appeared slightly hazy across a candlelit table of glittering wineglasses and delicate coffee cups. The hostess opened the door on three unshaven, dishevelled characters still in salt-stained jerseys, jeans and sea boots who tumbled across the threshold with a wonderful party-stopping greeting, 'Have the police been to see you?' and the gale began to earn us the first of many rounds of drinks.

MI issue 235. Episode 30.

<u>Milford Haven.</u>
<u>24 July - 27 July.</u>
The winter lasted until midway through May when it suddenly became total summer through June and into the beginning of July. Days which will be remembered by some as a 'golden summer of childhood', came and went whilst we sweated away at work looking out through windows with the envious eyes of Laurie Lee at shimmering fields heavy with the drone of bees and dragonflies. Soon it would be the holidays and we could burst free; but summer thunder storms heralded the end and in a flash it was gone. The Atlantic lows returned and my washing, done in readiness for the holiday, was removed from the washing line after three days, wetter than when it had been pegged out to dry.

My trusty old car was loaded until its mud flaps trailed on the ground and having completed all domestic arrangements I departed alone for South Wales at 09.30. I was heading for Caerleon near Newport to meet Dave Howell the secretary of the Telstar Owners

Association. As I arrived early I looked around the village which was built over the remains of a major Roman garrison town. The Roman baths were in fact a Roman leisure centre which would have been well equipped even today. One little display which caught my attention showed some of the stones lost from the bather's finger rings, which had been discovered during the excavation of the bath's drainage system; sieving the silt brought 80 of them to light. In the new museum I was able to look closely at the equipment of the Roman soldier and from the point of view of appreciating the problems in designing <u>practical</u> systems two technical points won my admiration. The spear had a long slender metal shank just behind the sharpened tip, designed to bend on impact, thus making it useless to the enemy who couldn't throw it back. The sword was very short so that it could be drawn by a right handed person wearing it on the right side of his body. This allowed the shield to always be correctly positioned by the left hand and arm.

In the evening Dave took me down to Newport to see the docks where the River Ebbw joins the Bristol Channel. We looked across to the English shore and Dave pointed out the navigational features from Avonmouth docks down to the twin islands of Steep Holme and Flat Holme. In Newport (for the technically minded again) there was the unique transporter bridge of ingenious French design from the beginning of the century. It looked a bit like the Eiffel Tower lying on its side and used a gondola suspended from a gantry. It was worth a detour to see it for any aspiring designer. Back at Dave's house, he and his wife Judy told me the fascinating story of their journey to the Mediterranean in a Heavenly Twins catamaran so it was midnight before the tale was told.

<u>Friday 25 July</u>.
Early start at 06.30. We had a quick breakfast and set off for Milford Haven (about 85 miles in the rain) taking Dave and his young son Stuart with me, so that after I had unloaded they could take my car back to Newport where it would be easier for me to return to it on completion of the sailing on *Starship*.

We arrived at Llangwm about 10.15 at high water and luckily John Barrett a local man who had been looking after some of my equipment was already out on the water, boat testing his outboard which he'd just mended, so he ferried all my gear in one trip, as well as running a shuttle for Dave and Stuart so they could have a quick look aboard before the tide fell leaving me marooned aboard by the mud for the rest of the day.

There is always a great deal to do when I return aboard. On this occasion it included fitting a new gas cooker as the previous one never really recovered from its violent treatment during the gale and rehanging the rudder. I'd given it a five star overhaul as a reward for not breaking in the gale when I'd realised just how much I was relying on it but, as always, work commenced with cleaning off the evidence of the resident incontinent seagulls.

In the early evening Dougal Hutchison came along to look over the boat. I'd met him on my previous visit and he had written to me whilst I had been away; now he came to invite me up to the Rugby club (proudly claimed as the oldest in Wales) which acted as a social centre. We yarned away all evening and he told me some lovely stories about sailing on *British Steel* with Chay Blyth and the leg of an Atlantic Race from Cape Town to Rio de Janero with Rob James as skipper. As the evening progressed other friends dropped in on the conversation. The best story of the night concerned the time that a bunch of them had gone across to a pub at Landshipping on the other side of the river and, past closing time, had ended up drunk in an overloaded boat for the return trip. Inevitably they all finished up in the river where they sobered up pretty quickly, but were carried down on the tide and would have drowned had not a local angler just happened upon them in his dinghy in the dark after two hours of clinging to their upturned boat. The details were well embroidered with their lovely Welsh accents and we roared with laughter at each twist in the tale. It was midnight again before I was in my bunk.

Saturday 26 July.

Domestic cleaning aboard, until I could get ashore with the tide. I went to arrange with Mr Brock, the moorings secretary, the best place to move to in the main channel when I went out of the pill. I discovered that his son was to be married later that day and everywhere that I went people were preparing to attend the ceremony, but they still all had time to talk to me and offer help and advice. It was a wonderful community.

My crew for the next stage arrived whilst I was talking to Mr. Brock, so I went to greet them. Bengy and Alexis were two young men who had just finished their examinations at school and had been volunteered for this trip by Bengy's elder sister. Neither of them had much idea of what to expect and neither had any sailing experience to speak of, but they were willing to learn and soon proved their adventurous spirits. I had to fix a new radar reflector at the masthead to replace the one which disappeared in the gale and they each asked to go up, having watched me ascend the steps. It's not an essential requirement (unless you sail with Chay Blyth) and it is quite frightening, but they both did it without any qualms, so I immediately promoted them from pressed men to midshipmen.

We moved the boat by extending the rear warp, retrieving the main anchor; returned for the rear anchor; three point turn under motor and left the pill to anchor in the mainstream. The midshipmen went for a run ashore in the evening, but returned with the impression that Llangwm wasn't the centre of the entertainment universe. Going to bed just after midnight I realised that the days were beginning to run together in a continuous string of happenings and I'd missed my own birthday.

Sunday 27 July.
The weather had been distinctly indifferent with rain and cloud about, but the sun did peep through occasionally to make it possible for the new crew to absorb all the information about the running of the ship in reasonable conditions. After checking gear, we hoisted about two thirds main and about a quarter genoa to go for our first sail to teach them about the handling systems. The breeze was quite strong for us as we ran upstream. There was plenty of water because we were sailing at high water and I went up to the confluence of the two tributaries just above Landshipping. I could have gone further but I knew that I would be the one to work the sheet winch, close tacking on the way back and it was a good force 5, so I did not venture into the restricted channels. The lads had a go on the steering and both picked it up rapidly as we tacked downstream below Llangwm where there was a windshadow from the forest. At the next corner the wind was howling down the narrow reach so violently that it would have been useless to have attempted sailing it. I was tempted to stay in the comparative calm and wait to see what the next day would bring, but cruisers don't make progress by staying in one place, so I dropped the sail and we motored through giving us a rough ride in the wind against tide conditions. Eventually we made it out under the bridge into the wider expanses of the lower Haven where the wind was not quite so funnelled. We saw a great bustle of activity amongst the yachts showing that some kind of regatta was in progress.

I spotted some people aboard a Mark III Telstar *Triumph* so we went over to ask if we could use a mooring and as they were just leaving for a sail they offered us theirs. This gave us time to prepare a meal, and to sit for a little while in the cockpit watching the world go by, which was all new to my crew who were really taking to this seafaring life. Some people on a nearby boat called across to us that they liked the boat, so they were invited across for a conducted tour and a multihull discussion. As three o'clock approached it was obvious that the regatta fleet was about to depart for an afternoon race so we hoisted a bit of sail and followed them down the Haven at a respectable distance. The wind gradually began to moderate. In the big bay off Milford Haven itself they sailed a couple of loops around some buoys. We just reached back and forth on the windward side of the course so that they all came past a couple of times. They gave us friendly waves and it was a good opportunity to explain to my crew what was happening aboard each craft as they twisted and turned around the course, trimming and changing their sails. Had we been fully rigged we would have been roughly comparable with the fast handicap class. We were faster than the slow handicap as we were and they had spinnakers for the runs and reaches. We eventually set full genoa, but kept a reefed main to come back up the Haven at roughly the same speed as the fast class under a three sail run/reach.

We picked up an inshore mooring at Hobbs Point near to where we had been earlier and prepared the evening meal when we were hailed from outside. Malcolm and Kathy (Telstar Owners that we had met at the MOCRA Exeter Symposium) hearing that we were in the vicinity had driven from Swansea (Over 50 miles) bringing their inflatable and outboard motor so that they could reach us. They went first to Llangwm, then hearing that we had left they drove to the bridge from where they spotted us on the mooring. They had come for their personal guided tour. We talked for quite some time and their local knowledge of the harbours that we intended to visit proved very useful. After they had gone at about 20.30 I began to pore over the charts in earnest, measuring distances, calculating courses. The first step would be at least 50 miles around hazardous rock-strewn headlands. The tide was favourable from about ten o'clock in the morning which meant getting out of the Haven early. In order to do that I'd have to get down to the Dale anchorage just inside the mouth ready for a start the following day. The welcome interlude of casual drifting was coming to an end and the time to move on was drawing near.

Serial Starship

MI issue 236. Episode 31.

To Fishguard.
28 July Pembroke - 29 July

The forecast was for heavy rain but that didn't quite do justice to it. Woken by the drumming of the rain on the roof I lay watching a mini torrent running across the window. The targets were to go shopping in Pembroke and later to sail for Dale at the mouth of the Haven ready to depart for Fishguard.

We wandered around the town in more torrential rain. The gutters were streams; gratings were blocked with water; filter tips from extinct cigarettes swirled in whirlpools. Flat-capped men in gabardine coats stood in shop doorways glumly watching the cascades from pipes and guttering down streets still decked with soddened bunting damply celebrating a recent Royal wedding. Just to prove that we were in Wales the shop sign said, Jones the Gas. After lunch it was pouring so hard that we could hardly get on deck so we sat around reading, waiting for a break in the weather. It was interesting to note that all the boats on the moorings here always faced downstream even though there was a big rise and fall and a strong tidal flow in the stream only 50 metres away. Having cleaned the toilet to while away a few idle moments, I noticed the rain easing.

14.30 Reefed main and two thirds genoa, set sail. The wind was varied by the form of the land and sometimes we were uncomfortably pushed to our limit by the gusts, whilst at other times we drifted almost becalmed. The actual wind outside the Haven we guessed at about force five. We really began to feel it when we reached the clear section just inside the entrance and had to reach across the open water under quite strong conditions with some biggish waves coming through, pushed by the south-westerly. It was grey and wet and uninviting. Bengy sat right up on top and really enjoyed it, which augured well for when we would go to sea.

Once we entered Dale we could see lots of moorings and yachts in calm sheltered conditions. I noticed a big catamaran that we'd seen upriver, so as we passed I asked if we could go visiting and they were pleased to invite us over. Called *Easytime* she looked like a larger, more slender version of an Ocean Winds, but with a big nacelle extending forwards to take forestay loads. Made of 30mm glued strip-planking she was the work of the Macadams, father and son. Their crew Bill Walker and his wife had constructed an even bigger foam sandwich trimaran designed by Dick Crowe. They had come from Barrow in the north-west of England and as they talked about the place it became clear that it had been very significant for the history of multihull development. It would appear that the combination of the shallow water there and the proximity of the technical skills fostered by the engineering firm Vickers had produced an interesting crop of multihull designer/builders. Pat Patterson of Heavenly Twins/Ocean Winds fame; Bernard Rhodes who sailed his trimaran *Klis* to New Zealand; Dick Crowe who took the trimaran *Mud Slide Slim* in the 1974 Round Britain Race before going on to New Zealand himself and Ernie Diamond designer of the Diamond Cat originated from the area. We chatted about these and other multi matters followed by a return visit to *Starship*. When they had departed I studied the charts, laid off courses, thought about the rock strewn headlands to be rounded in the forecast SW 5-7 going

NW and set my alarm watch for 05.30. Not a pleasant prospect was in sight.

29 July Tuesday.

The man on the radio said that it was quite a reasonable day for *November*. The forecast gave NW 4-5, backing SW later, it was already blowing more than that where we were and Scillies was giving Force 6. It was going to be a hard wet struggle with risk to the gear and the boat. I couldn't really justify departing, so we stayed on our nice big mooring and I tinkered with the old Autohelm 3000 I'd acquired. About lunch time I noticed the wind dropping and as we'd been sitting around long enough I decided to 'have a go'.

At about 13.00 with reefed main and a half genoa we ran out of Dale and sheeted in progressively as we turned to starboard to come close hauled heading for the harbour entrance. It became very sunny with the new air and the sea was sparkling but terrifically lumpy, so that we were being thrown about all over the place and had to sail free to make any progress. Needing to sail about 290°m, our southward tack was 220-230°m and the westward tack was 330°m. Although I had planned to go outside of the major hazards such as Skokholm Island, I could see immediately that tacking through Broad Sound was possible. I was even tempted to go through Jack Sound as there appeared to be plenty of space and a commanding wind, but I decided not to push my luck as I was still pretty inexperienced at sailing near to rocks in rough water with uncertain tidal effects. That would be a game of Russian roulette. We beat out through Broad Sound and straight up the middle of Wild Goose Race, which was so bumpy that I set full sail to give her more power to drive through. As we cleared Skomer Island heading north-west for the South Bishop which was low on the horizon we were being overpowered and I had to reef the genoa again. Unfortunately, Bengy had succumbed to seasickness shortly after leaving and although Alexis managed to steer through Broad Sound they were then both laid low, so I had to sail the rest of the journey myself. Fortunately *Starship* is set up with sail controls for singlehanding, even without the use of the autopilot which was not then functioning.

The course across Brides Bay was held at 330°m and at 15.30 we were roughly halfway over. Looking at the choice of channels ahead I decided to cut the corner by going through close to Ramsey Island instead of all the way around the off-lying Bishops and Clerks. There were some rocks awash but I could see their positions clearly as the sea broke across them. Accordingly I was able to free off and by 16.30 I was up to the top of Ramsey Island looking at its knarled and wrinkled red/grey granite structure. All the islands had a striated appearance where the wind and water had sought out the structural lines of flow and had penetrated the weakest points. Thin vegetation clung to the upper surface of any ledge or crevice to highlight it by colour contrast. From a distance the smooth rounded forms were similar to lumps of baker's dough, cut, rounded, and expanded ready to enter the oven. Closer, the striations gave an almost furry appearance like TV's *Magic Roundabout*, puppet dog Dougal, had it not been for their red/green colours. At the southern end Ramsey had stacks and bays, cliffs and the black gash of an immense cave where seagulls whirled like snowflakes against black velvet.

In half an hour with the slack tide, ample wind and a free course I'd covered five miles, but it couldn't last. The wind dropped off and the tide turned against me as I approached St David's Head. The course went more onto a dead run which was progressively blanketed by the land effect and we began to flop about so that the sails wouldn't fill properly. I could have done with my spinnaker/reacher but couldn't easily set it and tend it alone, so I had to sail a broad reach to the north, then gybe and sail a broad reach back again towards a distinctive Strumble Head where the powerful light beam could be seen even in daylight. At the headland the tide was strong enough to stop forward movement and I had to reach away northwards to where the flow was decreased sufficiently to allow progress again.

Along the coast to the east of Strumble Head I sailed gently across a smooth sea, seemingly alone on my boat with not another craft in sight. The breeze carried the smell of grass, animals, and newly cut hay across the water from the land. My distance off was such that no human occupant could be seen, but buildings, fields, lanes and tracks could be individually picked out as the clear sun came lower in the sky behind me. For almost an hour I was able to savour this model landscape, tracing its roads, admiring its beauty and neatness, drifting in its aroma.

The chart said that Fishguard was just around the corner, but of it there was no sign. As it was a ferry terminal I expected to see some kind of activity in, or around the port, but there was nothing. No ferries, no boats, no lobster pots, no yachts, no sailboarders, no houses, no power lines, no swimmers, no sound. Even the harbour breakwater blended into the background and if it hadn't been for the little white salt pot of a lighthouse on the end I might have sailed right past. Slowly the houses on the hill behind the town emerged and as the wind headed me I took in the sail and started the motor, then went below to put the kettle on and wake the crew from their slumbers; their only release from seasickness whilst under way.

We entered in an almost mirror calm to pick up a mooring off the lifeboat station just as darkness fell at nine o'clock having covered the 35 miles in a wide variety of conditions from a crunching beat, to a drifting run. It had been a super sail, because the sun had shone all along, but the thin cirrus now glazing the sky told us that tomorrow would be different.

MI issue 237. Episode 32.

30 July
Fishguard - Porth Cardigan.
I was prepared for bad weather, but this exceeded my expectations. I awoke to a sound like dried peas being shaken in a box as bullets of rain strafed the roof. Outside it was grey, grey, grey. I could just discern the low silhouette of a barge-like craft on the next mooring. Its edges were lined with gulls all crouched in line astern trying to shelter behind one another and looking distinctly unhappy. It was easily force six in the harbour, but getting up and gusting more. I had planned a trip ashore, but it would have been impossible, so it was

back to bed for a snooze to recover from the efforts of yesterday. The wind howled and the boat shuddered on a taught mooring line alone in our grey circle.

After a late breakfast about midday I decided on a personal clean up. Stripped to the waist with my head inverted in a bowl of suds, I heard a shout from outside over the roar of the wind. Something was happening, so I scrambled up into the cockpit and put my head out of the canopy into the world of waves, wind, water, blowing, bucking noise.

A rugged little launch crewed by about six uniformed men was trying to keep station with our port side. They had dark blue uniform coats, glistening with water and their heads were protected by naval-type flat caps with chin straps tightly deployed. They were hanging onto their boat and all leaning into the blast as the spray was being whipped off the water surface. It was hard to hear as one man shouted across through cupped hands, the usual questions. Where from? How many aboard? Any Stores? Who owns it? The words were being carried off on the wind. His face had a ruddy glow and water was streaming away from the tip of his nose and chin. My hair had been well rinsed and cold trickles were running down my back. I wondered at the fortitude of so many men setting out in such conditions to ask these questions.

A yellow oily-clad man sat flat on a broad hatch in the middle of the deck trying to maintain contact with the bouncing craft, he was sliding about. Above the thumping diesel a crewman shouted 'You're on somebody's mooring.' just as their bow was pushed away by a wave. The throttles came to full revs. The man in yellow produced a pad of pink papers from inside his oilskins which nearly disappeared downwind and was instantly soaked. He was obviously about to try to collect some dues or other. Perhaps this is the 'Welcome in the Hillside' I thought, that you get in Wales. I began to see the funny side of it. There was no way that I was going to cross the beam onto the float to pay up; he'd have to come to me. Their boat was being blown backwards. The oily-clad man looked in despair as the gap widened. Suddenly I noticed a woman also in oilskins wedged in a corner of the deck, her long hair being tugged by the wind. She was laughing. She'd maybe come out for the ride. All those men were earnestly doing their jobs, but she, like me, could see the humour of this boatload of officials forcing their way through incredible adversity, spending a fortune in wages, fuel and equipment to deliver a soddened piece of pink paper to a half-naked chap with a shampoo hairstyle, just to collect some paltry dues. The scend of a wave half obscured them, as they disappeared into the grey scud to leeward, a faint, faint voice could be heard ... 'They ... may come back....for the mooring...' I laughed 'til I ached, but I held that woman's smiling face in my memory, *that* was the genuine Welcome in the Hillside.

After lunch I spent the afternoon fitting up the Autohelm, calibrating the compass etc., but I needed a quiet sail to become accustomed to it. We also talked at length about seasickness and I explained to the boys what the causes were and how to overcome the problem. We needed to improve on their last performance.

The weather blasted away all day with amazing ferocity. I had just prepared the vegetables for the evening meal when suddenly the wind began to steady and within minutes shafts of sunlight broke through the cloud. We'd just received the 5.50pm forecast saying that another dose was on its way for the next day, so I grabbed the opportunity to give the lads another sail. Instead of putting the food on the table, we went out and hoisted sail to depart at 18.15 running goosewinged with enough wind once we were clear of the land to make us break into a little surf once in a while, despite being reefed. The boys steered her all the way. The main value of this journey was for them to sail her without getting seasick, to see the scenery and to enjoy some pale evening sunshine because up until now we had experienced a lot of inactivity with little actual sailing experience for them.

I would have liked to have made it right up to New Quay, but calculations showed that going against the tide we were only covering the ground at seven knots so we would arrive after darkness at ten o'clock. I did not consider it worth the risk and began to look at Cardigan Bay only half as far, which we could reach in daylight. It was better to have a successful sail, sort out the boat properly then eat a good meal, which would all act as a confidence builder.

As we approached Cemeas Head I aimed to enter and seek shelter against the southern shore of the bay. If the wind should go to the north we'd be in for a difficult time, but to some extent that was a risk which had to be faced in all of the anchorages along this coast. Closing the headland we were running fast and as we entered an area of turbulent overfalls with cresting waves I was looking ahead to gauge my distance from the cliffs and scanning charts to confirm that there were no off-lying rocks. We were rushing down the waves when suddenly four feet from the bow I saw the large black shape coming out of the water. Oh My God! We're on! flashed through my mind in an instant and I braced myself for the grinding crash as she hit. The next wave would sweep her, she'd be lost. No time to act; it was a heart-stopping moment.

The great grey shape exploded out of the water and its curving fin filled me with instant relief. *Starship* ran smoothly though the point where the crash should have come. The big porpoise was cutting across us at right angles to the bow and as he popped up again several others began to appear. They were all quite large and clearly enjoying the sport of racing with us as we surged between eight and ten knots on the waves. Some came right into the bay with us whilst others remained at sea. We estimated that we saw about six or eight of them.

Well inside the bay in a small indentation on the southern side there were three or four lobster pots and a little boat nestling against the shore, but apart from that the huge estuary was deserted. We were within an hour of low water and had the sounder running. We crept in to about six feet of water and then backed out to ten feet to set the hook. We were quite sheltered, but a sea swell kept the boat constantly on the move whilst we were there, similar to being in the Scilly Isles.

It is an odd thing, but we weekend cruisers sometimes profess that we'd like to sail away to find solitude. On the south and east coast cruising grounds we seek the unfrequented anchorages, knowing in our hearts that such privacy would be virtually impossible to find. Our rivers and estuaries are now cluttered with moorings. There are even men in launches who buzz around taking money from people who are lying to their own anchors. Sometimes we might fondly dream - What would it be like to discover a wide estuary all to oneself? Well maybe for the first time on our journey, in Porth Cardigan it happened to me. There were lovely tree clad shores, admittedly dotted with just the occasional white-painted cottage peeping through the foliage. There was a broad bay of smooth water and a family of porpoises to welcome us ... and how did I feel? I have to admit that I felt uneasy. I was plagued with doubt. If this was such a beautiful idyllic place why was there nobody else here? Had I made some dreadful mistake? What was the danger that I had not identified? I would have been much happier to have seen a few moorings, or a couple of other yachts anchored. I sat in my cockpit looking around and slowly came to realise that I have been conditioned and I suspect that I'm not the only one. I reluctantly had to recognise that I've become a certain type of sailor who rushes off at the weekend to join a traffic jam afloat, along with all the other characters who are also out to 'get away from it all'. We never do really. We actually go to look at each other's boats and compare them with our own. In sailing, we seek the competition of overtaking slower craft to prove our skill to ourselves, Perhaps we go to be entertained by the nautical tangles that misfortune or inexperience visit upon other sailors like us. I discovered that we certainly don't seek the totally deserted anchorage, because if we should accidently find it, the eerie solitude might turn out to be more than we've bargained for.

Alone in the gathering darkness I listened to the wash of the sea against the cliffs and imagined that I was amongst the islands of the southern tip of South America, or tucked into a remote cove in Nova Scotia, or British Columbia. Alone, totally alone ... except ... what is this? Out to sea a set of yacht's navigation lights was heading my way, suddenly I was back in Wales. As it neared I could make out the hull-form of a catamaran and as it arrived it became the crisp new shape of a Prout 33CS called *Idle Bug*. 'Is the holding ground good?' he called as he rounded up. He had the whole of the endless space of the bay in which to anchor, but with a splash I heard his hook go in so close to us that our respective turning circles overlapped. In an East Coast river I'd have been irate, but for once I felt reassured now that the two of us had created our own little traffic jam. I was much happier having the company to look at and to confirm in some way my attachment to the kind of cruising world that I'd become accustomed to.

Sitting in the darkness we talked across the water, disembodied voices in the still night. They had set off from North Wales to sail southwards towards the Scillies via Milford Haven but the awful weather had beaten them back. Frankly I was amazed at the progress they had made into the teeth of some atrocious weather.

In the middle of the night I woke up and lay wondering whether we might drift into a collision with the cat. I was looking up at the cabin roof, when a flash of light came through the window. I peered out into the dark and saw the flash again. He was on his foredeck measuring the distance between us with the torchlight. He swept an arc across the water then checked his anchor roller. He too was worried about being so close and as he was the last to arrive, it was his responsibility. The simplest thing would have been to move off a short distance, but he was reluctant to do that. I understood. With him keeping watch we'll be OK I thought and I relaxed back into sleep. What funny creatures we sailors are.

Serial Starship

MI issue 238. Episode 33.

31 July Thursday - 1 August Friday.
To North Wales.
I had hoped to visit Barmouth or Aberdovey, but I had to be in North Wales by the weekend to change crews for we had already lost too

much time during the week with bad weather and it had become essential to make progress. The 05.55 forecast gave us SW veering NW 5/7 decreasing 4/5. It was time to grasp the nettle and head out directly the 45 miles across the bay to Abersoch which is just inside the projecting tip of North Wales, so we prepared with a good breakfast then hoisted sail to depart at seven o'clock.

The wind had gone a shade westerly so that it crept into Cardigan Bay where we had stayed overnight, but once we cleared the shelter of the headland we immediately felt the strength of a good force five as we set off reaching northwards. It's an odd thing but I don't think that I have ever previously carried out a passage in heavy reaching conditions. For me, the weather seems to be ninety per cent on the nose and ten per cent on the stern. We had one third genoa and half a main and we flew along at eight knots for most of the time throwing water all over the place and the motion was rough and uncomfortable.

On the first sea-leg of this part of the journey from Milford Haven both of my young crew members had been desperately seasick, so we'd had a long talk about my methods for overcoming it. I really did need their help now, because a seven hour watch in such rugged and taxing conditions would have pushed me and our safety, to the limit. Our whole strategy was to overcome sea sickness for them and they were being put to the severest motion test. Both of them were magnificent in the way that they followed instructions and demonstrated belief and commitment to the method. Even though they were both taken to their personal limits they were able to work their watches and they completed the passage without being ill. 'Only just!' as one of them said, but it was a triumph for them and they remained cured and contributing heavily for the rest of their journey. It was this achievement which gave us the most pleasure.

The sea was rough enough for us to have to take everything that would move inside the boat and wedge it tightly down onto the floor. It was a bleak and grey scene that we sailed into, drawn only in charcoal and chalk on grey paper, then splattered with water so that any colour ran down towards the bottom right hand corner. Even sitting in my well protected cockpit behind my wonderful doghouse the water found its way into my old oilies and I had to have a change of clothes. It's hard to say that one enjoys a passage such as this. It was just a question of hanging on and bashing water as a means to an end. It was endured.

Fortunately we had odd little points of interest to break up the monotony. We could watch the land recede for a short while and then we found a small grey blob on the horizon near to our course which eventually became a large tug or oil rig tender that turned away and went downwind as we approached. The next horizon smudge turned out to be a frigate anchored close to a minesweeper and we passed within a mile or so of their sterns. A mystery object like a Lanby buoy and another flat yellow barge with half a dozen paddle-like structures arranged in pairs along its deck, held our attention for a while. They looked like research objects of some kind, but we didn't have time to investigate as we were intent on getting to our destination as rapidly as possible.

The first land that appeared was the distinct hump of Bardsey Island and then the peaks on the mainland came into sight to the right. We could have sailed straight up the outside of the Lleyn Peninsular because I had held to windward to avoid all hazards, but we bore away a bit and headed for the passage between St.Tudwal's Islands and the mainland. As we did so the land was obscured by a mighty rain squall which rapidly engulfed us also. It whistled around us and sent us scudding along pressed to our limit even with our tiny scraps of sail. It departed as quickly as it had arrived and we were suddenly in sunshine entering a broad sandy bay to port where strings of moored yachts, sailing boats and windsurfers contrasted vividly with the harsh sea world which we had just left behind. Around the bay racing yachts which had just completed their contest were heading back for their moorings, so we joined the procession.

Looking landwards near to the northern headland of the bay we could see the clubhouse building of what we discovered to be the South Caernarvonshire Yacht Club, built onto the side of the hill overlooking the water. It had a variety of different levels linked by steps on the outside so that we could see many people streaming up and down from the launches which constantly powered backwards and forwards taking people out to the yachts, or collecting them again when they signalled by waving 'something orange' (like a lifejacket).

A launch came up and directed us to a visitor's mooring by leading the way and then circling the chosen buoy. Amazingly we were then given a proper gold-edged invitation card welcoming us and asking us to partake of the Club's facilities. Later, having eaten lunch and prepared ourselves to go ashore we called a launch and crossed to the club steps where we landed along with many other people. Almost immediately a club official came down and picked us out from the crowd to heartily welcome us and offer directions and advice should we need help. We were most impressed, for we had rarely received this type of welcome anywhere before.

We went shopping in the village at Abersoch. The sandy beach adjoining the yacht club was a real holiday tourist trap and we were in mid-season. The village was designed to meet the needs of the thousands of day trippers heading to and from the beach and the local people could only retain their identities by speaking their natural Welsh tongue to each other as they were engulfed in the daily tide of foreigners.

When I took the evening shipping forecast they gave the usual north-westerly 5-7, but then backing south EAST, severe gale NINE. What a shock. We'd been battling away all week to find an anchorage sheltered from the westerlies (north and south) and finally when we'd made it, the wind was about to do a complete reversal and blow right into our secure bay from an almost unheard of direction as far as this part of the world was concerned.

Listening to the general forecast it seemed as though a deep depression was on its way, but that it wouldn't arrive until later the following day. We decided that there could be no relaxation and that we should depart early next morning to try to get ahead of the storm, then go around the end of the peninsular and up into Caernarvon which would offer more shelter. My alarm was set for 04.10. What an awful hour.

<u>August 1 Friday.</u>
It was still dark and we moved around like moles silently crunching our cornflakes and glumly staring at our coffee cups. Faint light began to illuminate the huge Tremadoc Bay, of which our Abersoch

143

bay was but a tiny part. The surrounding curtain of mountains created the impression of a closed lake, forming a mighty amphitheatre for sailing. It was a magnificent place especially in the still clear air of early morning. We motored gently away towards the southern headland absorbing the atmosphere. A solitary small porpoise played ahead of our bows, curving and flipping in and out of the water.

As we passed inside St. Tudwal's Islands again we looked across to the far mountains of Snowdonia in the east where the sun would rise. The clouds above the peaks were completely glowing with red bases and the sky grew lighter and brighter. The sun was just below the land and about to appear at any moment in a deep valley between the peaks. Suddenly the first spot of piercing liquid-gold light was there, projecting a single shaft across the water which drilled through our eyes with the intensity of a laser beam. It was a breath-taking sight. The smooth swift movement of the sun could easily be discerned taking less than a minute for the disc to rise upwards clearing the valley base and tracing the line of an ascending hillside. Its immediate warmth and colour filled the air and reflected from the sea, transforming the cold bleakness of the early dawn into day.

The significance of the sunrise was heightened for us by the proximity of the smooth bare islands of St.Tudwal lying in our wake. One could fully understand how ancient people trying to scrape a living from these inhospitable shores would have welcome the arrival of the sun as bringing renewed hope of life after the cold and damp discomfort of the night.

Early Christianity must have held a precarious toehold on these tiny islands protected from the superstitious shore-bound inhabitants by only the narrowest strip of water. We rounded the headland to go west across Hell's Mouth Bay, passing north of the Devil's Ridge; names which told of an ancient struggle. We wondered if we would find a safe haven before the severe gale arrived, or whether we were destined for another struggle with the elements.

Sea Sickness.
The strategies for dealing with sea sickness have proved to be successful for many sailors over the years. They are based on an understanding of the many factors affecting the sufferer. They are available in **Practical Cruiser's Guide to Seasickness** *(see the inside front cover of this book). Every yacht should have a copy to help new crew.*

Serial Starship

MI issue239. Episode 34.

To Caernarvon
Friday August 1.

A couple of biggish porpoise gambolled on the surface as we approached Bardsey Sound from the east but they paid us no attention, probably because we were motoring in the flat calm of early dawn; they'd have preferred us under sail.

The Sound was lumpy and we motored doggedly onwards with spouts of water being cast into the air all around us. Our craft was first wallowing then jumping, supported first on its mainhull, then on the tips of the floats. Bows up, then bows down, bumping and banging until we reached the smoother water beyond, where we were able to make our right turn to head up the outside of the Lleyn Peninsula towards Caernarvon. If the gale should come now, at least it would be from a favourable direction.

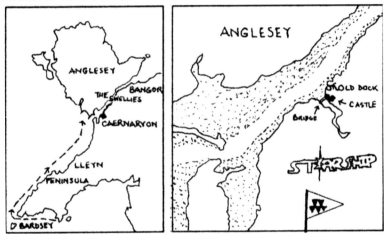

We'd progressed hardly a mile when the wind began to fill in from the land allowing us to set the main and then after another couple of miles out came the genoa for us to enjoy the bliss of turning off the engine to leave us close reaching alongside an interesting piece of land with mountains ahead to hold our attention and the boat slipping along so smoothly on a flat sea. It was a new experience for the crew who had become quite accustomed to fighting through every single wave to reach our destination. Their sea sickness cure was so complete that we were both cooking and munching for almost all of the rest of the journey.

Mountain tips on Anglesey appeared over the horizon far to our left, but we hugged the near shore to bring ourselves to the southern entrance of the Menai Strait. The shallow entrance bar was very extensive and it took some careful calculations to determine the optimum point to strike away from the mainland and sail about four miles out towards Anglesey seeking a small lighthouse which was in the proximity of the first two entrance channel marks. Once in the correct position we dropped sail and proceeded under motor as one dogleg in the channel was directly upwind. Eventually we passed through into the deeper water of the Strait itself where several craft were attempting to sail in the drifting conditions against the strong tidal flow.

Caernarvon is dominated by its castle which is a very impressive piece of masonry and the town itself is surrounded by a very complete wall with turrets and towers.

Alongside the castle is a shallow drying lake with a very narrow entrance beneath a low swing bridge which controls entry. Once through into the basin, yachts lie alongside a quay wall with halliards taken ashore to ensure that they don't fall over at low water. In summer, thousands of tourists flock the quay as it is the main town car park. I preferred not to enter this tightly restricted place, but sought to stay out in the Strait using a buoy just above the town where small craft moorings were marked on the chart. Some chaps in a launch indicated that we should use a bigger mooring just inshore, so we moved across and were quite comfortable throughout the afternoon until the rain started at about five o'clock. At the same moment loud noises from ashore told us that the owner of the mooring had arrived and he was apoplectic at the thought of us using his mooring. He was ranting and raving and shouting demands that we get off quick, before he exploded. It was another Welcome in the Hillside, I think. Never has a mooring been so vociferously verbally defended. There was absolutely no chance to reason, beg, barter or bribe, we just had to *go* and although we didn't know it at the time we were just beginning one of those convoluted incidents which take one to the limit of endurance that can be occasionally experienced when cruising.

The rain began to pour as we released the mooring and made ready the ground tackle, so that the two lads on deck were getting a mighty soaking. A big Rival-type yacht was anchored off the town and we tried to lay our hook inshore of him, but when I reversed to set it, we just kept on going. Getting the anchor back was hard work and when it surfaced we could see why. It was totally choked with

146

massive strands of kelp. We tried again with the same results, so I tried moving out to deeper water to get below the level where the kelp would grow. This meant putting out much more cable and my soddened crew were muttering words about Welsh mooring owners. The anchor held no better in the deeper water although this time there was no kelp. Something rather strange was happening though. When I went forward to investigate I could see that the anchor and its chain appeared to be polished, it was shining smooth and glistening like a newly caught mackerel. We went for another attempt and still it would not take, I knew the lads were getting exhausted. I tried one last time without tripping line to make the whole operation as simple as possible, but it was the same again. It was as if we had no anchor down at all. We could motor backwards at speed with the anchor just rumbling away on the bottom not checking us for an instant.

It was useless to try further and I was aware of how much effort the crew was expending, so we motored further into the Strait to an area of small moorings, but when we arrived it was clear that they were all too small, and we did not wish to incur further Welsh wrath. We tried to anchor again, but the result was the same as before and the anchor by now was polished to a mirror finish. We'd been struggling for over an hour in unrelenting rain and the wind was beginning to get up. The whole sky was darkening with thick racing clouds as night gathered prematurely. The storm was approaching and we were without a secure place to stop. I might have explored further up the Strait but I had a new crew to meet that evening in Caernarvon, so I could not go far. I motored down towards the town again and glimpsed as I passed a very narrow gap into an ancient silted dock with rusty fishing boats high and dry on the mud in there. I couldn't get in there. I had one chance left. Just below the town I'd seen four moorings together, which I had passed up earlier as they were in a more exposed place. I decided to return to them, but I had one last go with my big anchor. I did the foredeck work as this anchor with its associated chain approaches the limit of what a man can lift. It was useless. It had taken me a long time to believe it, but the bottom here was either smooth granite or thousands of small boulders or pebbles which scraped away at the galvanising on the ground tackle producing the polished appearance. I regretfully stowed the anchors realising that I had just discovered a new cruising situation where anchoring was not an option.

In the gathering gloom I managed to locate the moorings and secured to one, but I was now exposed to much windier conditions as there was no shelter from the town or higher land. I was feeling uneasy as I began to prepare the meal. Despite us being only a couple of hundred meters from the low lying shore gusts of wind came whipping across the water strongly enough for us to lift the mooring buoy out of the water and lay back tightly on the warp. Each twist and jerk of the boat made me feel more and more nervous. The noise in the rigging was increasing and the note it was singing was rising higher and higher. What could I do?

Our new crewmember Howard Snow was arriving on the 8.40pm bus in the market square and we had to meet him to bring him aboard. He had mainly dinghy experience and was coming to learn cruising; it was going to be a case of 'in at the deep end'. Bengy and I silently kitted up to go ashore in the inflatable. When we clambered out from under the cockpit canopy we suddenly appreciated the force of what was happening out there in the night. We had to keep the inflatable down to stop it behaving like a kite. The wind noise roared around us and flogged our oilskin hoods. Bengy worked full-time simply to hold down the bow of the boat as we went ashore and consequently a great deal of spray came aboard, even when travelling as slowly as possible. We headed for the pool by the castle and as we rounded the corner to pass below the swing bridge the wind was funnelled between the trees and the high castle walls. We were illuminated by the swinging street lights and saw a gust about to hit us which was lifting thousands of tiny spikes of water up from the surface. We both dived down to hold the dinghy and resist the force as it hit us. The rain and spray stung our faces. The forward motion of the boat stopped and we grimly looked at each other, both understanding that this was becoming dangerous.

We went alongside a metal ladder suspended on chains from the top of the quay wall which was about five or six feet higher than the water. I very carefully passed the dinghy painter below a rung and up the back of the ladder to secure it to the top step. In this way I could stop the bow from lifting and dunking the engine.

We felt pleased to be on the security of dry land and tried not to think of the return journey. We walked up and met the bus. Helping Howard with his bags we strolled back towards the dinghy, but as we approached I could see the bow of the inflatable occasionally appearing above the top of the quay. I rushed forward to see that the wind force had lifted the inflatable which in turn had lifted the metal ladder and cast it onto the quay. As I arrived the outboard was under water taking a bath.

The jollity of our meeting was draining away. Bengy and I had tried not to alarm Howard about our predicament, but now he intercepted our exchanged looks of concern and began to suspect that all was not well. We suddenly knew that we were about to undertake a very hazardous journey. The whole world was now a continuous roar of wind. Tree branches thrashed, lights swung dizzily back and forth casting eerie shadows and people clutching their coats tightly around them scurried for cover. What should we do?

We scrambled down into the boat, loading Howard's bags. The outboard wouldn't start. I pulled and pulled it, trying to dry it out. It coughed a bit, then suddenly burst into life. We cast off, and turned away from the quay. The engine died, then refused to start again. We had entered the wind funnel and we were gathering speed towards the arch of the swing bridge. Out there in the strait it was pure darkness and we were being propelled remorselessly towards that inky black hole. Once outside we would be lost for *Starship* was around the corner to the left and upwind. The engine would not start again. We were sliding out of the light into the night beyond. We must not go under that arch. We paddled like fury for the far shore where clinker hulks lined the shallows. It was impossible to go to windward. It was hopeless. We passed a hull closely but could not hold on. The arch came nearer as we finally grabbed a loose mooring rope and pulled ourselves into the tangle of stakes and lines between the beached craft. We were in trouble.

It was clear to me that I should not persist with the inflatable. It was now too dangerous. *Starship* was out on the exposed mooring of unknown strength with a lone inexperienced crew aboard in a situation where an anchor would not hold, a ferocious gale was building in the darkness; later we would learn of unfortunate people being killed as nearby hillside caravan sites were devastated in the storm. As we clung to the mooring lines in our dinghy, what on earth could we do now?

MI issue 240. Episode 35.

Harry and the Old Dock.
Friday August 1. Caernarvon.
We pulled our inflatable dinghy to the shore in the darkness. We had to shout to communicate over the wind noise. I had no idea what I should do next, but I repeated my words to myself out-loud so that I would accept my own decision. Going out into the strait with the failing engine was too dangerous. The risk to the three of us was

unacceptable. Knowing that using the boat was not an option forced me to begin again. I had no dinghy. Now what should I do? I must find a bigger stronger boat to get me back to *Starship* with the lone crewman aboard.

In my struggles to this point I had not had time to look around and weigh other possibilities, but when I shouted to the others that we would have to find another boat, they had both noticed the same open blue launch moving about in the little harbour and they pointed it out as it passed out through the entrance below the swing bridge. Despite the exceptionally bad conditions people had gathered on the bridge and were watching some kind of emergency on the other side just below the castle walls. I was busy with my own emergency and ran along the shore towards the bridge with Howard. The old man in the bridge control box said that there would be no Harbour Master about at this time of night, but he added that 'Harry' would help me. He pointed across towards the blue launch engaged in manoeuvers which still held the interest of the knot of people braving the driving wind and rain. As we crossed the bridge towards the stronger lights illuminating the castle I began to see what was happening below. A floating restaurant complete with all its customers still being served meals in the most cultivated manner had broken adrift from some of its mooring lines and was in danger of crashing into an access ramp which projected from the shore behind it. There was little danger of it disappearing out into the Strait, but the wave movement was crunching one corner against the concrete ramp causing a downpipe to break loose and buckling the guard railings on its pontoon. All this we could clearly see as we walked down the access ramp. If it hadn't been so serious it would have been humorous.

The restaurant owner was pacing up and down the ramp in his evening suit wringing his hands as the two hastily gathered craft tried to get lines on his restaurant to pull it clear. Harry had succeeded and was motoring upwind under the bridge. In the lulls he succeeded in dragging the restaurant clear of the quay, but then the next irresistible gust would drive it back with a nasty crash. The other craft attached to the far end of the restaurant attempting to assist was an open tripper launch complete with a frilly-edged canopy over the back section. The windage of the canopy would occasionally take over and make steering impossible. They only just avoided being driven through the side of the restaurant a couple of times. The poor owner was beside himself with anxiety, "Oh, it's no use," he grieved, "it weighs 130 tons, that *thing* (indicating Harry's boat with some disdain) hasn't got the GUTS to pull us off."

Harry had reached a similar conclusion, because shortly afterwards he gave it up as a bad job and began to return into the harbour. As he passed below the arch the bridge operator left his little control cabin and shouted to Harry then pointed towards us running along the shore. Harry brought his launch over to some steps nearby and called up to see what we wanted. I told him that I was unable to return to my boat and I expected him to start asking me lots of questions, but he somehow sensed the whole situation and did not hesitate for a moment. 'Is she the catamaran outside?' 'Yes.' (This wasn't the time to start correcting that misconception.) 'This gale will go round to the south-west and it will be too bad out there.' was his immediate reaction. He was a small man and an old man but there was no delay, he understood everything in totality. His face was earnest. "You must take her into the Old Dock." He was telling me, not asking me. "Get in." We scrambled aboard across the engine box amidships. "I've got a dinghy over there with another crewman." I shouted, pointing to where the orange form could just be distinguished beneath the trees. "Leave it. You can get it later." Harry commanded. It was my turn to wonder. I had only glimpsed the narrow granite entrance to the Old Dock very briefly earlier in the day. "Am I allowed in the Old Dock?" I asked over the pounding of the diesel. I could just make out his eyebrow raised to the cloud-covered sky. 'On a night like this they can't stop you.'

We were out now in the roaring darkness which overpowered even the smell and thump of the engine. The boat shook and stiffly rolled as walls of wind struck her. I put my face to Harry's ear, "How wide is the entrance? Will I get through?" "How wide are you?" he called back ..."Twenty two feet."... "You'll fit. I'll stand by you. You'll be OK." His decisive manner gave me confidence.

He brought her up astern between the mainhull and the float on the starboard side, balancing her against the considerable pull of the tide. His bow roller hooked a float stay with a twang as we crested a wave. I shouted to Howard to scramble across onto this strange craft, which he never even seen before. Alexis was holding the canopy flap open and trying to stop it from blowing away. I was fending, holding off, holding in, scrambling and pushing him clear with my feet. "I'll stand by you." was all that I heard as the diesel roared and he fell away.

Alexis' face said that he was very glad to see us. Howard was virtually speechless with all this happening so fast. Only half an hour ago he had been sitting on a nice warm bus driving across solid Welsh countryside. We checked lifejackets whilst I hurriedly explained what we would have to do. I was going to sit them on the port float with our big fenders. As we passed through the entrance if a collision seemed inevitable with the tide and crosswind driving us onto the solid wall they were to try to get the fenders in place to roll us through. First though we had to release ourselves from the mooring.

If ever we needed an inboard diesel engine this was the time. I started her up and we went forward, then cast off. My main worry was that Harry should not block me as I made a run at the narrow entrance. Twice before I had taken my boat through very narrow gaps of this type, both times in the Netherlands. Once was a lock only two feet wider than the boat. I tried that one slowly, jammed the boat diagonally and scraped us badly, as I found that I could no longer steer once she was dragging on the concrete walls. The second time was in Harlingen when a ship boxed me in, in the outer harbour and I had to pass between his full length of barnacled steel side, and the solid dock side with a tail wind. I did that one fast with crew on each float and everybody shouting, 'Stop we are going to crash!' We went through unscathed because with the speed, the steering was precise and the boat could be accurately guided. As we headed for the Old Dock I knew that we were going to go through *fast* and I hoped that Harry realised that we would not be hanging about giving little burst of engine to adjust our position. In such conditions the wind would take her if she slowed below a certain speed.

I thought carefully about the exact course of action that I wanted Harry to take and then looked across towards the small gap in the sea wall where he was preparing. He had rigged a big fender along his starboard gunwale and he was hovering just to the left of the entrance ready to move in alongside us squeezing himself between us and the leeward wall if necessary. This was exactly what I had decided I wanted him to do and I was encouraged and reassured by his judgement. We made a steady arc for the entrance and then straightened up. I could see the silhouettes of people on top of the sea wall on either side of the opening, pressing against the railings to see the outcome. Harry was coming in on our left, but I kept my eyes on the target. I gave her a boost of throttle and we went for it. The rain beat against my face as I strained to judge the line of approach. The crew on the float shuffled their fenders nervously. Would we hit the right hand side if we didn't get a gust in the next few seconds? We went faster. Harry dropped away behind us and we shot through beneath the people into the tiny rectangular basin, turning sharp right to head for the shelter of the windward end.

There was a small ship there with huge tyres hanging down her side for us to grab onto. My two crew were crossing the beams from one side to the other and I was holding back on the throttle to give them time to cross. The wind was tearing at the boat and we were pitching with the waves generated in only 25 metres of the dock. I went alongside and the crew grabbed hold. I set off walking forward with ropes to help secure us, but as I reached the forward crossbeam an incredibly powerful gust tore us away from the ship even though the wind hit us on our bow. I scampered back along the deck and dived into the cockpit, slammed her into gear and fought to regain control. Fortunately the wind was so strong that it held her stationary even against the engine revs, so I was able to use power without going forwards and managed to bring her in again long enough for ropes to secure us to the welcoming steel sides of the ship. What utter relief. We criss-crossed a spider's web of lines onto the ship and tied especially tightly to the notice forbidding mooring alongside. 'On a night like this …' Harry had said. He was nowhere to be seen. Like the Good Samaritan, he had gone on his way.

We still had our dinghy to collect and poor patient Bengy who had simply heard our shouted orders 'Stay there!' as we had disappeared into the night in the blue launch. We delayed not a moment, but walked through the town in our full 'lifeboat kit', drawing strange glances from late night drinkers. Our plan, after crossing the swing bridge again was to deflate, dismantle and hump everything, including a fairly hefty outboard and Howard's luggage, back to the Old Dock on foot. Luckily, as we struggled at the roadside to deflate the boat a passing motorist stopped and offered to help us. We gratefully accepted this kindness, lashing our boat onto his roof rack and nursing the motor in the back seat. Howard was still bemused by this action-packed introduction to the gentle art of cruising. Was it always like this? We, who had started the day at four in the morning, were too tired to explain by the time we had transferred all the gear back aboard *Starship*.

That night and the following day we were more than grateful that our outboard had failed to start and that Harry had brought us into the Old Dock. The strait became a horrifying maelstrom when the tide went against the wind and the moorings would have been untenable for us. We gained a great deal of peace of mind from being firmly fastened to the security of the solid Welsh rock of the Old Dock.

MI issue 241. Episode 36.

<u>Engines.</u>
<u>Caernarvon.</u>
<u>Saturday August 2 - Tuesday August 5.</u>
A windy day with strenuous activity warping the boat tightly into a corner at the end of the dock for maximum security and, I had a debt of gratitude that I paid to Harry who had saved us from the gale.

We were on the doorstep of the Caernarvon Yacht Club which was very convenient for it was well appointed and restfully quiet, an ideal place to stay for a couple of days to recover and replenish whilst changing crews as Bengy and Alexis departed.

We made a car journey on the Sunday up to Bangor at the top end of the Menai Straits to visit a good chandler and get charts for our crossing to Scotland. On our return we diverted to visit the yacht harbour at Port Dinorwic which was concealed in a narrow wooded valley utilising part of a canal once used for transporting slate to the coast. It had a fascinating, well preserved Victorian ship lock at the entrance.

<u>Monday August 4</u>.
The sailing crew which now consisted of Howard Snow, my youngest son Roland and myself, was awake at 07.30 on a bright gentle sunny day preparing to take *Starship* through the most dangerous and restricted section of the Strait known as the Swellies. It is an area of semi-submerged rocks with powerful currents and whirlpools. It rightly has an awesome reputation and must be passed at approximately high water slack. We'd carefully calculated the correct time to approach and having sorted out our other family visitors who had been staying aboard and who were now going ashore, we released our lines and waved goodbye.

There was hardly sufficient wind to sail so we kept the motor on at medium revolutions heading up the beautiful wooded valley. We had gone about 2 miles when there was a small pop from the engine which slowly came to a halt leaving us drifting in midstream. I immediately checked the fuel tank which was half full ... and this meant trouble. From lazing around on deck with a leisurely sunny passage in prospect we were immediately pitched into another cruising crisis and we'd only been going for a few minutes.

Diesel engines <u>don't</u> stop if they have fuel. I rushed below to check to see that nothing had fallen off the engine, but it looked OK. Then back on deck to deal with the immediate danger of being carried up on the tide with no wind to sail upon. We couldn't use the anchor here; we'd already learned that lesson. On most boats we'd have been in real difficulties, but we were saved again by the tender's outboard (operational again) being stored on a bracket on *Starship*'s transom. It gave us sufficient push to make up to some moorings off the Plas Menai sailing school.

I tackled the silent motor and confirmed my worst fears. The engine had decompressed, so it had to be a valve. I removed a cover on top of the engine to see the shattered remains of a spring under the valve ending. Oh, Woe is me! Replacements like that can only come from the makers or their comprehensively stocked representatives. I was looking at a big bill, a long delay, I had to be in Scotland in a matter of days and the tide was beginning to turn against me. Time to wallow in self-pity; to rage against fate. Time for self-recrimination, anger and anguish, but the old questions of Why Me? Why here? Why NOW? suddenly snapped me back into the real world.

What if it had been only TEN MINUTES earlier in the running time of the engine? Only that short while ago our boat and maybe our lives had depended on the motor as we had driven across the tide and the gathering night storm, heading for the narrow granite entrance to the Old Dock in Caernarvon. The thought of what our fate might have been had it expired at that moment sent a shiver down my spine which caused me to apologise to the beast and give it a quick rub over with an oily rag (that I know the engine appreciate). It had chosen an excellent time to expire, gentle weather, nice sunshine, not a million miles from civilisation, in restricted sheltered water. How lucky I was to have such an understanding engine. When I looked back in the log I even found that maybe it had given me warning (No.230 between Fowey and Falmouth) a long time ago?

My 'initiative test' was how to repair the broken motor? I decided that I had to find expert assistance. From what I'd seen at Bangor I felt my chances would be better there, than returning to Caernarvon, but first I would have to pass through the Swellies, without an engine; not an enticing prospect. The fitful wind was from astern, so I decided to give it a try, even though I had lost a lot of time and was well behind the planned programme. We ran goosewinged and kept the outboard on, but the opposing tide was gathering force and we were getting later and later. We pressed on past Port Dinorwic until around the bend we could see the first of the two bridges which marked the boundaries of the worst section of the passage. The closer we approached the faster was the flow against us until we found that despite doing five knots we had come to a halt. It was no use pursuing a lost cause. We'd given it a good try, but at the first bridge we were obliged to turn back.

The village of Port Dinorwic was set back in a bay to our left as we beat back from the bridge and we could see some large old sheds at the far end of the waterfront which had probably been a biggish boatyard in former days. We eventually managed to secure to a mooring on the outer edge of the many moorings within the bay. I went across in the tender to investigate possibilities at the boatyard then later, we moved *Starship* in alongside the quay.

The boatyard was not a place for hurry. The men were mainly elderly and like everyone in these parts they spoke Welsh, but their understanding of English was equally perfect and they could easily flow from one language to the other and back again in the same sentence, depending on how best the words fitted together. They worked from an old caravan that was unequally divided with a small office at one end and a 'works canteen' occupying the remainder. It was the world of men and working men at that. Nothing had been

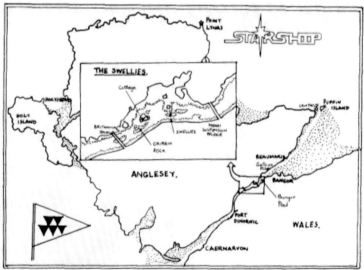

cleaned for years, especially the carpet, but possessions fitted their individual owners like old well loved, battered pairs of carpet slippers. There was no ostentation, no pretence, just work-a-day comradeship as they all pottered about their duties and met to discuss the happenings of the day over pint mugs of tea.

I was told that the engineer was over at the marina, but soon he returned to take a look at my engine. The elderly manager and engineer together advised me that the parts would have to come from the maker's suppliers. They escorted me to their telephone and left me to it. Recalling only that the address was somewhere near Poole I eventually made contact and ordered new springs, exhaust valve and gaskets. I arranged for an express overnight service which promised delivery for the following morning. The engineer removed the whole top of the engine and took it home with him to clean up and check over that evening. This left us with a chance to catch up on the domestic side, but first we explored the town.

It might be a fine place for the residents but for young Roland, who judged holiday quality by the number of arcades with Star Wars machines, it was an intense disappointment. I was most interested in a large dock basin which had obviously once been the heart of the town, but which was completely silted up. There were mechanical diggers in it making a deep channel around the edges to produce a Marina facility. The old buildings bordering it had been cleared away and it seemed that a new face for Port Dinorwic was about to be fashioned.

As our boat had taken the bottom on very firm ground against the quay I took the opportunity at low water to check the hull and scrub off the mud and weed which still adhered from Milford Haven. One of the major difficulties with not having access to my boat for most of the year was this question of maintenance. I was always having to move on in order to make progress; always a tide to catch, provisions to buy, people to pick up and there was a tendency for things to become neglected unless they showed signs of failure. Thankfully the engine was getting its share of attention right now. For a light, windborne cruising craft there was an absolute need for reliable back-up power on a journey like this.

Tuesday August 5.
The parts arrived and the engineer put the engine back together again in the afternoon, charging us less than the price of the postage on the parts for the work he'd done. A quick test run and we were as good as new again, but we had missed our tide for the Swellies, so we stayed for another day of enforced relaxation, repainting the bottom and renewing the deck paint. The day itself was reasonably warm and sunny but the shipping forecast was beginning to speak of another southerly gale on its way.

Readers may feel that perhaps I'm unduly pessimistic about the weather or maybe I am just making it sound worse than it actually was, for after all, these journeys were carried out in British Summer time.

The two summers involved to date had been characterised by a succession of low pressure systems following each other across the Atlantic. I am an East Coast sailor where we are usually sheltered from the worst of the westerly depressions. I was surprised at the difference when sailing on the West Coast where the systems still retained youthful vigour as they hit the land directly from the open ocean. In the east most of the energy has been expended by the time that they appear and it is not uncommon for forecasted rain not to arrive at all. The south-west wind, as experienced in the east can be mild and relatively gentle, but in the extreme and unprotected west the wind, coming unrestricted from the sea, felt cold and damp causing cloudy overcast skies as the air ascended to get over the mountains.

I have introduced the topic of weather because I found it to be one of my main concerns when cruising in the south west. On this day I knew that I had a longish crossing from Wales to the Isle of Mann ahead of me and I wanted reasonable conditions in which to undertake it. I was being told to expect gale force 6-8 from a favourable quarter. The weather which would follow this gale was north-westerly force 6 which was directly contrary to our intended course. It would make sailing almost impossibly uncomfortable and due to having to beat, it would double the distance to be sailed, increase the time of exposure, whilst reducing and taxing the stamina of the lightweight crew. These things may not be important factors for racing crews who have made a conscious choice to GO, almost irrespective of the weather, but for cruisers like us who were supposed to be enjoying ourselves and not getting too frightened or sustaining damage, this juggling with weather information dominated our sailing decisions.

As I applied the antifouling paint I knew that I was already days behind in my schedule to collect my Scottish crew. First I would have to get through the dangerous Swellies and then, would I be justified in setting out in a gale which was from a favourable direction or should I wait until it dropped to force 6 and turned against me?

Serial Starship

MI issue 242. Episode 37.

<u>Working the Weather.</u>
<u>August 6</u>
The passage that we were about to make from North Wales across to the Isle of Mann depended upon our ability to 'work the weather' by departing at precisely the right moment to catch a tiny weather window. It was going to be a gamble, but gambling with quite serious consequences, not to be taken lightly. There was always the easy answer open to us, which was not to sail at all unless things were perfect, but we met people who were taking that option everywhere we went. They made no progress and whilst their existence was easier and more comfortable they expressed dissatisfaction with their static situation and noted that they seemed to cruise less far as the years went by. Applying logic to that, seemed to show that comfort can become more important than cruising progress. They say that it's the harbours not the sea that rots the ships and the men. Our overall target for this project of sailing all the way around Britain provided the driving force which made us bored after a few days stuck in the one place. Our tolerance of the prospect of bad weather would increase until we'd become ready to face discomfort, just to get a change of scenery.

<u>August 6. Wednesday. Port Dinorwic</u>
The weather was sunny enough and the breeze was about south-east, just ahead of the starboard beam.   Approaching from our direction the Swellies had to be taken just before high water in order to take advantage of the tidal flow. Everybody used the same calculation to determine the time of H.W. in the Swellies which was 2 hours before H.W. Liverpool. This did NOT agree with the information in our tidal almanac, but it was the proper method to use.

Obviously we felt more than a tinge of excitement mixed with apprehension as we approached the arch of Telford's Britannia Bridge and began to feel the boat entering the swirling grip of the stream. We doused sails as we were blanketed in the gorge and proceeded under engine keeping tightly to the right hand shore to avoid the clutches of the Cribben Rock just below us. It was odd to be passing through such an inhospitable place to discover that someone had built a house and a home on a rocky islet in midstream. How did they get ashore? What epic struggles had they seen from their windows in the past? We had no time to seek answers because we were being carried through by the stream and we had to concentrate on the numerous angles and leading marks. Straight ahead was the Swellies buoy itself indicating a right hand turn in the tightest part of the channel. We firmly recalled that five boats had been lost here this season and we hoped that we were not going to be the sixth. We could see the sweeping form of the Menai suspension bridge ahead, but passing beneath its span and heading in our direction was a huge ship. A coasting oil tanker was going flat out to stem the tide, pushing a great angry wave aside as it powered for the narrow gap that we were filling. Fortunately we were through and clear by the time that he needed to pass. He demonstrated that there was sufficient depth in the channel at high water. Once we were through the worst we could afford the luxury of looking back at the beautiful wooded valley through which we had passed and before us we could see similar wooded shores and islands with luxury houses each set in its own little estate, each in its own idea of paradise.

There were now many moorings on either side of the channel and we went for one on the Anglesey side in the lee of some old concrete barges in the area known as Bangor Pool. We'd only been under way for about an hour but I'd decided to stop. The reason was the weather.

The Shipping Forecast

It was sunny, but the wind was beginning to blow strongly from the south and was being funnelled by the valley. It was force 5 when we picked up the mooring and looking at the chart I could see that if we were to go further out beyond Bangor Pier we would become increasingly exposed from the south east as the estuary broadened rapidly.

The Shipping Forecast
For us on this day and for our neighbouring areas was:

Fastnet   SW 7-9, veering NW 6.
Irish Sea   SE 6-8, cyclonic 6, becoming NW 6-8.
Shannon   Storm 10.

Reports from Coastal stations showed that Scilly to the south already had SW Force 7. These wind strengths could be physically dangerous to small yachts in the open sea and so I decided to wait for a certain moment before sailing.

The Weather System

The strong winds were the result of a depression whose centre was moving though our area. As the centre of this whirlpool of air passed, the wind direction would change, in this case from south-east (favourable to our course) to north-west (opposed to our course). This was confirmed by the Irish Sea forecast above which showed first one side of the circular pattern, then the centre (Cyclonic 6) and finally the opposite side of the swirl.

The change of the wind direction would not be immediate, but would take several hours. I have noticed that winds sometimes decrease in strength as a centre approaches and do not pick up again immediately after the passing. They take an hour or two, or even longer if it is night, aside from this difference being increased by the land/sea effect. Winds seem to increase during the daytime when the sun is present to fuel the weather engine. I've often been struggling against a gale at two in the afternoon, only to be struggling for lack of wind by seven in the evening. This gives an explanation of the critical moment that I had decided to wait for; the passing of the centre of the depression. If I was lucky I would get maybe a couple of hours of diminishing wind strength from the south, then an hour or so as the centre passed, followed by another couple of hours or more as we emerged into the new airstream on the far side. With luck we might have a six hour weather window. As we'd be going at night, it would probably be as gentle as it was possible to get, due to the lack of sun energy. The crux of this whole gamble would depend upon guessing precisely the right time to depart, which meant getting the position of the centre right.

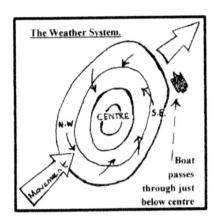

The Weather System.

N-W / CENTRE / S.E.

Boat passes through just below centre

Movement

Plotting the path.

The decisions being made at this stage of the journey are being explained in some detail because it illustrates the kind of tactical gambling which becomes necessary if progress is to be made in a situation where there is a succession of incoming depressions. I have had to do similar things to get boats back from the Netherlands across the North Sea. The decision relies heavily on keeping a constant mental picture of the weather pattern as it develops and **updating it over several days** prior to the journey. When I was caught out crossing the Bristol Channel earlier in the year I had not done this, but simply set out on the strength of a single forecast which made no mention of a Force 9 or worse. We almost paid the price for that oversight.

I was helped in plotting the position of the depression's centre by the general synopsis at the beginning of the forecast. On the morning broadcast they stated that the centre was expected Irish Sea 07.00 Thursday. On the midday forecast they said that the centre would be in sea area Tyne by 13.00 Thursday. I could expect its effects to be felt from about midnight onwards, which meant gambling on sailing Wednesday evening and so I was sitting waiting on the mooring to see if I could take advantage of that moment.

There was supposed to be a yacht race from Beaumaris to Caernarvon that day and we settled to see the fleet pass by. They'd have to pass quite soon in order to go through the Swellies at about the right time, but it soon became apparent that they weren't going to make their appearance. The wind was already up to about force 7 and the race had obviously been called off. During the afternoon we began to feel pleased that we had the concrete barges some 200 metres to windward as the gale howled around us. The wind was against the tide, but we lay very steadily to wind. The other cruisers that we could see on moorings around us were heeled well over and

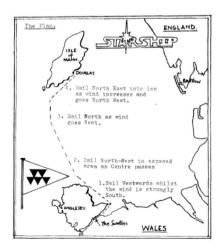

sailing about all over the place. Our cockpit canopy was being sucked up and flogging in the gusts, but most oddly the wind was tearing flakes of paint off the inside of our ventilators and sending them cascading down into the cabin in a mini snowstorm. Throughout the gale the sun shone and made the experience less frightening. By six o'clock in the evening I felt that there were occasional lulls, but I wanted to wait an hour to be sure that the worst was over. We had a good meal and then I explained what I hoped my plan would be.

The Plan.
The direct crossing to the Isle of Mann was about 45 miles to the north-north-west. I planned NOT to sail directly towards the island but to sail westwards along the north coast of Anglesey, trying to seek shelter near the shore whilst the southerly winds were strong. I would go westwards as far as possible, so that as the wind began to go around south-west, west and then north west I would always stay closehauled on the port tack and be gradually forced to turn to my right so that I would be sailing northwards towards the island, eventually I might even be forced to the north-east, but by that time I hoped to be coming into the lee of the land, where we'd be able to beat up to make it into Douglas. Young Roland would sleep. Howard and I would share the steering. Dusk was falling as we prepared to leave.

MI issue 243 Episode 38.

Wednesday evening August 6
Bangor Pool - August 8 Ramsey I.O.M..
The gale seemed to be abating rapidly so we dropped the mooring at 20.40. Night was falling prematurely as the sky was now overcast. I had set a tiny scrap of sail which turned out to be insufficient in the wind-shadowed area that we moved into, so after some waiting around I cautiously set more genoa to pull us out to where the wind might be. We slipped down with the ebb trying to pick out where the channel marks would be amongst the many moored craft. As we cleared Gallows Point and Beamaris we were suddenly out of the lee and into the real world of wind and water. Straight away the genoa came in as we began to race forwards desperately seeking the shapes of the unlit buoys in the darkening night. The wind gusted more and we were out into the gale, careering downhill as fast as we could go being overwhelmed by the tiny canvas that we had set. Looking astern we could see that we were absolutely committed and there was no chance of going back. Angry white waves were building to chase us down to the narrow gap through which the channel passed between the tip of Anglesey and Puffin Island.

I was struggling with the wheel to keep her straight as she was pulling like a wayward horse. Howard was valiantly peering over the doghouse into the driven spray trying to decipher the dim shapes rushing towards us to see how they related to the chart. I was shouting over the noise, even panicking a bit as I realised that we were too far to the right and returning left made her want to pull hard onto the reach rather than running easily. It seemed like someone had pulled out the plug as we were swept onwards by the power of the wind and stream, driving us faster than we wanted to go. The worst section came just before the narrow entrance where the wind was howling and even with no sail we would have been overpowered. There was water everywhere and I dreaded the thought of what we might experience once we got out into the open sea. The gap was tiny and with the tricks of the light I wondered if I broached I might hit one side or the other. As we reached the lighthouse apparently standing in the sea we momentarily got a lee and were able to regain control, making ourselves ready for the next onslaught. Fortunately it never came and as time passed it became clear that the wind had been heavily funnelled by the land. Once we were clear we began to experience the clean steady flow of wind that makes the boat pick up and begin to sail continuously. It was still very windy, but never again did it have the same venom.

We were well-reefed down as we sailed towards the guiding flash of Point Lynas light on the north-eastern tip of Anglesey. It was rough and bumpy, but we were speeding along under full control into the black and glistening night with the white wake unreeling from the float which said that we were making good progress. Somehow the degree of discomfort was reduced by seeing those miles falling away. We deeply breathed the fresh sea air. I patted the side of the boat thinking go, Go, GO. This is what we were meant to be doing. Far as possible; fast as possible; making west using this precious southerly wind. Riding up and over those waves, swooping onwards, with power to drive through, she didn't falter or slow, but pushed on, channelling the sail power in a constant energy stream. She was really sailing that night.

An hour after leaving Puffin Island we'd covered the ten miles to Point Lynas and I made a slight course adjustment to 330°m to begin to move out into the gap between Wales and the Isle of Mann. We would lose the shelter of the land effect and gradually as we went offshore we would become more exposed. Now we began to gamble more heavily. After half an hour of sailing I realised that the wind was dying and I constantly eased out a little more sail area, trying to keep her on the safe limit, as the wind fell off.

Serial Starship

August 7 Thursday.

By 02.15 we'd travelled another 16 miles with Howard and I continuing to stand two hour watches in rotation. We were now well out to the west of the direct track and at 02.45 things were gentle enough for me to try to snatch a little sleep by laying on the floor in the main cabin, being lulled into slumber by the rhythmical rocking and the constant rush of water past the hull.

Half an hour later I was awoken by a faint jingling sound. I knew that noise. It told me that the boat had almost stopped. It was caused by the topping lift shackle jangling on the boom end. I lay for a moment on the floor looking up and out of the companionway at the clear sky filled with bright twinkling stars. I realised immediately what the clear sky meant, we were into a different airstream, maybe the centre of the depression that I had been tracking with such care for the last few days. I clambered up into the cockpit. We were still on course, but in the starlight I could see the sails gently luffing, because the wind had come ahead. It was much cooler. The boat was just edging forwards, so I sheeted in and we began to move once more.

I unrolled another third of genoa and we were on our way. I gave her full sail and pulled her tight on the wind, to find we were heading due north, beginning to speed up on the relatively flat sea. Once more, this was our chance to make progress for I knew that we would be progressively headed as the breeze built in strength, then we would begin to have to endure the familiar battle to windward.

Out of the darkness came the welcome flash of the Calf of Man light, still probably more than twenty miles distant, but signifying that we were over the hump and our destination was in sight. It was heartening and encouraging. The wind continued to edge northwards and our course gradually went from north to 20°m then 30°m and at times 40°m pushing us away to the east.

As day dawned we could see that we were south of Port St. Mary, having averaged about six knots and we were driving hard to windward in about force four or five north-westerly. From about seven o'clock onwards we gained the lee of the land and were able to free sheets slightly, taking advantage of the tide. I estimated arrival in Douglas at about ten o'clock but the last thirteen miles took only an hour and a quarter so that we were off the harbour by eight o'clock and inside secured to a mooring buoy by nine. It was most gratifying to have made the journey in seemingly adverse conditions; to have taken a gamble on the weather and just for once, to have succeeded. Later we met several gale-bound small boat sailors,

165

waiting for a chance to return to the mainland and they were surprised to hear that we had crossed from Wales, because when they had gone to bed on the Wednesday it was blowing a gale, and when they woke up the following morning it was **still** blowing close to a gale. Not many of them noticed that the gale was from quite a different direction.

The harbour launch helped us secure to a large circular-shaped mooring with a short line from our stern, then they took out our anchor warp from the bow and we hauled tight upon it. It was wonderful to feel it bite and hold so firmly after our experiences in the granite lined Menai Straits where all our confidence in anchoring had been lost.

We had our usual celebration breakfast and leapt straight into our bunks to be asleep in moments. Later we were woken by the harbour patrol coming for our fees, so we went ashore to look around the town. Roland gave it a ten-star rating as every other building was an amusement arcade packed with Star Wars machines. This was the 'Promised Land' of which he had dreamed when trapped in Port Dinorwic.

The number one attraction for me was Nick Keig's new Kelsall Performance 52 catamaran. I'd seen drawings of it and heard about its kit-panel construction, but actually seeing it bobbing about against the harbour wall was quite a thrill. The wing mast was most impressive. I guess that every 'G' cramp in the Isle of Mann was pressed into service to make such a mighty mast as that. We also noticed a Triune trimaran *TAO*, a name that had been a topic of conversations whilst down in the Scilly Isles. There was a little race for some of the local boats around the bay during the evening so we went along to join them in their very sociable little club, returning late to the boat.

<u>August 8 Friday</u>.
The weather forecast said the weather would IMPROVE. They told us to expect a southerly three or four, which would be FAVOURABLE. Just the job. Wonderful. A wind tailor-made for the next step of the passage up to Scotland. Too good to be true?

We left Douglas at 09.30 after telephoning our Scottish crewman to tell him to expect us somewhere in the Galloway area overnight. Initially there was hardly a breath and we drifted about a bit in Douglas Bay, watching the toy traffic on the miniature landscape of the land. As soon as we'd cleared the bay's northern headland the breeze came in with a bang from the north-west at force 4 causing us to go shooting off close hauled with all sail set. We were in smooth water, so progress was very good at about nine knots.

Clearing Clay Head into Laxey Bay the wind went up a notch and we were really pressing on in a genuine force 5 and steady. Passing Manghold Point the waves had a fetch of two to three miles and we had to start riding them. We were back at our usual windward thrash, with the wind strength going on up. I knew that to make maximum progress I'd have to get up to the lee of the land, but I also knew that once we reached the Point of Ayre at the end of the island our course would be dead to windward and beating in virtually unrestricted seas was going to give us a good bashing all afternoon. I wasn't prepared to do that when the forecast was for gentle winds which would waft us across to Scotland without effort. Perhaps these winds would come later? Out came the pilot book and the harbour diagram for Ramsey as well as the tide tables to check the depth of water inside. We tacked for the land.

It wasn't a harbour that I would normally have chosen to enter as it dried at low water and had a long narrow entrance between breakwaters which made me nervous about being able to turn in strong winds. Once inside there was very restricted space, however, it was blowing wildly by this time and the upwind approach would give me maximum control over my craft in the entrance, so at 12.30 we dropped sail and began to motor in.

MI Int 244. Episode 39.

August 8   Ramsey Isle of Mann.
Making an Entrance.
Most of my sailing has been learned by the direct method, 'hands on experience', but every now and then I've tried to learn from books about the proper way to do things.

One of the trickiest cruising situations is taking your boat into a strange port and on this topic I've never really read a practical account which I could call definitive about the best way to tackle the task. I suppose it's because every harbour is a little different, so nobody has ventured to try to tell the world how it should be done. Could this be the end of the drought? These were my efforts at getting into Ramsey on a sunny midday tide, as the wind was becoming too strong to continue making comfortable progress on our journey. It raises some cruising issues.

<u>Pilot Books.</u>

I wanted to see what the place looked like so I went straight to a couple of pilot books that I had on board. One was for the Irish Sea and the other was for the Isle of Mann specifically. I also made a quick check of Reeds Nautical Almanac, just to see what was there. Attempting to read the pilot books whilst beating hard and trying to keep an eye on the lie of the land was a busy task. No sooner had the sail been sheeted in on one tack and the right place in the book been found than some important shore feature would catch my eye and my attention would wander from the text. I've found that even with the adequate preparation of having read the book well in advance, it is necessary to keep it available to constantly re-read relevant bits, trying to make them stick in the mind because of the heavy mental overload of distracting information when approaching a strange port. The pilot books were filled with pages of description, mainly irrelevant to the really desperate task of GETTING IN.

(Without an electronic chart plotter, this discussion remains relevant.)

I would dearly love to read an entrance description which commences:-

This is the way to enter:

Followed by FOUR or FIVE (at the most) numbered instructions on separate lines. All the rest of the local colour could wait until later. It wasn't until I read about *'how pleasant it was to tie up at the Town Quay and step ashore to be confronted with no less than six pubs to choose from each with differing appeal and standards'*, in **both** of my pilot books that I realised that they were the work of the same author and really the Irish Sea version was a diluted (not condensed) account of the other one. The sketch map was too small to be of much assistance whilst being thrown about in a seaway and the most useful aids were some rather grainy aerial photographs which gave the layout and some idea of scale at a glance.

In the old days when I used to scramble about on the mountains in the Lake District everybody used the guide books illustrated by Wainwright, which were masterpieces of detail and clarity. When I took up sailing on the East Coast I was encouraged to explore further because of the similar qualities found in Jack Coote's book East Coast Rivers. I have been interested to see that aerial photographs have taken an increasingly more important role as that book has been constantly updated, until now there is a version which is almost exclusively aerial photographs (of sharp quality) which I find gives the kind of information needed as rapidly as possible. When I travelled along the south coast I used the Stanford's Harbour

Guide, Christchurch to Mousehole which uses a similar technique. A friend was to lend me a Stanford's guide to the West Coast of Scotland that probably had the best blend of aerial photographs alongside large scale chart extracts which I think offers potentially the most successful way of cracking this problem of presenting the information clearly and in a book form which can be instantly absorbed.

Basically, Ramsey was a longish narrow entrance between two concrete piers with a left turn once inside where the quay then followed a natural semi-circular curve in the river. Whilst it was small it wasn't impossibly tiny and I did have room to manoeuver. As usual in most harbours there were fishing boats already moored against the wall and some yachts too. My ploy in situations such as this is to go alongside someone temporarily to give myself time to look around and get the boat organised.

Our general method when lying alongside anything rough like a harbour wall is to set a pair of fenders on the appropriate side of the boat and then suspend a wooden plank outside them. Add a couple of heaving lines to act as breast ropes and a bow fender to protect the float tip and you can see that this takes some setting up as we enter and cross the harbour. Once we are settled alongside there are additions to this arrangement so we need to be certain that we are finally in the right place before we invest a lot of time on a lot of warp.

In this case there were a couple of yachts on the far side of the harbour where I would be facing into the wind as I came to a stop. I approached very slowly stemming the outflowing stream of the river, using the wind to hold her virtually stationary. I asked the people on the yachts if I could come alongside and whether they would take my lines. People are usually happy enough to help except that we have the particular problem that most sailors are distracted by our boat. They just can't believe that what they are seeing is going to come right up to **them** and then involve them in some way. Most people have usually never seen a REAL modern trimaran moving on the water and they're usually slightly dazed, by looking at the boat instead of concentrating on the actions that will be required.

We went alongside, using only a couple of fenders between the craft and this gave me the breathing space that I needed. I called the Harbour Control on the VHF, because room was restricted and I thought that maybe I should get an approved parking space. I have yet to decide on the optimum time to call for such advice. Logically it would be best to call before entering, but if the place is strange I have my head whirling with the visual information and I find myself concentrating on getting in without hitting anything at the time when I should be calling. I prefer them to be able to see me out of their window when they are trying to place me, because over twenty feet of beam is a little unusual. Harbour Control asked us to re-cross the harbour and go alongside a small coaster just inside the entrance.

We prepared to release ourselves to move, when we had one of those tricky little cruising incidents. We shortened down to the very last line. The whole boat hung on that one piece of rope against the

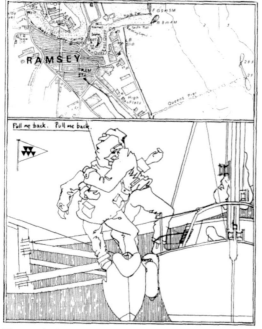

gusty wind and tidal flow. Both Howard and I were on the float and the rope was tight around a cleat that we could not reach on the other boat whose occupants had gone ashore. Howard held on to their toe rail and I stepped onto their boat to release the rope. I took it off and, in returning, stepped over the guard wire with one foot onto our float. At that instant a super gust of wind caught *Starship* and opened an immediate gap as she started to want to go backwards.

Howard, being pulled off balance forwards could either fall into the water or let go. Eight feet from *Starship's* stern was the curving concrete wall of the quay and there would be nobody on board to handle her if she got away from the boat that I was half on. She would crash then be turned by the wind and current to go around the harbour with increasing speed to smash into the steel side of a ship or the wall again. I would see bits splintering off her and hear the sickening grinding crashes. I wouldn't be able to get back on board her due to the height of the quay wall. I would only be able to watch her destruction.

In the very instant that Howard swayed backwards on the tip of the float I grabbed him like a Sumo wrestler in a passionate embrace. I gripped him as if my life depended on it. "Pull me back! PULL ME BACK." I hissed into his ear. I gave it every bit of power, urgency and threat that I could command. He was laying right back, as much to escape me, as to regain his balance. I had one foot over the guardrail, and I was being slowly stretched, but I would NOT let go. I could feel his body go taught as I locked him in an iron grip for an age. The people on the quay above were beginning to get rather embarrassed at these two chaps hugging each other. Too long at sea perhaps? Slowly through quivering muscles I felt the boats coming back together and as they touched I released Howard and regained a quick turn on the cleat with the short end of the line. Saved, but not without some red faces. We crossed the harbour and secured with springs and breast ropes to the coaster.

It was a lovely fresh and sunny day and our little stroll along the quay to absorb the holiday atmosphere revealed a real jewel for the cruising sailor. No, not the six pubs, but a launderette. It was the skipper's turn to give the place a five-star rating.

August 9 Saturday.
During the evening the wind finally began to die and when my alarm woke me at midnight the weather was calm again. I walked along the south harbour wall amongst the busy bustle of the fishing boats which had come in on the tide, unloading shells onto lorries high on the quay above them by using their powered deck winches to hoist the baskets on tackles suspended from their masts. Out in the inky black sea away from the bright illuminations, the stars were shining brightly and I could see the periodic flash of the Point of Ayre light, the northernmost point of the Isle of Mann. I turned and walked slowly back to the boat, roused Howard and we prepared to leave, departing under engine at 01.30.

The Point of Ayre has two lights which isn't clear from a quick glance at the chart. The lower, lesser light could be seen first, whereas the higher doubly powerful one wasn't spotted until later. It changed from red to white alternately with quite a slow period and I first took it to be a yacht following a weaving kind of course or even anchored and swinging with the tide.

At 02.22 we bumped our way through some choppy overfalls at the top of the island and made a sharp left turn to 310°m heading for another new country, Scotland.

171

Serial Starship

MI issue 245. Episode 40.

<u>August 9 Saturday.- August 11.</u>
<u>Heading for Scotland.</u>
Leaving the Isle of Mann the whole area to the north of us was the shore of the Solway Firth Looking at the chart I could see that this was a cruising area in its own right with many towns and bays to be visited, but unfortunately we just did not have the time. When we embarked upon this complete journey I wanted to linger wherever I found an area of interest, but I slowly discovered that the coast so abounds with cruising potential that I just could not afford the time to stop long enough to do justice to it. At this point in the journey I had concluded that Cardigan Bay and Anglesey would take a full season, the Isle of Mann would take the same. The Solway Firth from Morecambe Bay to the Mull of Galloway would require another year.

These areas are neglected by most sailing magazines and from reading I know better how to cross the Pacific or progress up through the islands in the West Indies than I do about getting into Kirkcudbright or any other of the promising sandy bays along this coast. I am unable to afford to keep *Starship* away from home indefinitely. Sail cruising is expensive enough as a hobby, but my project has the additional expenditure of the travelling and the recovery of vehicles (when I eventually reached Glasgow my car was still parked in South Wales). I began to think that trailing and sailing might be a more suitable method for really cruising the different parts of Britain.

When heading for Scotland by this route there was no clearly favoured harbour which could be defined as *the* place to head for. The nearest place to the Isle of Mann was The Isle of Whithorn on Burrow Head, but the corner to get around was the Mull of Galloway and finding a harbour with the right qualities of shelter and ease of access was difficult. Drummore is a little village to the east of the peninsular (actually called the Rhines of Galloway) which is a possibility, but most people head for the harbour of Portpatrick halfway up the western side. The most important point was to use the tide when going through the gap between Scotland and Ireland. We found that in the central portion of the Irish Sea there appeared to be little tidal flow. The time of high water at Liverpool would be almost the same anywhere within the sea itself, from Kirkcudbright in the north through the Isle of Mann to North Wales in the south ... BUT the water had to enter into this 'closed' sea by flowing in and out of two narrow entrances at north and south. We were heading for the North Channel, which had two notable restrictions, the first being the Mull of Galloway (only 20 miles from Ireland) and the second would be the Mull of Kintyre.

In the dark clear night we headed for the big flasher on the Mull of Galloway which had a range of 28 miles and to its left we could make out the loom of Crammag Head which marked the narrowest point of the channel.

We had a long dawn and hoped to see the sun rise clearly from the sea but low cloud formed to disappoint us. At about five in the morning we were rounding the mull on a perfect still morning with the blue frieze of the land standing on the dimpled surface of a sea hammered from reflective golden metal. The Isle of Mann still filled the horizon behind us as a separate distinctive land. To our left as the sun rose higher to pick out the headlands we could see the Northern Irish coast in the area of the Belfast Lough. This clarity of visibility which allowed us to see all the different lands around us was the most exciting part of the experience. I had not realised just how close all the places were to each other at this point and it gave us a feeling of an enclosed lake rather than an inhospitable sea, which I am sure that it can be. One could imagine the Viking longships using this important crossroads hundreds of years ago.

We were about four miles out from the Rhines (I used a point on the Irish side to establish that fix) and unable to see the land detail due to the morning sun, so we shaped our course in closer to Portpatrick to allow us to enjoy the passing scenery. The village was easy to see with its white houses being the only disturbance on a green-cliffed shore backed by a land of high rural hills. When we reached it at about 09.30 we could see that the tidal flow was now running hard against us and we toyed with the idea of going in, to wait out the foul tide, but it was such a lovely day for chugging along and we had the whole day ahead of us so I opted to go right up round the corner and into Stranraer. I must also mention that we used the old Autohelm 3000 that we strung up to do the steering for us. It was marvellous whilst motoring, because the course was steady anyway, so for long periods it had nothing to do. It kept a pinpoint accurate course and allowed us to wander about on board without disturbing the heading. We even spent a lot of time just watching it work.

At Black Rock there was a lighthouse and in the gulley just below the very light itself was the superstructure of a fairly modern ship. To see a wreck just below the light was quite an amazing sight. It acted like an advert warning against helmsmen who do not pay attention to where the boat is going; better just check our Autopilot again.

Nearing the northern tip of the Rhines we began to feel that we were sailing into a new area. Far out to the north stood the mysterious misty shape of the island of Ailsa Craig projecting from the sea as the isolated peak of a submerged mountain. Yet further away to our left we could see the Mull of Kintyre and at a similar distance behind Ailsa Craig the impressive mountains on Arran. Ireland was still visible over our port quarter.

We passed the lighthouse on Corsewall Point at 12.30 as the tide slackened and we entered Loch Ryan with a favourable flow. We'd been extracting information from the Irish Sea Cruising Guide and it became clear that the chartlet for the loch was so inaccurate as to be misleading, showing only one starboard mark where there were in fact five and even an incorrect harbour shape. The really effective pilotage information for this area came from the Clyde Cruising Club Guide, which was linked with an Imray chart of the Clyde. These two together were all that was necessary to cruise throughout the Clyde area right out to the Mull of Kintyre.

Stranraer has a large, square, empty harbour and we casually sailed in to do a few circuits to investigate. It was only as I was circling for the second time that I noted the echo sounder was only reading five feet at its maximum and this was close to high water. I sailed out again very rapidly. The reason for the place being so empty was that it had silted up and channels were maintained only for the steamer quay and a small gully just inside the West Pier for yachts and small local fishing craft which ran aground themselves attempting entry at low water. Having been saved from the ignominious arrival of running aground, in front of all the locals, by my shallow draught, I proceeded with greater caution, preparing my fenders and boards properly before going in.

The big problem that I usually have with a high quay is getting the warps ashore and secured. There are usually casual members of the public standing about watching, who have to be persuaded to take their hands out of their pockets and catch a couple of warps. If they succeed in this, they usually don't know what to do with the ropes they hold. We were lucky this time as a most helpful chap busied himself fastening us off and making constructive suggestions about the way the springs should lay etc. Next he gave us a hearty welcome and a quick description of the layout of the town, concluding with the information that the Harbour Office was closed and they wouldn't be about until Monday morning.

Our Irish Sea Guide said of Stranraer *'It is difficult to raise much enthusiasm about the rather grey little town which has so little maritime feeling.'* The patronising guide proved wrong again. The people of Stranraer should have the offending description removed, for it must discourage cruisers from visiting. We found the place filled with fun and atmosphere. The populace was having a week of fund raising for charities and there was music in the town square, with folks sitting on the grass enjoying the sunshine, whilst down at the waterside there was real entertainment. Three teams of young people from local firms were engaged in watery combat using surfboards, canoes, rowing boats and an inflatable octopus. Each contest involved all the combatants falling into the boating lake so it was a really good show with everybody in a summery mood. Stranraer was OK with us.

According to the locals a boat like *Starship* had never been seen there before and there was great curiosity, which was more openly and freely expressed than at any place that we had previously visited. All day, each day that we stayed we always had a little crowd looking down on us from the top of the wall above asking us how big our engines were, how fast could we go and whether it was possible to sleep in the floats. It is an odd thing but when you own a boat you find yourself open to public curiosity. As we loaded or unloaded crew or kit, people would come and stand right next to us or even in our way as we passed goods or bags. They would visually investigate each item as it came out of the back of the car, follow its progress down the ladder and below into the boat, then turn their attention to the next object which they tracked in a like manner. I'm sure that these same people wouldn't stand next to your car in the supermarket car park watching each detail of the unloading of the shopping trolley into the boot of your car because social convention would not allow it, but in the boating situation it becomes quite acceptable. There is no harm in it, just idle curiosity and we just had to accept that we would become part of the local attraction wherever we went.

Howard and young Roland left the boat and they were replaced by John Stewart from the local area and my eldest son Tristan. We departed the quay at about midday on August 11 moving further up Loch Ryan to investigate an anchorage known as The Wig where we stayed overnight. During the war flying boats such as the Sunderland operated from here against the 'U' boats in the Atlantic and their legacy is the broadest launching ramp in the land, used by a tiny sailing club which operates from there. There would be no difficulty in launching the biggest multihull. We watched the local dinghies trying to sail in next to no wind and generally extended our lazy holiday mood. We had a most peaceful night and were ready to explore further into the Clyde the following day.

The idea of trailing and sailing mentioned in this episode is a concept that I followed up on. I later designed and construct a 25ft estuary-cruising trimaran that was demountable and lived on its own trailer. I started dinghy cruising that resulted in the publication of the book **Practical Dinghy Cruiser** *(see inside front cover). One of the places I explored in the dinghy was Kirkcudbright.*

MI issue 246. Episode 31.

August 12 Tuesday. - August 13.
Entering the Firth of Clyde.
We left at 08.45 to take advantage of the last of the ebb out of Loch Ryan. This meant negotiating the shallow entrance channel to The Wig anchorage and once again our shallow draught paid off. At one point we had just two feet of water beneath our transducer. When we gained the main channel we turned northwards and as the conditions were so gentle we engaged the Autopilot. It was sunny, but there was a light mist which limited our visibility to about 5 or 6 miles. As Ailsa Craig was about 14 miles from the entrance to the loch we had to steer accurately as we motored along to our first waypoint which was invisible somewhere ahead.

Looking at the chart I slowly began to appreciate the cruising area which lay before us. We were just entering a large square basin measuring about 20 miles across its entrance to our left and extending about 30 miles to the north, ahead of us. The north-west quarter of the basin was filled with the island of Arran, but the basin's northern shore was a series of lochs, islands and channels extending for a further 30 miles or more. I followed the twists and turns of the deep but sheltered waters counting the cruising anchorages; at approximately 50 I began to realise the futility of the exercise. The muddy Thames Estuary can boast quite a few anchorages and the Solent to Swanage has its attractions, but roll them together and they would still fall well short of the Firth of Clyde. All this I realised as I entered the area in thick mist. I was to have the visual attractions unveiled slowly, so that I could savour each new view to the full and eventually understand that when it comes to scenery, the East Coast cruising ground and the Solent can be forgotten compared with this place.

It was a really lovely day apart from the restricted visibility and the water was so smooth that we spent time watching, as cruisers do, for jelly fish below the clear surface or guessing the identity of various pieces of floating rubbish as they entered our small circle and passed through to be left astern. Even the seabirds were lethargic, taking the opportunity to float around in colonies exchanging gossip and opinions. One area of water looked as if rain was falling upon it as thousands of dimples and swirls disturbed it. John said that it was caused by small fish being chased up to the surface by mackerel. There was always something to hold our attention as we progressed.

One of the most fascinating sights was the gannets. We'd first noticed individual birds off the southern tip of Wales, where I later discovered there is a colony on Grassholm. In my ignorance I only knew 'seagulls', but these were so much bigger and sleeker in flight, with lovely narrow streamlined wings, end-tipped with black. When we got close enough to them I was able to see the golden yellow tops to their heads. As we rounded the Mull of Galloway in Scotland we began to see them in their hundreds all flying northwards. They used the same kinds of techniques as cycle racers when travelling at speed in pelotons. One bird would lead and others would slipstream in huge 'V' formations. The lead bird would peel off when its work was done and join the tail of the 'V'. Small groups flew very low over the flat sea and individuals were often so close to the water that the wing tips would touch the surface leaving twin spots of ripples with every downbeat (ground effects?). Tired birds would rest on the water for a while and when they were recovered they would take to the air again to try to join one of the passing groups. It was only when this happened that one could see just how fast the group was managing to fly because individual birds had great difficulty in attaining sufficient speed to catch the tail of the 'V'.

As we had rounded the Rhines of Galloway I first saw one solitary gannet fishing and my interest in them became an enduring, instant fascination. I had often appreciated watching the tiny terns which fish by diving into the water from a height of 3–4 metres, but I never expected something the size of a goose to suddenly fold up in mid-flight and go rocketing into the sea from two or three times as high. It was spectacular and sensational witnessing a gannet crash diving out of the sky to disappear in an explosion of spray down into the sea.

We'd wondered where they might all be heading, but now as we motored into the mist it became obvious by their flight paths that

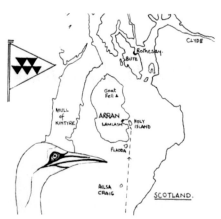

Ailsa Craig was the home of these magnificent birds. Almost imperceptibly the conical shape began to condense as a blue shadow out of the misty mixture of sea and sky ahead. The island riveted our attention for the next two hours as we approached and passed along its east side. It was extremely beautiful and one of the outstanding sights of our total journey to date. A rugged rock thinly skinned in sparse vegetation, often too steep to support life; painted white by the gannets on the southern side; some tiny white sunlit buildings surrounding the lighthouse to the east, totally dwarfed by the majestic mass of the high rock itself. The only features that we could make out were a small round castle tower and some quarry workings, but not the slightest sign of life or movement. Slowly the solid monolith began to dissolve as the definition drained back into the pale blue mist behind us. It became simply a shape again and then it was hard to see where it had been, leaving us only the circle of interest before us again. Another ten miles to go to the land.

What was that small black square on our course? It was a submarine on exercise and a reminder that big naval bases lay ahead. The tail fin just cut the surface and left a long white wake, rather as though they were towing a water skier. Could it be that their skipper was out for an afternoon's sport? As we watched his manoeuvres we noticed a distinct white patch glowing in the mist beyond him which became the lighthouse on Pladda Island at the southern tip of Arran. Our watery world was suddenly filling with many small traditional wooden fishing boats with their upright little wheelhouses at the stern, each one intent on fishing his own tiny patch of sea at the mouth of the Clyde itself.

We were heading for the enclosed bay at Lamlash on the eastern side of Arran. Holy Island (which is a popular name all down this coast), almost seals off the bay, leaving only a narrow entrance at north and south. Early Christians first made settlements in positions with difficult access, or good natural defence depending on how you regard it and this island off an island presented several natural defensive moats for any belligerent Pagans on foot, to cross.

We had arrived at the land without having seen Holy Island. My only image had been its outline on the chart where its small size gave it little significance. As it began to appear I was surprised to see that it was a mini-mountain rising to a considerable height, but it shrank almost to insignificance compared with the peaks on Arran which began to emerge out of the tops of the clouds. The tallest mountains on this relatively modest sized island were virtually as tall as any in the British Isles and clearly higher than anything on the nearby mainland. It was a complete surprise to motor into a notable anchorage surrounded by high forest-clad mountains, dark green and cool by contrast with the light, bright, glaring pale blue world in which we'd travelled all day.

There were moorings in front of the village of Lamlash in 40ft of water. One mooring had a sign on top - carrying a warning perhaps? We crossed to investigate and found an advert for the local restaurant. Going to the shore we could see the bottom in at least 20ft depth. We secured to the worn granite pier and went shopping only to find that we were five minutes after the five o'clock closing time.

We passed the evening in the usual way watching other craft arrive, cooking and repairing as necessary. On my final rounds removing the ensign, putting on the cockpit cover and pulling up the rudder I glimpsed, just for a moment a tiny strand of orange passing beneath my transom,- floating rubbish maybe? I packed up and went below to write the log.

August 13. Wednesday.
We had the most uncomfortable night that I could remember, including going aground in the Scilly Isles, which was a further surprise in such a sheltered anchorage. It proved once more that there is always plenty to learn in cruising. The trouble was that the boat laid head to wind, roughly south, but there was an entrance

channel from the sea to the east, our left hand side, through which came a small reflected swell. This tiny swell was at just the right height to lift each float in turn from the water making them bang back in again with the passing of each wave. In all my time sailing on *Starship* I'd never experienced such circumstances before. I should have heavily weighted one float to permanently lift the other one clear of the water.

The day was grey overcast and raining. Visible distance was quite short and Holy Island disappeared into the low cloud base. On shore we wandered damply dripping around the Co-op shop with everyone else, being cheerful about the weather. This was quite a different place from the others that we had visited. We were back in the land of fell walkers and climbers, stout boots and backpacks, damp maps and plans to ascend Goat Fell. Activity here was dominated by the mountains not the maritime element; sea-goers were of secondary interest as incidental picturesque visitors arriving on the local lake.

There was a southerly breeze about force 3 blowing, but there was an ominous forecast for later and I decided to find even greater shelter in Rothesay harbour on the Isle of Bute so we prepared to leave. I was dropping the rudder blade when I caught a tiny orange fleck under the transom out of the corner of my eye. There must be a piece of orange rope under there. Oh dear. There was only one object that it could be snagged upon and that was the propeller. It appeared that someone was in for an early morning swim in a cold Scottish firth. I went back inboard and prepared to get in the water, taking off my clothes and putting on an old sailing suit to keep the cold wind off me when I was on the surface. Tristan prepared me a sharp knife with a rope loop and we launched the rubber dinghy. Instead of getting straight into the icy water I tried lying on the side of the dinghy and by stretching underneath the hull I reached for the rope which had been tightly coiled by the propeller into a knotted ball. Pulling it up to the surface I saw that I had both tangled ends and a couple of twisted strands disappearing down to the propeller. I cut through the rope being careful to keep plenty of length on the strands emerging from the water to allow me to manipulate them. I kept a firm grasp and started untwisting. After two or three turns on them I felt the grip of the cord on the propeller relax and with a few more twists I was able to release one end and pull it through to clear the propeller. I'd been very lucky. Thinking back, I had actually felt the boat pick up the rope the previous day as we'd passed through rafts of floating seaweed in Loch Ryan. I'd thought that it was just seaweed at the time. When we straightened out the rope it was about 50ft in length, and turned out to be quite useful. My propeller and bits of ropes seem destined to find each other, but as can be seen, my shallow draught can alleviate some of the difficulties involved in solving the problem as I can reach the propeller lying on my side on the edge of the inflatable.

It was 11.30 when we finally dropped the mooring and headed out of the north-eastern end of the anchorage with full plain sail set and the wind on the starboard quarter.

MI issue 247. Episode 32.

August 13 - August 14.
Arran - Rothesay - Great Cumbrae.
There was an eleven mile crossing of the Firth of Clyde from Lamlash on Arran to a narrow entrance between the Isle of Bute and Little Cumbrae Island. With such poor, grey, cold and misty conditions I had feared that the visibility would make accurate navigation essential, but in the event we could discern our destination in plenty of time. We could also make out, a couple of miles ahead of us a big modern 39' ketch which had left our anchorage to sail on a similar course to ourselves a short while before. He was under full main and genoa with a force four on the starboard quarter.

Now if there's one thing that we really like when cruising, it's a bit of opposition of the right kind, on the correct point of sail. It happens so rarely but it adds a bit of spice. This opposition really qualified, because he had a couple of important qualities. He was longer than us and I knew that the basic price for such a craft was in the region of £loads-of-money, which needless to say, was just fractionally more than our back-garden-built *Starship*. Had he not been there it might have been a very boring crossing, but instead there was all the thrill of the pirate chase and we soon had him sorted out. It took us only about three or four miles, so by the time that we reached the narrows at Little Cumbrae Island he was but a distant speck behind us - most gratifying for ... we hasten to add ... cruisers.

As we passed onto a run in the wind shadow of the lee of Bute we saw another craft which had shared our anchorage at Lamlash. This was a Seawolf-class craft which whilst being nowhere near our size was nevertheless quite a slippery customer. He'd departed earlier just as I was deploying my inflatable to go to free my fouled propeller, so we'd given him a good lead. When he saw us coming in the very light conditions he commenced a fair bit of sheet trimming and whisker poling. They decided to air one of their spare jibs in addition to the genoa already in use and even pegged out some spare tea towels on the pushpit. Did they really need to peg them top and **bottom**?

All this was too much for me. Down the fore hatch I went and for the first time that year out came the spinnaker bag and up the mast went the blue sausage. Tristan pulled the release line and out cracked our big blue stripy. We were just in the right weight of wind to go from an idling lollop to a smooth continuous fizzing movement, easily doubling the speed and bye-bye went the opposition. Aah! - What a wondrous sail. The only problem was that it took us to our destination so rapidly, we could only use it for just a short while before we had to pull the tube down and stow it away again.

We rounded the next corner and headed for Rothesay Harbour. I called harbour control on the V.H.F. as space seemed so restricted. The simplest description of the harbour would be to say that it was based on a 'T' shaped pier which faced north. The right-hand top of the 'T' was longer than the left hand. Most of the boats sheltered inside the right-hand side which was to the east, but I was blocking the entrance so they redirected me to the less popular western side, which was used mainly by fishing craft. We went alongside a fishing boat on the inside of the pier. There was a flat rate of £3 per day for any boat.

Rothesay was a small town with a distinctive Victorian seafront; it was like going back in time and very interesting to see. I was lucky that I had John Stewart aboard to explain how this area of the Clyde developed. We southerners imagine Glasgow to be a solid industrial sprawl rather like our own urban conurbations, Leeds, Manchester, Birmingham and London, but it's not really like them because it is a 'city in a landscape'. Big, it may be, but it is well spread and although it uses space it does not overpower the natural setting in which it is placed. Nature is bigger than man in these parts. Once one is away from the immediate city centre one has only to glance up and around to see the hills, mountains, or the river itself cutting into the suburbs.

Historically the working population of the industrialised areas needed holidays and the richer folks wanted somewhere select to live. With the countryside being so visibly close there was a strong attraction to move out of the centre of the town to have a break from work. The islands in the Clyde were linked to Glasgow by ferries and it was easy to embark on them and cross to somewhere new to get away from it all. It was as simple a matter as boarding the local bus in other major towns. Gradually the more wealthy people began to have holiday homes or retirement homes built in the little towns which had sprung up on the islands and as communications improved it even became possible for some people to commute to work from these more desirable outer areas. In London it was the train that made it possible to commute from Brighton; here it was the steamer ferries coming from places like Rothesay and in both places the holiday trade generated additional finance to fuel the lifestyle. Of course, things have now changed. The motor car and foreign package tours have overtaken this former life, but Rothesay retains much of the fabric of that age in a wonderful state of preservation.

One of the most unique monuments to this faded age are the famous public toilets, which are magnificent solid marble structures, sometimes with fireplaces to keep the customers warm, but also with broad solid wooden seats to ensure comfort.

We had heard about the public baths, so we went along to experience them for ourselves. Each individual bath was in a separate spacious cubicle. The lady attendant ran the bath and set the correct temperature to the liking of each customer, then added soothing salts to ease away rheumatic pains if needed. The interesting thing was the size of the baths. They were enormous; so big and deep that they resembled a horse trough and one could literally float without touching the bottom. Tristan was making a lot of squealing noises in his bath and it transpired that he was having a similar difficulty to myself, in that he was unable to sit upright because he simply floated off the bottom and then capsized.

Everything was built to last at least a hundred years. The huge mixer taps resembled a boiler valve from the Titanic and the plug chain would have fitted the pawl wheel on any anchor winch. The turbulence and suction when the plug was removed looked and sounded like the Coryvrekin; but the piece-de-resistance was the shower whose gleaming copper pipework dominated the far end of the bath. It reinforced the stereotype image of the Scots as dour, thrifty people for apart from 'OFF', it had only two other settings deeply cut into its cast handle. One was 'COLD' and the other was 'TEPID' (No luxuries in those days.) The towel was also intended to be durable; it was about as soft as the storm topsail of the Cutty Sark woven in asbestos. It was as good as new although stamped with the date 1964. A quick rub down with that was a most invigorating experience, never to be forgotten.

At this time I still had almost a fortnight of my cruise left, but I knew that I would have to leave the boat somewhere for the winter at the end of that time, so when I was walking past the eastern arm of the harbour and I saw a Prout Sirocco 26 cat moored there, I went along and introduced myself. This was a most fortunate action for I found myself talking to Ed and Marion Crangle who had excellent local knowledge and eventually they were to help me enormously.

They had sailed the whole area for a number of years in their Bobcat before moving to the Sirocco and not only did they suggest a place to lay-up for the winter, but during a very pleasant evening they took me through a guided tour of the chart giving me good outline descriptions of the qualities of many of the anchorages. In time we got to yarning and Ed told a wonderful story about the delivery trip of his Sirocco from Poole Harbour to the Clyde, one February. After rounding Land's End he'd had a similar experience to ours when they found themselves in a winter gale-force 9. In his gale the wind direction had been north of west and it had veered at a crucial moment forcing them further and further out into the open Atlantic. Eventually the lifeboat at Wexford in Eire came out and escorted them in there. Needless to say Ed was impressed with the performance of his boat under such extreme conditions.

Ed and Marion offered me every assistance and advice and their help with my boat continued throughout our time in the Clyde.

August 14 Thursday.

Whilst in Rothesay I began to learn some sailing lessons about piers which were a new experience to me.

The top surface of the pier was a tarmac road, with buildings, car parks, street lamps, barriers, people and it was solid, solid, solid. Viewed from afar it was a unified structure of great mass, seeming to be only a shaped extension of the land. I classified it in my mind with harbour walls which offer great protection from the elements, but I'd made a mistake. The lower structure of the pier, not seen nor considered by those who walked upon it, was an open latticework of mighty proportions and great strength, but most importantly, **open**. There was a minor incident which was to have significance later, but I did not appreciate it at the time.

The Roll-on-Roll-off ferry which linked frequently across to the mainland was a big ship. It came along the outside of the pier at the junction of the two strokes of the 'T'. As he came alongside to secure, there was considerable surge and prop-wash which came in through the pier. We became accustomed to this disturbance and thought little of it. On this day our fishing boat went out and we secured in the normal way to the pier. The ferry docked apparently normally on the other side of the pier, something that we were hardly aware of until its CAPTAIN appeared and told us that if we remained where we were we would be liable to be damaged. He explained that he had spotted that our fishing boat had departed as he was making his approach and so had come in much more slowly than usual to reduce the wash effect upon us as we were now secured directly to the pier. This took up too much time within their schedule and he wouldn't be able to continue using the slow approach.

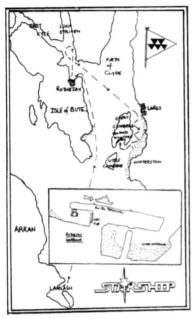

At the time I was more impressed by his sharpness of observation in seeing that one small craft on the opposite side of the pier had moved, than I was in trying to understand what he was saying. I did not have his depth of experience to understand the implications. I confess that I did wonder what all the fuss was about. Later I was to wish that I had given this apparently minor matter some more thought.

It was a lovely bright sunny day and the forecast gale had not appeared. I was also learning that sea-area forecasts didn't really apply in here, tucked away behind so many islands. I decided that we might as well solve our immediate problems by going for a sail, even if we returned again in the evening. We raised our sails and went on a broad reach up to the junction of the East Kyle and Loch Striven. It was absolutely perfect sailing with a force 2-3 southerly wind, lovely sun, blue water and good visibility to see the exceptional view of the mountains flanking the sides of Loch Striven. We turned back towards Rothesay then eased away on a long single tack towards Great Cumbrae Island across the Firth. I wanted to look at Inverkip or Largs Marina.

If only the weather could have been like that for more than ONE day in August then maybe everybody might take up sailing. It was a pleasure to be gliding across smooth water as a small reward for some of the discomforts endured in reaching the place.

At the north end of Great Cumbrae two identical ferries plied back and forth to Largs, arriving and leaving with a precise clockwork motion working in mirror image. The wind had dropped very light and as we had no particular destination we tacked slowly southwards towards the British Steel terminal at Hunterston. We were cheating the tide a bit at the edges sailing well outside the buoyed channel. Our echo sounder battery was getting a bit low and we were getting erratic readings, but we risked it a bit because we had a biggish monohull ahead and further inshore than us. We weren't racing you understand, but there was a fair bit of tweaking going on when all of a sudden he went aground with quite a bang, so we tacked out of there quickly. It's probably safer to have a functioning echo sounder than to follow other cruisers until they hit the bottom.

The wind had almost died, so I decided to visit Millport the capital of Great Cumbrae island. It was a light decision, taken on a sunny afternoon which was to become a fateful step for me.

MI issue 248. Episode 33.

<u>August 14 - August 20.</u>
For a cruiser, the major problem with the little village of Millport on Great Cumbrae is that the bay is open to the south where the prevailing winds are supposed to come from. If the weather should deteriorate we might be exposed, but the breeze had almost exhausted itself. When I looked at the sketch chart in the Clyde Cruising Club guide I could see several small rocky islands which could afford a little protection and there was even a small pier that we might wriggle behind.

It was late afternoon and the wind had finally died so we motored in following behind a vintage Clyde Puffer, an old steam-powered fishing boat which secured across the very end of Millport's pier. I wanted to see behind the pier to gauge the space in there and so I did a couple of circles just off the end. There were a couple of yachts and some small fishing boats fastened alongside. Could I get in beside them or was there sufficient space between the craft for me to squeeze in? Only 20 metres from that side of the pier a stick projected from the water indicating the presence of a rock. Would I be able to turn in such a space?

A soft distinctive bump from beneath my boat cut right across these calculations. My hand was actually resting on the engine controls so I dropped her out of gear immediately. I felt instant annoyance, because I had noticed the small floating buoy and made a mental note to avoid it, but as I was occupied looking at the pier it had gone from my mind ... but not, it seemed from my propeller. A glance over the transom showed the tell-tale line tightly stretched at an angle going down into the water. I sprang to the foredeck and put the anchor in, cursing myself for forgetting the little mooring.

I changed clothes and launched the dinghy to investigate. The buoy was bobbing against the hull just beneath the surface, held there by the pressure of the boat pulling on its line. The first task would be to relieve this load and this was where it was quite handy

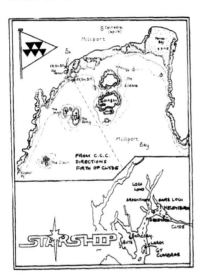

having a trimaran, for I was able to go to the rear of the float to have a nice firm platform to operate from. I fastened another rope onto the one which we had snagged and heaved it up until it could be secured to the float cleat. More heaving and the float now took the strain, relaxing the pull on the propeller end of the line. I went back down into the dinghy and was able to start unravelling the buoy. A few twists and it came away entirely. It was only secured with a line about the size of a bootlace and had been unused for so long that it had just crumbled away. Digging into the assorted seaweed and shrimps all mixed with barnacles I was able to find the end of the line and start untwisting it. I was lucky, for the quick reaction of going out of gear had reduced the twist and it soon came free to allow me to float clear and hang on my anchor with the buoy reattached to its troublesome line.

During this little fracas the two yachts which had been alongside the pier had cast off and departed leaving a lovely clear space for us. We placed our fenders on the starboard float and approached in a tight arc of circle so that with the help of the tourists and fishing enthusiasts on the pier we managed to secure ourselves with our bows facing outwards and almost level with the end of the structure. At high water our decks were about a couple of meters below the level at which people walked and there was a range of about two and a half metres.

We certainly were a great attraction. The Clyde Puffer at the end of the pier was the tourist equivalent of a steam locomotive and it was parked there specifically as a visitor attraction, but the crowd looking at our craft at rest on the still water often outnumbered those that gathered to view the steam trawler. Multihulls were extremely rare in this part of the world. The only ones encountered would usually be accommodation catamarans, so our fine lines caught the imagination of our admirers who likened us to racing cars. We wandered ashore and generally whiled away the evening in domestic duties, planning to stay another day to hire cycles to explore the island. We were well settled when the first faint breeze began to blow from the south.

In the beginning we thought nothing of it, but as it began to increase in strength, so it began to generate waves, small at first, but then increasing as time went on. I had thought that tucked snugly behind the pier we might be adequately protected, but that was due to my inexperience with piers. I was about to learn about them the hard way, which is the usual method with sailing and me.

The pier had the same open wooden structure as the one in Rothesay and as the waves were driven directly against its side they simply passed straight through it and it afforded little or no protection. The motion of the boat was similar to that experienced at Lamlash where the swell had run across the wind, but this time it was much more violently uncomfortable.

When a boat is on a mooring it is free to swing until it comes head to wind and usually the waves. When the wind is against the tide it may take up a position of relative discomfort facing neither one way nor another, but at least it still has a freedom of movement to take the line of least resistance. Here we found ourselves to be in a totally false situation with regard to the forces operating on the boat. We were held beam on, so that each wave imparted a severe rocking motion causing the floats to begin to slap with increasing severity.

The wind's arrival had coincided with the onset of darkness and as it was near high water the rocks which bordered the entry passage to windward of the pier were covered allowing a lengthy fetch for the incoming waves. It was very uncomfortable and I might have decided to depart immediately, but there is inertia in actions.

We'd been on the go all day; we were secured by a number of lines which meant somebody clambering off the boat and jumping back on again and the ropes might prove tricky to free with the boat snatching up on them; the rocks around the channel were now submerged; and there was at least one small mooring waiting for us on our direct exit line; there was no alternative anchorage close at hand, so we stayed where we were, allowing the crew to get some fitful sleep, but not so the skipper who had to remain on deck.

The situation was a constantly changing one due to slight fluctuations of the wind direction and the fall and rise of the tide. She was secured alongside in the standard manner with two breast ropes and two diagonal springs running up to bollards on the quay. She was protected from hitting the pier by two pairs of fenders, each pair with a plank rigged across the outside of them. This arrangement worked reasonably well in the area of the forward cross beam where the float was relatively deep and had a vertical outer surface for the fenders and the plank to push against, but at the rear beam the float was curving and of such little freeboard that the buoyant fenders were lifted and thrown onto the deck as the float banging down onto the water.

As the water level descended so we were pulled more tightly against the pier legs and the lines had to be extended for the force of the contact could be quite severe. In the middle of the night one of the boards which measured 250mm deep and 30mm thick was snapped clean in two and I had to hurriedly substitute two thinner pieces of packing case lashed together which I had picked up from rubbish in a dock some time earlier. Imagine the discomfort of sitting on the float fending off with booted feet whilst awash with black water, fumbling to retrieve broken wooden chunks thrashing like insane animals on the ends of their rope tethers in the surf, untying knots in the darkness and using the ropes to lash boards together to be inserted in a gap which surged and snapped and would crush a hand or foot in an instant given the smallest misjudgement. All the time there was the thought of what would be the next line of defence if the last plank should snap.

Another difficulty concerned the very tips of the float, especially at the stern where the narrow pointed sloping transom defied every attempt to fender it. I tried to pull the boat forwards, but at one stage whilst I was dealing with another crisis a horrible rending sound told me that the barnacled pier had begun to eat the rear of the float despite my best efforts.

Standing on the rolling deck, often awash, precariously balanced in the darkness with the snatch of the lines, the jarring thump of the float hitting the water, being sprayed by the deflected splatter of wave tops as they clipped the beams and cross struts coming through the pier, I learned quite a lot about fenders and

189

fendering that night. If I had to select one little gem of information to pass on, it would be to lead lines **under** the float to pull the boards tightly **down** trapping and securing the fenders inside them.

All night I worked backwards and forwards, retying, making up new lines, sitting observing the actions of my lashings and as I was always involved in devising some new scheme to improve protection it was surprising just how quickly the night passed, but at first light the following morning I had no hesitation in getting out of there just as rapidly as possible. We motored across to the marina at Largs which we had passed the previous day and at last I was able to catch up on some sleep.

It had been a bad experience going to Millport; in fact the majority of the week had been a little disappointing due to the lack of a proper sailing breeze, poor visibility and an assortment of uncomfortable learning situations. We were now well into the Clyde and I determined not to make life difficult for myself, but to slowly potter towards our winter quarters in a boatyard near Renfrew well up the Clyde. I spent some time travelling ashore to visit the yard. We changed crew and gently cruised towards our destination.

We went up Loch Long to moorings at Ardentinny where we had a lovely evening walk in the forest which reminded me of our trip to Norway. Next we sailed round into the Gare Loch for a visit to Rhu Marina and then Helensburgh. We were on the north side of the Clyde and had to cross to the southern side. There was an odd smooth island close to our route which was quite different from anything that I had seen previously. It wasn't until we had passed around it that I suddenly realised it was the upturned bottom of a sunken ship known as the Sugar Ship. As we sailed towards Greenock and followed the channel up the Clyde my preconceptions were shattered again. I had expected something like the lower reaches of the Thames. A deep metallic-grey flow of murky water between industrial banks set close on either hand, but instead we found something more like a grand version of the verdant River Orwell. It is a very broad river but extremely shallow, lined with green shores and only a narrow dredged channel to give access to the upper reaches.

We followed it up almost to Glasgow and then turned south into a tributary river where we secured to a wooden barge to await the opening of a bridge. Once through we motored to the yard where *Starship* was lifted out to spend the winter ashore

The year ahead promised well for the Hebrides lay before us.

Year 3
Refitting problems
Finding windfalls
The Clyde, the Kyles, the Mull
All about injectors
Iona, Staffa, Coll, Rhum, Oronsay
Outer Hebrides. North Uist
St Kilda go–no-go?
Cruising on a mooring
Transport for the trapped
Barra, Canna
Drumbuie
Loch Sunart. Loch Aline. Loch Spelve

Pic. The family on an earlier trip.   *(Fisheye lens, Norway.)*

Serial Starship

A reminder. Many things have changed in sailing in the relatively short time since this voyage was made. Actions that were acceptable then may now be regarded as unsafe, but right or wrong, this is what happened and you can compare it with how you would respond today using current methods and modern communication systems.
Also, much of the information about electronic technology, prices, locations and facilities will have changed. Some of our decisions and evaluations relevant at that time may no longer be so, today.

<u>MI issue 249. Episode 44.</u>

<u>Problems.</u>
We had left *Starship* to overwinter in a Renfrew boatyard near to the city of Glasgow on the Clyde and at Easter we had to go north with two targets in mind. We had to attempt some maintenance such as painting the antifouling whilst she was out of the water and we had to find another stopping place further west so that when we sailed her during Whitsuntide we would have a target to aim for.

My first surprise upon arriving at the boat was that the mast had been unstepped; something which I'd specified should not happen. Climbing aboard I noticed that the entrance hatch boards were damaged, caused by a lack of understanding as to the way they worked. Somebody had tried to force them inwards. The most disturbing discovery was a large blank space below where the cooker had been. It had been a brand new one which replaced the previous one that was irreparably damaged following several attempts at flight whilst crossing the Bristol Channel. Sure enough this new cooker had actually flown. It was a severe loss for in total the cost approached £200 to replace it again.

I was lucky, for the situation had been explained to me previously when I had left the boat. My good friends Ed and Marion Crangle had prevailed upon me to remove most of the gear from the boat to store at their home for the winter. I had taken off all the obviously attractive items such as radio and echo sounder without really realising that the new cooker was a more expensive item than they were.

It appeared that in the poorer areas of the big city there had grown up a tradition of 'opportunism', which involved making the best use of things 'found'. It was 'enterprising' never to overlook a 'windfall' and this habit of picking things up had translated itself into a generally accepting attitude towards what was really crime, because

192

it was only a small step from exploiting articles genuinely lost and 'found', to removing items if the opportunity presented itself. We saw and heard of many incidents which demonstrated a high level of petty theft and with hindsight it was unwise to have left anything which could have been unfastened on board in that area.

I might add that this was not the first time that I had suffered a loss of this type. One of the hidden problems of having a very distinctive boat is that it gets noticed when you arrive and if you are cruising it is pretty clear that you will soon be leaving again. The criminal mind puts these observations together and sees easy pickings. In Norway I lost an outboard motor and the police placed the responsibility for the investigation with an officer who was away on a fortnight's holiday at the time. Their first question had been: Are you insured? An affirmative answer meant that they had no further interest. It was an insurance job. In Cornwall I lost a number of items to a thief close to someone I had trusted, but who went through the boat selectively removing only those things needed to complete his own inventory; a scattering of items such as kitchen utensils, lights and a spanner set whose loss only became apparent over a period of time.

The theft changed my plans for the year. I had intended to cruise in the greater Firth of Clyde area at Whitsuntide and only go around the Mull of Kintyre and on to the Hebrides in my summer holiday, but now I decided that I should distance myself from the urban influence, for I would have to leave *Starship* fully equipped through June and July until my return in August. This meant that I had to go exploring overland in the area around Oban on the west coast for a stopping place, so with Ed's help we identified the likely places on the map and then set off on our search.

A marina just to the north of Oban mentioned a figure of about £200 for the two month stopover and as my shock was difficult to disguise they mentioned that I might lay a temporary mooring for myself in a shallow area of the bay. They suggested a couple of 90lb CQRs that I didn't have aboard *Starship* at the time, and which would have cost the same as the stay, but they were just trying to be helpful and it was an interesting observation/strategy.

Opposite Oban was the island of Kerrera which had moorings, but this was too close to the town for my liking at the time, so we drove on southwards to a privately run operation on Loch Feochan where we spotted the racing trimaran *Memec and Chips* on a mooring. Unfortunately this place was tightly restricted by the environmental restraint of being in the middle of a sanctuary area for wildlife that placed a tight limit on the number of craft and the only option was to take a half-season contract which was about £250.

Feeling a little disheartened we went to our next place which was a small bay where an old slate working area had been roughly converted to allow a Travelift-hoist to carry boats ashore. It was a bare and uninviting landing place with a black slate beach, but we talked to the owner who was most pleasant and encouraging, quoting about £30 a month for us to stay. We'd found our next target.

On our return overland journey we drove further down the Mull of Kintyre to visit Tarbert. We took a small car ferry across to Loch Ranza on Arran and drove over the mountains to catch the ship which would carry us back to the mainland. This mainland ferry was late arriving because it was packed with hundreds of motor bikers who had come over for some kind of impromptu Easter rally where they could race around the island. The mighty roar of their engines issued from the bowels of the ship as the unloading ramps were deployed and then commenced a continuous stream of ominous leather-clad riders, streaming off the ship in a crescendo of noise and unbridled power ... all except the last one who was devoid of all threat as he was pushing a machine that wouldn't start.

We boarded and the ship began to leave half an hour late when three people, man, wife, son and dog came running along the pier shouting to the ferry to come back as they'd missed it. They were clad in light sunbathing clothes, it was almost nightfall and this was the last ferry of the day. The man waved and whistled for the ship to come back, up to the bridge two decks above us and we were three decks above him. We, the passengers lined the rails looking down thinking 'No Chance', but all of a sudden the bow thrusters began to operate and the ship began to manoeuver to return; an exercise which took a further half an hour as the entry platforms had to be re-rigged. There was applause all round as they finally scrambled aboard the ship. It later became clear from announcements on the intercom whilst we were eating the most awful meal in the world in the ship's cafeteria, that many passengers had missed their rail-link transport as a result.

We returned home and I prepared for the journey to deliver *Starship* round the Mull of Kintyre. Extracts from the Clyde Cruising Club guide had this to say: *'The passage round the Mull of Kintyre is one which requires great care owing to the tremendous seas which arise when wind and tide are opposed. Conditions can deteriorate rapidly. A small craft unless properly equipped and able to batten all hatches securely should not attempt this passage.'*

<u>Friday-Saturday May 23.</u> There were logistical considerations with the land transport, so keeping our numbers down to three meant that we and the gear could fit in one car. Ray Weston had previous experience with me (and an excellent car). Ian Goodrum was a resourceful dinghy sailor making the transition up to cruisers. We drove overnight to arrive at Renfrew at 06.30 where the boat had been launched, re-rigged and transferred by the yard to a small dock where she lay afloat,

Marvellous Ed Crangle had arranged for a friend Steve to sleep aboard overnight to ensure that nothing else disappeared and had brought the heavy gear down in his car, which he helped us load aboard. We had set aside Saturday and Sunday to refit the boat and as we did so a number of details came to light which were to have significance as time passed.

There was a loose coil of rope on the deck which turned out to be half of our spinnaker halliard. Whilst the mast had been lowered in the yard someone had taken a liking to the swivel block attached to the masthead and to remove it easily they had simply cut the halliard, leaving the section inside the mast to fall down and be lost as the mast was stepped.

Down below I turned on the water tap to be greeted with silence and not the slightest trickle. The oven burglar had also removed the pump which powered my water supply. Still no cup of tea from yet another new cooker.

It became clear that there had been problems, for the men from the yard, in understanding how to use the engine. The floorboards were adrift (in their search for the seacocks?) and the carpets holed. I got a message that they had recommissioned the engine, but they'd had to 'reconnect' my cooling water supply. They were unable to operate the fuel cut off to stop the motor and I had water in my fuel, all of which was a bit of a mystery to me. I went and looked at the engine to find that my temperature sensor was broken off the top and a plastic, low pressure diesel return pipe had been left in contact with the hot exhaust which was welded to it. The fuel cut off worked perfectly, but at least I was reassured that they had stopped the engine correctly without just turning off the ignition switch which could have burned out my alternator.

Next I learned that they thought my rudder was a bit tight and so they 'loosened a few bolts'. This sent me straight to the transom to discover that the bolts which might have put excess pressure on the sliding blade remained untouched, so I was puzzled, until I noticed that other bolts fastening the tiller to the rudder box were about to fall off. Somebody had tinkered who had little idea of how things work. Whilst at the stern I notice the back of the boat was covered in soot, and another yachtsman mentioned that my diesel appeared to be producing a lot of black smoke. This informed me that it had been running at full throttle trying to force the boat along faster than was comfortable for the engine trying to turn the big propeller or running with no water in the cooling system.

Everywhere I found signs of ignorance and incompetence. Perhaps I should have known when I read their business card advert which listed the services that they offered, one of which was 'Laying up and Dismasting' The only redeeming feature was that they were cheap when one discounted the cost of the repairs.

Finally on this topic, all my split pins had been carefully removed from the rigging and lost, oh, and the V.H.F. aerial had been disconnected by cutting it close to the deck plug. Needless to say there was much work to be done, including shopping at the chandlers, but eventually Ray, Ian, Ed and I got an operational craft together from the ruins, so that on Monday 25 May at about 13.00 we were able, with a slight sense of relief, to wave goodbye as we motored out into the Clyde and pointed our bows downstream at the beginning of another season's adventures.

MI issue 250. Episode 45.

The Clyde, the Kyles, and the Mull.
Monday May 25 - Wednesday May 27.

The upper Clyde has some really interesting sights. The Erskine Bridge must take suspension bridge building to its zenith in the slenderness/distance spanned, ratio. Trimariners have an obsessive interest in beam structures so this impressively lean span is a reassuring confirmation of the strength of engineering calculation and modern materials. We drifted beneath it on a warm sunny afternoon using only our genoa despite there being very little wind. We were sightseeing. The next sight across the bright reflecting water was the distinctive castle at Dumbarton standing on an island as a defensive doorway to the upper reaches. At Greenock the oil rigs, cranes and shipyards were so fascinating that we rolled up the sail so as to get unrestricted photographs as we chugged past.

Having rounded Cloch Point we headed south and tried to sail again but the breeze was so fitful that we twice went from close hauled on one tack to close hauled on the other tack without deviating from a straight line course. Having struggled down to Toward Point we turned with relief to sail more freely to the north-west, the wind died a little and then returned directly on the nose. Back to beating. When I tell people that I always seem to be beating they don't seem to appreciate just how acute the problem is with me.

Entering the East Kyle the wind died completely so we motored into the dusk along the beautiful valley looking at the houses and trees scattered along the lower slopes. Before us the way appeared blocked by mountains rising on top of other mountains which were darkly silhouetted against the misty setting sun.

Searching ahead with our binoculars we saw only a silvery path beneath the rising brooding mass of the mountainside.

*Kyles
of Bute*

Where the East and West Kyles met there was a pattern of broken rocky islands studded with bushes like the finest horticultural rock garden or Japanese Bonsai. The channel narrowed to a tiny constricted passage through which our trimaran could barely squeeze. It was a place of great beauty and worth travelling a long way to experience.

We crossed the West Kyle to Caladh Harbour which is a tiny bay almost sealed off by an island that leaves a narrow entrance at the north and south ends. When we had first heard of this place I had doubted whether there was space enough inside for us, but we had been assured that there was plenty of room. There wasn't. We were fortunate that the other occupants were two chaps in a twelve foot cruising dinghy, camping beneath their boom tent. We took the best place and were fortunate because another yacht arrived but left again unable to find sufficient space to anchor. The other yacht that did succeed in staying used the catamaran technique of sailing in at low water until it ran aground on the soft mud and then throwing in the anchor. As an anchorage of outstanding beauty and shelter this would be hard to better. It is totally surrounded by trees and grass with woods extending up the steep hillsides and distant mountains rising over all to fill the gaps and complete the perfection.

I was woken in the night by lapping sounds from outside and I saw that a little breeze had set a few waves in motion which lapped against the sides of the clinker cruising dinghy. I had forgotten just how noisy they could be and I wondered as I looked across the water at the dim shape, how it sounded aboard if it was sufficient to raise me from my bunk at three in the morning. I certainly felt no nostalgia for the bad old days. Give me smooth plastic every time.

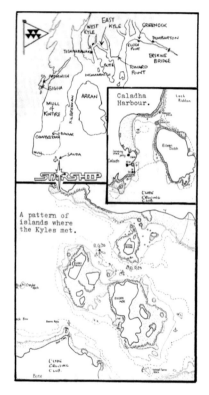

A pattern of islands where the Kyles met.

Tuesday 26 May We started the day with some gentle maintenance until the tides became favourable and then in force nil, warm and misty conditions, we departed Caladh (pronounced Clada) heading for Campbeltown. We motored down past the little town of Tighnabruaich then out to where the West Kyle joined Inchmarnoch Water.

At first the breeze was force 3 southerly so we started to sail, but after a half hour calm it went north-easterly and we hoisted our spinnaker as a reacher tacked down at the stem head. We began speeding along for the very first time. Oh what joy. We remembered why we sailed multihulls as she accelerated effortlessly up to nine knots and smoothly ran on rails. Ian who hadn't sailed on such a craft before had a delighted look which spread from ear to ear as he suddenly appreciated this novel feeling of just skimming along. The whole machine of tubes, ropes and cloth which had lain dormant for so long sprang to life and carried us in its wings down the west side of Arran.

The visibility was very poor and it was hardly possible to see both sides of Kilbrennan Sound at the same time. We stayed close to Arran surrounded by a heavy shroud of mist which locked us into

198

isolation with its overwhelmingly mountainous nature. We saw little ahead or behind except the unfolding of high crags with tiny houses clinging to the narrow coastal strip or dotted in solitude amongst the patchwork of fields higher up. Even higher and only rarely glimpsed were peaks upon peaks, behind peaks. We could almost smell their cold hard bones scraped clean by the wind and obscured by the cloud. In our closed misty world we might have been looking at an isolated island anywhere in the world, in the deep southern latitudes, passed in mid Atlantic, or as an oceanic waypoint on an extended world cruise.

Occasional wind shifts had us hauling on sheets as we gradually left Arran and drifted over towards the Kintyre side, our eyes straining to identify scant details on the sullen mass of land and our ears resounding to the words of the song. 'Oh mist rolling in from the sea ...' The wind eased as the Sound became wider and with five miles to go to Campbeltown we were back on motor to enter the loch whose mouth was constricted by the bulk of Davaar Island. At the town we first went alongside an Ocean Youth Club ketch and then transferred inside the harbour wall secured to a fishing boat.

Just before leaving the Clyde I reflected how lucky we had been with the weather. When we had first arrived from the instant weather of Cornwall and Wales I was reacting without delay to the shipping forecast. Here in the Clyde when it said a gale was approaching the nearest sea area Malin, I got myself into a secure harbour triple lashed to the windward shore and couldn't understand why the locals were sailing out in shirt sleeves with a picnic basket on the foredeck. They knew that by the time south westerly weather systems had traversed Ireland and all the outer islands there was usually little left for the Clyde. A much more important weather factor was the reshaping of the wind direction by the various mountains and valleys; but if the wind should blow there was always some island to hide behind.

We sailed the Clyde in holiday times and found it to be deserted by the standards of the south and east coasts. Onshore the towns and villages had a Sunday feel of quiet calm with few people about and on the water we seemed to sail almost alone. Caladh Harbour was referred to in the Clyde Cruising Club guide as a popular harbour, but only a couple of other craft wanted to share it with us. For a sailor used to our River Deben, or to Newtown (IOW), or East Head (Chichester Harbour) where 'popular anchorage' could mean boats deck to deck almost across it, having the scenery and the water exclusively to ourselves was a novel experience. The whole area seemed almost designed for cruising, with attractive anchorages set apart at comfortable distances and clean sea water mainly free from tricky obstructions. For us it was a super sailing place with years of exploration potential which only needed more reliable sunshine to make it absolutely perfect.

<u>Wednesday May 27.</u>
Rounding the Mull is one of those sailing passages which comes high on the sailor's list of things not to do. Like the major headlands of Portland Bill or Land's End the cruiser is committed to a lengthy passage on the other side before reaching a secure resting place. The Mull can develop a tremendous race and as we approached this passage we couldn't help wishing for weather conditions which were not too extreme. For once we were fortunate.

We did the calculations to catch the tide at the right moment as described in the guide but we came across an instruction to *'reach Sanda Sound as the ebb began (+0230 Greenock)'*. The actual meaning of the plus sign was ambiguous and whilst we found explanations later in other guides we were unable to find one at this time and had to engage in lengthy debate trying to confirm what it meant for it made a difference of five hours according to interpretation. We eventually became convinced that +0230 meant it had to be subtracted from high water time, which gave us a critical time of 10.40. We went to the harbourmaster's office for confirmation and were advised that the critical time was 15.00 which was most disconcerting. Eventually we stuck to our own calculations and were relieved to find them correct as the day progressed. Our target was the Gigha Islands.

The Mull of Kintyre is a much mightier headland than Portland Bill and the cliffs, valleys, villages, roads and rocks presented constant interest as we progressed. We had almost a flat sea, misty sunny conditions and as it turned out, a favourable tide all the way. One of the navigational marks had the lovely name of Arranman's Barrels which certainly provoked our conversation.

To the south east of the Mull stands Sanda Island with several outliers in its group. Little islands on the chart were always imagined by us to be low rocky outcrops so it was a surprise to find a huge chunk of land like Sanda was inhabited and farmed. We wondered what life must be like living in such isolation. Either Heaven or Hell?

We made the whole trip from Campbeltown around the Mull under engine helped by the three knot tide until about five miles north of the Mull when a gentle breeze filled in from the south-west and we were able to set the spinnaker which was a blessed relief. For an hour or more we skimmed northwards at about seven knots watching the land go by. Eventually the wind died and we did the last hour to the islands under motor to carry the tide.

The Gigha islands were low lying with many shoals and rocky outcrops, but the main island was rolling farmland with seven miles of road. Apparently thirty-three thousand tourists cross from the mainland two miles away to visit every year, but we didn't see a single one. There were three main anchorages on the eastern side, but we chose to go to the main centre of population at Ardminish Bay where we found only half a dozen houses visible but a string of ten strong mooring buoys near to the landing stage, put in by the Highlands and Islands Development Board for the free use of visiting yachts such as ourselves. This was most welcome and surely an excellent way to attract yachtsmen to a particular location.

Onshore there were good facilities for rubbish disposal and information displayed about where to go and what to see on the island. We were immediately struck by the clarity of the water as we rowed in and the pure white sand which looked almost like salt or snow. There was an industry in egg timers just waiting to be started on this the first of our Hebridean Islands.

MI issue 251. Episode 46.

Gigha Islands - Seil Island. May 28 - 30.
There was a cold, feeble, fickle south-westerly and it was misty and overcast when we departed Gigha at 10.15 having stayed the night and walked the island. Just for once we went away under sail and tried very hard to make progress in the light conditions, but an hour later having only covered two miles and with another thirty-eight still to go, we had to turn the key in order to make some progress.

We were close to the aptly named Badh Rock guarded by a cardinal mark which demonstrated the classic situation found in textbooks where the buoy has lost its distinctive coned top that indicates in which sector the danger lies. We had to resort to confirming it by reference to its colour scheme. This is a system not as easy to remember as the one used for topmarks. Ray's method of memorising the principle was the best.
'The arrows (formed by the topmark) **point to the black bands.'** This buoy was yellow with a black belt around its middle, so you can work it out for yourself.

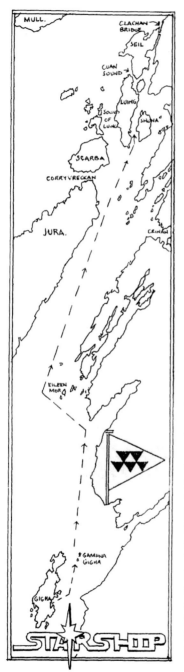

We were busy discussing these fascinating facts whilst passing close to another group of rocks called Gamhna Gigha when the engine note changed and a quick glance over the side showed that the seabed was visible, so a sharp turn was required to avoid becoming a permanent part of the islands. Half an hour later the misty weather was closing right in and soon it began to rain. We went from casual-coast-glancing pilotage to rigid night-class-plotting as we motored on in our own little world for another hour heading northwards up the Sound of Jura.

Luckily a breeze sprang up from the west and faintly at first the rugged mountainous beauty of the island of Jura began to materialise. We set the genoa and cut the motor to sail on 330°m. over towards the Jura shore. Just south of the MacCormaig Islands there was a great turbulence of the water which was disconcerting to see. A distinct line between smooth and rough tumbling water seemed to indicate a possible underwater obstruction but it was a product of the tidal streams now assisting us at 2 knots, so as we were already moving up to 6 or 7 knots in the strengthening breeze we flew over the rough water and didn't even disturb our kettle on the cooker. The largest island in the group Eilean Mor (Big Island) was less than half a mile in length, but the sailing directions said that an anchorage on its north east corner was alleged to have been the headquarters of the pirate John Paul Jones.

By now we had a good breeze which cleared the mist all around us and allowed us to absorb some of the finest sailing scenery to be found anywhere. Hills and mountains on all sides yet a steady breeze and the flat water that we love; we sped along appreciating our good fortune. Ahead of us, to port, lay the Corryvreckan, the Witch's Cauldron or Whirlpool.

The chart showed a tidal flow of 8.5 knots on springs and we were on springs. I must extract a little from the Clyde Cruising Club sailing directions.

'Between the Islands of Jura and Scarba is the Gulf of Corryvreckan 1½ miles long and ½ a mile wide at its narrowest point. The tide surges over the deep and uneven bottom (depth 219 metres) and is impeded by a high shelf ending at the 29 metre sounding. The overfalls close to the 29m sounding are invariably the most awesome, on occasion with breaking crests and spume on their tops. In CALM weather at Springs the first overfall can rise to a height of 4 metres (FOUR metres in calm weather, Wow!) *but a Westerly swell can double its height. The roar in extreme conditions is audible even at Crinan six miles distant. On the Ebb huge overfalls can extend over five miles out to sea in what is called 'The Great Race.'* This place was well known to the Vikings and woven into their legends. To be fair, we did not have to pass through the gulf, we simply had to cross the entrance to it in clear and settled weather. As we approached at eight knots it was interesting to speculate that if we turned into the Gulf and tried to sail through at this speed we would probably come out backwards at half a knot. The whole area at the top end of Jura was an intricate crossroads of channels between many islands. One could turn right to go through the Crinan canal to arrive back in the Clyde not terribly far from Caladh where we had anchored overnight a few days earlier; it was just over 20 miles as the crow flies. Turning north-west by bearing slightly left up the Sound of Luing would take us out towards the distant misty mountains of Mull. Instead, we chose to sail straight ahead across the centre stage of this natural amphitheatre of hills and islands forming a ring about four miles in diameter. We were reaching at about nine knots average on the fresh sea air which funnelled through the Gulf of Corryvreckan. The water beneath us swirled and eddied, welling up from great depth to form intricate moving-mosaic carpets for our keels to cross. Only once were we deflected bodily sideways, but we enjoyed the sensation as we were immediately entering into another of the intertwining pattern of bubbles and streams snaking like the Runic straps to be found intricately carved

on a longship's prow. There was a magic there but nothing sinister. We saw isolated dolphin fins ahead and around us as we entered and a whole pod of arching backs as we exited towards Shuna Sound. We liked the place and we all felt it to be a highpoint of our journey, well worth the week of work that had been the price of arriving there.

By 16.00 Shuna Sound was before us. Only half a mile wide and disappearing as straight as an arrow northwards, it was a little like sailing down a tree-lined highway with the lovely green islands on either hand.

There was a neat little village at Tobernochy to port; a man standing near to a black car was watching us through his binoculars. We spotted our second sailing yacht of the day disappearing to the right across Loch Shuna just before we crossed the entrance to Cuan Sound on our left. This narrow doglegged channel exits through to the sea, totally isolating the island of Luing from the next island north which is Seil. Seil is linked to the mainland at its northern end by a beautiful high-arched stone bridge at Clachan. We began to take off sail to enter our anchorage.

At one time this place had been a point of export for slate, so the landing was not typical of the Hebrides. The site had been levelled and shaped from the slate beach to give access for a huge Travelift-crane to take boats from the water. It could carry my 22 foot beam trimaran complete inside its mighty arch with room to spare ... not that I thought I would need it. My plan was to leave *Starship* here only for a couple of months until the beginning of the summer holiday. As we picked up a mooring only a lone man ashore next to a black car noticed our arrival.

Whilst our sailing was complete we still had much to do for our car was a hundred miles away in a world incredibly different from this isolated place. When our sails were furled and the boat finally at rest, we were assailed by a silence so powerful as to be unnatural to our ears which had rarely escaped the constant sounds of 'civilisation'. We were made most welcome by the yard's owner. He could only recall one previous visit by a trimaran, which from its description must have been a Lodestar type. We were kindly invited to visit the owner's home.

That evening Ian and I were guided across open fields, climbing ridges and following valleys to reach a secluded little house tucked close into the edge of a sheltering forest with a southerly view towards Shuna and Jura which in the evening light were set darkly on silver shafts of water. We were offered wonderful hospitality; had showers and talked sailing until quite late around a cosy log fire.

Ray had disappeared earlier, sitting astride the back of a motor bike on which he'd been offered a lift towards the village. His job was to find his way back to Glasgow by public transport and to bring the car up; our job was to tidy the boat and be ready to leave when he returned. We knew, by enquiring at the Post Office, that Ray had to catch the school bus going to Oban at some unearthly hour in the morning, so he thought it best to take bed and breakfast in the village. His motives were not exactly one hundred per cent those of catching the bus early, for he had other plans, but my enquiries revealed that the nearest pub was, supposedly, two miles distant.

When Ian and I walked back over the moors to the boat after eleven o'clock that night it was still quite light enough, being so far north, for us to find our way with ease.

<u>29 May</u>.
Ian and I were engaged in stripping the boat of valuables and locking them away following our earlier experience with thieves. Top of our list for security was the cooker. We were advised not to bother, everything would be safe. The security advice for a 2 month stay was:-
a) Don't leave the inflatable in the water, lift it on deck or the seagulls will mess it up.
b) Don't leave the outboard on deck, put it below.
Well obviously that was insufficient for me after the Glasgow experience and we engaged on a dismantling process which soon had the decks thickly covered with all the valuable gear from below. That was when the rain started. It was gentle at first, but then it became a downpour and the wind started blowing until, in the end, we had to rush out and pile everything below again. Total chaos. We reconnected the cooker to warm things up and dry out.

Darkness came early, so bad was the storm. As evening came on we expected Ray to return. We cooked a meal and waited. No Ray. We warmed our portions up and ate them. Perhaps he'd be back about nine? It was raining very hard and blowing quite a bit. At ten thirty we knew he wouldn't get back that day. I donned oilskins, braved the black night and driving rain, went out, hauled the dinghy aboard and got it triple lashed down. If he did come back, he'd go to the B&B again. I was really glad to get below once more and cheered myself up by reheating Ray's meal and scoffing it for my supper. Ian was in his bunk and I was just scraping the plate when I noticed a flash of light from the shore. I went up in the doghouse and flashed a torch into the darkness to receive an answering flash that said that Ray had returned. Back into oilies then re-launch the inflatable in sheeting rain and howling wind to row ashore to collect Ray.

His adventures were too convoluted to record in full here, but the previous evening he had ventured out from his lodgings to walk the two miles to the pub. They turned out to be 'Irish' miles and suffering from exhaustion he fell in with some locals who took him drinking until two o'clock in the morning before returning him back home in a fisherman's truck. Upon arrival he found himself locked out as his landlady, taking him to be a Christian gentleman, thought him to be safely tucked up in bed. He didn't have the heart to disturb the old dear and spent a fair proportion of the night shivering out in the cold before gaining entry.

We'll draw a veil over what happened on the way to Glasgow and relate only that he managed to return to the boat about 9.30 that evening but decided to go off again for a few drams with his new-found friends whilst there was still time. He was tired and hungry, to say the least. Supper … what supper?

Sat. 30 May. Returning home.
We left the boat on her mooring and drove south for twelve hours stopping only a couple of times en route. Firstly, after only three miles for Ray to have a final drink with the locals and next at a motorway service station where a slice of toast cost 14p, a glass of water was 55p and my sandwich, drink and slice of cake cost an arm and a leg. What a contrast that packed and sweating service area made with the solitude that we had left behind.

We drove in fine weather until we reached East Anglia where we caught up again with the same weather front that had given us the rain for unloading the boat in Scotland. By the time we were home it was the same torrential rain that had been wetting us in the morning that was wetting us again that night.

Ray, one of my favourite crewmembers, departed to join another yacht the next day to sail across the North Sea for his Sailing Certificate. I had a quiet day washing, cutting the grass, writing and of particular pleasure, baking a bit of bread.

MI issue 252. Episode 48.

<u>August 1 - August 3</u>
Start of the Summer Cruise.
<u>All about injectors.</u>
You really know that the great departure day has arrived when you defrost the fridge, and write a note for the milkman.

Plans are sometimes made to sail to exotic places years in advance and at the time the plan may seem unreal, but gradually the day draws nearer and then realisation actually dawns when you wake up in the morning and say to yourself THIS is the day that I committed myself to years ago, when I embarked on this scheme. When I did that I must have known that I'd be involved in going to some remote places but I don't know if I realised that I would be buying a chart with St Kilda on it and hoping as I closed my front door behind me that I would be able to reach islands such as these far out in the North Atlantic. It had all gone beyond the everyday sail as understood by most yachtsmen. The whole thing had somehow stopped being an extended daysail and started to be more in the nature of an expedition involving more than a degree of danger.

The understanding of what it now involved began to produce mixed feelings in me and in particular, one of not being really sure that I wished to continue any longer. Why couldn't I just book a package tour to a sunny place like everybody else? Or simply sail up and down the local river like I used to? Thinking back though, it wasn't all that easy in those days when I was learning the game. I had my fair share of failed motors at moments of extreme crisis; fouled anchors in front of the yacht club; dragging onto neighbour's boats in the middle of the night; running aground, dismastings, lost rudders and falling overboard and I didn't give it up and take a package tour did I? So why should I stop now? Well, because somehow it was more remote, unknown, frightening. Atlantic seas, fast deteriorating weather, barren islands, rocky snares and no chance of help. It had all turned rather serious and I was filled with doubt about the risks. Could this have been a case of the weekend sailor getting out of his depth?

We departed just after midnight to drive north on deserted roads. In my friend Paul Brown's car was Adrian his son and Roland my son as well as myself and all our gear including a new outboard motor. We went to Oban via Inverary which is an outstandingly beautiful Scottish village. By the time that we had loaded supermarket stores in Oban and driven on to where the boat was moored, ferried out and loaded the gear aboard, we were exhausted. It was a case of sleeping amongst the debris and then waking to move, pack and store a bit more.

<u>August 2 Sunday.</u>
The boat was in need of some urgent repairs. Floorboards needed sorting out, the marine toilet wanted rebuilding, cooker connecting, the usual maintenance jobs which build up all year had to be done in just a day or two.

It wasn't until the end of the afternoon that we tried the motor but it refused to start. I primed it, bled it, cleaned it, Easi-started it, but it wasn't inclined to work and I had to take care to preserve the battery power. I began to check back in detail. I discovered water in the injector, then water in the pipes and eventually a whole system full of watery sludge. My mind went back to the yard near Glasgow where I had received lots of vague messages about 'water in the fuel' and that they'd eventually 'got it to start'. I had wondered at the time what they were trying to tell me; everything else that they'd touched had needed repairing afterwards. I always religiously sieved everything that went into the fuel tank and couldn't understand the huge lumps of dirt now in there. We had to drain the tank and pipes into buckets and bowls which were stored all around the boat. We eventually took out the whole fuel system to clean it except for the final high pressure pipe from the injection pump to the injector. I was down below checking this when we almost had a very bizarre accident.

Paul was in the cockpit and he had been helping me by turning over the engine with the ignition key, so that I could check the pulsing of the fuel in the injector which was out of the engine, but didn't seem to be firing. We had finished that process and the loose injector was no longer suspect. I popped it back in the top of its cylinder. Fuel was coming through the pump continuously instead of in little bursts. I called up to Paul near the cockpit tank, 'Switch off the fuel.' He did. I was sitting on the cabin floor with one foot on either side of the engine about 450mm away from it. I checked the fuel had stopped running and wanted to see if it would start flowing again. I shouted 'Switch on.' and immediately a mighty explosion hit me with a force sufficient to blow me backwards onto the floor with hands clutched over my face. Paul was mortified, thinking for a fleeting second from the sound that I was either dead or terribly injured.

Early Trimarans.

Left. *Mistral* 6mm plywood 20ft

Below. *Endeavour*
Sheathed ply. 25ft
Designed/built Tony Smith.
Owner Sq. Ldr. A.R. Williams

Lower page.
Starship at Thornham Marina
Myself with Auntie Joyce and
John Morton

Top. View from my lounge window, before and after turning the hull over

Above. Turning the hull in the garden

Above. Naming Day. Woodbridge

Left. Float stored in garden prior to assembly

Some changes, mainly made by Malcolm Legg

<u>Above left</u>. Owned by Norman Reed
Queenborough, River Medway

<u>Above</u>. Mudberth, Weston-super-mare
Owned by Richard Topham
Aft cabin windows and hatch

Below. Fins on floats

Below. Fabric cover and trampolines

Starship's Big Rig

Picture from
Richard Topham

Below and on previous page.
Starship prior to final sale.
River Avon
Pictures John Perry

What on earth had happened? We had been 'switching' on and off the ignition for some time as we checked the engine and naturally when then I said 'Switch on.' again, this time referring to the fuel, Paul had turned the ignition key not the fuel tap. The unsecured injector had literally been fired by the engine as a massive bullet at my head at very close range, but a small teak bar 30mm x 20mm lay between the motor and my face, level with my nose and eyes. The blast of particles from the cylinder alone was sufficient to knock me back on the floor. When we checked the wooden bar it had a big splinter dug out of the back and the injector was lying in the bilge below the engine. I had a lucky escape.

It became clear that the injector was not operating and I needed to have it tested, but what chance was there of doing this on a Hebridean Island? I was not hopeful.

Monday August 3.

Enquiries revealed that a man called Floris could help me, so I walked down to the village telephone to ring him. He asked me a few questions and when he heard that I had brought the injector ashore he said he'd come and pick me up.

Ten minutes later he arrived. He was a tall slender chap of wiry build, a heavy moustache and a clear Dutch accent at the very edge of his most fluent English. After he'd visited the shop to buy his breakfast we set off in his car along a series of remote tracks towards the isolated place where he lived. When we apparently had almost reached the ends of the earth we came upon an old house and tucked away behind it, a small wooden cabin with a different world inside it. What a surprise it was to walk into a place filled with sophisticated equipment, pumps, microscopes, micrometres, neatly racked tools, injectors, shims, in fact a scientifically precise laboratory for testing and rebuilding diesel injectors, pumps, etc.

As we had travelled, we had talked. Floris told me of how he had worked in the Middle East and as a break from sun and sand had come to the Western Isles for a holiday. Hearing that he was a diesel expert somebody had asked him to look at a tractor engine. He found it difficult to believe that with all the agricultural machinery around this rural area there was no specialist facility for diesels nearer than Glasgow, 100 miles distant. When the Iraq-Iran conflict hotted up and he could hear the sound of approaching gunfire he remembered his peaceful holiday, so he moved to find the quiet life. His workshop and house took their water supply from the local stream and he had a turbine under a nearby waterfall providing his electricity so there was never any need to switch off the lights.

209

Now, as he worked he explained to me what he was doing throughout the procedure, showing me all the working parts so that I could understand how it operated. Most of us have an idea about how a spark plug sparks, but know nothing about how an injector injects. The basic principle was this. Fuel was forced into a gap around a needle which was being pushed forward by a spring. The needle was closing the injection holes. As the fuel built up pressure in the cavity, it pushed back on a shoulder around the needle, so that the spring was compressed and the needle was forced back, releasing diesel from the holes at the tip. Pressure was immediately released as the fuel escaped and the needle went forward to close the holes allowing pressure to build again, sufficient to open the needle once more.

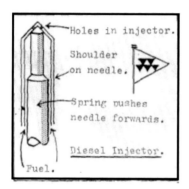

For testing, the injector was held in a device where fuel could be hand pumped into it and fired into a chamber coloured black inside. By directing a strong light at the injector tip the pattern of the diesel spray could be seen. The injecting of the fuel resulted in a constant cracking noise as it fired the fuel in a pre-defined pattern. Floris got the injector working properly as far as I could see, but he said that it didn't make the right noise. By changing components he got it to work more sharply. He showed me the water corrosion damage to the injector holes of the old nozzle and the change this made in the pattern of the diesel spray.

We had a further discussion about the motor's symptoms and he diagnosed improper functioning of the injector pump, so he returned with me to the boat to check it. He was right. The nut which locked the mechanism together was a turn too loose, allowing fuel to escape back into the pump so that it couldn't hold the high pressure. With a twist of his spanner the system worked perfectly again and we were all smiling.

He asked only a moderate fee and was dragged away from the quay to look at somebody's car as soon as he was spotted. He was a busy man in great demand for anything mechanical in the area so life was far from peaceful. I blessed my good luck for having unknowingly broken down on the very doorstep of the 'Diesel wizard' of Western Scotland.

In the anchorage was a chap named Tony in a Wharram catamaran called *Faoileag* (Gaelic for seagull) and (as cruisers do) I went over to look around. He'd built the boat which was schooner-rigged with a junk main. Having sailed it for a while he sold it, but after a year without it, bought it back. As with most home-build live-aboards there were a number of good ideas, but one which caught my eye as being particularly neat was the Dorade-type ventilator cowl on the float hatches. Tony said that the idea came originally from Moitessier. I think maybe that it is worth passing on how to make a cowl from an old inner tube to another generation of boat builders.

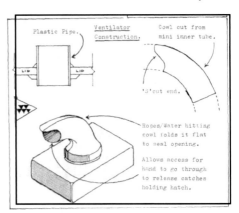

MI issue 253. Episode 48.

August 3 - August 6. Departing.

We were at the very beginning of our holiday, but I was already thinking about its end. I was going to sail away from our anchorage just south of Oban in north-west Scotland, but where would we be heading for at the conclusion of our summer cruise? Despite a number of enquiries we seemed to have run out of ideas, it appeared that there wasn't the demand for boatyard and marina facilities once north of Ardnamurchan Point. I had written to a couple of likely places, but had received no replies, so before we finally cut our ties with wheeled transport we explored a bit further overland.

We headed off on a day trip towards Arisaig and Mallaig, driving through super scenery alongside Loch Linnhe towards Fort William. The scenery improved as we crossed the Caledonian Canal and turned west towards the coast. After passing the monument at Gallanish to Bonnie Prince Charlie, at the spot where he was proclaimed King and waited to gather the fighting men of the Highland clans together, the scenery actually improved again.

The road became winding, the mountains ever more precipitous and the forests thicker. Around each corner there were stunning sights to see. Waterfalls to the road's edge, gradients to gasp at and then suddenly, sea views that were absolutely stupendous. On a scale of 1 - 10 the first view across to Skye and the jagged islands of Rhum and Eigg easily topped 15. It was totally breath-taking beauty which could not be conveyed in words or pictures because the vastness of scale would defeat any mechanism short of the human brain. We were just compelled to stop and gaze in wonder at this scenery beyond description. I had heard that it was good but had not really appreciated that the sun, sea and distant islands could work such magic.

As winter stopping places Arisaig and Mallaig seemed potentially good on the map because they are served by the railway and although they are incredibly remote, they are still accessible. We found Arisaig to be open and windswept. The waterside was littered like a derelict graveyard with old cars and defunct machinery. There was a feeling that leaving a boat there might result in it being the last place I'd leave it.

Mallaig was completely different, but even less suitable. It was a very commercial, fishy-smelling harbour with rugged little steel fishing craft packed tightly against precipitous granite walls. There was the raucous call of the gulls and lines of cars waiting to be loaded onto the Skye ferry. The chandler's shop was a very distant cousin of those on the south coast. It dealt with sledgehammers, chain and galvanised buckets rather than designer waterproofs and dinghy fittings. A cold northerly carried a swell into the harbour and swirled fish and chip wrapping paper into blank concrete corners. Mallaig was a transit place where tourists crossed the road from train to the ferry and fish boxes were swung from scraped steel decks onto railway trucks, it wasn't a snug resting place for delicate hibernating private yachts.

We had the delight of the return journey, seeing all the beautiful scenery in reverse. I was no nearer to solving our problem.

August 4. Wednesday.

Paul had to take the car to Oban so that he could recover it there at the end of the first week when we changed crew. Whilst he was away I prepared the boat and generally pottered about ashore. I happened to fall in with some chaps who were involved with fishing boats and diving.

There was a fishing boat alongside a little stone pier with a rope around its prop. These two characters were freeing the warp and whilst one was down in the crystal clear water the other one was yarning away about similar jobs that they'd been on.

We sat in the warm sunshine as he told about the coaster up in Inverness that had a log jammed inside the protective circular propeller shield and they were called out of their warm beds on a dark night, to arrive in a rough sea to have a look. Down into the cold inhospitable water they went, only to find that the log had been washed out by the motion of the ship. They came up to the surface and asked for a big hammer; went down and bashed the hull a few times and then came up again. This time they wanted a sledgehammer, which was eventually produced so that they could go below and whack the hull some more. Returning exhausted but triumphant from such a tough task they submitted their bill. On another job a freighter had wrapped miles of big warp around the prop which was an ideal mooring line, so when it was all unravelled and cut free they took it down to the bottom and left it there so that they could come back later and pick it up.

We were having quite a laugh and it was being explained how on every dive they always searched the bottom to see if there was fishing tackle or anything useful which had been dropped overboard. Suddenly the other diver surfaced and handed over a live 303 bullet to his buddy. It shone in the sunshine, pristine and new. 'Have the IRA been through here?' said one of them in jest. A cloud passed across the sun. Where was that man with the binoculars and the black car?

After Paul returned we checked the engine, ran it and tanked up water and stores ready to leave the next day.

August 5 Wednesday. Bound for Iona.
The weather had been pretty exceptional. On the first day it had been very changeable going from downpour to sunshine in seconds and we had seven days of weather in the first afternoon, but since then it had steadily improved. We were getting sunshine all day with

a patchy northerly 0-3. On this morning it was mirror calm and we could watch crabs and starfish leading their hum-drum lives beneath us, down in the pool-i-verse.

We unshackled our mooring at 09.30 and motored down towards Cuan Sound wishing we could take 360 degree photographs because the greens and blues of land and sea begged to be captured on celluloid. The dog-legged sound had swirling, twisting upwellings which spun the boat as we passed through into what appeared to be the open sea. We chugged slowly out towards the blue mountains of Mull looking around us to the south to try to identify the numerous rock groups and islands that were visible. We made out Jura with its distinctive mountains; Islay and Colonsay were also to the left. Just behind us to the right was the island of Inch at the entrance to the Firth of Lorne. Ahead was the southern coast of Mull which looked straight, apart from a couple of bumps. We began to follow it.

The breeze was now very light on the nose and the tide was about half a knot adverse. We cut the motor and sailed because we wanted to, not because we wanted to make progress. Up to the first bump, Malcolm's Point, about a third of the way along, it was a bit of a struggle. After that we made gentle progress as the breeze strengthened a little. The last one third of the trip demanded some accurate navigation as we tacked through a narrow passage between the Torran Rocks and the south-west tip of Mull. The coast just here was similar to parts of Sweden where the shoreline itself appears to be almost a blank wall of sea-smoothed granite sculpture, but for those that know, there are intricate passages through into tightly sheltered anchorages such as Tinker's Hole to the south and Bull Hole to the north of the Sound of Iona. We glimpsed the odd sail disappearing behind stacks or saw the flash of a red or blue hull in some crevice as we passed.

We approached Iona in the evening and could clearly see the Abbey standing above the tiny hamlet on the island. The anchorage off the landing was fairly exposed with this wind and open to shifts. The Clyde Cruising Club guide indicated that a sheltered anchorage wasn't possible on the island itself, but we had been told of a certain spot to the south of the village where we might cross into a lagoon inside a protective reef of rocks. When we arrived we were encouraged by seeing two other boats already inside there. We crossed where we had been instructed to, noting that the depth was only four feet, but once inside it was immediately deep again and so absolutely clear it was as if we were suspended in flight, hovering above the weed patches and snowy white sand. There was an old Uffa Fox designed Atalanta called *Grace* already moored and, following their advice we set our anchors front and rear, being able to place them with absolute precision for fifteen feet of water appeared to be only a couple of feet deep. It was 9.30 pm. so we'd been sailing for twelve hours to cover about forty five miles direct, but we had enjoyed the views, the sunshine and just the feeling of sailing again.

August 6. Thursday.

The forecast was for the winds to increase through the day but I wanted to visit the Abbey and do a bit of shopping before leaving, so I decided to move up and anchor off the village, ready for a quick getaway after the shore trip. After breakfast we bid our friends on *Grace* goodbye and motored down to the anchorage entrance. I was feeling a bit nervous about getting out because the wind was behind me and she was difficult to slow down. *Grace's* skipper was signalling 'Go Right', so I had one crew watching him through binoculars for instructions and the other two crew were in the bows watching the bottom to see that it was safe. I made the turn and was edging ahead through the gap when there was a grinding bumping crunch and we shuddered to a halt by riding up onto solid rock. What a wonderful start. It was only the second day.

There was plenty of flailing about with the inflatable, anchors, and 'weight off into the dinghy' etc. but she was seen to be firmly on and unlikely to shift. Our friends came down in their dinghy to offer condolences and assistance, but as it was fairly low water the best course of action was to leave her to re-float herself. They were worried in case she was holed, but, dare I confess it, I knew from having done similar things a couple of times in Scandinavia that she would probably not be badly damaged. Being of foam sandwich construction it is like having a boat inside another boat with a lifejacket in between them. The worst that could happen would be to damage the propeller or bend the prop shaft in such a situation. Taking weight off her was the most useful thing that we could do.

Paul B stayed aboard and Adrian and Roland came with me across to the white sand beach from where we walked up to the village. The island was an absolutely perfect place for camping. In sheltered grassy gullies isolated tents bathed in sunshine had children playing before them in unmarked sandy bays. The blue water of the Sound of Iona was only disturbed by the occasional passing of a white sail. Sheep stood unafraid giving us their puzzled stare. We scrambled over hills and down onto the cropped grassy shore, through a gate and onto a sandy road. A woman sat before her home enjoying the sun and winding newly spun wool yarn onto a large rotating wooden frame. 'Weaving' said the sign, 'Knock on the Second Door'.

After two small shops we were at the pier head which smelled strongly of horses and was lined with lobster pots and markers. Two pony traps stood waiting to take visitors up the road to the Abbey. We walked up the twisting lane past a tiny corrugated iron Post Office, then through the old ruined nunnery built in the 1200s. We passed Maclean's Cross, a tall beautifully slim and elegant Celtic cross richly carved with elaborate decoration and found ourselves approaching the Abbey itself. It was founded in about 563 when Columba crossed from Ireland to establish a settlement on this site. He and his followers were responsible for converting Scotland and parts of Europe to Christianity. The present building is of a much later date and has of necessity, been much restored.

For me, contact with the realities of what those men saw and felt, came from their choice of site and from my own experiences as a sailor. When we think of these pioneers I am sure that we have misconceptions about the kind of men that they were. Our images are perhaps more shaped by the modern concept of life in an established monastery, but such a life would have been impossible in a frontier situation like that known to Columba.

Imagine making a longish sea journey in an open boat built like a coracle of flexed wood and skins. Imagine landing on an open beach, dragging the gear ashore, digging defensive ditches and living out in the open. Sustaining life in such a wilderness for the first few seasons demanded men of action, tough, resourceful and ... workers; working day and night at hard physical labour on a minimal diet.

Standing on the uneven ground, littered deep with the anonymous bones of men, be they kings or serfs, it didn't matter now. The only really common link with them that we have now is the view of the land as they saw it and the sea as they felt it. Our eyes looked across the same Sound, our faces felt the same wind, the sand and the grass were the same, as was the noise of the waves falling on the shore. I felt humbled in some way, across the great gulf of time, by their strength of conviction. They showed me the frailty of mine.

We headed back for the boat.

Serial Starship

MI issue 254. Episode 49.

Thursday August 6. Iona - Coll.

We scrambled down the grassy-green valley and collected our bright orange dinghy from the edge of the brilliant white sand beach which surely belonged on a desert island. Our footprints marred the sand's perfection and the water was so clear that in the strong sunshine its edge with the sand could not be seen, until suddenly our feet splashed when we put them down. Out of the shelter of the cove a stiffish breeze blew from the north-west, making little waves inside the rocky reef. The forecast was for heavier winds later in the day but my earlier attempts to make progress to our next destination, before the onset of the gale, had resulted in *Starship* grounding on a reef at low water. We had made the best of a bad job by going shopping and visiting the world famous Abbey on this remote island of Iona.

Starship was afloat again and Paul who had stayed aboard said she'd come off easily with the rising tide. We motored northwards at about midday into a fresh force four, hoisting sail as we passed the village. We cleared the sound beating up towards Staffa an island famous for its geology, because it is principally basalt columns standing on end, always reminding me of a handful of matches 130ft tall. It is part of the same structure as the Giant's Causeway in Northern Ireland. It is perhaps more famous for one of its two south-facing caves; one is Cormorant's Cave and the other Fingal's Cave.

Apparently when in 1829 the composer Mendelssohn got over his seasickness sufficiently, he immortalised the cave with the lovely repetitive tune.... Daa-da, dada, Daaah-da ... which sounds so much like the sea. The island is only three-quarters of a mile long and noticeable, on this day, mainly because in such a remote and empty area there were perhaps four or five other craft in close proximity. Yachts like ours were sailing in close to take a look; launches were coming across from Mull to attempt landing tourists to walk around and go into the cave which is about 50ft. across at the mouth and 230 ft. long.

My MOCRA friends Pam and Gordon Hobday had loaned me many charts that I used for reference in the Hebridean area and the one that gave the best detail here was based on a survey in 1857 and actually engraved in 1859. It was so much more interesting than its modern equivalent and in a number of respects much better for navigation. I have noticed, by referring to the information always present but often tucked away in a corner of charts, that the most modern-looking metric charts are often extracted and updated from ancient surveys and older charts without any major recent additions. The added colours and deleted details are what separate modern charts from the old ones. Going back to the 1800's is quite common in areas such as this where a solid and rocky coast will have changed little in such a relatively short time. This old chart, bought at the beginning of the 1960's gave excellent land detail to assist with building a clear visual picture. It even contained a metric conversion chart and if ever it is finally finished with, it can be framed as a piece of artwork. I can vouch for the fact that Staffa, on a breezy day, still looks the same, except that now there should be a multihull in the drawing.

Staffa might be famous but, to some extent, it was just as we had expected it to be. Four miles to seaward is another island in the Treshnish group called Bac More (Gaelic) or Dutchman's Cap, which is much more notable from a navigational point of view. It is long, low and flat with vertical (basalt?) edges. In the middle stands a high cone-shaped peak which for its absolutely perfect geometrical

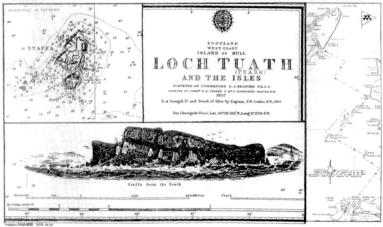

symmetry would shame the builders of the Great Pyramid. Seen from a distance, through mist, the island resembles a huge aircraft carrier with a flat hull and raised superstructure. As we were tacking past the southern tip of Staffa my interest was being taken by the unique shape of Dutchman's Cap ahead which was a much more compelling sight, made greater by being so unexpected.

The scattered group of the Treshnish Isles had two islands at the northern end called Cairn na Burghs, each island being no more than a couple of hundred metres in length yet each topped by ruined fortifications. In the 1715 rebellion men had fought and died here. In 1691 the Macleans had made their last stand here. What other stories of carnage had this place seen? Wherever we went we saw things which directed our conversations back to the days of early settlements and habitation. The whole area is one of such great contrast. The natural beauty is spellbinding but the power of nature is apparent. Men are smaller than ants in this landscape and it is difficult to imagine that their struggle to exist here was not a greater binding force than the urge to kill one another. The signs left behind by man's occupation of this lovely land tell a story of continuous death and violence.

There are bare and cold mountains dominating the scene, yet sheltered green havens whose only link would have been by sea. We were now beating up into a gusting five with the tide just beginning to go against us and we had the benefit of glassfibre, Terylene and stainless steel to push us against the adversity of the elements. How was it for them, the early seafarers? They had no modern oilskins, just heavy, wet, absorbent clothes in open boats. Their diet must have relied heavily on coarse, stone-ground grain, dried fish and meats with little ability to heat or cook unless the weather was calm. I have seen in the Norwegian Boat Museum open clinker craft so crude in construction which must have been similar to craft used in these parts and I noted the flat frying-pan scoop bailers which accompanied every craft. They bailed to stay afloat. They faced the unkind sea just as we do and they shivered in the biting northerly winds. They went without charts or real compasses and their minds were filled with the constant knowledge of witches, sea monsters and evil spirits. Perhaps Christianity was so acceptable when it came, because it simplified much of this pressure of superstition? It must have been a message which carried a ray of hope that life is not really ruled by the forces of dark oppression, but by a benevolent presence. Maybe Columba had a message that the people were relieved to hear?

Whilst all on board were discussing these things I was below in the galley preparing lunch humming strains of Fingal's Cave. A lurch of the boat and the knife which was slicing the loaf, sliced me. After an initial flurry with cotton wool and bits of tape I was stuck back together again and our modern means had calmed the situation. How was it for marauding Vikings or their victims, nursing an open sword or axe wound with the prospect of a long, wet, cold sea journey to face?

Once clear of the Treshnish Islands we headed out west towards Tiree and Coll, a pair of islands some 20 miles in combined length to the north-west. We were making for Arinagour on Coll for we knew that the inlet had Highland & Island Development Board moorings. These were big, in this case, craft up to 15 tons, secure, FREE moorings conveniently spaced for visiting yachts near shore facilities. Knowing that strong winds were coming, we wanted to find shelter to allow us to sleep easily knowing the security of our ground tackle.

Note. We used HIDB moorings at Ardminish in Gigha Islands, Tobermory on Mull and Portree in Skye. They were being introduced in Kilchoan opposite Tobermory, Craignure on Mull, Scalasaig on Colonsay and pontoons were being placed in Campbeltown on Mull of Kintyre and Millport, Great Cumbrae Island that I remember so well.

The wind really began to increase as we neared the middle of the passage of Tiree and we rolled our first reef into the genoa as we tacked north. The gusts were getting over force six and we were tearing along at 8-10 knots with a float in the air smoothing the waves with our speed. Closing the shore the wind grew stronger and it was soon time for another reef. The low valley seemed to funnel the wind and the white horses on the water went right in to the narrowest part at the head of the creek. Visibility was deteriorating so that we almost didn't see the dark blue moorings even though their seaward end was marked by a big yellow can buoy not marked in our guide book.

We motored across and picked up the mooring at 18.30, not a moment too soon for it was blowing in earnest and turning very cold. We were pleased to get all snugged down and a meal on the cooker. Roland was defeating all-comers at chess; Adrian doing well at cards. We read and wrote. Part of the crew attacked the whisky and outside the rain lashed the deck whilst the wind whined in the rigging.

MI issue 255. Episode 50.

<u>August 7 Coll - August 9 Loch Scresort, Rhum (or Rum)</u>.
It certainly blew very hard during the night and it would have been a sleepless one for me had we not been firmly secured to our lovely HIDB mooring. The shipping forecast spoke only of force 5 but it was

topping seven at times, so perhaps the land was having a funnelling effect? The morning was grey and visibility was restricted in the flurries of hard drizzle that drove across us from time to time.

We had a long stay in bed and extended breakfast until dinner, waiting for the wind to abate sufficiently for us to get across the gap between Coll and Mull to reach Tobermory where we had to change crews the following day. About mid-afternoon I decided that if I was staying I had better make a quick trip ashore so Adrian and I donned our oiles. We zipped, buttoned and laced ourselves inside so as to become as impervious as possible to the raging elements and then we set off in the inflatable to motor up to the quay. Adrian had the job of holding the bow down as water crashed over us, so that when we did finally make it into the lee of the shore we were half filled with water.

The tiny white houses made neat white rows. Sheep wandered slowly down the street browsing the trim grass. Rudimentary outboard motors hung on garden fences opposite every door and yellow-eyed seagulls gazed unafraid from the roofs of garden sheds.

In the shop the girl on the cash till was acting as baby-sitter to someone else's baby; she jiggled it on her knee whilst ringing in the prices. In the Post Office the policeman was just taking leave of the sprightly grey haired post mistress. "I'll be round to see you." he said. "My door is always open Donald." she replied with a hopeful, mischievous twinkle in her eye.

We posted a card, bought some potatoes and trudged back through the empty village. A glass-fronted sign in the centre offered information. We wiped the rain from the glass and read that there were 150 inhabitants; we also read that this was the sunniest spot in Britain. On a deserted, wet Friday afternoon near closing time we were difficult to convince. We loaded a container of brown drinking water and departed.

It was 4.30pm and we'd adjusted to being outside in the strong wind. The forecast had insisted at midday that it was only force 5 and the visibility had cleared sufficiently to at least catch an occasional glimpse of a dark outline distantly at sea which told us that Mull was still there. I had been worrying and wondering all day about whether I could make it across the ten miles of open water, where the waves funnelled between the islands, to reach Mull to meet my new crew. I knew that my worries would extend through the night unless I made a move, so I decided that we'd have a go. We readied the boat and set off.

The main was down to three quarters its size and we had half of the genoa. We sheeted in and went upwind keeping reasonably close to the island. The sky and the land were gloomy. White horses flecked the sea but shafts of sunlight came through to illuminate headlands here and there. At an average of eight knots we went up to the northern tip of the island and then bore away onto a reach, out into the exposed seas towards the hidden black mass of Mull. Now the waves had dimension enough to slew her sideways as they caught her and angry white crests slapped, then cascaded into a million crystal missiles splattering across the deck and doghouse in front of us. It was uncomfortable, but safe enough. The two boys loved it and Paul manfully picked his way through it because the steering was quite a handful. I tried to keep track of our position for it would have been embarrassing to have missed the entrance to the Sound of Mull.

We had a period of being slewed around then a period of exploding our way through waves. A brief period in the middle saw an illuminating spotlight of sunshine break through the black overcast and pick us out in its base as a splash of colour surrounded by white foam. As we became more sheltered approaching the lee of Ardnamurchan Point my period of anxiety dwindled away and I knew that the worst was over.

There had been a couple of other sails going in the opposite direction and as we looked up to the dark northern shore of the sound we could see another yacht running in ahead of us. I jokingly suggested setting more sail to catch him up, because at the time we were crashing through water and using every stitch of canvas to the full. I expected to slowly overhaul him as we went into the sound, because that's what we always did, but oddly he seemed to hold our speed and at one point even went away from us until we set more sail as the wind became progressively sheltered. I vaguely remembered thinking that this red boat was quite fast and if I could find him in Tobermory I would be interested to see what type he was.

The bay that contains the town had similarities with Fishguard in that the natural qualities of the land didn't betray the presence of the town. Apart from a small lighthouse it was necessary to sail right around the corner before suddenly finding oneself looking at the houses. As we came around we immediately met the red yacht. The trimaran *Memec and Chips*, oft-times victor of the Three Peaks Race was manoeuvring under sail in and out of the moorings. We had a little chat across the water and they anchored close in, whilst we picked up a mooring. They had pondered on what kind of a yacht it

222

was that they couldn't leave behind, because that was what they always did. In the shelter of the bay it was difficult to imagine that it could be blowing hard only a couple of miles distant. We wondered if they were still being battered on Coll as we tucked into our evening meal feeling invigorated because we had made the effort to do the journey. All the crew agreed was a fitting end to their week's cruise.

<u>August 8 Saturday.</u> Time to change the crews.

The bus stood at the far end of the promenade; we were nearest to the landing place at the other end. The bus boarding point was in the middle and the time to be there was 09.45. I took Paul ashore with the heavy luggage so that he could carry it along to the bus stop and then I returned for the boys.

The outboard wasn't running smoothly. Halfway back with the lads on board, it stopped. Cardinal sin. We were out of fuel. It was 09.43. No time to return. The paddles came out and began to stroke. Paul was at the bus stop looking at his watch and making powerful rowing motions with his hands. The paddles whirred. The bus started from the far end of the promenade. We rowed faster. The bus was held up by the traffic. Paul jumped up and down. The bus started again. We reached the steps 200 metres from the stop. I leapt out to steady the boat. Paul was making vigorous running motions on the spot. The bus approached him. He was picking up the luggage as slowly as possible. The boys were running. Paul was lingering on the steps. The bus edged forwards. The boys leapt aboard. They drove away. Exhausting to watch.

Suddenly I had a little time to spare and a lovely little village to explore on a sunny gentle day. I rowed across to talk about multihulls to Nick and Roland aboard *Memec*. They had been cruising to the north and they told me about a strategy for getting out to St. Kilda in which I was interested. They hadn't made it there themselves as they had been exploring other areas and didn't have time.

I got supplies for the boat, tanked up the water and then had lunch in the Gannets restaurant. I was investigating the Mishnish Hotel prospecting for a shower and as I entered there were two elderly yachtsmen following close behind me on their way to meet friends in the bar. One was saying, 'He started off in Suffolk and every holiday he sails a little further round the coast. Looks like he's got to here now. I never miss an episode, I find it all most amusing.' and then they disappeared into the bar, leaving me standing holding the door for them and wondering who they were talking about? The bath cost £2 as opposed to the launderette which cost £1.20 so the hotel water must have been quite expensive.

14.30 I emerged sparkling clean and saw across the road, looking over the harbour wall, my friend John Morton seeking amongst the assorted dinghies tied at the base of the steps. As a wily old cruiser he was looking for my tender to ascertain whether I was aboard or ashore. He'd already met up with David and Rita our other crew on the bus that came up from Craignure and they'd all just alighted in the middle of town. They had greatly enjoyed the bus ride because of the character of the driver. He'd explained to the passengers that he wasn't allowed to give them a conducted tour so instead he'd just explained what he was seeing as they went along. He delivered papers and even a bouquet of flowers by stopping at the appropriate houses en route. Then when the bus became too full to take any more passengers he halted to apologise to people waiting at the bus stops and to explain to them when the next bus would be along.

After we'd all met, John came out with me to sort out the boat whilst David and Rita looked around ashore. It is a very picturesque place with a lovely atmosphere, made even better by a one man band playing a wide variety of Scottish and modern music in the little central square. We stayed moored overnight.

August 9 Sunday.
It was a gloriously sunny day, but with next to no wind. We got under way at about 10.30 and motored out into the sound. David and Rita were learning all about the boat systems and we did some exercises in checking the boat's position. I observed once again that a most important element in finding out where you are when taking fixes is trying to get a sense of scale. I've never seen it written about as part of any teaching system, yet is appears that the fundamental problem of working out 'how big and how far away', is the first principle to try to grasp.

Much tacking brought us just south of Ardnamurchan Point where the wind died entirely, so we motored over a glassy sea up the east side of Muck and through the gap between it and Eigg. The islands stand in groups together, but they have totally different characters. Canna and Muck are relatively flat in outline, whereas Rhum standing between them is memorably mountainous and stunningly impressive.

Avoiding rocks on the corner of Eigg we entered the waters between Eigg and Rhum (Sound of Rhum) which swirled with turbulent eddies, betraying an uneven bottom with ridges to cause upwellings of water. Food was carried to the surface for the birds to

224

feed on and they gathered in great rafts, the like of which we had never seen previously. We city dwellers were fascinated with the great variety of birds squabbling like youngsters at a party, on the waters all around us. We just had to expand our knowledge, which was mainly restricted to sparrows and starlings prior to this, with the aid of a bird spotter's book.

To begin with, the commonest birds appeared to be guillemots, but as we were far from certain of this we called them guill-e-whats? Herring gulls we thought we knew, also the superb gannets sitting like swans, airily aloof in the screeching flocks. We read in our bird book about the special Manx shearwaters, which until then we had been calling big black swallow-like things. Our next discovery was that all the gille-whats didn't have the same call. Some whistled and others had a raucous rasping

cry, until we grasped that the whistlers were the real guillemots with pointed beaks. The new species with the broad parrot-like beaks made an Awk-Awk sound to call their young to their side. The young we called little awks which turned out to be more or less correct as they were actually auks or razorbills. There were black-headed gulls and dirty brown skuas as well as the super-gliding fulmar petrels. They surrounded us on all sides and their constant noise and activity totally occupied us as we motored towards our haven for the night, Loch Scresort on Rhum.

At last we rounded the headland to find quite a good breeze being funnelled down from the high mountains so we hoisted sail to tack up the couple of miles to anchor some way off the head of the loch in seven metres of water.

This is a special loch because at some time in the past a millionaire mill owner took the place over and transformed it from a near barren wilderness into his own little Shangri-La. Apparently he imported the soil to plant the trees and brought the plants as well as the building materials to construct his own special castle which now doubles as a hotel. There are guided tours around the place but we came on a 'Closed' day, so when we went ashore we contented ourselves by peeping through the windows and having a tiptoed excursion around the main hall which has an incredibly ornate interior with everything that a Victorian, Scottish castle hall should have; deer heads on the wall, pictures of ancient ancestors, massive grandfather clock, grand staircase etc. We gazed in awe at these ornate splendours, all done in the best (worst?) possible taste.

We walked back along the loch side to find the Post Office still open at 7.30 in the evening with absolutely no customers other than people who might land from a boat such as ourselves. We took a sprig of heather back aboard with us to tie to the pulpit rail in lieu of a bowsprit, to signify that we had cruised north of Ardnamurchan Point the most westerly point of the British mainland, roughly the same as the Scillies. It was a place of great interest with outstanding scenery and we gained a strong impression that we were now really using our boat to reach remoter parts, difficult to attain by other means. Our interest in St. Kilda was growing.

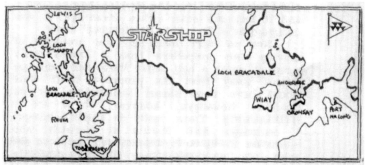

MI issue 256. Episode 51.

August 10 Rhum - August 11. North Uist.
To the Outer Hebrides.
The day dawned sunny, still and clear and remained so throughout. The scenery was superb. Looking towards the mainland a continuous chain of mountains stretched right around the western horizon from north to south. They weren't just in a single line. There were mountains behind mountains and all painted in such subtle colours. They went on and on and they changed and kept changing with every little trick of light, sun and cloud, reflection and angle. It was possible to sit and look for a whole day at the same scene and observe a constantly changing panorama - and we did.

226

A light breeze tempted us to try to sail from Loch Scresort whilst breakfast was still scattered all about the boat, but the breeze expired before we'd even gone a mile and so we reluctantly started the motor and ran all day on barely tick-over revs. We were heading north-westwards for Loch Bracadale.

I have already exhausted superlatives on the scenery and I can't really add any more. The earlier trip to Mallaig by land had been crowned by the view of the mountainous island of Rhum and on the opposite shore the Cuillin mountains on Skye and here we were again, sailing right between these two ranges. When the clouds lifted from the top of the Cuillins the razor sharp tops and surprising lines and shapes produced their magical effect. This area is, for me, an absolute jewel and it is relatively easy to reach. It is an essential pilgrimage for the cruising sailor.

Loch Bracadale is a large area of water composed of three lochs branching into Skye with numerous islands scattered about at their junction. The two northernmost lochs seemed unlikely to offer us shelter if the wind should change to the predicted south-east, so we looked into Loch Harport for Port-na-Long which our old Clyde Cruising Club directions said was a good place to go. We noticed that the directions said that a telephone was available from the Temperance Hotel and, water from the Talisker Distillery. We rounded the corner to our chosen spot to find that it had been 'developed'. Onshore were sheds and heavy machines, in the water were moored fishing boats and the little bay was blocked by fish farm floats so we had to do a quick rethink.

We returned around the island of Oronsay and then slowly inched our way into an almost closed rock pool formed by the strip of water which divided Oronsay from the shore. At low water the island joined the shore, but this rocky link was submerged when we entered.

We had found the marvellous dream anchorage that imagination can sometimes conjure up. It was a still, sheltered place all to ourselves with a shore and an island to explore. The inflatable was soon overboard and we motored slowly over a sea-plant garden in clear water 12 or 15 feet deep, admiring the individual plants growing below us. Ashore we beachcombed a little for it is always fascinating to see what has washed up in a deserted place where no human has recently passed by. We could not long resist beginning to follow the sheep paths upwards through the lush and springy grass, heading for the top of the island. We had noticed when we had first entered the loch that from seaward Oronsay had a vertical cliff face, but it tapers back inland like a huge wedge of cheese lying on its side. It wasn't too stiff a scramble up this side, but when we reached the summit ridge we were speechless, not from climbing but from the view that we found.

It was possible, with heart in mouth, to lie in the tussock grass and look down the precipitous cliff at the raucous seabird tenements and then on down into the depths of the sea at the foot. Raising your gaze in the windy up-draught you looked out at a silhouetted headland against the declining sun burning a golden path across the sea bordered by the distinctive peaks on distant islands below the horizon. It was a sensational place to be. The sight, the awesome altitude, the sound of the gulls wheeling below, the wash of the sea; it could not have been improved.

Looking back *Starship* was a tiny white petal on a blue pool in an endless land-and-seascape. Each of us wended our way down exploring separately as we went and then after more beachcombing we brought our discoveries together to share the interests of our finds. The evening was calm and still, so we enjoyed another night of perfect sleep in our snug little anchorage.

Tuesday August 11.
The 05.55 forecast said south-easterly 5-7. They had been talking about south-easterlies for two days but we had experienced only fickle northerlies. Now, we were assured, the REAL thing was bound to turn up. Force seven can be unpleasant, so we made an early start whilst it was still calm. There was insufficient wind to sail so we motored until well clear of the harbour where we found a bumpy irregular sea which banged us about until after about half an hour there was sufficient wind to blow the cobwebs off the spinnaker. Last year it was set for about two hours and this was its first appearance this year.

The wind settled at about force 3 with a dull overcast sky. Visibility varied, but we were always able to see the three mountain peaks on South Uist around Hecla (604m) and our guiding mountain was Eaval (345m) on North Uist. These two were cross-referenced with the lighthouse on Neist Point, Skye, as we skimmed along at about four or five knots. Navigating on peaks projecting above the horizon was a new experience, but it makes sailing in the whole of this area so much easier. We were using a new Imray Chart C66 which is another in the series linked to the Clyde Cruising Club guides. The chart had an error in the height of a mountain called South Lee which was given as 88m instead of 288m which caused some cross checking to confirm that we were heading for the correct rocky headland.

We doused the spinnaker at Maddy Island and set the genoa for manoeuvrability inside the harbour which has a series of low rocky islands and a choice of waterways apt to confuse a stranger. In the busy south of England it is possible to just head for where all the other yachts are, but here we had finally come beyond the normal yachty range. We had to make our decisions without the copious signs and symbols which we had come to expect in the land of the private yacht.

Each of our little trips in the last few days had been only 30 - 40 miles, but we had noted a distinct geographical change at each of the different locations. Tobermory has a green forest growing along the shore. It is busy. People and boats are constantly arriving and departing. Rhum was quieter, but there were many of the domestic marks of comfort that man adds to a place to make life easier. On Skye the remote ribbons of lochs had grassy surrounds and there were distant farms, but trees were very scarce. Now we had passed through some kind of frontier by coming to North Uist. Here it was hard rock hills with spare grey grass. The village of Lochmaddy was a single line of council-type houses which hardly marked the vast open landscape. Man seemed to hold only a tenuous grip on this world and my romantic notion of life in the outer Hebridean islands was about to be shattered. There was no romance in the struggle to live here.

There was a new pier to the left of the town as it is approached from the sea, but the old stone landing was on the right hand side and our directions encouraged us to go that way. The final channel was so narrow that we rounded up and dropped an anchor back and front. Just when we were about to go ashore in the tender some local fishermen arrived and offered to take me in their boat to show me another spot, close by, where the holding was good and where there was room to swing. After re-anchoring we went ashore and any last idea of romance disappeared forever.

The rocky, muddy foreshore was liberally strewn with broken bottles, scrap metal and discarded refuse. The rubbish on the shore even included the recognisable frame of a motor scooter. Our friendly fishermen had been tending their fish farms and spoke to us in beautifully soft Hebridean accents. When we asked where the public toilets were, the reply was 'Well the Council do keep talking about installing some, but that's as far as it goes.'

Our first task ashore was to get water and we were horrified at its colour. We had seen brown water up here before, but it had a peat-stained brown tinge, or specks of brown in suspension. This stuff was so dense that you couldn't see the bottom of the container. We had debates about boiling it, but amazingly it was perfectly OK and after using it a couple of times we stopped regarding it with suspicion. We noticed that fresh streams coming directly from the mountains had the same coffee colour, so we ceased applying our urban values.

In the shop they spoke Gaelic and threw in the odd word of English to greet newcomers, then drifted back into Gaelic if the newcomer was local and could follow the tongue.

Two little boys had their shopping list and a shopping bag. The list said, a tin of peas and the shop lady went to select the tin. "Is it big or small?" she asked. They exchanged puzzled looks.
"Who is it for?" she went on.
"For Grandma."
"Grandma who?"
"MacDonald."
"That will be small." said another customer, busy selecting her own tins from a shelf at the back of the shop. "Small one." said the shop lady slipping the can into the bag.

There were two shops. The grocers and the Weehaveit which sold trinkets to tourists, tea towels, sticks of rock and postcards with local views, printed in Norwich.

Another of my misconceptions, that of self-sufficient islanders ingeniously producing all their requirements, quickly crumbled away at the grocers. Everything happened at twelve o'clock, exactly a quarter of an hour after the ferry arrived from Uig on Skye. Until that time there was no milk, no bread and nothing fresh. No self-sufficiency, no cow in sight, nobody kneaded dough or tried to coax summer vegetables from the sparse soil; there was only the throb of diesel engines as the lorries revved up the ramp and the Mother's Pride truck made its first stop of the day. By midday precisely seven lorries were lined up in front of the shop and the goods were being unloaded. People and cars were homing in like bees to a honey pot. For an hour there was frenzied activity as the town came alive, then the street became silent and only the tourists, cycling explorers and skinny dogs meandered occasionally along the windswept strand.

The man in the ferry office (where we found some public toilets) had pointed out a visitors mooring just inside the harbour entrance in the shelter of the bay. So we tanked up with diesel, visited the Weehaveit and upped anchor to motor into the evening gloom with driving rain to secure ourselves well clear of the town, ready for a quick departure for St. Kilda.

MI issue 257. Episode 52.

North Uist. Outer Hebrides.
St. Kilda is a legend. It is a small group of islands in complete isolation far out in the Atlantic. The complete tale of its occupation has to be read from a book devoted to the story to be fully appreciated, but perhaps I can sketch an outline.

The people who lived there were as completely cut off from contact with 'civilisation' as it was possible to be. They always owed some allegiance to a clan chief based on the mainland, which they paid partly with feathers, but most of the time they were left untroubled to live in delicate balance with nature, locked into the seasons for collecting plants or harvesting seabird eggs and chicks for food and fuel. Originally they lived in black houses with low walls and turf roofs; later they had houses in a more modern style. They survived by hard work over endless hours, operating a communal system of deciding what work had to be done each day.

The reasons for their decline is left to the judgement of each person who reads their story, but there are striking similarities with the decline of any primitive peoples coming into contact with 'civilisation' even to the present day. Was it religion? Was it the tourists? Was it contact with an easier life-style? Was it their reduced numbers? Their end was well documented and it makes sad reading; one can weep at their trusting simplicity which led to the final evacuation. 'Civilisation' eventually swallowed them.

Their islands and their spirits remain, together with the seabirds on the precipitous cliffs which supported them, but to reach those islands is still an ultimate challenge in small boat sailing. One must sail fifty miles out from the Outer Hebrides and upon arrival the only anchorage at Village Bay is not secure, offering shelter only from south and westerly winds. There are dangers in getting there, in staying there and in returning. To go there one needs to be granted the favour, by the elements.

<u>Wednesday 12 August.</u>
The morning forecast wasn't good. We were going to get up to force 6 with the tail of a gale coming in later. I had an uneasy feeling. I wasn't looking forward to this.

To depart from the islands we had to go north to the Sound of Harris, a rock strewn and tortuously narrow passage between the islands. It would take an hour to get there and then maybe two to go through into the open Atlantic. Once out with a following wind we'd be committed to making the voyage out to the tiny group. Good visibility was needed to pick up the islands which soar out of the sea. The only anchorage would be an untenable lee shore and we'd have to rely on the wind going south at just the right moment to allow us to stay and then, go into the south-west for our return.

I looked out of the fore hatch at the grey morning. The Loch Maddy village was half obscured by low scudding cloud. I should call it off. The rain was just ending and the sky looked a little lighter. Was I afraid at the thought of this final leg after coming all this way? This was my chance, was I going to take it? Was I about to chicken out? I sniffed the fresh damp air. 'Stop thinking about it and get on with it,' I thought, 'this isn't the time to hesitate.' I decided to go. Bury my doubts in the many actions required to organise the breakfast, get the crew moving and prepare the boat. I set to.

It was now seven o'clock and we were in the final stages of preparation. I was on deck having just lowered the rudder blade and was about to hoist the main when David called from below that the light in the toilet wasn't working. 'Have you got a battery fault?' he asked. I wondered for a moment and then switched on the VHF which has a low voltage warning. It whirred its siren sound. I switched it off and dropped into the cockpit to find the navigation light switched ON. Last night when we'd strewn our wet oilies around the cockpit a loose sleeve had caught the switch and the thirsty light had drained the battery. I understood this in a moment and explained it to the crew.

The immediate question was: Can you start the engine? I could, because I keep a separate battery for that and I went to operate its small test light. It lit. Back in the cockpit I turned the ignition key. Nothing. No warning light. I turned to start the engine. Nothing. I couldn't believe it. I should get a glimmer or a faint and feeble wheeze but the system was dead. It was impossible, but I had to accept the physical evidence that somehow it had been drained. I was devastated.

Both David and John were electrical engineers and had a thousand questions to ask about the circuits and systems but I could hardly answer, because I knew that my chance of getting to St. Kilda was evaporating due to something as stupidly simple as a switch being left on.

Talk doesn't put things right. Only actions. We had to get the batteries charged in order to start the motor. We couldn't risk entering the Sound of Harris without the ability to use it. We disconnected the batteries, loaded them into the inflatable and David and I set off to the village 2 miles downwind to see about recharging.

It was still early morning and things were quiet. We pulled the dinghy up near to the pier, unloading our two batteries. I asked a man in his car where we might charge our batteries. 'Benbecular.' 'How far is it?' 'Twenty miles.' That wasn't a good start. We found another man in a storage shed. He only served to confirm the distance to the nearest garage. We tried harder to make him explore possibilities. Do fishermen charge their own batteries? Is there an electrician about? Who dabbles with cars? Whilst he was pondering we watched a mobile crane unloading a mixed cargo from a coastal tramp ship onto a lorry. Who runs the lorry? Can a ship charge batteries? Yes, maybe the ship can help, why not go and see the captain? We picked up our batteries.

We stepped across onto a real old rust bucket and dropped with a clang onto her smooth plate deck, passing the batteries as we went aft and up the steps to the bridge. No sign of uniform or gold braid here. The young bearded chap with the overalls and a woolly hat turned out to be in charge. He listened and nodded, maybe he could help? The problem would be leads; he sent for the engineer. The engineer was doubtful, unless we had some leads. Could we take a look at the difficulty please? Follow the engineer.

We set off down into the ship. She had a Gaelic name, but every sign was in Dutch. Down and down we went following a narrow well-worn track through a steel maze until we entered a room, greasy green, dimly lit by a grimy bulb with the floor awash in slippery diesel. Assorted bits of unrecognisable, unused machinery stood around the edge and in a corner was a workbench deep with scattered tools. A big steel trunk with a heavy lid was opened to reveal a bank of batteries. The lid was wedged with a timber prop.

Their supply was 24 volts and our batteries were 12 volts. We raked around, along with the engineer amongst the assorted junk that lay in and around the trunk and by borrowing a lead from another battery bank we connected our batteries (negative to positive) to each other and then ran charging cables made of scrap, from the boat's batteries to ours. The engineer started a generator, which made an almighty racket, to begin to charge their batteries and ours too.

We had time to kill whilst waiting for the process to charge our batteries so we drifted up to the bridge to see the rate of charge on the dials and to chat to the captain. He had a very large scale chart of the Sound of Harris and it was helpful to make notes to compare with our sketchy maps. We watched the unloading of the ship through the windows and fell into conversation with a crewman who explained that this old tub was part of a two-ship shipping company, and it chugged around the Western Isles delivering anything anywhere.

We noticed the rest of the crew sliding ashore, so we set off to join them, to buy the engineer and friends a drink as thanks for their assistance. One chap was small and swarthy with a permanent grin and thick glasses below his woolly hat. He had bright orange overalls covered in congealed grease; the engineer had dull green ones covered in the same stuff. The third chap was an elderly heavily-built Irishman, forty years too long in coasting tramps; world weary, he had seen skippers come and go and had forgotten ... how many craft?

They were seated in the bright bare billiard hall with its hard lino floor, the only three drinkers at that time of day. We joked together. Hail fellow, well met. Their drinking capacity was matched only by their cigarette consumption. They told us stories of their waterfront world, temporary, transient, rootless. They cared not where they went, nor what the job was; they simply lived and anaesthetised themselves around bentwood tables in harshly lit bars at 11.30 on Wednesday mornings. They made us laugh. They were likeable rogues full of the tricks of evasion and survival. You might have thought that they didn't have a care in the world, but when the conversation drifted around to us and what we did for a living, they were strangely subdued, listening with care, interested. Briefly they sat and reflected, wondering what another life might be like, but then the moment was gone and they set up another round.

We returned to the ship, collected our batteries then motored back out to *Starship*. It was a wet ride in the rising wind. We re-rigged everything and turned the ignition key. Still nothing. Lengthy investigation showed that we had two faults together. The domestic battery had been drained by the light, but a corroded terminal was to blame for the engine not starting. The engine battery had been protected and functioning, but it had suffered this mechanical fault at the same time as the other battery was run down.

To some extent I believe that on this earth we do what we are meant to do and when fate deals a card in our lives then we should take heed. I had that feeling strongly at this moment. The weather was not good and I had missed the optimum moment to leave. Worse weather was coming. Should I go now?

I noticed that in ten minutes time we should hear the early afternoon shipping forecast. I decided to throw myself totally into the hands of fate to have my message clarified. Was I meant to go, or not?

I told the crew that we would wait for the forecast.

If we had a GALE in the forecast we would NOT go.

If there was no gale, even if it was force seven we would GO.

We sat down to wait and see what card Fate would play for us.

MI issue 258. Episode 53.

August 12 - August 16 Lochmaddy.
Cruising on a mooring, and Transport for the Trapped.
Would we depart for St Kilda? The shipping forecast would decide. If we received a gale warning we could not depart and all our efforts to reach North Uist in the Outer Hebrides would have been to no avail.

The oracle said Gale. I experienced only a numbed acceptance. This was a life-risking journey with tremendous hazards into the open Atlantic to windblown, precipitous, rocky islands and there was no way that I could disregard such a forecast whether it was right or wrong.

13 August.
It turned out to be right. The gale started in the evening after being very breezy all day. During the night we were bucking and snatching at the mooring and as day dawned it was quite clear that even though we had the shelter of the land we could not get on deck. It diminished my disappointment at not going when I saw that the conditions were severe and it was confirmed that the right decision had been made. Not only was there a gale but the cloud was down to ground level and for much of the time the land was not visible even within the confines of the bay.

We were going to have a day doing nothing, a real cruising day, but it wasn't a day without difficulties for me. I had crew transport problems to untangle and as we were gale bound and going nowhere for this day it might be worth looking at something that I have often been asked about and which is probably my biggest cruising problem, that of meeting up with the crew.

When I cruised to foreign lands I discovered that I was not pursuing my cruise as I wished to, namely, casually drifting from place to place as the vagaries of the weather dictated. Instead I was actually sailing from one railway station to another, in order to collect my crew. Travelling abroad has the complications of currency, customs and passports to add to the insecurity of not speaking the language. This always made crews a little uneasy about the journey. When the boat was away the incoming crewmember had to be informed where to find it (though some have managed with only the name of the country to start from) and this meant having to achieve certain destinations to a set timescale. Often the crew had a great distance to travel on various linking transport networks and so once they embarked upon their journey they were almost impossible to contact, yet sometimes it meant that they were probably heading for the wrong place.

One of the attractions of this sail around Britain was to cut out the international and language difficulties, but we still experienced communication problems such as on this occasion, because the crew was heading for Castlebay on Barra by Friday, an island 50 miles to the south, whilst we were trapped on a mooring unable to get ashore to make contact and it was Thursday. Travelling in the outer islands involves a very complex series of possible links between many transport systems including the Postbus which meant getting a lift with the van delivering mail.

At this time, before mobile phones, the contact method I found to be of greatest value in these situations was for the incoming crew and I to have a third person to telephone (next-door neighbour), so that we and they, could ring back to base when it became convenient for each of us.

Transport in the islands by coach, railway, ferry, bus, air and postbus is scheduled in a single book and sitting on my boat I was able to track my incoming crew through its pages. She had to be told not to get off the steamer at Castlebay, but to go on to the next stop. Arrival there would be at night and accommodation would be needed. Next morning she would have to ride in the mail van going to the aircraft landing place on a beach and transfer to another postbus which would go from Lochmaddy where we were, to meet the same aeroplane. Using the VHF I contacted the ferry office of Caledonian MacBayne and explained what I wanted so that telexes could be sent and bookings made. The extra journey meant that the crew would not arrive until the Saturday.

These preparations took me most of the gale-bound day, whilst the rest of the crew were entertained by John cooking a loaf of bread to supplement our supply. I had brought packets of supermarket bread mix and a suitable tin for just such an occasion as this. John baked a delicious loaf and proved that his major problem was stopping the rest of the crew from devouring it as soon as it came out of the oven. The smell was tantalising and the taste tremendous.

In the late afternoon the gale abated sufficiently to go on deck to discover that our mooring securing line had stranded, so we struggled to replace and parcel it to ensure our peace of mind overnight.

August 14.
We'd been surrounded by mist, rain and inactivity for far too long and it was getting to the crew. We had to have a little blow. In the shelter it had moderated to force 4 southerly with occasional gusts, so we reefed down and sailed in the harbour and at sea within the wind shadow of the headland. When we'd had sufficient fun we went back right inshore to the anchorage close to the old pier to enable us to get ashore for shopping and crew collection. We wandered around the deserted town meeting only a charming young German artist Silke who had been sketching in the harbour area. In that bleak, rain-soddened place there seemed to be only her and us, both trapped by our inability to transport ourselves out. To brighten both of our days we invited her aboard in the evening as a change from her youth hostel. She'd never been on a little boat despite having been brought up on the Frisian island of Langhof. It was a treat for both parties.

August 15.
There was still no let-up in the wet and miserable weather, so we went to the Lochmaddy Hotel for a bath. If I haven't stressed this sufficiently already, I will do so now. The water's tea-brown colouring comes from permeating through the peat. In a container it is very dark, but in a bath it is intimidating. It does not seem possible to get cleaner by immersing in that stuff. There is a strong inner revulsion about stepping naked into a tea bath so it took quite a bit of courage and not a little curiosity about whether it would stain the skin a nice shade of suntan. As with its use for making drinks we soon discovered that it was perfectly alright in every respect.

Our new crew Gill made it after travelling for three days on a mystery tour and our next problem became how to return David and Rita to our kind of civilisation. There was no service on Sunday, except in church. When we enquired about leaving, all the locals were philosophical. Their attitude was simple. Why leave at all? They were quite serious. Why not just stay here? They lived at quite a different pace from ours and we noticed that almost all outsiders were frustrated by the slowness of life until they managed to detune and accept the speed of the islands. Once one gave in and accepted, life became liveable again.

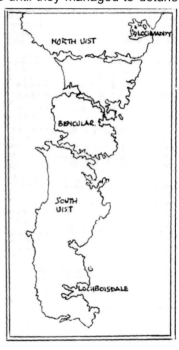

We spent quite some time in the Lochmaddy Hotel, the centre of all life, talking to potential travellers seeking a lift for David and Rita down to the south of the islands, but without success. We met the crew of a big patrol boat which had been out at St Kilda over the last few days and they said that it had been as bad as they had ever experienced. Somehow, I was pleased to hear it.

We each engaged in the Timetable Game where we attempted to design a travel itinery to transport by ferry, coach and railway David and Rita back, by all manner of different routes, but we always ended up stuck in some remote highland spot awaiting transport for the next link the following day. The game was compulsive and more taxing than Monopoly and Trivial Pursuits combined. Eventually it was crystal clear to all players that overnight stops were required unless they could start off from a different square in the game. That square was called Loch Boisdale, Monday morning, 06.30, but it was fifty miles away against appalling weather in thick fog.

Sunday 16 August.
For the sake of sanity we had a morning session in the hotel again. We had never been stuck in one place for so long. At dinnertime as we all squeezed into the dinghy to return to the boat I noticed a

sudden forty degree wind-shift to the west. I was explaining the significance of this development when, as I spoke, the mist began to clear and there was an amazing transformation. We looked around and could see the place (to a height of about 200ft) for the first time in a week.

The weather had dealt a new card in the game and we were all so fed up with being in the same place for so long that I instantly decided to have a change of scenery now that it had materialised and go for Loch Boisdale. Getting caught halfway there and having to pull into an even more remote spot was a strong possibility, but that was all part of the gamble in the game. Twenty minutes later at 13.30 the sails were up, the anchor aboard, and the boat was speeding down the harbour on a run for the entrance.

MI issue 259. Episode 54.

North Uist - Barra - Canna.
August 16 - August 18.
We were so pleased to have escaped from the claustrophobic mists of Lochmaddy after having been trapped there for almost a week. The wind shift which had allowed the cloud to lift might only last for a short while, but we were desperate to leave after having been cooped up there for so long. We headed for the entrance as soon as it was visible, still lashing things down on board and getting ready to put to sea. We were attempting to reach Loch Boisdale, to allow two of our crew to catch the ferry the following morning and we wanted to make it there before nightfall.

Rounding the headland we sheeted in tight and felt the boat begin to rise and fall, cutting through the clean sparkling waves as we took deep breaths of the fresh sea air, enjoying our freedom at last. We went south, close hauled on starboard averaging eight knots and with the boat running on rails, eagerly responding to our urge to make progress before the weather closed in again. It wasn't long before we were passing the island of Ronay and then Benbecula. The whole crew was on deck trying to identify each distant lump and bump of land as we rounded headlands and new navigational sights came into view. Pure white gulls soared around us, accompanying us as official outriders, calling their appreciation over our wake as we sped along.

Clearing Wiay Island the wind dropped in strength and our magic eight knot average became five. By the time we were passing Loch Skiport we were struggling to make three or four knots and the wind was falling lighter. Usinish lighthouse was the two thirds stage of our journey and in order to reach it we had to resort to motoring.

Behind Usinish stood the impressive mountains of Hecla and Ben More; we were treated to some superb weather effects as the clouds, looking solidly white, came rolling over the high ridges and tumbling down the mountain sides resembling dry ice on a theatre set. The sunlight played constant tricks with the colours and we were all impressed and enjoying the journey.

At 17.00 the lighthouse was abeam and we were just beginning to congratulate ourselves on our progress when the weather played another card in the game. The wind returned but from dead ahead and kicked up sufficient waves to slow our progress and force us to set the sails again, but this time we had to tack out to sea.

The southerly wind always felt colder and brought fog with it. We now began to understand the meaning of those pretty white clouds we'd been admiring up on the mountain tops. Soon the land disappeared and we were alone in an eerie blank world. Fog, when sailing close to land is not a pleasant feeling. All the bright conversations aboard became rather muted. The wind was dying again. We slowed right down. The wind headed us, we tacked and we began to go back in towards the coast. Conversations had now ceased. Everyone aboard peered forward into the fog, disoriented, wondering if the compass was right, experiencing strong sensations of heading in the wrong direction; worrying that a cliff would suddenly loom up ahead, or a rock would rise from the water. We sailed on. What would this be like when darkness eventually fell?

The fog ahead brightened. A headland at Rubha na Brataich appeared at a safe distance and we heaved a sigh of relief, lifting our spirits again. The theatrical nature of the way the land came and went as the sunlight pierced the cloud or a puff of wind revealed it, was worth a front row seat. In the light wind we started our engine again to allow us to hold a course which maintained visible contact with the land about a mile offshore. At 16.15 we were off the entrance to Loch Eynort when the wind shifted very firmly to the south-east. We set the genoa once more, and sailed on the same southerly heading as we had done earlier on the trip, but this time we were on port instead of starboard tack. The mist lifted and we made good progress again to arrive off Loch Boisdale at 19.34, eventually anchoring in the small harbour near the ferry pier. Within an hour the fog clamped down finally and shortly afterwards it grew dark. We were very pleased to have made it in a very tight weather window and to some extent to have rounded off a less than satisfactory week, on a slightly better note.

David and Rita were able to transfer directly to the ferry ship, because the system allows passengers to stay aboard in overnight accommodation cabins so that they are ready for the 06.30 start the following morning.

Monday 17 August.
When the ferry left, I glanced out of the window to see its stern light disappearing into the fog. The mist didn't lift until about midday. We had a lazy morning and went to the shop. I say **the** shop because there really was only one, which was organised by some kind of farming cooperative. The hardware section took us right back to the sights and smells of childhood, many years ago. This was still a land before the age of supermarkets. The floors were of patterned linoleum and all the goods were displayed in their original brown cardboard packing boxes. The only decorations were the multi-coloured cards which stored lines of pens, combs or packets of rubber bands. There were stiff-bristled long brushes and galvanised mop-pails. Racked high on the wall were shepherd's crooks in a choice of either wood or aluminium. In the cupboard store were cans of sheep dip and de-wormer.

We left Loch Boisdale for Castlebay on Barra ten or twelve miles to the south at about 15.00. We had conditions similar to those for our previous journey. We got off to a good start and then we were becalmed. We occasionally lost the land in mist patches, and finally we resorted to the engine to take us south, down Vatersay Sound to Castlebay itself. In one or two places the channel was very narrow, about 400 metres and we were amazed to see that these points were the favourite places to set lobster pots, not just at the edges but right in the middle of the fairway. Thinking that the harbour might be a little exposed to a south westerly we explored a small bay on the Vatersay side, but found it very shallow and so returned to anchor in the bay to the north-west of the ferry pier, right in front of the town.

Castlebay was of interest to me mainly because I had read about it so frequently as a stopover place in the Round Britain Race. It was more populous and more visually interesting than the places that we had recently visited. The castle looked rather mouldy with the greenery growing on its walls and it was not a remarkable feature when viewed from the water. The town itself was spread around the shores of a nicely circular hillside and we were anchored close to the centre of that circle. The result was that sounds from all around the bay were reflected to us across the water, making it appear to be very noisy to ears that had become accustomed to more remote anchorages.

Whilst we were at Castlebay there was only one other yacht there. The same could be said for Loch Boisdale. When we sailed from place to place we rarely saw more than three yachts in the day and these were usually so distant that only the sails could be distinguished. The area around Castlebay was studded with coves and beaches so there was no real need to stay near the town as there was the option of many other anchorages. This was true of the majority of the Hebrides in our experience. The sailing was there, the anchorages were, so were the views and the only problem was the weather, which could not be relied upon.

Tuesday 18 August

The forecast was for the usual force five but we looked forward to having the wind in our favour, just for once, to run back across the Little Minch to the island of Canna. We struggled out of the harbour at 10.15 with a barely lifting spinnaker. An hour later we'd only reached the outer harbour buoy with a very limp sail. After another hour we simply came to a stop, with everything including our faces hanging vertically. The weather had won again, so we started the engine and set off across a flat sea for the 35 mile crossing to Canna. The sun shone and we started to peel off our oiles, then we dug out the autopilot to free everyone aboard to set about cleaning and airing the interior of the boat which had become so damp in the prolonged period of wet, cool, dreary days that had just passed.

Carpets, bedding and clothes were lugged on deck until we looked like a floating Chinese laundry motoring towards the mountains of Rhum which acted as our beacon. We scrubbed, cleaned and tidied our way across the Sea of the Hebrides to arrive off Canna's northern coast about 16.00

Compared to its near neighbour Rhum, Canna appears to be rather flat, but the sea cliffs on the northern side go up to about 600ft high. We'd tidied up and we were beginning to watch the many cormorants fishing in the waters around us when we noticed what appeared to be distant small explosions in the water just below the cliffs. Against the high dark backcloth of the land we spotted the elegant, wide white wingspan of the gannets.

We were treated to the sight of a lifetime, the spectacular aerial display of the gannets feeding time. They flew at a height of between 150 to 200ft, going slowly into the wind. On spotting a fish they half folded their wings into a supersonic sweptback mode which allowed instant descent. They fell like stones, crash diving at enormous speed into the sea. At the final instant their wings folded right back like an umbrella, into a sharp white dart and they plunged deep under the water in an explosion of white spray. We passed the binoculars around and gave each other running commentaries about the location of birds about to dive. We shouted with approval as bird after bird peeled away and plummeted downwards in a breath-taking performance. It was thrilling to see and as a cruising experience, akin to meeting dolphins or porpoise at sea, but more rarely seen.

We'd come to Canna Harbour, because it is a classic and it is often chosen by cruising writers to illustrate the quality of Hebridean anchorages. We were not to be disappointed.

MI issue 260. Episode 55.
<u>August 18 - August 20. Canna - Sound of Mull.</u>
Canna harbour is one of the classic Hebridean anchorages. It was lush and green. It was one of the places that we saw cultivated fields, which was an indication of the sheltered quality of its surroundings. The main features on land were two tiny churches standing in isolation on either shore. The one on the island of Sanday to the south resembles the ornately-roofed Scandinavian churches. The one to the north on the island of Canna had a starkly bare, pencil-like tower similar to the protective towers that I have seen in Ireland, into which the people fled to escape the Vikings.

The small cliff headland on the starboard side of the entrance was decorated with the painted names of the many yachts that had visited the harbour. There was plenty of anchoring space and the water was clear. Small fishing boats came in to tie alongside a little pier just inside the entrance on the Canna side whilst their crews processed their catch. We went that way when we were ashore for our evening walk.

Gulls wheeled and dipped around the boats where the men were gutting their fish. Heads emerged from the water as inquisitive seals patrolled backwards and forwards about 20 metres away trying to pluck up courage to come in closer to where the fishermen were throwing food scraps directly into the water from their cutting and trimming table in the waist of the craft.

The gulls were making a great commotion scooping up all the tit-bits almost before they hit the water and the seals were becoming more and more agitated in the knowledge of what they were missing. Eventually one very large mottled seal submerged and came in underwater, quite easy for us to see from our vantage point on the quay above the boat. The fisherman sitting with his back to the gunwale was unaware of the seal as it rose up close against the side of the boat. It blasted through the water surface blowing a great

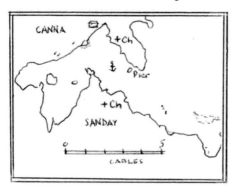

cloud of spray up and over him as it expelled its breath. He almost jumped overboard in surprise, much to our amusement. Even the seal seemed to appreciate the joke.

The fisherman was actually picking out huge prawns from the catch and tossing the fish overboard. Having been reminded by the seal that he should give them an equal chance with the seagulls, he selected a biggish fish and tossed it well out for the seals. Half in jest, I called down to him that we could have eaten that one (as it was bigger than we'd seen in the shops). He asked if we wanted some fish and promptly went off to find a plastic carrier bag. He started throwing fish into it until we protested that we'd not be able to eat such a quantity. He accepted no payment for about a dozen biggish whiting. Rather than waste them we selected six for ourselves and then I took the remainder around the other yachts which had come into the anchorage. This was the busiest anchorage that we came across outside Tobermory as there were six boats in that evening. I had a pleasant time chatting to the other people as I toured with my gifts of fish. All the other craft were chartered.

One other abiding memory of Canna was the telephone. The traditional, red public box retained the old Button A, Button B - call the operator system. All subscribers on the island were listed on a board inside the box. As they only went to double figures there was no need for a phone book. There were instructions that if (when you were using the phone to call off the island) you were 'beeped', would you please complete your call rapidly, as it was an indication that someone else wanted to use one of the other phones.

<u>Wed August 19</u>.
The morning was quite pleasant, but we waited until the afternoon to sail back to Loch Scresort on Rhum. No sooner had we left than the weather clouded over and a strong south-easterly began to blow. We were returned to the grey, misty, cold place that we'd experienced at Lochmaddy. The wind went up to force 6 as we tore along the north-western side of Rhum fast reaching. The land kept disappearing in the cloud and the rain fell in torrents. If it hadn't been for the speed it would have been a most miserable experience. Clearing the northern tip of Rhum we had a very lumpy beat to get into the loch, which being open to the east was far from being a smooth anchorage. We managed to find some shelter by using our shallow draught and getting close against the southern shore at the head of the loch.

The weather was terrible with rain cascading down and strong winds. In a brief respite in the deluge we attempted to catch up on our washing. Our socks were taken up on deck in our plastic washing-up bowl, to be pegged to the rigging in the belief that either the wind would dry them or the rain would rinse them more thoroughly. The pegs were in an old polythene bread bag. The wind was so strong that a gust blew the empty bowl and bag straight off the deck into the water. I scrambled to launch our tender, mentally trying to choose which to save first before it sank; either the bowl or the bag of pegs? I was making for the bowl, but the bag was sinking, when a gull which had been perched on a nearby boat swooped down and seized the bread bag. It struggled to take-off into the air with the bag in its beak but when it realised that this was futile it attempted to get inside the bag instead, all the time keeping it afloat. This gave me time to rescue the bowl and then head for the gull, which appeared to be re-reading the words on the bag to check that the meal would be worth the effort. It gave up the struggle as I approached and I grabbed the bag as it slowly sank beneath the surface. We threw him a crust later as a reward for saving our pegs.

245

<u>Thursday 20 August</u>
It bucketed with rain all night and we felt very sorry for the hardy people who were in a couple of tents on the shore side. A big passenger ferry came into the loch early in the morning and people were transferred ashore in an open blue launch looking very dejected and bedraggled. Visibility was so bad that it was questionable as to whether we should leave, but we had an incoming crew to meet at Tobermory so there was little choice. The wind dropped temporarily as we motored out on a compass course to take us to the east of Eigg. Just after passing the northern tip of Eigg, which was dimly visible to starboard the wind returned exactly on the nose and began to kick up waves. We were close hauled heading due east for half an hour until I estimated that on the other tack we would hopefully clear Eigg's southern corner which was an off lying island called Eillean More. We tacked and had to make 210°m to clear the island but could only do 200°m sailing freely enough to minimise leeway. We sped along into the mist, making good progress and the wind freed slightly to allow us to clear the land. The lighthouse on the island was visible abeam at 14.15 and our course freed further to 220°m as we sped towards the headland of Ardnamurchan hidden somewhere about nine miles ahead.

We were calculating on a fast crossing and even beginning to keep a special eye out to port for signs of approaching land when suddenly the wind increased. I immediately began rolling in the genoa, but the change was happening so rapidly that even as I was doing it, I was forced to revise the amount of sail area that we could use. As I wound the handle I had to wind it further for we needed less and less sail. I scrambled up on deck and began reefing the main, rolling it well down as I sensed that I might not get another chance. The wind had already risen to force 6 and the sea was cutting up very rough. We were being headed and finding it difficult to steer; the boat was being thrown around with water going everywhere. We'd been exploiting the tide going south through this channel between the islands, but we now found ourselves in wind against tide conditions off a notorious headland, in bad visibility, with the wind at force 7 and gusting over 8. I'd fallen into the trap of cruising complacency once again and was being sharply reminded that even a routine passage could become a serious test.

We were wrestling to keep control in such rough conditions because the waves were throwing her all over the place and steering was somewhere between 270 and 210. I wryly wondered how

246

evening-class plotters would calculate the variation/deviation on a course like that.

The wind was on the move again and as it went south the visibility cleared briefly, to allow us one last fix on the Adrnamurchan lighthouse. To seaward we spotted another yacht also doing battle in the same way as ourselves. It was comforting to think that we were not alone in our suffering. We could see that we were having to head westwards, further out to sea and might even get driven as far across as Coll before we would find any shelter. With this short message clearly delivered, the fog descended once more and we were alone in our little circle of mist with waves attacking us from every direction, crashing water all over us.

The wind headed us even more as it continued to move south west, so I decided to go for the inshore tack. Executing the tack itself was a bad experience with the sheets lashing the doghouse like demented pythons and the effort on the sheet winch, whilst being deluge with salt water, sufficient to exhaust the crew. Now we were sailing towards an invisible rocky shore, climbing over lines of watery hurdles that came foaming and hissing into our tiny sphere. We

 anxiously peered ahead, but it was difficult to look upwind with rain stinging the eyeballs. What was that? Was it an island ahead? Was it rocks? Everybody strained to see. Go about! Go about! Tack NOW! TACK NOW! The crew were shouting over the howl of the wind. White water crashed into foam on a jagged black rock projecting from the water 20 metres off the port bow. The loosened sail thundered. The boat smashed and slewed by waves, headed up and came through the wind. Tired muscles found the strength of desperation on the sheet winch. We inched forward, picking up speed, hoping, praying that we were not ringed by the sharp rocky teeth in the driven mist and spray. If we hit now it would cut through her hull and open her up like a can. We felt the unease beneath our feet and a shiver down our spines. We desperately scanned our little grey circle but as the seconds ticked away we gradually allowed ourselves to feel rising relief. "I didn't like that."

said a small voice, to break our silence. 'Neither did anybody else."
came the grim reply.

I was beginning to wonder about our options. We were taking a real pasting and to turn and run would not ease the situation. Finding our way to shelter behind an island involved the very real risk of hitting the island at considerable speed. It would be very dangerous. We weren't out of danger by doing what we were doing. Where was that other yacht? It would be just our luck to come together. Things were looking very tough.

Suddenly the mist ended and the wind disappeared. It was astonishing. We were all caught completely unawares. We were actually braced against the blast, shielding our eyes against ... against - nothing. It was a total surprise. It just stopped. The sea was still hurling us about and crashing all around us, but the wind had gone in a vertical wall of mist that receded to the north. I did not believe that such an instant change in the weather was possible. We looked in disbelief at each other, water still streaming off our oilskins and then ventured to look around in amazement. Our partner yacht had gone out to sea.

We had to start the motor to give us steering control, because we had no forward movement. I unrolled the main and sheeted it flat to resist the rolling of the boat in the rough waves and flat calm. The first of a new breeze came in from the west allowing us to head south towards the headland about two miles distant. The other boat was a big ketch setting full main and a big headsail. He was going our way. We cut our motor and set three-quarters of our genoa, being cautious of sudden wind changes. He was a mile and a half back and half a mile to windward. He was quite fast. I remembered the saying: If there are two boats on the water, they are racing. He gradually came closer by sailing a freer course and cutting the corner at the headland.

Once around the corner we ran with the wind on the quarter, and our full genoa came out. He set more sail too. We both tried tacking downwind and running goosewinged as we came further into the Sound of Mull. He piled sail on, but made no impression on us. I was feeling very smug and contented in a cruising kind of way, having escaped the rocks, survived the gale, made the passage and was holding off the opposition, when looking forward I noticed something odd about my roller-genoa luff spar.

Examination revealed that the alloy tube of the spar had snapped in two about 150mm above the roller drum. The wire forestay had cut upwards into the tube which had dropped down alongside the broken bottom section. This serious compound fracture could mean that I would be unable to roll the sail, or remove it from the spar when I reached Tobermory. I had less than 30 minutes to find a solution.

When would I learn not to get too smug about this cruising game?

MI issue 261. Episode 56.

20 August Tobermory - 24 August Loch Aline.

We were heading in towards Tobermory and my mind was wrestling with the problems of my shattered genoa luff spar. Would I be able to roll up the big sail when I reached the harbour? I had visions of sailing around unable to douse the sail; we sailed on and I pondered.

The aluminium tube had broken near to the bottom and it had dropped down alongside the lower section of tube attached to the drum. My first action was to lash the two pieces of tube together as it looked as though twist could be imparted from the roller drum to the luff spar with them firmly tied to each other. We experimented with rolling the sail and fortunately it worked. As we approached Tobermory entrance we managed to roll the whole sail, with sighs of relief from all on board.

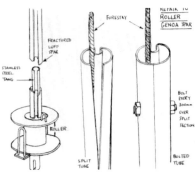

The moorings were full, but we used a useful dodge that I have learned for just such a situation, tying up alongside an abandoned derelict yacht which occupied one of the moorings. I was pleased to get in after such a rough passage down from Rhum and pleased that I could pick up my new crew next day, but the pleasure was overshadowed by the problem with the luff spar.

Friday 21 August.

John Morton left on the 9.50 bus and Alison arrived, as did previous crews, on the 14.20 bus which did not appear to feature on any timetable, such are the vagaries of Hebridean transport. The major challenge was, of course, the luff spar which turned out to be in a much worse condition than I had first suspected. After removing the sail it became clear that not only was the bottom of the tube sheared across but the top had become detached from its swivel and the upper sections of tube had split down the front. The top tube had developed a permanent twist of more than 180 degrees so that the luff groove faced forward at the top. This was all a disaster because the sail cannot be used without its spar. I had tried to do this in the past and had discovered that the sail's power simply destroyed any equipment used to try to control it. The real solution was to try to replace the tubes but that wasn't possible in our remote situation.

I went up the mast; dismantled the whole arrangement and brought it down on deck. From a cruiser's viewpoint I would stress, as I have done previously, that having steps up the mast made this relatively straightforward. Having a 'safety' forestay about 300mm ahead of the roller stay which supports the mast in the event of failure of the roller system also eased the whole operation.

I applied three solutions to make the system serviceable again. I trimmed the broken ends of the tube with a hacksaw and file which shortened it by only a few inches. The tube was then secured to the roller drum at the bottom by being forced onto its stainless steel tang.

The split tubes were pulled back together by drilling holes in opposite sides and putting stainless steel bolts through, taking care to allow space for the forestay to rotate inside the tube. Finally the re-assembled tube was untwisted as much as possible and re-attached to its upper swivel with self-tapping screws.

To begin with we did not trust the lashed-up system and we sailed with three rolls in the genoa to reduce stress, but gradually as it stood the test of time we gained confidence and soon we used it as normal. One source of worry was the projecting bolt heads which could have torn the sail. They were taped over. The tape could not be wrapped all around the tube as it would have fouled the sail track. Thinking of how to make the taping neater triggered another solution in my mind. At a later stage I brought down the spar once again and used glassfibre onto the tube across the split. Once this was set the bolts were removed and further glass applied. The temporary repair became permanent and the boat continued to sail with this system.

What had appeared to be an almost hopeless task had yielded to simple solutions evolved slowly, following careful thinking about each separate aspect of the problem. The initial reaction had been to think that nothing less than the expensive replacement of the whole tube system would be sufficient, but eventually a few stainless bolts and screws then some glass tape and dabs of resin did the trick.

<u>Saturday afternoon 22 August</u>
Back in working order and with no pressing schedule, *Starship* with myself, Gill and Alison aboard departed for some wanderings around the local lochs with only the rough idea of making our way towards our winter quarters.

We went across to Drumbuie which is known as one of the best anchorages in the Hebrides. We shaped a visual course for its entrance only to notice a rock breaking the surface ahead, delivering another sharp reminder to me not to be too casual about pilotage in these parts where size and scale can trick the senses.

Drumbuie has a narrow rock entrance but once inside it opens into a perfect pirate's lair, completely enclosed with lush green wooded shores. There are two preferred stopping places. In the south-west corner a brook meanders through trees and grassy banks to a beach which is idyllically beautiful. If the midges were removed it might be totally perfect. From the water we could see the names of visiting yachts written in white across the flat black rocks ashore, similar to those painted on the cliffs at Canna harbour. Once ashore we found that the names weren't painted, but were written in sea-shells which had been gathered from the beach and painstakingly arranged into intricate shapes. Each of us explored individually, enchanted by the perfection of the grass, the trees, the stream, the whole setting. I climbed high up the hill to look

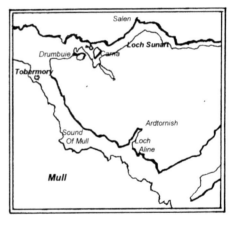

down on the bay with its single white trimaran and beyond it to the varied bays and islands of Loch Sunart to the north. It was a sight to savour. The night was mirror calm as usual in these inner bays.

<u>Sunday August 23</u>.
There was a gentle north-easterly so we decided to sail up Loch Sunart, which has seventeen miles of navigable water. If by some magical trick this loch could be moved to the south-east corner of Britain it would be absolutely packed with every type of floating craft and its shores would be studded with habitation of the most

expensive kind. Situated where it is, it's virtually empty and other craft are so rare that one can make-believe that the whole loch is your very own as you sail along.

I augmented the charts by following the Clyde Cruising Club directions for the area. They frequently used descriptions such as the following: *'...keep the northern extremity of Carna in line with the 41m peak on Risga (bearing 273) to clear Dun Ghallian rock.'* Despite having done quite a lot of sailing over the years I had never previously bothered too much with such descriptions as I have usually been too busy to absorb their complexity, or have found that the wind would not allow me to hold the courses described anyway. I have preferred charts or sketches which made the information more graphically clear, but on this occasion I did try to follow the descriptions and found that they worked very well.

We leisurely sailed through the forest seeing only the occasional house apparently perched in the tree-tops, until we reached a little hamlet called Salen, when the wind, which had been fitful suddenly piped up and we began to sail at around 10 knots. We turned and ran back down the loch in double quick time. When we reached the narrow channels nearer to the entrance around the islands of Risga and Carna we suddenly found significant tide rips as the water tumbled towards us, building rapids as it forced its way through the constrictions to build up the seventeen miles of head water. In general we had not been aware of heavy tidal flows except at restricted places such as this, but when we met this considerable flow we were pleased to be able to use our boat-speed to skim over the top and make light of the turbulence.

We returned to Drumbuie and this time chose to go into its northern anchorage that has a sheltered bay with vegetation so lush that we discovered ruined cottages buried in jungles of irises like a lost village in the deepest Amazon rainforest. We climbed the hills, to enjoy the panorama of lakes and mountains and sunbathed on the shore or casually beachcombed.

Drumbuie was the tops with us.

Monday 24 August.
We returned to Tobermory to replenish our stores and then departed again to sail down through the Sound of Mull to Loch Aline. The wind was force two, northerly, which would lead one to expect that the wind would blow from that direction. This was not so. The wind was funnelled by the valleys which meant that we ran down the sound using the wind deflected in from the western end until we reached a

mid-point where we were becalmed for about a mile and had to motor until we met the wind which was channelled into the sound from the opposite end. As we sailed close hauled to the east, we noticed a change in the world around us. We counted twelve sailing craft in sight at one moment. In the outer isles that we had become accustomed to, we would not have seen that number in a week. The shores became softer, the hills greener and we felt that we were crossing a broad threshold into a more velvet scenery.

We caught up with some friends in a Rival yacht *Vane Jane* who were heading for Loch Aline like ourselves, so we agreed to meet up there. The entrance to the loch is narrow and a ferry is marked on the chart. I understood this to mean that a small craft plied across its mouth. As I headed for the entrance a large car-carrying passenger ferry emerged to cross to Mull causing me to make some swift adjustments to my course. We anchored near the head of the loch near other moored craft and later walked ashore to admire the impressive Ardtornish House which stands like a castle amongst the trees. From a bridge over a fast-flowing stream we watched a fisherman standing in the rapids fly fishing in the traditional manner. We climbed to the ruined keep of Kinlochaline castle to look at it stark walls and rusting iron-barred windows; returning, we discussed such weighty problems as the technical distinction between swifts, swallows and martins that wheeled and swooped all around us, making the most of the many midges and, can herons float on water? We watched them fly across it and stand at the edge of it, but if they should land in the middle of it, do they sink?

It will be seen that, for once, we were in true touring mode, without targets or deadlines, not stressed by weather nor gear problems, with scenery, feeling secure and with stores on board. Free to meander, to read, to sail or to walk. Wouldn't it be nice if cruising was always like this?

MI issue 262. Episode 57.

Tuesday 25 August Loch Aline
Season's end.
We were wandering. Cruising as it should be, drifting around the Inner Hebrides slowly heading towards our winter quarters.

On a fine still morning we motored gently out of Loch Aline south-eastwards from the Sound of Mull for Loch Spelve, timing our arrival there for low water at about 13.30. The entrance channel was narrow and curved against the northern shore. The written description relating to how to enter had many instructions about a particular rock which was waiting to ensnare the unwary. It all read so horrendously that we were very anxious about attempting what appeared to be such a dangerous entrance. It turned out to be a lot of fuss about almost nothing. Some kind-hearted person had spent much time painting crosses and circles on boulders ashore to

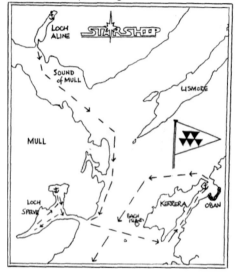

indicate the position of the hazard by transits and entering at low water we could actually see the offending rock awash. By keeping to the southern side with twelve feet on the echo sounder we managed to steer well clear of this particular danger which seemed to us to be on the northern limit of the navigable channel.

Outside in the firth a cold southerly wind had sprung up but inside the loch the air was warm, soft and completely different. We motored gently down the southern arm of the loch appreciating the western shore which was dominated by impressive mountains rising over 2,000ft above us.

At the misty loch side there was cattle-grazing pasture which gradually ascended into sheep-grazing, then heather fells and finally the lofty granite buttresses projecting through the clouds. As we went along a light breeze came to clear the misty veil allowing the sun to break through onto the fell side. Visibility improved so that individual plants and stones emerged over the whole surface. The greys became greens and purple shadows formed as the true texture of the land became evident. Moments of great visual beauty such as this are commonplace in this area. They happen many times a day and to furnish a true cruise account each one would have to be described, for they were the sights which most occupied us. It is not possible to convey them adequately, so they are omitted and instead, we simple tell of going from place to place, and our cruise becomes a catalogue of names.

On this Hebridean cruise every crew member was at some stage deeply impressed with the quality of the changing scene due to variations in light and visibility. Every crew member gave up trying to photograph their impressions of these effects, because it was as futile as trying to capture the intricate sensory qualities of a firework display in black and white on an eight shot box-Brownie camera. You had to be there and to be surrounded by it, to look around and see it working, moving, shifting. It was only there for a moment and then it had evolved into something else too vast and too wonderful for a mere camera to catch.

At the head of the Loch we turned, set a little of the genoa and drifted back along its length to eventually anchor in the north-west corner near to the delta of a river which entered there. A friendly seal came to check us over, but we weren't too interested because we had come in search of a sea otter, or even more exciting, an eagle which we had been given to understand sometimes made its appearance there. Needless to say, we almost wore out our binoculars scanning every inch of mountain and loch without any success, except that we found a solitary snipe feeding on the mud. Whoever held the binoculars entertained or bored the rest of the crew with an interminable running commentary about every action of this little celebrity.

<u>Wed 26 August.</u>
In the night the wind got up and the boat began to snatch at her anchor. The wind was being funnelled by the mountain to the west of us and our anchorage was exposed. I didn't need my alarm for the 05.55 shipping forecast which gave us gale force. I immediately dressed and roused the crew, for the longer we stayed, the worse it might become. It was grey outside with flurries of white horses rushing across the water towards us. In the general activity to get away the boat sailed herself sideways over her anchor rode and the wind held her in such a way that she sailed her anchor out which gave us a few anxious moments.

The wind was right behind us, so we set one third genoa and departed for the entrance. The water was entering at two to three knots and the wind was exiting at force 5 and rising. We cut straight through the tidal overfalls, looking out into the firth to see what conditions were like. It didn't seem too rough, but that was only a temporary illusion. Once clear of the land we began to feel the wind coming down the Sound of Mull and we set off at quite a rate. We headed across towards Bach Island with an awkward quartering sea then rounded the southern tip of Kerrera into the narrow sound which took us up to Oban.

It is an odd thing, but when one visits a remote anchorage it is usually an easy matter to seek out the best place to anchor. The more urban a place becomes the more difficult it can be to discover the approved mooring place. Oban becomes a tricky lee shore with a strong north-westerly blowing, so we went across to Ardantrive Bay and attached ourselves to a sheltered mooring buoy, there to catch up on our sleep.

August 27 - 28

We loitered around Oban and then went south in clear conditions to pass back through Cuan Sound to sail inside Shuna. A biggish monohull followed us through the sound and cut a few corners to catch up with us with the intention of testing his speed against ours. Unfortunately he chose close-reaching in force 4 over flat water, which meant that he was never really in the hunt as we went off like a rocket at well over ten knots in sparkling sunshine and clear water. We were sailing up-sun over the blinding reflections of pure light on the water which was a sensual delight and one of those memorable moments which will live with us forever. It was a fitting conclusion to our sailing season. We eventually turned and ran back. The weather broke later that day and we had to spend a day or so at anchor cooking and reading whilst listening to the rain drumming on the deck before heading for our over-wintering place.

We left the boat and drove south to home. After Christmas we heard that the yard where we had left the boat was in financial difficulties and *Starship* had not be stored ashore, but had remained on a mooring through the winter.

She came to no harm and the following Easter we were travelling north again to prepare her for a journey to the far north. Our plan was to round Cape Wrath and sail along the north coast of Scotland to Orkney and then go even further north to Shetland.

We still regarded ourselves as day-sailors who simply kept on going a little further and a little further, so the thought of getting up to the farthest tip of Shetland at Muckle Flugga was daunting. Once at that turning point, further north even than Bergen in Norway, we would have to work our way back to the tip of the Scottish mainland and on down the east coast. Aberdeen would feel to be a long way south. Tyneside would be almost next to London from this far-north perspective. We'd have to cross the Firth of Forth, visit the Yorkshire coast, traverse the Wash and hopefully return to East Anglia.

Year 4.

Serial Starship

Much of the information about electronic technology, prices, locations and facilities will have changed and improved. Some of our decisions and evaluations will no longer be relevant, but they are included for the sake of continuity and understanding the relevance of the decisions taken at the time.

MI issue 278. Episode 58.

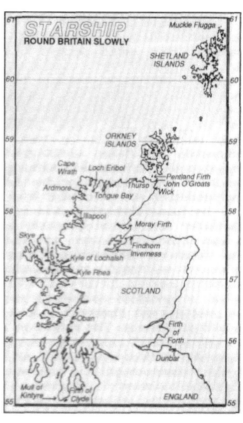

The final year.
It is only fair to warn purist cruisers that this final season had more than its fair share of appalling cruising incidents for which the skipper alone was to blame. One learns the complexities of cruising by experience and the account which follows will include all of my terrible mistakes in the hope that others may benefit from our experiences.

The situation.
Starship was on a mooring in a sheltered bay just to the south of Oban on the Scottish west coast. It may seem to be already a long way north, but it was still 200 sailing miles to the south of Cape Wrath which is the name given to the north-west corner of Scotland. In order to make the best use of our summer holiday sail we had to get *Starship* nearer to that corner during the Spring Bank Holiday week in May, but we had a problem. Where is there a suitable place to leave a boat up there from May until August?

We had searched for a place without success until I chanced to see the adventurer John Ridgeway MBE on the television one evening. He is most famous for rowing across the North Atlantic with Chay Blyth, but he has also led expeditions in the Sahara and up the Amazon as well as circumnavigating the globe under sail. He has an adventure school close to Cape Wrath where he keeps his sailing boats and I wondered if he could help me to find somewhere for *Starship*. I had one of his books 'Round the World with Ridgeway' on my shelves and taking it down I was surprised and pleased to see photographs of the area near to his house which appeared to offer the shelter that I was looking for. Carefully reading the first chapter of the book and referring to a road map, allowed me to conjure up an address and I sent off a letter. He replied quickly and positively, so we set off by car at Eastertime to seek him out and confirm an arrangement.

The 1,850 mile Recce.

My wife Alison and I drove north on Scotland's east coast to investigate likely harbours and possible anchorages. We stayed overnight at Dunbar on the south side of the Firth of Forth where the harbour had a very narrow rock-bound entrance which we decided we would prefer not to use. We crossed the Grampian mountains to Findhorn on the south side of the Moray Firth near Inverness, where we were welcomed by Phemie Davidson and the members of the Royal Findhorn Yacht Club. We had met Phemie through her late husband Hugh who had been an enthusiastic Telstar trimaran sailor. Findhorn is a special place with superb sailing and we decided to use it as a staging post on our journey.

Another 200 miles northwards via Wick harbour brought us to John O'Groats to resolve a question that we'd previously been unable to answer. Can you see across the Pentland Firth to the Orkney Islands? The answer was yes, easily. In fact the view was magnificent, breath taking and we were surprised that it has not been more widely publicised as a tourist attraction, because it was well worth the journey from the opposite end of the country. Staying overnight in Thurso we made the mistake of ordering true Scottish porridge for breakfast. One instantly discovers when the first spoonful hits the tongue that it is made with heavy quantities of salt as a 'sweetener'. It is like drinking a glassful of seawater and the immediate shock reaction is to spray it across the breakfast table or to be violently ill, both of which we narrowly avoided.

The single-track road which winds along the northern coast of Scotland is a holiday experience in itself, for the scenery is very beautiful with many deserted, sheltered, sandy beaches to seaward and snow-capped mountains (at this time of year) inland. The valleys at Tongue Bay and Loch Eribol to the west were visual highlights of the journey after which we turned southwards for the first time in several days to seek out John Ridgeway.

Ardmore Adventure School.
We drove down a track towards Ardmore until it ended 1½ miles later in the middle of a barren moor. We parked and began walking down a path for another three quarters of a mile until it gradually diminished, then ended. Ahead was a climb up a boggy waterfall which tested calf muscles and lungs. At the top we were lost, so began searching, wondering which sheep path to take. We scrambled around in a wood, picked a narrow path and followed it down into a steep meadow where there were prefabricated buildings which had been brought in by water. Here, in a house on the hillside, overlooking a magnificent panorama of lochs and mountains we found John Ridgeway. We chatted about our trip here, for which he used the military term 'recce' i.e. reconnaissance. He indicated the area where he thought *Starship* might be moored for her stay and also told us how to gain access to the loch at a different point to make it a little easier to load stores aboard.

From Ardmore we went southwards trying to follow the coast, but the mountains don't allow a true coast road. The alignment of the valleys means that the narrow roads must zigzag back and forth, making swift progress impossible and doubling distances as the car in effect 'tacks' towards its destination. The constant reward is the scenery which makes one wish to linger at every turn in the road and every hill crest.

The Kyles.
We stayed overnight in Ullapool which was originally founded as a fishing base by Dutch herring fleets and then we drove to the Kyle of Lochalsh. The word kyle means a narrow strip of water, a bit like the word strait and the kyle we were looking at was between the island of Skye and the mainland. Skye is probably the best known of all Scottish islands because of the song which begins:
Speed bonnie boat, like a bird on the wing,
Over the sea to Skye,
Giving the impression that Skye is far offshore, which it clearly is not. It is just across the strip of water a few hundred metres wide, known as the Kyle of Lochalsh. (*We understand the song relates to a boat*

coming IN from the outer islands, rather than crossing this narrow piece of water, that has since been bridged.) When one is sailing up the west coast of Scotland one can choose a longer route outside Skye or a shorter one through this kyle and another one just to the south called Kyle Rhea. They are aligned at roughly 90 degrees to each other, so a commanding wind is important if they are to be negotiated under sail. The tides are funnelled through the Kyles and the passage is studded with islands, so we took a good look to get a feel for the place and wondered whether we could use this scenic route with the boat.

One hundred and twenty miles to the south we found *Starship* swinging on a mooring. The boatyard where she had been left over the winter was bankrupt, so she had stayed afloat, but she was no worse for the experience except that she needed antifouling. We put her ashore and allowed her to heel on either side to be painted.

Ashore for antifouling

The range was not great and we had to work swiftly before the incoming tide halted progress. The next day the weather was bad which stopped any further external work on her so we packed our things and headed home. The next time that we'd see her would be in late May when we would have a week to get her up to Ardmore. We hoped for better weather. Our car had clocked up 1,850 miles on the recce by the time we reached home again.

MI issue 279. Episode 59.
<u>Cuan Sound - Kyleakin.</u>
Friday May 27
I'd arrived home in Suffolk from a visit to a Netherlands multihull meeting at seven in the evening and my alarm was set for one o'clock in the morning; not the best start for the long journey up to Scotland to recommission the boat for the season.

Saturday May 28
Ray Weston our first crewman called for Alison and me at two in the morning and we drove through patchy fog across to Cheshire to link up with Chris Nurney and his wife Lindsay to complete our crew. We took two cars for the rest of the journey. This was not only for comfort, but because we needed a car for the return journey from the eventual destination of this week's cruise to John Ridgeway's adventure school at Ardmore. We stopped for shopping in Glasgow and again in Oban to shorten the distance that we would have to transport stores. We arrived at the boat on the island of Seil, which is connected by a bridge to the mainland, in the early evening. By the time we and all of the gear were ferried aboard we were exhausted.

Sunday May 29.
Ray and Chris went north with both cars on a two day round trip to leave the return vehicle in position at Ardmore. If the weather should stop us from managing to sail there during the week we could be stuck midway in some remote location with our two cars in similarly remote places 100 miles to the north and south of us. This produced plenty of incentive to make the delivery passage successfully. Whilst they were away the remaining three had to prepare the boat.

Monday May 30.
At 15.20 Chris and Ray returned having succeeded in placing the car for our return. The boat was ready to leave following the day-and-a-half of feverish activity. We were reluctant to leave Ray's car here in case we did fall short with the delivery of the boat. We might then find it difficult to cover the last few miles back to the car overland as access to this place wasn't easy. Ray drove it to Dunstaffnage Marina just to the north of Oban, whilst we dropped the mooring at 16.30 to sail the boat there to collect him. It's an unusual time of day to begin sailing, but we were exploiting the fact that it stays light until quite late in these latitudes.

   We motored through Cuan Sound and raised sail in a favourable F3 gusting 4, steering 330°m out into the Firth of Lorne. We were overtaken by rain showers which blotted out Mull and diminished the wind to the point where the motor had to be started, whereupon the wind returned to allow us to sail close-hauled towards the marina. There were a couple of islands at the marina entrance and we wondered whether we dare pass through the gap inside them, but decided on the more cautious but longer route of sailing outside them, not wishing to run aground on the first sail of the year.

We arrived at 20.30, picked up Ray so that now our complex preparations were finally complete.

Tuesday May 31.
The sound of a cuckoo ashore woke me just in time for the 05.55 shipping forecast on a cold grey day with occasional showers. The favourable tides in the Sound of Mull during the afternoon allowed us a leisurely start after tanking up with water and diesel.

We cast off at about 11.30 and cautiously headed for the narrow gap inside the islands that we'd not dared to take the previous evening. We passed slowly through with the echo sounder reading 45ft deep. Ah well, better safe than sorry. The wind was only F2 to 3 occasionally dying, but we reached the bottom end of Lismore and turned for the sound at about 12.30. The wind allowed us to run, then died and came ahead forcing us to tack. After a while it picked up from the Mull shore giving us a close reach and we creamed away over the flat water watching the misty scenery passing on either side. We made steady progress and as Tobermory approached a decision was needed. The original intention had been only to sail this far, but it became clear that we would reach the entrance by 15.30 which was quite early in the day and we would lose good sailing time by stopping. We resisted the siren call of the picturesque little harbour to try to make distance whilst the tide and wind were favourable, but this meant a much longer sail up to Loch Scridain on the island of Rhum (or Rum).

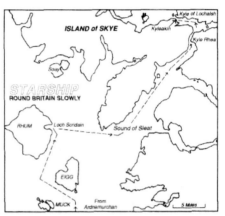

Until this time the water had been flat but as we began to leave the sound so we felt the first surge of the incoming waves and the boat began to move in a more lively fashion. It wasn't possible to see the islands further out to sea. The sea was grey, lumpy and reminiscent of the short random waves of the southern North Sea. Through the mist the white line formed by waves breaking at the base of the hard cliffs around Ardnamurchan told us that we were sailing different seas.

The island of Muck was a bluer patch of grey which came and went periodically, but gradually resolved to stay with us. The crew were rather silent as they hung on. The island of Rhum has a massively mountainous bulk but it remained invisible inside its wreath of captured cloud. Wherever it was hiding it blended so perfectly with grey sea and sky that absolutely nothing could be seen. We had uneasy feelings knowing that it was virtually on top of us but giving no sign of being there. The odd seabird flapped across the swirling water.

The cloud only lifted slightly off the sea to show a dark line when we came right up to the island, but it did not allow us to see the mountains above. As we slid between the walls of Rhum on our left and Eigg on our right we gradually lost the wind and had to motor up into the loch. There were several other craft at anchor but due to our shallow draught we could snuggle right into the south west corner for the most sheltered berth. We were all pretty tired and it was raining fairly heavily, so there was no suggestion of going ashore.

Wednesday June 1

I could have done with a long lie-in to recover from my exhaustion but a pesky cuckoo was seeking a mate at 04.30 in the morning and judging from the number of answering calls it was having a degree of success. It was fine and sunny when we emerged on deck to admire ashore the little white cottages with smoke gently rising from their chimneys, all tucked into forest clearings just like the cottages in fairy stories.

We took advantage of a fresh southerly wind in the loch to sail out and we made good progress for a couple of miles, until a shout from one of the crew

In holiday mood aboard

alerted us to incoming dolphins (Common Porpoise). As I turned to look over the port quarter one of them was completely out of the sea in an exuberant leap and other fins and backs were cutting the water in a wide patch about thirty metres square. They came in fast heading for our bows and everybody aboard was leaping about shouting "Look at that one." "Wow!" "Did you see that?" Ray who has seen them many times before was just saying "What lovely creatures they are." in a reflective kind of way. Every contact that I have had with them I have found to be quite precious. They somehow seem to communicate their sense of joy and fun so well; they're truly wonderful to watch. We were lucky and they stayed for almost five minutes, arcing, leaping and cutting past us from stern to bow at incredible speed just below the surface. When they dropped away from our stern they left us in a happy mood, even though they took the wind away with them.

We had no alternative but to motor on, as the surface of the Sound of Sleat which we were entering, became more and more glassy. The sun burned hotter and at first, trousers were rolled to the knees to reveal stick-white shins, then pullovers were removed and sleeves were rolled up, until it was clear that the crew was in holiday mood. The Autohelm was engaged to free everyone to sunbathe or spring-clean the ship as we progressed.

We moved steadily onwards into increasingly spectacular scenery with the mountains soaring higher on the mainland and a green and rural countryside studded with white houses on Skye to port. At 13.45 the wind came from astern with sufficient strength for us to set the spinnaker which carried us up to the first narrows at Kyle Rhea.

There was a small ferry carrying cars across the entrance which had to be dodged and then we entered the stream of swirling, upwelling pools which rushed us along through the narrow channel. We had learned when passing similar areas of disturbance such as the Swellies in the Menai Straits or the Corryvreckan that they generate food for the sea life and this was no exception. Heads popped out of the surface swirls as seals casually observed our passing. There would be three or four black faces watching us and then with an easy flick of the tail or a flipper slap they'd be gone, down into the soup we sailed upon. Soon we emerged into Loch Alsh being blown along by bitterly cold winds which descended from the high mountains on either side of the pass. We could see the second narrows at the Kyle of Lochalsh where we planned to break our journey for shopping.

On either side of the kyle there is a small village which owes its existence to the ferries constantly moving backwards and forwards. We had chosen to visit the northern (mainland) side, but when we arrived we found it difficult to come alongside easily. There were high piers, no moorings and the constant wash of the commercial craft. In such circumstances I usually resort to asking to come alongside bigger craft already moored. In this way they act as a big fender, allowing me to use shorter warps and lighter gear. As we came nearer we saw the distinctive shape of an Ocean Youth Club ketch which is one of the best craft to go alongside. Their helpful crews are interested in distinctive craft such as ours. Their freeboard makes them easy to transfer onto when going ashore, yet their weight allows them to be sympathetic to the movement of our size of craft whilst still providing a steady platform.

We made a pass and asked permission to come alongside, which they agreed to, but I could see that it was going to be difficult for us. The strong, gusty wind was now blowing in opposition to the tide which was moving at about three knots. If I stemmed the tide, the blasts of wind on our stern sailed us by, even with no sail. If I approached from the other direction using the wind to stop the boat, the tide would catch her in a lull of the wind and spin the stern out into the stream holding her at ninety degrees to the side of the ketch unless we got our stern warps across smartly. The water was rough.

I had a line across with lots of eager young people ready to pull, but I did not have the control that I wanted so I asked to be cast off and we motored over to Kyleakin village on Skye which was considerably more sheltered.

The tiny harbour was very constricted, so as the tide was rising I went further north close up to a muddy beach and anchored in about five feet of water. We were near to a small row of houses and we could see their occupants all looking out to see what this unusual visitor was doing anchoring in front of their windows.

MI issue 280.
Episode 60.

<u>Kyleakin - Ardmore.</u>
<u>Wednesday 1 June</u>.
We had taken a short break in our day's sailing whilst our shopping party went ashore to the small village of Kyleakin on Skye. The boat was anchored near to the shore and when the crew returned with our additional stores we made sail even though it was early evening. As we departed the narrow waters of the Kyle of Lochalsh we sailed into an enormous cruising area centred on the Inner Sound.

Having now sailed all the way around Britain and having seen most of the scenery, for me, the sheltered waters and lochs to the east of the Isle of Skye compose the most beautiful scenic cruising area to be found anywhere in these islands.

A glance at the chart showed a wide choice of anchorages, with many islands and channels so that it was difficult to choose a route to follow. As we were looking for shelter from the west we headed that way toward the windward shore.

Our course took us close hauled across to Longay and along the eastern side of Scalpay where the wind piped up. We were tight on the wind through the Caol Mor and then we turned right into the Raasey Narrows. We had in mind to anchor in The Aird, but when we arrived we found that it was only sheltered from waves made by the south-westerly wind. There was a big swell coming down from the north against the flow of wind and water. In the open waters of the Inner Sound it had not been noticeable, but Raasey Sound being a long and narrow funnel, it amplified the swell within its constrictions, making the anchorage untenable.

We turned away and headed for Portree which might be regarded as the capital village of Skye. There was a rainstorm gathering and it was getting quite dark when we arrived, but our problems of where to moor were immediately solved when we spotted the distinctive big blue buoys of the Highland and Islands Development Board. These strong moorings are free for visiting yachts, so they are always a welcome sight. My interest was taken by a small trimaran on one of the other moorings and whilst I was looking at it, the rest of the crew launched the inflatable and disappeared in the direction of the town, so as to arrive before the calling of 'last orders'. They might have saved themselves the hurry in this isolated spot. It was midnight before they reappeared.

Thursday 2 June.

The weather during the night was very mixed and it blew sufficiently hard for me to be pleased that we were on the nice tough mooring. The morning dawned brighter and we moved over nearer to the town for more shopping and to fill up with water. The single row of houses and shops near to the quay was painted in many bright colours similar to those in Tobermory. There was also the same pleasant air of gentle activity as men worked on fishing boats, travellers wandered and people went about their daily business.

Our general sailing progress had been a little slow because the winds had been light, so we decided that rather than daysail and stop in another anchorage we would continue to travel right through the day and night ahead to arrive at our destination at Ardmore. This would mean working watches and trying to get a seagoing rhythm established rather than all of us being in the cockpit at the same time during the day.

We took our time and left at about 11.30 with quite a good following breeze using goosewinged main and genoa. This carried us to the top end of Raasey where the wind began to drop as we lost the funnelling effect of the land. We hoisted the spinnaker but the wind progressively failed to the point where the sails kept collapsing and the tell tales hung vertically.

We did not motor, because the sun was strong and the scenery superb to the point of being almost unbelievable. It was an ideal place to linger. The mountains were magnificent, the sea blue, and we lay snoozing on deck or lazily scanning the islands and the horizon through binoculars. We wondered if the smudges of land to the far north-west could be the island of Lewis and we admired the mountains grouped around Loch Torridon on the mainland.

In the afternoon as we approached the little white lighthouse on the headland known as Rubha Reigh I tore myself from the scenery and went below to try to catch some sleep in readiness for the night. The wind fell further and our progress stopped completely. I was dimly aware of the motor being started. Shortly afterwards Chris opened the hatch into my cabin to say "We've got dolphins with us and they're staying ... and there are some more coming in." This was worth being woken for. I scrambled out expecting to see a similar event to the previous ones that I had always experienced where we saw the odd tail and shadowy shape here and there beneath the surface, but this time it was different.

The visitors

We had a school of about 10-12 individuals who came to play on our pressure waves for about half an hour as we motored steadily along. Looking down into the crystal water we could see their large clearly marked bodies only inches beneath the surface. They held station so that we could study them in great detail. When they cut away, flashed across or leaped to breathe, they were so near that we could recognise them as individuals. At first we looked and then we tried to photograph them. This was difficult for the water surface reflected light patches, but their bodies and the water itself appeared to be dark, so setting exposure times was a problem. After a while we put our cameras away and just studied them intently. I hadn't noticed them breathing gulps of air through the blowholes in the tops of their heads previously; neither had I studied their markings. Several of them had strong white spots that appeared to be scars from old injuries which when they had healed remained white instead of grey and black which are the dominant colours on the upper sides of their bodies. In this first school one individual had a 'V' shaped mark on its side; another had a round spot halfway down the left hand side of its body.

As they gambolled in the water they attracted seabirds to hover above, waiting for them to drive food to the surface. Noticing this, we were able to follow their progress by watching the birds whenever they departed. Sometimes they would all shoot away to one side and have a quick snack, chasing fish. We could see their fins cutting the surface and even small fish jumping out of the water. When they dropped back for about half a mile we expected them to go away, but no, after they had finished their detour they caught up again, travelling effortlessly at speed with hardly a flick of their tails.

Eventually they did go and we were left alone for a while heading across the bay for a far distant Point of Stoer using a little easterly breeze which allowed the motor to be cut. We still had the unbroken sunshine and the Summer Isles to our right to identify. Suddenly the rippled surface of the sea was being stirred again by the fins of more dolphins racing in to play all around us, but this time we had a different group with new individuals to get to know.

We had 'double white spot' and 'white tipped tail' and they proved even more adventurous than our previous visitors as they cut backwards and forwards just below the surface at the bows. They were so close that we felt that we could touch them, especially from our fine float tips and we had a strong impression that our shouts of joy and surprise were a strong part of the attraction for them.

269

Previously our contact with porpoise had been relatively fleeting. On this day we had almost continuous contact throughout the afternoon and well into the evening. We passed through our rushing-about phase, the camera phase and in our studying phase we began to gather more understanding of why they interact as they do with one another. We discussed their size, their markings, their breathing, swimming and hunting. We played with them and most surprising of all, we watched them watching us. In order to do this they had to take up a distinctive position to one side of the boat and roll slightly on their sides to bring an eye to focus. It was quite clear to us when it was done, why they were doing it and it had a powerful psychological effect upon us to look down into the water to see that eye looking back, examining us, assessing us and attempting to understand us on its own terms.

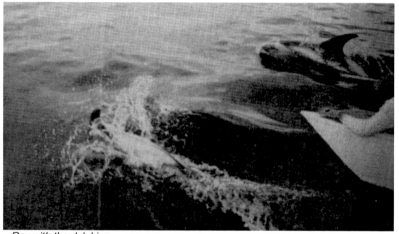

Ray with the dolphins.

Ultimately, each one of us aboard had to leave them to tend to the boat or carry on ship-board life as normal, leaving them to their games as we had other things to do. They were still out there as dusk fell on what had been one of the most memorable days of the circumnavigation.

Throughout this time we had been passing across the wide mouth of Loch Broom. The scattered Summer Isles had appeared ahead and to the right, like the backs of so many blue whales. Then far beyond came the first signs of the northern shore of the projecting mainland where we could just distinguish tiny white specks in the merged blue of sea and sky. This mirage effect was caused as the white buildings on the land glowed when the sun's rays caught them.

270

Serial Starship

I began to calculate our expected time of arrival and realised that we were going too fast. The darkness of night was very short; lasting only from about 23.30 to 03.30 and it appeared that we would arrive off the entrance at about 02.30 - 03.00 if we continued under sail at our present speed. All manner of juggling with figures still made us arrive in darkness and so I decided that I would just have to sail off-and-on near the entrance until it became light enough to see to go in safely. No sooner had I decided this than the wind rose another notch and *Starship* moved into her next gear. All calculations went out of the porthole and it became a matter for me of getting some sleep and accepting whatever progress we made until we came within striking distance.

I returned on deck at about 23.15 in the twilight to find us just dropping the lighthouse at Cluas Deas astern on the starboard quarter. The wind had really piped up to about force 4 from the east so that we were just nicely close-hauled going at maybe seven knots

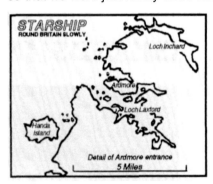

occasionally shouldering a sea aside with a slight bump. At this speed we were moving swiftly across our last bay towards Handa Island which lies just to the south of the entrance that we wished to make. I could see the island clearly, but as time ticked away and darkness gathered, so it imperceptibly dissolved into its background. I stared hard, took bearings and memorised its position, willed the light to stay, prayed for just a little more speed, wondered why I hadn't started an hour earlier in the morning, or used a bit more engine during the day, but it was to no avail. The sliding scales of visibility, darkness, time and speed, coincided, crossed and there came that moment when it had to be admitted that it was now no longer safe to continue in. We had to stay out at sea for the sake of arriving about twenty minutes too late.

Friday 3 June.
The wind died again as we closed the land and once round the mass of Handa Island we were virtually becalmed. I have never previously had to stand off an entrance overnight, sailing as I do in populated areas where leading lights are usually arranged to guide craft into

harbour. I had wondered what it would be like, but in the event it was a very simple procedure as we didn't have sufficient wind to move us and the sea fell to a glassy calm. Just for once, that evil servant of Murphy's Law, the terrible serpent Snagar who waits upon the unwary sailor to dispense misfortune, was asleep. Ray sat watch in our enclosed cockpit whilst the rest of the crew slept soundly below until I joined him as the first grey glimmer separated the land from the sea once more. Without waking the rest of the crew we started the engine and headed for the gap in the wall of striated granite which opened ahead of us. This rock-bound coast was almost exactly like that I'd seen in Sweden and we were pleased to have such favourable conditions for our entry into this secret place.

We turned to port into another narrow channel and passed through into the surprising green haven of Ardmore which is such a contrast with the forbidding entrance. All was silent and bathed in the sunlight of the early hours. Not knowing exactly where to go nor wishing to disturb anyone ashore, we secured to the vacant, massive mooring belonging to John's 57' ketch *English Rose VI* and went back to sleep. About eight o'clock I heard a commanding voice in my ear telling me that *English Rose* was expected back soon and it was time to move my boat. Mr Ridgeway was actually on the shore opposite, but there was no mistaking the strength of his rightful request.

During the day we were grateful for valuable help and advice from the Adventure School as we prepared to leave by moving our car and ferrying gear ashore. The final move involved getting the last person ashore without using our tender. I knew another local friend would be passing *Starship* in an outboard dinghy and made an arrangement for me to be picked up and ferried ashore. I was actively involved in positioning the boat and setting two anchors when the friend arrived earlier than expected. I had to rush the job, and didn't feel easy about the result, but I had no choice except to leave it as it was and transfer ashore. As our heavily ladened car struggled away up the valley I looked back at the tiny white speck, insignificant in such a rugged landscape and wondered how she would fare until we saw her again two months later.

At the beginning of July my phone rang at home.
"Paul Constantine? ... John Ridgeway here.
It's about your boat ..."

MI issue 281. Episode 62.

Logistics again.

Problems, problems.

The boat was in an almost inaccessibly remote loch in the far north west of Scotland. If I went there with my car and sailed the boat back to Suffolk at the end of the holiday as I intended, how could I get my car back? This was a cruising problem just as real as any problem relating to sail changes or courses to steer. Could I hire a one-way car? Could I find a volunteer to drive the car back? What would it cost in fuel, in food? Cruising generates a steady stream of unexpected challenges to tax the inventive mind. I console myself with the thought that the solutions to these difficulties offer an opportunity for experiences of greater cruising interest. The solution involved using my own car and the discovery of an apparently insignificant hamlet called Lairg on the opposite side of Scotland.

The night before I departed for Scotland saw me defrosting the fridge, always a sure sign that a major cruise was about to begin. The next-door neighbour received my last five frozen fish fingers as a reward for minding our actual gold fish.

Sunday July 31

My time of departure was 03.10 to collect Ian Goodrum the first crewman at 04.15 then on, up across country towards Lancashire to collect Alison from a relative's house. As we passed through a deserted, sleeping Northampton Ian said 'Be careful of the fox.' The creature had seen our approach as it started to cross the road, so it returned to its own side and waited for us to drive slowly by. We eyed each other with interest. We, with excitement at the privilege; the fox with unconcerned confidence. After we'd passed, it ambled gently across behind us.

Alison had ten carrier bags full of food to add to our already overloaded car and by the time the contents had been slotted into every available spare space the rear mud flaps were trailing on the ground causing a dragging noise on uneven roads until we had used up most of our petrol.

550 miles further north we drove through Lairg without noticing it, even though we were looking for it. We returned to seek out a deserted group of antiquated, overgrown buildings which constituted a railway station. The key to our plan was to return the car here after unloading it at the boat, which was still some 60 miles to the north-west. Ian would sail with us to Orkney, then cross back

to the mainland and catch a train to Lairg to pick up the car for the return to Suffolk. We found a bed and breakfast accommodation nearby and the landlady kindly agreed to us parking our car there for a week once we had explained what we were up to.

Monday August 1.

I approached Ardmore, where I had left *Starship* moored by her own anchors, with some trepidation. I did not know if the boat had survived unscathed. John Ridgeway had agreed to keep an eye on her, but he had contacted me to say that she had broken loose in a severe gale and that he had retrieved her. Amongst the weighty gear presently overloading the car was a generator and power tools in case repairs were needed. As we bumped and scraped over the rough terrain towards our first sight of the loch my anxiety increased. We parked and walked until we crested a ridge from where we could see the distant ribbon of sparkling water with, at one end, *Starship* secured to John Ridgeway's big mooring usually reserved for his own world-girdling 57ft ketch *English Rose VI*. I looked long and hard through Ian's binoculars and was relieved to see that my boat seemed to be OK.

Starship at Ardmore

We eventually reached the Ridgeway's house and learned from Marie Christine, John's wife, that our boat had been rescued at least three times. On each occasion in extreme gales the craft had gone on a walkabout. She had fouled her anchors and then dragged across the loch, only to re-anchor herself 10-20 metres from the lee shore. On the last occurrence in desperate weather there had been no option but to cut the anchor warps and take her to the big mooring. The anchors were retrieved and we found them aboard ready for reattachment. Only a very short length of warp had been cut and apart from a rather bent bow roller there was no other damage. I was very grateful for the efforts that John Ridgeway and his team at the Adventure School had made in looking after the boat. When I spoke to him he said that maybe he'd revised just how bad the conditions could become in the loch. He now considered that two 75lb CQR anchors would be necessary to really feel secure. His own mooring had been laid by a trawler.

Tuesday August 2
Alison took the unloaded car across to Lairg and caught a lift back to us in the post office van which we knew departed from there at 13.45 each weekday for Kinlochbervie just to the north of us. Ian and I prepared the boat and I took the weather forecast which was south-westerly force 4-6 accompanied by cold, misty weather. It rained heavily all night and we were buffeted by strong winds swirling in the loch.

MI issue 282 Episode 62

Ardmore to Loch Eribol around Cape Wrath...
Wednesday August 3
It was pouring with rain and we could hardly see across the loch at times, but I went to see John to take my leave. He was optimistic about the weather and said it would clear. His curiosity about the boat was revealed when he asked if we could go to windward. The limits of his interest were discovered when I offered to give him a sail. In jocular mood he indicated that the boundaries of safe nautical adventure probably didn't stretch to going to sea in something like our craft. John cannot lack courage but maybe we found one of his limits. We laughed and parted amicably.

Around Cape Wrath.
At 10.40 we dropped the mooring and motored out in low misty conditions heading into a westerly 4-5. In Loch Laxford we set two thirds main and half a genoa and shot off towards the sea with the smooth granite shores on either side. We departed the entrance at 11.20 and it was really quite rough as the incoming Atlantic rollers crashed over the rocks and white spume flew everywhere. It was a steady force five outside which gave us the sail power to attack and climb the waves. She drove rapidly out cresting the incoming waves and speeding on to meet the next ones. Could we go to windward? ... indeed!

Once clear of the rocks to our right we were able to bear away northwards to bring the wind further aft. This was a mixed blessing for the sea was mightily confused and we had our hands full with the steering. It rained steadily, the wind blew hard, the sea was rough and the land disappeared in the mist. It wasn't fun. Why did I spend my holidays doing this kind of thing instead of lying in the sun on a Spanish beach?

With our scrap of sail we sped onwards and we managed to find our position from the grey shape of Am Bag island which emerged from time to time. Half an hour later we'd covered the last five miles to Cape Wrath of which there was little to be seen or heard except a slight thickening of the clouds and the sound of the dismal foghorn's moan. We'd been almost surfing on the waves, but gradually the seas subsided to indicate that we were rounding the corner and sailing an easterly course for a change.

On the flat water the motion was much more comfortable and the crew brightened visibly, along with the weather as we crossed the Kyle of Dourness. The clouds lifted to allow us to see the land which was filled with variety and interest. Rocky stacks and islands, small white cottages nestling in green velvet and the waters around

us teemed with activity as all manner of seabirds from puffins to gannets went about their daily business of feeding. Afraid Head had some kind of lookout building atop its precipitous cliffs, probably for observing firing on the range there. We sailed past the target buoy feeling rather vulnerable.

Our target was Respond Bay, a tiny sheltered inlet on the west side of the entrance to Loch Eribol. We followed the entrance instructions for the loch passing around Black Rocks and the Louring islands before heading for our selected bay. The cruising guide advised that this was the best stopping place as it had a beach and perfect shelter whilst Loch Eribol itself was subject to fierce squalls due to the hills funnelling the south-westerly winds. Imagine our dismay when we found that the tiny bay had a fish farm in the centre and all around there were strategically placed 'lobster pot' markers which made anchoring impossible. The only place available for anchoring on the outer edge of the bay was occupied by a black fishing boat with someone in the wheelhouse. We approached gingerly to take a look and could see lengths of rope trailing across the surface from the pot markers to provide maximum obstruction.

It seemed to me that the place had been appropriated for the fish farm and the markers were arranged to discourage unwanted visitors. As we drew near, a man appeared from the wheelhouse of the guarding fishing boat. He shouted that we should take care not to foul the pots and suggested that we should go to a neighbouring bay which was clear. We asked what the holding was like there and he said that there was no problem. We went south as he'd indicated to take a look, but it was no good. There were a few pots in the middle of the bay, but it was at the end of a valley through which the wind whistled and there was little shelter. I was quite furious that this fellow had appropriated Respond Harbour and was sitting there discouraging yachts from using a legitimate anchorage. Finding shelter in the rest of the loch would be difficult. I decided to try Arid Necktie which I had spotted on my exploratory recce at Easter.

Halfway down the loch on the eastern side a rocky island is connected to the shore by a shingle and sand spit which forms the north and south bays of Arid Necktie. We set half the genoa and sailed across close hauled to enter the northern bay which appeared reasonably sheltered with flat water. It seemed an ideal place, but when we tried to lay our big anchor it would not take. The first time it came up clean, but the second time it was heavy with weed and we had to put a line on it to capsize the weed off. Just as we tried to set it for the third time two chaps came by in a dory filled with diving

Ard Neakie linked to the shore

gear. One of them explained that to his knowledge no yacht had ever managed to successfully anchor in the bay as the weed and shingle bottom wouldn't allow it. They suggested that we should go round to the south side to use their mooring near to the pier. This bay was much more exposed to the present wind direction and I was explaining our need for shelter when one of them remembered a 'dinghy outhaul' tucked right into the corner of the north bay which our shallow draught would allow us to use. They said that it had been there many years and they had maintained it for their own diving use. It was very strong. The mooring was close to the rocky island, with ropes running to the shore, so we secured to it with a running bow rope and laid our anchor at full scope towards the east to keep us from swinging inshore.

The wind turned out to be very gusty and it was a good thing that we didn't trust to our anchor alone. During the very dark night, with the rain beating heavily on the deck, I was up six times checking the boat as severe squalls looped round the island to tug at us. On each occasion I blessed the decision to secure to the old outhaul which was the only feasible way to ensure against dragging.

We were well and truly cruising again with the problems of the land exchanged for the uncertainties of the sea. We stood on the brink of even greater adventurous uncertainties, for tomorrow we might sail for the Orkneys.

MI issue 283. Episode 63.

Loch Eriboll - Stromness.
4 August Thursday.
It was alternately raining and clearing on our side of Loch Eriboll, but the western side was almost continuously in cloud. As the daylight increased I was pleased and relieved to be still tucked close in behind Ard Neackie where the shelter appeared good with flat water, but where fierce gusts of wind whipped round the island to pull at the boat.

We departed at 09.45 hoping to sail to Stromness in Orkney a total distance of about 54 miles. The information which dominated the passage was to be found in the Clyde Cruising Club guide to Orkney and concerned Hoy Sound through which we would have to pass at journey's end to enter Stromness.
'The tidal streams in Hoy Sound are very strong and entry should not be attempted in bad weather or with wind against tide, or on the ebb (i.e. westgoing). Spring rate may exceed 7 knots.'

We were three days after the spring tide. As we had been forced to go well down into Loch Eribol we had an hour's journey to clear the entrance. This gave us roughly six hours sailing to do approximately 48 miles to the entrance of Hoy Sound at about 16.30 which appeared to be the end of the favourable flood, meaning that we would have to average 7 knots just to get there, and then of course we'd have to contend with the passage through. We had an alternative which was to follow the north coast of Scotland to Scrabster and then sail from there to Stromness the following day. This would become the preferred option if the visibility became poor.

As we sailed up Loch Eriboll we saw another yacht. This was quite an occasion. In this area it is possible to sail for long periods without seeing another sailing craft. It appeared to emerge from the vicinity of Rishold Bay about half an hour ahead of us. It is surprising what a sail on the horizon can do, especially a traditional brown sail. Ian said that it felt a bit like the old days of revenue cutters and smugglers. My eyes were on our sails wondering if I could take a couple of rolls out of the genoa. All other eyes were on that tiny brown speck heading out to sea. Were we catching up? What was his length and how much sail did he have set?

We hardly noticed the incoming waves, the white crests, the lift and surge of the bows as we sped out to meet the sea. Then the rain came in and blanketed out the coast. The wind began to drop from the N.W. force 4/5 and we were soon being thrown about by the residual swell and waves. It was terribly uncomfortable and setting full sail hardly helped. Instead of bearing away as we wished to do, we had to continue sailing northwards just to get enough power to keep the boat moving. We were still clearing the headland to our right, but this wasn't going to get us to Hoy Sound.

Eventually we made our turn and found that a goosewinged course gave the best power, but the motion of the lumpy waves overlying a big swell threw the boat about so that the wind was shaken out of the sails, or the sea would push the stern around to gybe the main or collapse the genoa. We might have set the genoa on one side and the spinnaker on the other but the light sail would have been flogged mercilessly. Whilst I was mentally wrestling with what I might do next the wind began to return and rose sufficiently to steady the boat so that we could get down to the serious business of overhauling the boat ahead.

We were now on an easterly course crossing the entrance to the Kyle of Tongue which we knew to be a beautiful, shallow, sandy sea loch. The craft that we were chasing occasionally oscillated

279

violently from side to side appearing to dip the boom in the water and as a consequence he had to shorten sail. He disappeared from time to time as either he, or we, sank into the troughs. As we crested waves we spotted his rolling goose-winged shape. The wind increased again to force 4/5 and we really started creaming along, sailing more steadily with the greater strength. He was a traditionally shaped G.R.P. monohull of about 32ft, in good cruising trim. We overhauled him at a distance of about half a mile watching him gybe and resetting his whisker pole. We had our genoa sheet passed through a snatch block secured to our cap shroud about a metre up from its base on the float. This gave us the sheeting width without having to resort to poles. It was fascinating to watch the behaviour of the other boat under these conditions. There was a strict limit on the amount of power that they could force into their hull. They were obliged to wallow slowly due to their narrow deep draught hull form. If they raised more sail they just rolled more in the gusts. We could catch the gusts and translate them into forward motion and then on waves steep enough to give us a little kick, we'd break into a little surf travelling at 10/12 knots, so they were soon left behind.

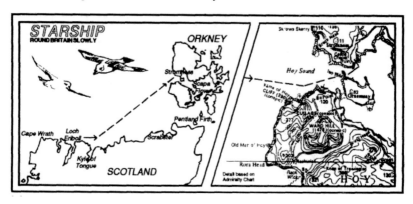

At midday I decided that the weather was sufficiently clear to make a shot at crossing to Orkney. I had 35 miles to do in four and a half hours. The course would be 040°m broad reaching which should increase my speed and I was hoping for 1½ - 2 knots of tide, so maybe 7½ knots wasn't out of the question. The option of sailing directly to Stromness was made possible by our boat speed; the craft we had just passed would have to overnight at Scrabster and come up the next day if he intended to make the same destination in daylight, I realised that we were probably making a passage which would not have been possible in most comparably-sized, cruising craft that we might have used for a journey such as this only 30 years or so previously.

When we turned left we sailed away from the misty mainland out into the open sea for a couple of hours. We had nothing but the turbulent water, the sound of the wind and the constant interest of the seabirds. These northern waters are teeming with sea life. We had a complete variety of birds from the largest to the smallest, but the ace performers in this world of wind and big water were the fulmar petrels. Built like balsa wood gliders they soared in endless flight right across the wave faces seeming to enjoy their game of getting closer to the water as the waves grew bigger. They rode them like surfers lazily trailing a fingered wing tip as if to caress the sharp danger of the wall of water to prove it was tame, smooth-soft velvet, not overwhelming iron might. Each individual was gliding, gliding, scanning with coal black eyes. They were masters of this inhospitable environment.

By three in the afternoon a hard edge in the low cloud ahead showed where the island of Hoy might be. We could still see the mainland distantly to the south. The edge proved to be the Kame of Hoy an impressive cliff to the right of the entrance we wished to pass through. For a while it looked as though we would arrive in time, but the wind which had held so well began to die on us and a distinct lack of power between 15.00 to 16.00 saw our chance slipping away. I desperately combed my pilot books for a hope that the tide would be favourable longer, but only succeeded in finding that the tide in the sound might have begun ebbing 1hr 10minutes before my Almanac had indicated. Although we did eventually arrive at a position almost due north of the Kame of Hoy at 16.30 we were too late. By any calculation it was clear that the tide was visibly against us.

The incoming waves from the open sea were entering the funnel-shaped sound and steepening as they came. The entrance channel was on the northern side of the funnel and as we approached we watched the inter-island ferry enter well to the south. I decided to do the same. We went from a dead run to a reach, moving to starboard away from a direct line with the entrance. Immediately we began to make progress. Once into the bay we could see the broken white caps of the waves set up by the race which ran as a distinct line along the northern shore. We picked up the increased wind being deflected into the bay from the high cliffs on the south side and began to accelerate again.

Graemsay Islands formed the constriction through which the water tumbled outwards like a river in spate. We could see that once up to the corner we would have no option but to sail into the stream, however, the wind was now up again and we were sailing fast. We were doing about eight or nine knots but entering at about three, skimming across the rapids, making light of the standing waves that we crossed. We sailed a balanced path between maximum reaching power and heading into the flow, keeping our speed going but allowing ourselves to ferry-glide across to where we could see calmer water beckoning. Our magical boat speed had the power to open up even this door and offered us a chance denied to most cruising boats. Once we were past the beacon on the end of the Ness we were able to relax, for the stream was now behind us and we were on still water with the town of Stromness before us. We doused sails and motored in at about six o'clock.

There was plenty of water and space with several piers to choose from and we didn't quite know where to go. Some chaps on a quay said 'Try the harbourmaster on Channel 16', but there was no reply. We went well up the harbour and picked up a mooring to try the V.H.F. again. An American yacht *Star,* moored against the quay, came on to inform me that the harbourmaster stopped at five o'clock, but they invited us to go alongside them, so we prepared warps and moved over. *Star's* skipper was most helpful and by coincidence he and his wife, Ian and Alison, the same names as our crew.

Before it grew too dark we decided to have a quick walk around the town. Many places that one visits are very much like many others, but Stromness was very, very different from anywhere that I have ever visited.

MI issue 284. Episode 64.

Stromness - Hunda Sound 4 - 6 August.
Stromness.
We didn't expect to find anything remarkable about Stromness when we arrived late in the day in Orkney after a fairly strenuous daysail from Loch Eriboll on the Scottish mainland, but we were immediately impressed with the place. It belonged in a different world.

The single main street ran roughly parallel to the waterfront and zigzagged around as it rose up, or descended. It was very narrow and every building had a very individual character with interesting architectural features. Whilst the buildings were basically square-shaped they often had the corner which faced onto the street cut off at an angle to form what a woodworker might call a chamfer. This shaping which could have begun as a way of easing the space at ground level for the passage of traffic had evolved into a major design feature creating an angled wall which was specially favoured by decorating it with windows. The bottom two floors had normal vertical rectangular windows, but the upper stories each had a small square window. Extra little gables and windows in the roof were very popular as the buildings stretched ever taller in a seeming attempt to secure views over each other of the harbour which was the focus of all activity around here.

More unusual was the roadway which consisted of a series of enormous paving slabs with a central band of cobbles or sets. The overriding impression of the jumbled houses was of some kind of medieval street, but with stone as the sole building material. It was startling to see cars driving along sometimes at quite high speeds, because not only did they appear to be in the wrong century, but in places there was only sufficient width for a single vehicle and the many blind corners and numerous pedestrians created quite a problem.

The shops were reminiscent of the 1940's or 50's and most proclaimed their names and trades with hand painted wooden signs in a primitive art kind of way. The overall effect was delightful, because it was so unexpected. To find oneself in a place with such an aura, one normally has to visit a working museum where one is mentally prepared prior to arrival. Stromness was not striving to re-create a false period, it was not artificially preserving anything; it was natural, it was itself, in an active human way and we just sailed into it as if we were time-travellers. It was the most distinctive place that we visited on our journey.

I fell into bed exhausted at about 11 o'clock after a long and busy day. We had travelled far and I looked forward to a long-earned rest. At two in the morning I was woken by the noise and movement of the boat.

The wind had gone to the south which created small waves from the only direction from which we were vulnerable. Each boat in our line worked one against the other so that they bumped and jarred occasionally. The inside boat against the quay was taking the full compression of the rest of the line and looking out of my window I could see her owners repositioning their fenders by the light of the street lamps. For half an hour I lay listening to the snatching of the boats and the rising wind in the rigging. We were stern to the waves and the odd one slapped the transom. Then I heard a different sound as an infrequent squeaking bump became a jarring snatch, indicating that maybe our hulls were touching our neighbour.

One lies in the warmth of a nice cosy bed hoping against hope that you won't have to go out into the cold night, but knowing the inevitability of it. Suddenly with a scraping crunch the decision is made for you and you can't get out there fast enough. It is a time to take special care if you are in a half-drugged, sleep-like condition. It is very easy to fall. I pulled on my clothes and went out in my bare feet. I preferred them bare, because I know my boat well enough not to stub my toes and I find it makes me most sure-footed; getting the swiftest warning of a rope underfoot; having the best grip in wet conditions and being brought fully awake by the shock of the cold deck under my feet.

The fenders on my neighbour's boat were on too short a lead and had been lifted onto my float deck by the movement. I readjusted their length and slipped them back between the boats. I checked my own lines and found that the spring which was taking all the strain needed re-leading outside the shroud as it was grating up and down. I had to substitute another rope to carry the load in order to release the spring and make it run directly. After adjusting everything to my satisfaction I returned below after being outside for about half an hour.

It is an odd thing, but once such a task has been tackled, one's mind gets lost in the problems being set by the situation and if the night is relatively mild it can even be enjoyable being out there. Scrambling back into the nice warm bed and feeling those icy feet gradually thawing out was joined with the peace of mind of knowing that all was secure. The reward for facing up to the unpleasant prospect was doubly rewarded this time, for within a couple of minutes of my return I heard the rain drumming on the roof and as it grew heavier and the wind subsided I slumbered with a happier heart.

Friday was a day of rain. An almost endless downpour raised the humidity level close to 100%. All the local people were busy explaining to the tourists that this was most unusual; that this was the worst day of the year and the rain couldn't last much longer. The tourists were unconvinced, but pleased to be offered the profuse apologies.

We showered at the Ferry Boat inn; washed our clothes at the launderette, wandered round the bookshops and visited the museum. We learned of the Orkney Hoy (local fishing boat) and saw sepia tint pictures of the heyday of the herring fishing when the harbour was packed tight with hundreds of luggers. Most fascinating of all was the amazing display about Franklin's disastrous North-West Passage expedition which resulted in the disappearance of all concerned. Bodies of the unfortunate mariners have recently been discovered perfectly preserved by the cold and investigations have indicated that deaths were in some measure attributable to the lead solder in the rudimentary tin cans which carried their food. We read of Scapa Flow and the scuttling of the German fleet and of Captain Cook's ships making their landfall here after returning from the Pacific, in short, we generally revelled in a mixed maritime nostalgia which seemed to permeate not only the museum, but the very stones of Stromness itself.

Ian our crewman crossed to the mainland on the ferry and then returned home using the car we'd placed at Lairg. He was replaced for the rest of our journey in the islands by Gavin and Carol Hall a New Zealand/Scottish couple; both were experienced sailors. Gavin had built an Ian Farrier designed Trailertri 680 *Magic* and cruised it from North Cape to Bluff in New Zealand, a total journey approaching 1,000 miles in a small boat often in open ocean conditions. He and Carol had travelled overland from New Zealand and more recently Gavin had been working with British boat builders including Derek Kelsall to learn the latest constructional methods. Carol had the rare gift of total immunity to sea sickness and in some of the rough times to follow would save us by chirpily preparing food when conditions pinned the remaining crew on deck, watching the horizon and taking deep breaths of fresh air. Following their return to New Zealand to build boats again Gavin was appointed as an authorised commercial builder of Ian Farrier designs and plan agent.

The open friendliness of everyone we met in Stromness was refreshing. The Customs man had missed us during the working day, but he wanted to talk about the boat and how it sailed so he came back later in his own time. The Americans on the boat next to us had sailed across the Atlantic via Iceland where the prices had provided them with a nasty shock. They told us that car hire was £135 per day and lettuces (which were usually sold in quarters) were £4 each. Prices in Orkney were quite cheap, so upon their arrival they jumped at the offer of car hire at £20 a day, only to later discover that the going rate could be £10 a day.

We met a local man Jim Hunter who was at that time running a small sailing school enterprise. He was most interested in our boat and invited us to his home on Saturday to talk about our journey, foam sandwich boatbuilding and the flat-table building technique. In exchange he told us about Scapa Flow and gave us one of his large scale charts, which was very useful for we didn't have good coverage of the western side. Whilst we were at Jim's home the weather brightened, so we hurriedly returned to *Starship* and departed in a solid burst of sunshine which lasted for at least half an hour. As we went down the harbour Jim could be seen waving enthusiastically from his garden, wishing us well.

Navigation by tea towel.

The wind was light westerly and we ran along the northern shore towards Houton Head and then crossed towards Hoy going down the western side of Cava. I got out my illustrated souvenir tea towel which showed the positions of the old battleships below the placid surface of the flow. We first passed over the Konigsberg Class SMS *Karlsruhe* (5,354 tons) now resting at a depth of 24 metres. Rounding the southern tip of Cava we headed east following the northern shore of Flotta where the oil terminal is the major industrial blot in this beautiful rural landscape. At least they have managed to concentrate it in one place with only two massive loading moorings out in the flow, unlike Milford Haven which had a similar rural beauty, but which was ruined by pipes and tanks casually strewn along its length.

The next ship to pass beneath our keels according to our tea towel was HMS *Vanguard* (19,560 tons) lying in 34 metres, which blew up on July 9 1917 killing 1,000 men. The water over the spot looked just the same as anywhere else in this historic place.

As we crossed the Sound of Hoxa we looked south to the blue smudge of the Scottish mainland across the Pentland Firth. Far to the north in Scapa Bay we could make out the cathedral tower above the town of Kirkwall. We entered Hunda Sound between Hunda and Burray to spend the night in the shelter of the island. The usual fish farm had been positioned in the best spot, but there was plenty of space and we anchored close in against the island in 15ft over pure white sand which gave firm holding. The next day we planned to sail into what many regard as the most dangerous stretch of water in the British Isles, the Pentland Firth.

MI issue 285. Episode 65.

Scapa Flow towards Kirkwall .
7 August. Sunday.
The forecast was V3 becoming SE3/4. Our intention for the day was

to go to Kirkwall, which we could easily see from our overnight anchorage in Hunda Sound. To reach it directly we could go to the northern shore of Scapa Flow and walk 1½ miles across a narrow neck of land, the problem was that we needed to take our boat there. To **sail** to Kirkwall was not quite so simple. It was a long and dangerous voyage due to an event which occurred long ago, on October 14 1939.

The eastern side of Scapa Flow is formed not of a continuous land mass, but of a string of small islands between which were a series of sounds or channels through which boats could once pass. As Scapa Flow was a navy anchorage there was a danger that enemy craft might penetrate one of these sounds and attack the warships at anchor. To deter such an audacious action, blockships were sunk in the sounds and it was thought that the fleet was secure until in October 1939 the unthinkable happened. A submarine U47, entered and escaped through the most northerly channel Kirk Sound and whilst in the Flow torpedoed HMS *Royal Oak* (29,150 tons) killing 800 men.

Winston Churchill determined to remove the possibility of this ever happening again by having dams built across the sounds. The work was done by Italian prisoners of war. The Churchill barriers now provide the road links between islands, but they also mean that to get from one side of the road to the other in Kirk Sound by sea, involves a 26 mile journey around all of the other islands to the south. Kirkwall is much further into the flow so a sailing distance of 45 miles is the alternative distance to crossing the 1½ miles of land.

In addition to the distance, there is also the danger, for to round the southernmost island one must enter the Pentland Firth which is probably one of the most hazardous places to take a boat in the British Isles. The tidal flow squeezing through the firth can cause enormous overfalls. The Clyde Cruising Club pilot in its preamble says *'Any swell opposing the tide causes such severe conditions that the safety of a small vessel can be in jeopardy. The hatches and scuttles of all yachts should be secured and the safety harnesses of the crew should be attached before the passage is started.'* The guide also instructed us that the correct time to pass the tip of South Ronaldsay (on this particular day) was at two in the afternoon, so we had some time to spare whilst we waited for the conditions to come right.

We raised our anchor on a pleasantly sunny day and ran with the south-easterly up the flow towards Kirkwall. My mental image of this place had always been cold, grey and harsh. 'flow' sounds a bit

287

like 'ice flow' and this had been an important staging post for the Russian convoys and Arctic explorers. I had thought it to be a remote and desolate place suited only as a refuge for the steel war machines of a bygone age. I'd got it all wrong. It is a rural lake, sparkling and blue and excellent for cruising around the many islands. Its shores are farmland, green fields with animals grazing and cottages, any reminders of warfare are relatively few, insignificant and difficult to find. One of the easiest to discover was the green starboard buoy for which we now headed. It marked the sunken hull of the *Royal Oak* which was only 15-20ft below the surface. In still water we might just have seen the hull; we were told that it was clear from an aircraft, but there was nothing visible except the wreaths on the buoy and a special marker reminding us that this was a war grave. There **was** a sense of what had happened there. I thought that I might put on the echo sounder to see exactly when we passed over the wreck, but I decided not to as my imagination was

sufficient. We turned and sailed slowly to the south.

We entered the Sound of Hoxa at about one o'clock when we had about eight miles to go to round South Ronaldsay. The book said that I should have a favourable tide and with the breeze which was blowing we could make about six knots close reaching so I felt that I had timed it about right. We passed through the narrowest part of the sound still guarded by the old lookout towers at the same time as our American friends on *Star*, who motored out heading south for Inverness and the Caledonian Canal. We waved goodbye. As I watched them pull away I noticed that the clouds seemed to be down to the fields on top of the cliffs to our left and wisps of mist spilled over to cascade down into the sound.

The wind had fallen in strength and our speed dropped to four knots. The tide seemed adverse and this was increasing our leeway. We tacked to find a more favourable current, but it wasn't there. I was falling behind my schedule to reach the point by two o'clock, it would be nearer three o'clock and I had only a two hour tidal gate to catch. I looked ahead for the distant American yacht and just managed to catch a glimpse as he disappeared into the fog. Looking back at the land I saw the cloud was now cascading down like a waterfall over the cliff face. I grabbed my handbearing compass and took a quick single fix on a headland as it disappeared. Within seconds we were completely enveloped and into quite a different white world. I laid off the bearing on the chart and looked out to see that visibility could be no more than 200 metres, but it felt like much less. I had to take a decision, so I looked at the charts, the distance to go and the hazards that I faced. I weighed my chances of making the journey on another day. I had no electronic position fixing devices; I simply had the charts, the rule and the pencil. I evaluated my crew strength. When I returned on deck somebody asked, Can we go on in these conditions? I tried to sound casual but definite in my reply, "Oh yes."

I had my starting point and I drew a track towards the island of Swona intending a kind of test run. The approach to the shore was reasonably steep-to and I thought that I would see it with sufficient time to take avoiding action. The sea was relatively calm. I marked my positions on the chart for each 5 minute interval down the track making allowance for a 'worst case' leeway or tidal action. I noted the time and went on deck to watch. The minutes ticked away as we sailed into the blank white wall.

My time was up and within the next couple of minutes I should see the signs of land, or tack away. I actually saw the darker edge of the top of the island at what I estimated might be about a quarter of a mile and took what I considered to be a good bearing. I held the tack closer and closer, slowly closing the shore until I felt certain of my position and then we tacked towards South Ronaldsay.

Again I followed the procedure of using a very 'realistic' track and marking the distances at ten minute intervals. The wind was up sufficiently for us to make 5/6 knots which is a mile every 10 minutes. My first test on Swona had worked well and I hoped for a repeat performance. I gave our time of arrival at the cliffs to the rest of the crew and everyone stared into the fog eager to be the first to see something. Within a couple of minutes of the predicted time we spotted the land, confirmed our position and tacked away out into the Pentland Firth itself. I noticed that the pilot book had additional advice especially for me. *'The passage of the Firth should not be undertaken in fog.'*

Why is it that I find myself in these positions? I try to plan carefully and sail reasonably safely. It's never my intention to set out to do foolish things. I somehow seem fated to allow them to creep up on me and ensnare me whilst my mind is otherwise occupied. One minute we were on schedule, making good time with everything in our favour and less than five minutes later it had all evaporated as the tide went against us, the wind fell off and visibility had gone. Suddenly we were struggling.

It is easy to be wise after the event, but at the time the warning signs were not so clear. For almost three years we had sailed the south and west coasts where a south-easterly breeze brings nothing but fair weather. We were learning with a vengeance that this is not necessarily true on the east coast. Did alarm bells ring when you read that gentle weather forecast? It had not prompted any warning bells for me and I had heard no mention of fog. Maybe I should have turned the boat and run back up the sound, but running into the narrowing neck of a funnel, with the tide, in fog, isn't an easy option either. We had almost reached the corner and once around it we would have more sea room and a favourable wind for the rest of the passage. Should these advantages have been thrown away at this stage by trying to get back into the flow? I opted to continue.

As we moved further out into the firth on the southwards tack we were greatly aided by the tiny bleat of a foghorn on Muckle Skerry and the mighty groans of a device on Stroma. It was clear that we were getting close to Stroma as the sound increased and Muckle Skerry could no longer be heard. At 15.10 we tacked north-eastwards and slowly Stroma receded as Muckle Skerry returned, increasing in strength on our starboard side.

At 15.30 we entered the Liddel Eddy race as a direct confirmation of my ten minute track position and as we reached 15.55 I knew that we were into the real danger zone just off Old Head. It was difficult to know just how close we were, so we kept our eyes glued ahead and to port. Suddenly there was a shout and the cliffs with rocks at their base emerged within about 25 metres. It was a heart stopping moment.

MI issue 286. Episode 66.

<u>Orkneys. Old Head - Kirkwall.</u>
I had banked on the visibility being at about 200 metres but the rocks cutting through the white foaming water just off the port bow proved

that now that we were upwind of the land we could not rely on seeing through the fog even this distance. We drove outwards over the overfalls around the tip of South Ronaldsay and when we were finally clear we were able to free sheets to go shooting off on 030°m towards the north leaving the Pentland Firth behind us.

I now faced a deepening dilemma. Since entering the thick fog on leaving Scapa Flow I had sailed relatively short tacks and confirmed my position at the end of each of them with a positive land sighting. If I lost contact with the land entirely for a long period of time I would become less certain of my position the longer I was away, for I was without any position-fixing devices. Now that I had the possibility of sea room, should I use it? Should I try to sail directly for Mull Head (avoiding the hazard of Copinsay on the way) a journey of several hours, or should I try for one or two position confirmations on the way? I reasoned that I would have to find the island group of Copinsay whatever I did as it was such a major hazard across my course and in order to get this right I would first have to close the coast in the region of Grimness.

We made good speed with the wind behind the beam and I checked my position off. An hour later at 16.50 I calculated that I had run my time and distance to Grimness, but having seen no land I still made my right turn onto a starboard reach to go out to sea. We had travelled for about two minutes and picked up to a speed of about six knots. I was about to go below to the chart table when both Gavin and Carol who were on watch together called simultaneously that there was land ahead. Land! This should have been impossible but there it was, a vertical cliff and really very close.

The dark cliff loomed out of the blank wall of fog only yards ahead of the bow. We rushed towards the land which just should not have been there. I called for a crash tack and the sails thundered; sheets thrashed against the deck and winches chattered like machine guns as we strove to turn the craft around as fast as possible. The boat heeled as the sails filled and I looked back at the black shape dissolving back into the fog. There was something odd about the right hand edge of the image. It appeared to end, as if it was a headland. We sailed on for a short while then tried the outgoing tack once more. Within seconds we came back on the same section of headland, so that I could take another look at it. I realised that I was embayed in the tiny bay to the south of Grimness. Through pure chance, as any blindfolded sailing exercise will soon prove, I was almost precisely where I had calculated to be. By using carefully timed tacks we climbed out until we were clear at 17.15 and headed for the next hazard.

We had already had some moments of extreme anxiety, feeling our way around the cliffs, but I could now see that the potential dangers of the Copinsay island group was worse than anything we had yet faced. I made all the avoiding calculations but I also exploited Murphy's Law and assumed that wind, tide, course and leeway would conspire to place me in the worst situation possible, so I looked at the chart to see what I would least like to happen. Copinsay had a string of islands linked by rock skerries. The worst thing that could happen would be for us to sail into the main bay which had a reef across it at the far end, so this was what I mentally prepared for.

For an hour we sailed on in total blindness with our speed

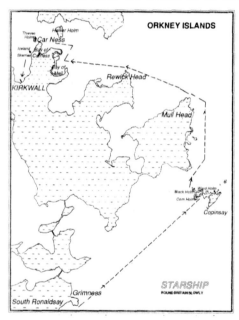

varying between 4 and 6 knots according to wind strength. Our heading was designed to sail us clear of the outside of the islands on a close reach. We knew that slowing would increase our leeway and the wind and waves would push against our starboard side sliding us into the danger zone. The precise tidal direction wasn't known, but it was assumed to be unhelpful.

At 18.05 we began to hear the faint sound of a foghorn and it came from dead ahead. We were sliding inside the main island towards the reef-barred bay. A tiny brown sparrow fluttered across our path, flying in disorientated semi-exhaustion directly into the wind, desperately searching for a landing place. It sank lower and lower towards the waves. Would it make it? Was there land to windward of us? There was a lull in the wind. The water was getting flatter. We strained for some sign as the sea sounds subsided. There was a sense of waiting. The echo sounder read 65ft.

Suddenly Carol broke the silence with "It's there." and sliding past close to port was an immense grey block, silently passing in the mist perhaps 35 - 40ft away. We were in the bay at Copinsay. I held my course for a short while watching for confirmation on the echo sounder but the depth remained almost constant. The reef had to be just ahead. The high block of land had disappeared in the mist again and we were gliding over the eerily smooth, grey surface of the water.

Beating out to windward to round Copinsay would take us much time and effort, and carried with it a strong risk of running onto the Horse of Copinsay just to the north of the main group. I decided to use the inside pass as I had such a well-defined position from which to calculate the course. We went about onto the reciprocal course searching for the land that we had just passed which I knew to be Ward Holm. By creeping round it at the very limit of our visible range we picked up its neighbour Corn Holm and then Black Holm, being careful not to pass too close to the north in order to stay clear of its rocky ledges. We did pass through a turbulent band of water where the depth fell to about 12ft and then we gradually picked up a steadier breeze as we sailed clear of the islands. It was wonderful to hear the small foghorn receding behind us and to feel the lift of the waves again knowing that the worst hazard on our course was now behind us.

At 19.05 we turned northwards and in difficult running conditions held our course for half an hour then I cautiously changed course slightly more to the west to close the land. When I thought that I had cleared Mull Head I went further west hoping to feel the signs of shelter as we passed into its lee. We were getting smoother water at 20.00 and looking back over the port quarter we momentarily glimpsed the edge of the headland around which we had passed without visual contact.

With a general course of 290°m we picked up the grey form of Rewick Head at 20.45 and feeling that we would be safe from this point inwards due to the frequency of landmarks I relaxed the rigid system of timing the track and watching the compass like a hawk every time that a slight course change was required. We all spotted bits of land here and there which confirmed our position so that general advice to the helmsman and lookouts about what to expect was sufficient.

Heading across the little bay towards Car Ness I suddenly felt that the bay to my left was not indented sufficiently. I had an overwhelming feeling that there was land right across our course. Searching the water ahead I thought I saw rocks to our right where no rocks should be. I hastily shouted orders to the helm so that we turned rapidly and began sailing north-eastwards towards the safest sector. We had drifted a few degrees to the south of our intended course and had entered the Bay of Meil instead of the Bay of Carness. It was a classic case of Channel Fever, causing me to relax when the major hazards were perceived as being conquered. It was also a strong case of fitting the evidence which was before our eyes into the situation that we thought ourselves to be in.

The lighthouse on Hellier Holm became visible to confirm that we were back on track and we rounded Car Ness going inside Thieves Holm, cleared the Iceland Skerries then sailed down the bay in increasing darkness towards the cluster of lights around the harbour at Kirkwall.

We thought that we would pick up one of the shallow water moorings at the head of the bay, but on hoisting it we found it supported a bag of crabs so we entered the harbour under motor at about 22.00 after a long and hazardous day's sailing.

Upon reflection after the event, I concluded that a number of things might have been done differently on this day and that our margins of safety were far too small. To look on the brighter side I also know that having come through the experience I learned a great deal from it.

MI issue 287. Episode 67.

Orkney. Kirkwall - Stronsay.
August 8. Monday.
To compensate for the strains of sailing a complex passage in thick fog the previous day we remained in Kirkwall all day, which was fortunate, for visibility remained poor outside the town and the swirling gusty wind reached force 6 at times.

We took part in the usual activities when arriving at any new port, visiting the laundrette, going to the sailing club for showers, finding the post office for sending cards, not to mention sampling the wares of the various cake shops as we sauntered around the usual tourist haunts.

One cannot visit Kirkwall without going to the St Magnus Cathedral whose tower is such a dominant landmark throughout the islands. The most notable exterior feature of the building is its distinctive red colour derived from the stone which was quarried close by. My casual curiosity had been aroused by the name St Magnus. I was accustomed to the more usual saint's names, especially those applied to churches, St Paul, St John etc. and I had a rough idea of their biographical details, but who was Magnus? I'd never heard of him. What part did he play in history?

My curiosity about Magnus was quenched by a display that I found inside the cathedral. The local school children had illustrated some episodes from his life with a series of drawings. In essence, he was an early Christian living in Orkney who had a joint claim to be the Earl of Orkney along with his cousin Hakon. A meeting was arranged between the two of them to resolve their right to succession and Magnus went along in good faith, but Hakon arrived with a large force of armed men to take the Earldom. Such a betrayal of trust was commonplace in those days. Hakon felt unable to execute Magnus himself and ordered one of his followers to do it. This man refused, so Hakon detailed another who also did not wish to strike the blow. Magnus seeing no escape from the situation encouraged this second man to be brave enough to wield the axe and make a clean job of it, which he did and Magnus was martyred. The story of his death spread and eventually the cult which grew up canonised Magnus and the Cathedral was built.

Whilst I was wandering fairly aimlessly around the building I came across an apparently insignificant genealogy (family tree) of Magnus and was immediately surprised to see William the Conqueror included there. For me, this known name suddenly lifted Magnus out of a vague mythological world into the real one. An even greater surprise was the name of another relative included in the family tree, a character called Thorfinn Skullsplitter. Did we really have chaps with names like Skullsplitter roaming around the pages of our history? I gradually realised that I knew very little history prior to 1066. Until this visit I didn't even know that Harold's (the loser at the Battle of Hastings) surname was Godwinsson a distinctly Norse-sounding name. There was a flash of recognition within me that Orkney wasn't remote at all, it had solid factual links that made it an essential cog in the historical machine that I had not previously suspected. The men who had lived and died here had been involved in shaping the world we know. I was ignorant and somewhere there was a story waiting to be discovered.

Whilst musing on our discoveries we drifted further down the main street and entered a cafe. This was an event of pure nostalgia as the atmosphere and decor was exactly 1950's. How times have changed. The purchases were totalled with pencil and paper on the counter, not in an electronic cash till. When a bun or a cake was selected, the serving assistant simply picked it up by hand and put it on your plate, reaching across the old lady washing up in the sink behind the counter. The plates were of mixed designs and well chipped, so were the assorted Victorian chairs. The tables had cotton cloths on them. Two teenage girls at the table behind me were dreaming of escaping from here to go far to the south, to the big city, where, they'd heard, the life was great. They were talking about Glasgow. I loved it all just as it was.

We were eventually driven back aboard by the deteriorating weather. The rain poured and the wind howled, so we were pleased to be in harbour.

August 9. Tuesday.
I was awoken by the torrential rain hammering on the roof and the

local fishing boats powering up to leave. Looking outside I could see the fishermen clad in ordinary sweaters and trousers with no oilskins on, wandering around in rain that descended like a waterfall. Did they have different blood from ours?

We departed at 10.20 in a break in the rain. The forecast was south-easterly, but the wind was consistently north-westerly all day. As we were leaving, a white plastic cabin cruiser which looked as though it had escaped from the Norfolk Broads came into the

harbour. It was overloaded with people who disembarked. Another similar craft followed it in. As we cleared the entrance we could see an enormous cruise liner *Vistafjord* had anchored out in the bay and was ferrying its passengers ashore in these craft, to double the population for a day and provide a bonanza for the gift shops.

We were heading north-eastwards through the islands looking for a place from which to make our crossing to Shetland. All around us lay the low green undulating hills of Orkney which we should have seen previously when we entered, but which had been hidden in the fog. As we rounded the cruise liner the weather was darkening and black rain clouds gathered in the north. We sailed north along the west side of Shapinsay admiring the baroque turrets and monolithic mass of Balfour Castle that dominated the corner of the island. Interestingly, there was a large walled garden behind the castle containing trees. This disproved the one fact that most people seem to know about Orkney and Shetland, namely that trees don't grow there. Given the right shelter, they do.

There is a whole minefield of rocky skerries blocking the gap between Shapinsay and its western neighbour Gairsay. The safe channel was only a couple of hundred metres wide between the first of these skerries and Shapinsay as we approached Vasa Point. The Vasa Skerry turned out to be more than just wave-washed rocks, for

as we passed by black heads popped out of the water all around us. Seals always know where you are, even when you drift silently by under sail. The wind dropped almost to nothing and the rain began to fall. Visibility remained good enough for safe navigation which was fortunate, because we were about to cross the Stronsay Firth a broad band of water which cuts diagonally through Orkney dividing it into the north-east and the south-west groups. As usual the pilot books were loud in their warnings of tide rips and races, wind against tide etc. but in the almost calm conditions and with neap tides we found little of note and we've faced far worse on the East Coast rivers where there is a greater flow at all times.

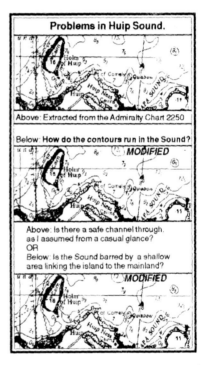

Problems in Huip Sound.

Above: Extracted from the Admiralty Chart 2250

Below: How do the contours run in the Sound?

Above: Is there a safe channel through, as I assumed from a casual glance?
OR
Below: Is the Sound barred by a shallow area linking the island to the mainland?

Just after crossing Veantrow Bay on the northern side of Shapinsay the rain stopped suddenly and the visibility cleared. From 12.30 to 13.30 we crossed to the south-eastern corner of Eday and then on across Eday Sound passing east of Little Linga. Here the seals were lounging on the sandy beach, swimming and diving in a totally relaxed manner.

I was heading through Huip Sound to creep around the northern tip of the island of Stronsay when Gavin who was sitting up on the roof of the aft cabin casually said 'The water's shallow through here.' I jumped up from my cockpit seat and looked over the side to see the bottom VERY clearly indeed, apparently only a few inches down. We did a panic tack to come out of there and I was quite shaken that I had unknowingly sailed the boat into such a trap. Why hadn't I picked it up from the chart? As soon as we were sailing clear again I looked more closely at the chart to see that the shallow contour was obscured by the name of the sound 'Huip' being printed over it (see illustration) and I had assumed a depth of between 2.7m and 4.6m all the way through rather than a ridge of 0.9 m linking the island to the land. Being of shallow draft we might have passed through safely, but then, we might not.

Passing north of Huip we ran goosewinged against the tide to the entrance marker for Stronsay harbour and then turned south towards a village called Whitehall.

A single row of houses runs along the shore with a couple of small piers projecting. The place appeared deserted except that two men were driving some cows along the street. We secured alongside a small fishing boat on the inside of the west pier as directed by the pilot book. The weather was now quite bright and the place was silent. Black-throated divers frolicked in the water as the only sign of life. We had sailed into a ghost town. A Cortina car raced along the front, turned up the pier and screeched to a halt beside us. Some men jumped out and asked us where had we come from, where were we going and how fast could we sail? We told them, they said 'Thanks.' jumped back in their car and raced away.

There was silence once more. The wind rippled the water. Clouds passed overhead as sunshine and shade crossed the bay. A battered yellow car appeared speeding along the street and turned up the pier to stop alongside us. The man said that this was his fishing boat and he'd like to paint the outside in a little while. Could we go alongside the wall until he'd painted? The paint would dry quickly and we could then go back alongside if we wished. We agreed. He jumped into his car and sped away. Once the noise of his engine had faded into the distance the silence returned. It was far too silent for our urban ears. We busied ourselves moving the boat in order to create some sounds to fill the void.

When we walked along the street we discovered the reason for the silence. Sadly, most of the houses although still in quite a good state of repair were empty. The struggle to survive in this remote place was clearly difficult. One house had a register of marriages for the island displayed in the window. There was one for this year and one for last year. Time passed in this timeless place. The small adverts in the local shop window included one for the services of a bull.

The silence of the evening was broken only by the sound of the brush as the fishing boat was painted. The sunset was superb. We had nothing to disturb our contemplation of the crossing to Shetland on the morrow.

MI issue 288. Episode 68.

Towards Shetland.
August 10 Wednesday.
Wonder of wonders, the sun was shining, but the forecast for the crossing to Shetland wasn't encouraging. Gales were promised to the south and west of us, yet as I took the early morning forecast there was a flat calm. This was the one day when we needed some wind to power us across the widest expanse of sea with which we'd be involved on this section of our journey. We wanted to make a dash for Shetland across 50 miles of open water, with the total distance to Lerwick being about 77 miles which is quite a good daysail. The tide was arranged to sweep across our track or be directly opposed to us except for two hours in the late evening. There was no choice except to motor away from Stronsay at 06.30 noticing the high cirrus which had now glazed the sun and worrying slightly about the cloud banks gathering in the south-west. We headed north-eastwards being guided by the black and white vertically striped lighthouse at Start Point on Sanday. As the sun receded the breeze came up, so that by 08.30 just off the point we were able to cut the engine and proceeded under all plain sail. We had another lighthouse on North Ronaldsay, this time with horizontal stripes, to guide us and by cross fixing we could easily check our position as we left the land behind us.

What's in a name?
Throughout our sailing in the islands I had always been very conscious of the very strong links with the Vikings who sailed these waters in their open boats. I was mentally putting myself in their place and checking with the chart when I fleetingly wondered about the names North Ronaldsay and South Ronaldsay; why did these two islands have such similar names? I remembered sailing in Norway where many of the islands have names ending in 'oy' (Notteroy, Husoy) or just 'o' (Hanko, Vestero) to signify that they are

islands. 'Oy' means 'the island of'. Why had I not realised before now that the 'ay' sound on the end of names of the Orkney (*Ork-nay*) islands (Eday, Gairsay, Shapinsay) was being used in exactly the same way? Ronaldsay was actually 'Ronald's island; Sanday probably meant Sand Island. 'Egilsay' reminded me of the French word 'eglise' for 'church', so I was pleased to see my theory confirmed by the presence of the symbol for a church on this tiny island. I could suddenly distinguish between the Norse and the English place names on the chart and for me the Norse names were much more descriptive. 'Ness' means 'headland' or 'projecting into the sea' and 'wick' means 'landing place'; 'bister' is a farm.

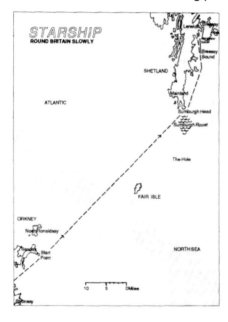

Across the gap.
What would the Vikings have given for the modern chart that I had before me? I was in the situation of having charts which covered Orkney and charts that covered Shetland, but they did not quite overlap. There was a blank bit of sea a few miles wide missing between the two sets of charts which were of different scales anyway. Vikings wouldn't have had the problem, but it's amazing how disturbing it feels to be sailing in the unrecorded gap between two charts. To set my mind at ease I taped a spare piece of writing paper to the top corner of my Orkney chart and marked latitude and longitude lines onto it so that my track did not fall off the edge of the navigation table. Anxiety allayed, I went on deck for an hour or so until I had crossed the gap and could return to mark myself onto a real chart again.

We were making good speed, reaching in a south-easterly across a moderate, lumpy grey sea out into the Fair Isle Channel. We aimed to pass to the west of Fair Isle which lies as an isolated stepping stone exactly half way between the two main island groups. The grey mass of the island became visible at about 11.30 and was used for position fixing until about 14.30. The limit of our visible range on this now murky day appeared to be about six miles and we were due north of the island by about 13.45.

<u>The Rost</u>.
Water from the Atlantic squeezes through the gap between Orkney and Shetland to fill up the North Sea, so the tidal flow can be powerful. When a gale of wind blows against the tide, great areas of turbulence can be created. All of the pilotage information about Shetland usually begins with awesome descriptions of the tide races or rosts, or roosts, as they are called. The mother and father of all rosts seems to be the Sumburgh Rost which forms between Fair Isle and the southern tip of Shetland at Sumburgh Head. The Clyde Cruising Club guide says *'South of Sumburgh Head a violent roost forms under conditions of wind against tide and/or swell. This can be three miles wide and extends six miles or more to the south. In bad weather very bad sea conditions have been reported right across The Hole* (name of this stretch of water) *to Fair Isle. The race forms in both directions with practically no slack period on the turn.* As we were sailing towards this area we did so with some trepidation.

Sumburgh Head and the other headlands just to the west of it began to become visible in mid-afternoon. At first they were grey smudges and then tall masts could be seen. Aeroplanes periodically passed overhead aiming for the airport at Sumburgh. The isolated lumps of land linked together and then took on shades of green, buildings could be seen, followed by rocks, cliffs and then the white water breaking against their foot. We were fortunate that there was no sign of the dreaded rost. By 16.40 we were clearing the rocky tip of Sumburgh and the whole of the eastern side of Mainland (obviously an English word) was opening up to us. The land was much higher than the low smooth shapes of Orkney, but it was no less green. It was varied and interesting to look at as we picked out its features whilst continuing to make progress towards Lerwick. Strings of gannets flew by, homing in on the island of Noss which lay like a huge misty wedge of cheese ahead, with its steep face to the east and its tapered face sloping down to Bressay (Norse word) indicating where we might find the entrance to Lerwick.

The wind fell lighter and lighter as we neared Bressay Sound, until we were just drifting along. Within the sound many big ships were anchored; they were mainly Eastern-bloc factory ships known locally as Klondikers, there for the purpose of picking up fish from their fleets of massive, deep sea trawlers which called in constantly.

We had not expected to come upon such an industrious scene in so remote a place.

As we passed the lighthouse on Kirkabister Ness we doused sail and started to motor for we anticipated wind-shadows as we moved between the steel-hulled giants which formed the floating town. Suddenly, from behind one of the ships ahead sailed a Viking longship. Her square sail caught a dying puff of wind from the shore to heel her down to the row of ornate shields fixed along her gunwales whilst she shot forwards with good speed. As she slowed, the yard was lowered and her oars came out to make a few hesitant strokes to take her towards the harbour. We passed close by and both crews eyed one another in wonder for we were each accustomed to being the most unusual, eye-catching craft afloat. Actually she is a modern 40ft replica (called *Dim Riv* (Norse) *Morning Light* (English) which takes tourists for trips. She was a most unexpected yet welcoming sight upon our arrival and a fine contrast to *Starship* in her sailing systems. We entered the harbour at about 19.30 having covered our 77 miles in 13 hours.

August 11 Thursday.
Lerwick is a very busy town with noisy traffic and the constant movement of crews and workers coming ashore from the ships out in the sound. There were many people both local and tourists who frequented the quay, because it is the town's main car parking area. We were now a very long way away from England and it was quite noticeable that there was a strong Scandinavian influence. Norway is about 160 miles away. Scandinavians were as much in evidence as Shetlanders, but English people were few and far between.

We moored alongside a superbly constructed Swedish 50ft steel yacht on her way to Iceland. Ahead of us were boats from the Faeroes with dried fish hanging around the cockpit as part of their standard food supply. Behind us were Norwegian motor cruisers whose occupants celebrated by photographing themselves holding bottles of alcoholic drink. There was the feeling of being in a frontier town, of standing at a crossroads where cultures intermixed freely. Yet there was no rowdy behaviour and the standard of honesty was extremely high; bicycles with full shopping baskets or dinghies complete with equipment were left unattended around the car park without fear of theft.

I called at the harbour office to record my arrival and was given a full tourist information pack along with a key to the Lerwick Boating Club and an invitation to use the showers and the bar. The club itself had new facilities even though it is more than 100 years old. We read the visitor's book which confirmed the heavy proportion of Scandinavian visitors. There were also visitors from many other parts of the globe particularly Americans, Germans and French, but only isolated English people, usually from the north-eastern area. One of the pictures which graced the walls was of *Colt Cars* and a wall painting was by Katie Clemson who first came here as a Round Britain Race competitor.

MI issue 289. Episode 69.

<u>Lerwick towards Muckle Flugga.</u>

<u>Friday August 12.</u>
We paid the modest harbour dues just prior to leaving so as to get a late-dated receipt as it remained valid for a stay of 10 days even if one departed and returned again as we intended to do. After shopping we departed at about 13.30 to catch the favourable tide up the coast. There was strong sunshine but almost no wind. We motored gently up Bressay Sound and out across the bay. We set sail and spent an hour or so drifting. In the silence we could hear strange howls coming from Green Holm which we took to be the sound of seals. For once it was very hot and the companionway was blocked by the crew's discarded oilies. The scenery was very beautiful with the high green land fringing the blue water dotted with islands and rocks standing on white foam bases. We started motoring again to make progress.

The Moul of Eswick is a high rocky headland topped with a lighthouse. Just as we were passing it, swooping round the corner at only

303

mast height came a Loganair fixed-wing aeroplane which had to hop over our mast before heading off northwards, still virtually skimming the sea.

The sun began to disappear behind clouds as we passed through the narrow gap between the Climnie Rock to port and the isolated post of the Inner Voder beacon to starboard. When I see such an isolated post projecting from the sea it always makes me wonder who has the job of going out and cementing it in place and who it is that nips out with a paint pot to keep it looking smart.

The bright day had gone by the next headland on Whalsay Island and as we entered Linga Sound a cold, fine rain had started to fall. The lovely green scenery had faded, but there was beauty in the many shades of grey ahead, illuminated by a strong rainbow as the only dash of colour against the drab background. As rain showers passed we could at times look forward at a misty grey prospect of desolation with restricted visibility, whilst behind us it might be clear and sunny with green fields, white houses and sparkling sea.

We trended left towards Lunna Ness for I had decided that motoring much further would not really be worthwhile and I should find an anchorage for the night. I would have liked to have stayed in one of the voes (inlets) on the south side of Yell, but they were not sheltered from all directions like the one that I had selected inside Lunna Ness called Boatsroom Voe. One of the Yell anchorages Burra Voe had a wonderful description in the Clyde Cruising Club pilot book of the leading marks for the entrance. *'The leading line is the two middle doors of the council house block with red-brown roof visible between the shop (warehouse building on the quay) and the white house with four dormer windows beside it bearing North.'*

As we sailed up the east side of Lunna Ness we could see over its top to the west, two very strange and contrasting sights. One was a modern wind generator like a huge aeroplane propeller on a tower and the second, what appeared to be an enormous bonfire. The fire on the hilltop was somehow filled with ancient primitive symbolism, whereas by contrast, the propeller dominating this island setting looked very futuristic. In fact the 'Indian bonfire' was as modern as the wind generator as it was a flare for the oil terminal at Sullom Voe.

We rounded Lunna Holm at six o'clock and headed south west in cold drizzle. I was distracted by a fish farm and passed the entrance to the inlet as it was partially obscured by a shingle ridge which protects the anchorage, but we returned to enter the voe which to a large extent was filled by the fish farm. At least they had left enough room to anchor.

It is a great pity that the most enclosed little anchorages are the very places best suited to farm fish. One has to expect the presence of farms if the stopping place looks at all sheltered. The fish farmers are obviously nervous about boats visiting, for fear of losing some of their stock to poachers, so some of them litter the surrounding area with floats and lines in an apparent attempt to discourage visiting craft. I felt that they would fare better if they defined their own area more clearly with yellow buoys and signs, then either advised on where to anchor or supplied a couple of mooring buoys for visitors, away from their fish pens.

Only a couple of days previously we had sailed into the village of Whitehouse on the island of Stronsay to find it empty and silent. Here we sailed into an apparently empty rural bay and after dropping our hook we were taken aback by the noise of the place. Our arrival had coincided with lambs losing their mothers on the hillside, flocks of seagulls engaged in aerial squabbles, cows with stomach ache, the fish in the pens thrashing and jumping and guard dogs at the local farm demanding to be released. We sat astonished at this bombardment of our senses. It was a stark contrast to silent Stronsay. All that night the flares lit the sky to the west.

August 13 Saturday.
It was a thirteenth day and the one on which we planned our final assault to round the remote rock of Muckle Flugga at the northern extremity of the British Isles. The rain was pouring, it was cold, but visibility wasn't too bad. We departed at 10.30 as the rain was abating to get the best tidal conditions which were never very good. The wind was westerly about force 3 so we crossed the swirling pools and eddies of Yell Sound and passed close against Heoga Ness inside the Muckle Skerry of Neapaback, discussing the meaning of the word 'muckle' (large) which was relevant to our destination. The fine weather overtook us along the east coast of Yell and for the rest of the day we had magnificent scenery.

What one sees is composed of a complex balance of elements. Nature has its prime share. The main islands are huge pieces of land, high and hilly with cliffs and bays and whilst they are rugged they are not bare. Man takes his proportion with green fields, small hamlets, sheep everywhere, the odd road, ferry or small fishing boat. The sea weaves between, providing the link, whilst the sun and shadows guarantee the variety and the change. Seabirds are always in evidence, soaring and diving. The scene isn't hostile or remote because these people, these creatures, live here. It is their home and they are not distanced from any other location nor from each other. It was we who were from the outside, looking odd; Summer visitors who were soon to leave. Here man is in a kind of balance with nature, surrounded by it but allowed his part within it.

Hascosay Sound had groups of gannets swooping to fish the swirling waters whilst ahead on the island we watched a shepherd with three dogs rounding up sheep on the high ground and driving them down to the farm on the lower levels at the northern end. He waved to us enthusiastically as he strode on, calling to his dogs. At Burra Ness an ancient Broch lay in ruins; much of its stone raided to build rough sheep pens. These round 'castles' were once homes to the local chief and defendable sites for the whole community who could shelter inside whenever marauding raiders passed by. Passing through our third Linga Sound we spotted the ferry linking Yell to Unst. It's amazing but no matter how hard one tries to time the approach correctly, one always arrives at the landing slipway just as the ferry approaches. We might have been only the second yacht during the past week but we still managed to time it just right. Unlike ferries met elsewhere on our travels, this one throttled back and the helmsman came out onto the bridge wing to give us a cheery wave and allow us to pass before he went on about his business.

We were now passing up Bluemull Sound which takes its name from an impressive blue granite headland on the eastern shore. The pilotage description of the sound was roughly as follows. '*The Spring rate in both directions is 7 knots in the narrowest parts and races form off the points on either side. Turbulence forms across certain bays, with wind against tide dangerous seas develop.*' Not very inviting, but we had become accustomed to such descriptions and had found that timing it roughly right and having the sail power to produce boat speed makes them much less of a problem than might be expected. We had a good reaching breeze and went through at six or seven knots meeting no real opposition until we met the incoming waves from the open sea. We had the wind power to push through some rough stuff without undue discomfort. For a mile or so we drove out directly into it and then we were able to go onto a smoother, broader reach following the coast up, admiring the scenery. Just after 14.00 we spotted Muckle Flugga lighthouse atop its bleak rock as it appeared to pass between a headland and an off-lying stack.

An hour later it was bearing due east and at 15.30 it was due south. Technically speaking I suppose it was just another corner with a lighthouse on it, but visually it was quite special. The area has a

306

number of bird colonies and the turbulent waters were filled with activity. The rocks themselves were particularly striking being angled and grouped to provide more interest than the best that any sculptor could make. The rock with the lighthouse on it is not the most northerly point, for the Out Stack lays another half a mile further out. Neither is Muckle Flugga the point where a craft can turn southwards, that place is another three and a half miles along the north coast at Skaw. The beautiful high hills, topped with a radar station which we called the Taj Mahal, and the deep inlet of the Burra Firth provided the perfect backdrop to the rugged scene of this turning point for the year's cruise.

The area of rough overfalls known as the Skaw Rost marked prominently on the charts was fortunately not present as we turned south. We came close-hauled heading for the north-channel entrance to Balta Sound and found a sail to chase. We nearly caught him, but dropped sail outside the entrance and motored up to anchor just to the west of the pier at the completion of the most scenic and satisfying day of the Summer's cruise. Later we were to meet the crew of the 40ft steel yacht, home based in the Firth of Forth that we'd chased. They had actually stopped at Muckle Flugga and then had sailed along the north coast. They felt themselves to be sailing rather well and were at a loss to understand why the craft behind them was overtaking them, until we came close enough for them to see the extra hulls.

We were content to stay aboard reading and writing, whilst sounds from the village fete and disco drifted across the water long after our eyes had closed for a well-earned rest.

MI issue 290. Episode 70.

Balta Sound - Mid Yell Voe.
14 August. Sunday
The forecast was for easterly force 4 with the wind increasing throughout the day as a depression neared. After examining the chart I decided that if I could weather Fetlar I'd be able to sail all the way down to Lerwick virtually on the one tack, even in bad weather. I could have stayed in harbour, but the pilotage guide warned of the length of the fetch that could be generated in Balta Sound with the wind in its present direction, a wind which was due to rise to force 7 maybe? Getting down to Lerwick before the conditions deteriorated was a strong temptation.

The tide went our way at nine o'clock so we set off to motor down the harbour raising our mainsail as we went. Hard on the wind under motor and main we could just point for the narrow southern entrance. There was a rocky shore on either hand and the lumpy sea was being forced straight into the entrance. I was holding her under main and engine until I could clear the entrance. We were on the port tack and closing the rocks to starboard when suddenly the engine stopped firing properly and we lost its power. There was white water all around and absolutely no time to investigate mechanical matters. We immediately tacked the boat whilst we had the momentum to put her through the wind. As we only had the main raised we had to rapidly deploy the roller genoa, fighting to get it sheeted in with the strong wind filling it and waves crashing all around us. We slowly moved forwards and then began to pick up speed. The rocks receded behind us to be replaced by newer, equally menacing ones as the opposite shore of the entrance rushed towards us. To immediately tack again so quickly risked a possible snarl up with the sheet, losing speed and drifting sideways onto the rocks. There was just a chance that by holding the tack we could clear the entrance and sail into open water. By taking the time to think this thought, it was already too late to make the choice. We held our tack, cresting the incoming waves and watching the water falling beneath us to explode on the rocks just metres away from our port float. We sped out of the foaming trap with our sails stretched to bursting and the boat gripping the water as tightly as she knew how to. Only when we were clear could we breathe more freely again and take stock of our situation.

I knew without needing further confirmation that the engine needed attention, I also knew that to sail without it being available reduced our safety margin substantially, so I had to find a sheltered anchorage where I might enter with ease, under sail. Balta Sound that we had just departed might have served well except for it being exposed to this wind direction. I chose therefore to go to Mid Yell Voe, because when we had passed it on the previous day it had appeared to be a well-populated area which promised the possibility of assistance if I should need it.

We took a lumpy tack out to sea on 095°m and then turned onto 185°m which wasn't quite so uncomfortable and we continued to throw a lot of water around. We held up to windward quite well and I was able to bear away to 210°m heading for Haaf Grunay. This Norse name meaning *'Green island in the deep sea'* marked the northern edge of a broad bay which has an historic link with the Vikings. They used this area as an important staging post on their journeys from Norway westwards towards Faeroes, Iceland, Greenland and eventually the land we now call America. They re-provisioned and rested here on the outward trip before going north through Bluemull Sound into the Atlantic. We intended to turn southwards from this bay to stay in the North Sea. We progressively bore away into the sound. We were no longer thrashing to windward so the motion eased as the water became flatter under the shelter of Fetlar.

To enter Mid Yell Voe I could pass either to the north or south of the island of Hascosay. The tide was going from north to south; the wind which followed the channels was going south to north. Unable to see any great advantage in either route I chose to pass to the south of the island to avoid having to tack in the narrow Hascosay Sound. Passing between the islets of Urie Lingey and Sound Gruney we met our first rost and as soon as we saw it we knew what all the fuss about rosts was for. The wind was funnelled along the Fetlar shore to hit this spot where the water squeezed between the islands. The line where the turbulence started was as clearly drawn across the water as a weir marks a river. The smooth flow of water pitched over this line into a tumbling cataract resembling rapids and it demanded much checking of the chart to determine that we were not about to sail the boat onto a hidden rock skerry. The anticipation and apprehension on board mounted as we came closer to the line, then suddenly we were over it and into the roar of the water crashing and falling all about us. Still sailing free, we just surfed along skipping over the wave tops at between eight and ten knots. The day before we had sailed through the biggest rost area marked on the chart at Skaw and found it as flat as a pancake; today we approached a clear area and met a sizeable rost.

The wind was rising to about force 5 as we began sheeting in to pull closer to Fetlar, so I rolled in a third of the genoa which still gave her the power to sustain six to eight knots as we squeezed her closer and closer into the wind funnelling between the islands ahead. Once through the gap we were able to ease off a touch to cross Colgrave Sound heading for Whitehill lighthouse. Just off the corner of Hascosay we met a really big rost that gave us quite a thrashing as we were beating into it. We were really powering through everything with water going absolutely everywhere. There was one memorably mighty crunch when all three bows together went straight through a wall of blue/green water and we felt like canoeists with water over the coaming and spray deck, going down rapids. We were underwater sailing. As Gavin pointed out, it wasn't the waves that were the problem, you can get over them, it was the holes in between that were proving difficult as we crashed down into them. We had the roughest five to ten minutes sailing that I could recall, but throughout it the boat never faltered, she just went speeding along cutting cleanly, shaking off cascades of streaming sea and leaping forward to meet the next watery obstacle.

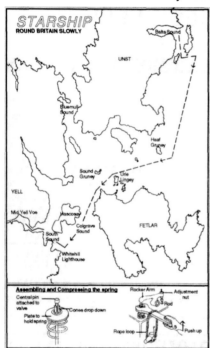

We found a brief respite as we neared the lighthouse before we bore away to go up South Sound. Only the previous day we had drifted casually through here waving to a shepherd rounding up his sheep. On this day we found the sound filled from shore to shore with another Rost. This time we were running again and we sped lightly over the waves to enter Mid Yell Voe. This confirmed the lesson we were learning that tackling a rost going to windward gives the boat a very rough ride, whereas off-the-wind the boat can pass over it relatively unscathed.

I was later to wonder if with a bit more experience, I could perhaps have escaped altogether by passing around Hascosay to the north, for then I might have avoided the roosts which appeared to form only on the down-tide sides of islands when the wind and tide are violently opposed.

The wind did not abate inside the Voe at Mid Yell for it followed the contours of the valley and we found it equally windy inside as out. The anchorage was again taken by a fish farm with many pot markers taking the remaining relatively sheltered space. Fortunately there were three enormous mooring buoys as part of the enterprise and we made an effort to pick one up. The wind was now approaching gale force and with the noise it was hard to communicate with the crew on the foredeck. It was also difficult to exercise the fine judgement required to halt the boat alongside the buoy. We had to reef the boat down to gain control, by which time we had torrential rain and a driving mist was descending in the semi-darkness even though it was only midday. We finally secured and it was a great relief to get below for a hot meal, ignoring our difficulties for a while until we had warmed up a bit. In the next couple of hours the wind was gusting well over gale force and we appreciated being attached to the nice solid mooring.

We checked the engine in the afternoon and discovered the worst. We had a broken valve spring. Fortunately we had a spare spring aboard as a result of the previous similar failure in the Menai Strait a couple of years earlier. The real problem was that I didn't carry the powerful spanners aboard which were needed for dismantling the motor to insert the new spring correctly. In addition we had no device to compress the spring to hook it underneath its retaining washer.

Such little trials are sent to tax the ingenuity of the cruising sailor. There is no advantage to be gained by moaning about a problem, one has to look at the tools available and work out how to get the job done in an unconventional way if that is what is needed. We had to look on the bright side. At least we had the replacement valve spring.

It was a combined crew effort. We managed to slip the spring in underneath the rocker arm and I compressed it by using mole grips on a spanner handle to increase leverage, passed through a rope looped onto a projecting piece of the engine. Gavin used Carol's tweezers to slip the small locking cones into the retaining washer as Alison directed the torch to illuminate the dark recesses of the engine in which we worked. We were rather proud of our improvisation, but our feelings of superiority evaporated immediately when we discovered that the rod which pushed the rocker was bent so badly that it could not engage the rocker to operate it. We withdrew the rod and carefully straightened it using a 'G' cramp and the tube of our bilge-pump handle. To extract and replace the rod we had to compress and remove our new spring once more. With each dismantling and refitting operation we ran the risk of dropping those tiny, vital, locking cones down into the inaccessible depths of the bilge beneath the engine, or even worse, into the engine crankcase itself. 'Sailing' can be so exciting.

Reassembled, crossed fingers, turn the ignition key ... and ... it worked. How sweet the sound of a working diesel. I made a note to lay in a stock of spare springs for future use.

The 17.50 shipping forecast extended its gale warnings to our area, a little too late. It was really blowing rather strongly. The gale was intended to go from east to north-west the following day so there was a chance of using it to take us down to Lerwick. We enjoyed a good meal and lay cosily rocking in our bunks listening to the extremes of the weather outside. I was pleased that we weren't out there trying to sail down to Lerwick.

MI issue 291. Episode 71.

<u>Mid Yell Voe   Lerwick. Shetland.</u>
<u>15 August. Monday.</u>
Although we awoke to a flat calm, the shipping forecast told us that a gale was on its way. The Butt of Lewis was already experiencing north-westerly force 8. In the light of our memory of the gale the previous day we decided to take no risks but to have a lazy day staying tied to our big mooring in Mid Yell Voe. Such decisions are an advantage of being true cruisers. Visibility remained poor for most of the day with low cloud and mist.

We prepared the inflatable dinghy and went across to the comprehensively stocked shop at Mid Yell. Upon landing at the sandy beach beside the small pier we were met by one of those scruffy dogs that carries its own battered beer can which it places at your feet to be kicked or thrown, so that it can be retrieved. You could throw the can anywhere, but the dog just wasn't interested unless you threw it into the sea. He then felt that he had adequate excuse to fling himself with gay abandon into the water. He loved it and just to prove it, he came back and shook himself all over you, unless you threw the can into the sea again without delay. Mid Yell is not the busiest place in the world. Two local people just happened to arrive at the Post Office at the same time, so when we four stood in line behind them, we formed the longest queue seen in Mid Yell that month. Extra staff had to be called into the shop to deal with such a rush.

It goes almost without saying that the forecast gale stayed away and the westerly wind rarely exceeded force 3 all day, but we had a nice rest with plenty of reading.

16 August Tuesday.
It did blow a bit in the night with rain drumming on the roof, so technically the shipping forecast was correct as the gale arrived in the last two hours of the 24 hour span of the forecast. The wind was quite strong when we awoke, but had dropped to about three or four when we were preparing to leave to catch the favourable tide at

about ten o'clock. With a west wind we could sail free all the way to Lerwick and we departed under ideal conditions with the most gloriously intense green hills dotted with white sheep and the azure sparkling sea specked with white seabirds.

We went through a calm South Sound and rounded the Whitehill lighthouse watching the beautiful cliffs and rocks which were clear and coloured as never before. Carol casually noticed a tiny dot on the horizon far to the south which might have been a fishing boat, but was too distant to distinguish. We followed the coast identifying the headlands from the chart and generally enjoying the warmth and the superb sail. The sound of the water was a continuous gurgling, as though we were sitting beside a stream; it was smooth and relaxing. The dot to the south seemed a little nearer; looking through binoculars I saw an unusual sight. The sail was tan coloured, but it was squarish with the yard peaked higher at the stern. It seemed for all the world like a Shetland sixareen (or sixern) the traditional fishing craft once used in these parts but which was now extinct. How could it be then that I had this ghost boat in my binocular's lens?

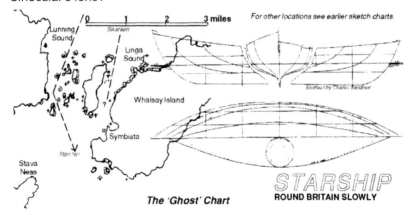

The 'Ghost' Chart

STARSHIP
ROUND BRITAIN SLOWLY

The wind was dropping as we approached the crossing of Yell Sound where the waters are made more turbulent by flowing through a maze of reefs, rocks and small islands. To produce more power we unwrapped our spinnaker/drifter. For a while we made swifter progress, but the apparition of the sixareen refused to dematerialise and return to the history books. As we came nearer he was becoming an irrefutable reality, sailing towards Linga Sound past Whalsay Island.

Our course took us through Lunning Sound on a parallel

course. The black-hulled sixareen was disappearing behind an island as I went below for my camera. I returned to find the wind even lighter, but we were now in a position to sail down onto him. Hunting for signs of him I caught a glimpse of the peak of his sail just going behind an island about a mile to leeward of us. As soon as he emerged I could get a picture to prove that sixareens still exist.

We were almost becalmed and suffered a spinnaker collapse, because I was concentrating on the sixareen. The wind changed direction slightly. Where was that sixareen? We reset our sail. He should have emerged by now. We worked eastwards towards where he should be but as we cleared Stava Ness to open Linga Sound to our view, we found it to be empty. The last sixareen to be seen in Shetland had sailed right through into its own timeframe and disappeared. My camera lay unused. There was nothing except the sparkle of bright light on the water and a tangible emptiness. It was a mystery. Nobody would ever now believe that when the sun shines, the gentle westerly blows and gannets dive into clear seas through the simple joy of living, the ghost of the sixareen can still be seen sailing in Shetland. Sadly, we turned and drifted southwards once more.

Just when I thought we might have to resort to motoring to get across South Nesting Bay the wind returned with enough south in it to make us reduce sail to genoa again. By the time that we were passing through the narrow gap between the Climnie Rocks and the Inner Voder beacon just to the north of the Moul of Eswick we were back at full power on a flat sea. It was one of those magic sails that we dream about, with the sun's glare on the water ahead and the right weight of wind to push the boat at six or eight knots without creating the waves to disturb the endless sensation of accelerating across the sea. We goosewinged into Bressay Sound carrying our sail right up to the harbour entrance and tied up alongside the same Swedish yacht which had acted as our fender when we were here previously.

Lerwick is such a contrast with the rest of the quiet islands. There were at least 20 ships within the sound off the harbour and at least another 20 Klondikers in Brei Voe just to the south. The whole place was full of Soviet factory workers. In Lerwick the smell is of fish; engine noise is like a motorway; the equipment is rugged; the motors are diesels; the atmosphere is frontier and there's money to be made by getting hands dirty. An observer on the quayside calling down to ask about our unusual boat began with 'Do you speak English?'

We were straight ashore to get our Boating Club key, top up with water and deposit our rubbish. Returning with fresh bread and milk I saw, crossing the harbour, my earlier apparition, the sixareen. She was as large as life. The tan sailed, clinker, open fishing boat *Far Haaf* had her crew just shipping their oars as she approached the landing where misty-eyed Shetlanders gathered to reach out to touch her with pride. She had been constructed only a year previously in Balta Sound as an exact replica of recorded sixareens. They had sailed her down to join the fun of the Combined Clubs Regatta which was being held over the next three days. Her skipper later told me that he had seen us emerge from Mid Yell Voe and overhaul them just as they stopped for a lunch break in the little village of Symbister on Whalsay Island at the bottom of Linga Sound.

It's worth just recording that, when working, these small open boats were rowed and sailed about 40 miles out into the Atlantic and there the crew of six men laid handlines up to seven miles long in depths of 50 - 100 fathoms (300 - 600ft). The lines had baited hooks at 30ft intervals. Once the lines were laid the boats were effectively anchored to them. The gear had to be retrieved whatever the weather, for the men would lose their livelihood if the lines were cut. Without weather forecasting, this was a very dangerous way to live. In 16 July 1832 thirty-one boats were lost; on 20 July 1881 ten boats were lost to freak storms. The numbers of men killed in such incidents represented a high proportion of the working population of the areas from which they came. The fishermen had inadequate protective clothing and survived on meagre meals of oatmeal bread when at sea. Each boat made two, three-day trips each week. Let nobody speak of the 'romance of sail' when talking about such craft.

The regatta had all the usual classes of boat racing with the addition of the Shetland model. To ignorant outsiders such as ourselves, they looked like miniature Viking boats complete with a dipping square lugsail which had to be lowered and reset on the opposite side of the mast with each tack. There was a crew of three. A bow man to pull the yard forward of the mast, a halliard man to drop the yard and re-hoist it and the helmsman who steered and manipulated the mainsheet. The tack of the sail was secured to the end of a short bowsprit and hauled tight to create a luff which rose from the stem, right up to the peak of the yard which tilted under tension, to make the sail almost triangular like an Arab Dhow.

The boats had a broad wineglass cross-section. They were speedy and initially very tender. We saw them having their bottoms polished whilst still afloat by simply standing the crew along the gunwhale holding onto the mast. This heeled the boat far enough for one whole side to be scrubbed off from gunwhale to keel by a man ashore. In this attitude the boat was developing its maximum righting moment. A unique advantage of the long-keeled shape was that launching trolleys were not required. When ashore the three-man crew could balance them upright and ski them along. As the fleet sailed in from racing the crew disembarked, the bows were lifted slightly onto the ramp and the boat slid away as an almost continuous movement, causing no delay.

The fastest of these craft had Bermudian sails and all the go-faster goodies such as barber haulers, bendy rigs with shroud adjuster and mast rams, but all the hulls were subtly different from each other. The older ones were solid clinker planked, but the newer ones were epoxy/ply planked with laminated stems and stern posts etc. It's worth noting again the impressive level of public honesty, proved by leaving up to 50 craft on the public car park, complete with all their gear.

17 August Wednesday.
We had southerly winds which were no good for travelling south so we decided to stay a while and maybe explore overland. We took the opportunity to tackle lots of cleaning jobs, do shopping and washing and visit some of the local sights. We helped the Swedish boat inside us to get out and leave for Iceland. The weather deteriorated in the afternoon as the regatta got underway. There were rowing races where the rival crews all used the same boat, being timed over the roughly triangular course. The rain poured and it was dark early, but this had absolutely no effect on the continuation of the event.

As we had no time to properly cover the west side of Shetland under sail we decided to hire a car which we booked for the following day.

MI issue 292. Episode 72.

Voyaging Shetland - Overland
Lerwick to Fair Isle. 18 August Thursday.
The wind was adverse, so in order to explore Shetland quickly we hired a car for the day. Together with insurance, VAT, fuel etc. the cost was less than £30 so it was a cheap deal for four people. We had just two problems. The first was that there was thick fog and drizzly rain, which wasn't good for sightseeing as we couldn't even see where we were going. The second difficulty was that we

departed without a road map and had only a small leaflet illustrating Ancient Norse Shetland, so we were reduced to interpreting its place names to compare with roadside signs when we found them to discover roughly where we were heading.

We first went to Scalloway (Bay of Huts) which is only six miles from Lerwick, but over on the west coast. It was formerly the capital of Shetland, but now it is hardly more than a sleepy village. The point of interest for us was the busy little boatyard which had on its ways a big (80ft) wooden fishing vessel being refurbished, which gave us a fascinating discussion about bending wooden planks of these dimensions.

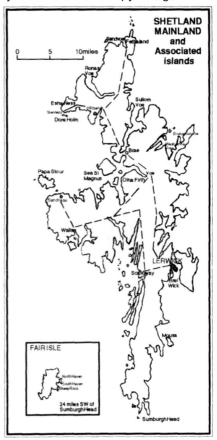

There were two other attractions, a ruined castle built 1600 and a tiny two-roomed museum at the end of the main street. The museum was supposed to be closed until later in the afternoon, but as we passed by we saw some people going in and we were told that we could join them if we wished. Whilst we were looking around the usual exhibits of carved whale teeth and seamen's kit chests, more and more people kept coming in. Where they came from was a mystery for we had hardly seen a soul about on the streets. The place was getting very crowded when suddenly without warning a tall, distinguished man stepped into the middle of the room and began an emotional speech … in Norwegian. Everyone stopped and listen intently, so I ceased studying an antique ship-in-a-bottle and did likewise. The man stopped speaking and to my relief, a lady gave a translation at the sentence end. He said it was a special day for him to return once more to Scalloway to represent his close friends. He had come to thank the people of the town for their generous support when he and his compatriots had arrived without possessions during the last war.

It emerged that this man was a major figure in the Shetland Bus group of Scandinavians who had used small fishing craft to cross to Norway taking weapons, men and evacuating refugees during the last war. They had first tried to operate from West Lunna Voe, just south of Boatsroom Voe where we had stayed overnight on our journey north, but they had no engineering facilities to refurbish their craft so they had moved to Scalloway where the local boatyard gave them all that they needed. He presented a special pennant to the former owner of the yard amidst flashing cameras and Press questions about the wartime operation. (*The story is told in a book, The Shetland Bus by David Howarth*.)

As we drove out of Scalloway the fog lifted sufficiently for us to see one of the enormous modern windmills operating on a hilltop. We passed up the valley of Tingwall where the old Viking parliament used to meet. Politics in those days was even more back-stabbingly dangerous than today. To reduce the number of such casualties the meetings were held on a small island in a lake; the isolated island could only be reached across stepping stones.

The further west we went the more the fog lifted and we gradually began to see more of the Shetland scenery. Generally speaking, the centre of the main island is high moorland very similar to the Pennines in northern England except that there are extensive peat workings everywhere. It's not at all like Orkney which is a group of green, low lying, farming islands. Shetland is of such a size and character that in places one could easily forget that it is an island. Passing through the south western area there were many valleys cutting far inland making long sheltered lakes interlocking to form a labyrinth of waterways for a cruiser to explore.

We went out to Walls which had an excellent secluded harbour with only a single sailing dinghy drifting around. We drove over rugged moorland to drop down to the green oasis of Sandness to look across the shallow sound to the island of Papa Stour, wishing that we had time to explore its caves and secluded bays.

Back inland we came across wild Shetland ponies which took off at a frisky gallop whenever we stopped to take their pictures. Going north we skirted the edges of many voes and islands passing an especially good anchorage at Voe at the head of Olna Firth. At Brae we stood on a narrow neck of land which only just links all the

318

land to the north-west with the mainland. It is possible to see Sullom Voe to the north and the Sea of St. Magnus to the south. It's a mystery why someone hasn't dug a short cut to link the two.

We briefly passed through Hillswick the largest centre of population in these parts and drove onwards to the end of the road at Stenness. This was the most scenic part of our tour for the coast has high cliffs and on the offlying island of Dore Holm was the highest and most impressive natural arch that we had seen. Having appreciated the views from the rocky headland we followed a sign 'To the lighthouse.' and came, by chance, to the top of the cliffs at Esha Ness. The sight from these heights was awe inspiring. The precipitous cliffs had the open Atlantic crashing in slow motion onto rock formations far below as we looked down on the many seabirds returning to their rock-ledge nests beneath us. Approaching the edge of such a frightening fall gave an overpowering sensation which

created a very hollow feeling in the pit of the stomach. We lay on the overhanging lip of the cliff in the rising blast of air which carried the roar of the ocean up to fill our ears and hypnotise our senses.

Esha Ness

Returning from the brink of the precipice we passed along the southern edge of Ronas Voe and up to the northern extremity of Mainland to the promontory called Fethaland finding a beautiful, almost enclosed bay at Sandvoe. Along the way the scenery became more and more Nordic. The houses were clad with vertical wooden boarding, the fields were filled with tall stooks of hay stacked around wooden frames designed to improve the drying process. It seemed as though farming had changed little over the centuries in these outlying areas.

As we went south again we found the rain and mist exactly where we had left it at the beginning of our voyage around the interior of Shetland. Lerwick in the drizzle seemed most uninviting, but the locals were cheerfully treating it all as Summer. The Shetland model evening race was being keenly contested by the dripping competitors in the half light. We joined the rest of the spectators parked in a line at the pier head with our engines ticking over to keep the windscreen wipers and heaters going.

19 August Friday.

When it is time to leave, it takes about 2½ hours to just do all those last little things. Just to top up the water, just to tank up the diesel, just to get the fresh bread, just to take back the clubhouse key, just to take in the washing, just to leave the last bit of rubbish, post the last postcard, confirm the weather report, shorten the lines, then one casts off, to discover what one has just forgotten to do.

The weather was poor initially but brightened for us to leave on our return journey towards Orkney about midday. The forecast wasn't too promising. A north-west gale was on its way somewhere but we were supposed to be having variable four. In fact we had north-west as we departed which became south-west as we sailed out through the factory ships in Brei Wick. Thousands of gulls filled the air and gorged themselves on the outflow from the ships. Thousands more covered the headlands all around, feeling too full to take flight. The stench was nose numbing.

We had a fine breeze to help us crest through the incoming swell and we swooped away, waving to the workers on deck enjoying the sunshine. Gusts of wind came rushing across the water from the land a mile and a half away and our progress was good. There was a powerful feeling of 'leaving'. Although we had turned southwards several days earlier shortly after rounding Muckle Flugga we had remained in Shetland, but now we were about to leave these islands behind and there was a sense of finality almost as though our summer holidays were ending.

After the first hour at eight knots we were down to the island of Mousa, pointing out the rounded form of the Pictish broch which survives as the most complete example of these fortified towers used for protecting the whole community. The P&O ferry was sailing up inside the island which gave its passengers a better chance to observe the broch. If only the weary people who constructed its defensive walls against seaborne raiders could have imagined that the structure they were building in their desperation would one day become a tourist attraction, what would they have thought?

The wind dropped a little and we set full genoa to take us down to Sumburgh Head at seven knots. We gave it a two mile offing to avoid contact with the rost, but once clear of the land the wind began to die and we only achieved four knots on a southerly course until we lost the wind entirely about halfway between Shetland and Fair Isle.

We ghosted along for a while and were intercepted by a group of porpoise which played around us for ten minutes but then disappeared when we tried a tack to the west to try to bring us nearer to Fair Isle which we could see about ten miles distant. There was virtually no progress after the tide turned at about 17.30. At 19.00 realising that I had about two hours of good light left I had to decide between lolling about at sea all night, or being in harbour, I turned on the motor.

The harbour on Fair Isle has a north-facing entrance but there is an alternative south-facing bay. The slight breeze that we felt was from the south, but there was the northerly gale forecast to arrive at some time. Should we go in the north or the south haven?

We arrived just as night fell, guided in by the distinctive mass of Sheep Rock. The haven was very tight and surrounded by vertical jagged cliff faces except where the high shingle bar linked the island of Bu Ness to the mainland. The lazy south-easterly swell agitated against the foot of the rock walls filling the basin with continuous wave sounds. It was essential to guard against being trapped if the wind should begin to blow in. We were anchored in only twelve feet of water with limited swing and on a short scope. Should we anchor to resist the incoming swell or the gale which might arrive? As we laid the anchor I was mindful of the pilot book warning that anchoring was difficult due to the bottom being rock and boulders.

The boat was never at rest, but was continuously rocked by the reflections of the refracted swell which echoed round and round the rocky arena. It was not a night to be dressed in pyjamas and carpets slippers. The restless skipper remained wakeful all night with his ears twitching at every sound and movement.

MI issue 293. Episode 73.

Fair Isle - Tankerness.
August 20 Saturday.
The night had passed peacefully enough for the crew, but the skipper had never changed out of oilies and had cat-napped only fitfully, constantly checking the proximity of the dark cliffs in Fair Isle's South Haven.

The calm
The forecast confirmed that the northerly gale was on its way, without any doubt, so there was little time to lose. We had an early breakfast and began to leave the wave-washed anchorage to its

nesting seabirds once again. The enormous mass of Sheep Rock towered high above us, whilst to seaward we marvelled at immense slabs of rock hundreds of feet high which were separated by angled fissures passing right through the headland. We motored over a calm sea anxious to clock up as many miles as possible before the onset of the storm.

At the southern tip of the island we could see the rural beauty of the green pastures surrounding the houses behind the lighthouse then we were bouncing about in a lumpy rost which extended for about a mile even in the flat calm. It was a steady slog under motor until about 09.30 when a little breeze from ahead encouraged us to motor-sail southwards on 210°m, hoping for a westerly tack when the northerlies set in. All morning we chugged gently along apparently in the middle of nowhere, but grateful to be on a flat sea. Suddenly the wind came in from the south. The gentle force 2-3 allowed us the same rate of progress towards the west, but under full sail in silence.

Oh, isn't it wonderful, when after five hours of donking diesel, it is turned off and progress continues in smooth silence embellished only with the sound of a trickling wake? For two peaceful hours we slid westwards until we fell becalmed and had to endure further noise disturbance in the cause of progress.

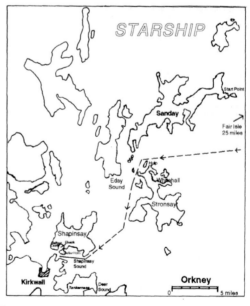

At 14.20 we saw the lighthouse at Start Point on Sanday and sailed back onto the chart again. At 16.15 after three days of waiting the first breath of the northerly wind it finally came in, but by this time we were well into Sanday Sound hoping to retrace our outgoing route around Stronsay to the south. The wind had a steadiness which immediately picked the boat up onto a broad reach at about six knots so that she steered perfectly with nobody at the wheel, freeing me to trim the sails and enjoy the skimming sensation

as we aimed for the top end of the Holm of Huip where a rost had formed to indicate that there was a strong adverse tide.

We turned southwards and began goosewinging, holding tightly to the side of Stronsay to minimise the two knots of tide against us. The channel we were crossing can have tides running at up to 7.2 knots on big Springs. From the corner of Stronsay we cut across to Shapinsay on a broad reach. The sea and sky behind us looked dark and angry. The water was covered in white caps but our speed of seven or eight knots made for level sailing until we entered Shapinsay Sound where we began close-reaching in force six winds under full sail doing ten or more knots. We really began to move and it was like riding on a speedboat under perfect control. Most of the time our heavy cruiser is fairly well overloaded with gear-for-all-situations and she rarely gets up and goes. We are usually quite happy with four to six knots in comfort, so when she climbs over ten knots to windward on flat water we really appreciate the feeling. It was a glorious sail and we revelled in it.

Just past Hellier Holm there was a biggish tide rost, but we knew what to expect by this time. We went in with a bang, whooping and hollering whilst cascades of water went smashing everywhere like a beach cat going out through the surf. We had to make a sharp right turn into Elwick the small enclosed bay in which we had chosen to ride out the incoming gale. We tacked and reduced the genoa in one operation then went speeding up the harbour like a dinghy in a wind now steady at force six. We tucked in tight to the northern shore and dropped anchor only to find it dragging back again, choked with weed. Pulling up a 35lb CQR with a similar weight of chain and another similar weight of kelp and attached rocks amounts to unhealthy exercise, but it was cleared and reset again on a sandy patch in 25ft of water. The anchor rode was parcelled at the stem head fitting and everything was made secure on deck.

The gale

The wind really began to blow at around 23.30 and it increased in power until it began to shake the boat. Luckily there were almost no waves as we were so close to the shore, but the wind noise was extreme and for the skipper at least, it was difficult to sleep. The back of the mainsail escaped from its tying at about two o'clock and I had to go up on deck to secure it. The noise and the wind force out there were much greater than I had thought from being down below. I crawled along the deck to the bow and looked at the single warp that we were all relying on now. It was stretched as tight as a bowstring and humming when the boat strained from one side to the other as she did in a constant cycle. Under extreme load the rope became visibly thinner. For a while, in the deafening roar of the darkness there was just me and that anchor warp. At such times one prays for the anchor to hold and the warp to withstand the tons of strain being imposed upon it. The thought of what might happen if either should fail was too chilling to contemplate.

I secured extra lashings over my cockpit canopy for it was being sucked off by the wind's power then I returned below to the comparative calm and warmth. I needed a rest for I had hardly slept the previous night in Fair Isle's rock-ringed haven, but I had to periodically monitor the boat by looking out of the window to make sure that she did not begin to drag backwards. I learned a trick for keeping watch in comfort, which has proved useful to me on several occasions since then.

There were one or two distant lights ashore and their illumination entered through the window to be reflected on the opposite side of the cabin and roof. As the boat sheared about the light patches moved back and forth, back and forth. I noticed that their movement which appeared to be haphazard, was in fact following a regular cycle. I could lay in comfort and watch the light patterns, for whilst they were there and moving in a regular pattern, we were remaining stationary. If they altered, we would be dragging. In this way I could rest physically by lying relaxing and rest mentally knowing that we had not dragged. I hoped that after a couple of hours the worst would be over, but the gale was sustained and went right through until mid-morning before it began to abate. It was my second very disturbed night in a row, which is not unknown to cruising people.

From Kirkwall Heritage Guide.
The tower of St. Magnus at Kirkwall an aid to navigation throughout the islands.

21 August Sunday.
This was unanimously proclaimed as a lazy day by total crew-inaction. Nobody bothered to get up. We just lay reading and listening to the violent wind. The skipper took his oilies off and slept on his bunk for the first time in several days.

When it cleared and abated somewhat in the afternoon Gavin, Carol and Alison went ashore in the dinghy to walk around Balfour Castle. Unfortunately it wasn't open, but there was sufficient of interest to make the trip worthwhile. On the return trip the outboard on the inflatable hiccupped due to a dirty plug, reinforcing the fact that a most essential piece of equipment in an inflatable is an effective anchor. How many inflatables do we see kitted out with them?

22 August Monday.
A quiet night for a change. When we awoke it was almost calm with just a gentle force 1 from the south west. After breakfast we upped anchor and sailed across to Kirkwall. It was a nice sail in force 3 winds. Moored outside the harbour was a Russian cruise ship. The harbour was virtually empty and we went alongside the eastern wall as virtually the only yacht in the harbour. Russian tourists could be seen wandering back to the pier, looking exactly like the archetypical American tourist with loud holiday clothes and cameras around their necks. The locals said that the number of such ships calling was in the teens this year. It was a great surprise to me for this was still the time of the Iron Curtain and the Soviet bloc. Was this the Russian Bus?

We'd called only to top up our supplies and we went rapidly through our harbour routine of washing, shopping and loading to be ready to depart again about three o'clock in the afternoon. Our one moment of excitement came when we heard lots of shouting and whistling on the dockside above us. A large flock of sheep was being herded off a ship and taken along into the town. There was a dog in charge. The dog ran ahead to stop the traffic on the busy main road and then held the centre of the road whilst keeping his eye on the arriving flock. The single farmer was well to the rear, but the dog knew his way. Along the road he went and then turned into the town, not in the least put out by not being on the open fells. Pedestrians, cars and lorries were just minor hazards on his route which he controlled in the same way as his flock, getting on with his job in a single-minded way.

It was a lovely day and we thought to take advantage of a favourable breeze as we departed under sail. We had a lovely reach for five minutes then the wind died and went to the west. As we turned to run we had to goosewing the genoa on one side with the spinnaker/reacher on the other. In the lightest of airs we sailed in glorious hot sunshine for the second time that summer, for half an hour, lounging about and enjoying the beautiful green islands and the sea. What a superb cruising area this is when the weather is clear enough to allow it to be seen.

We turned south to enter Deer Sound following the coast reaching under spinnaker down the side of Tankerness. On the end of the Ness stands a cannon facing seaward, as a reminder of days gone by. We motored up to an anchorage near the pier close to Tankerness Hall. The evening clouded over and became very still. We watched a fisherman tending his pots and had a quiet evening reading and writing.

MI issue 294. Episode 74.

<u>Tankerness - towards Findhorn</u>.
23 August. Tuesday.
Starship had spent a quiet night in Deer Sound and we were about to leave Orkney for the Scottish mainland. In a way we were sad to be leaving for we had greatly enjoyed the two island groups of Orkney and Shetland. A boat is the ideal form of transport for exploring them, for they are linked not divided, by the water. This fact has always been essential to the social structure and history of Orkney and Shetland. The islands are steeped in history more than any other place that I have visited. Scapa Flow echoes with the ironclad era of the First World War, but the rest of the islands are deeply dyed in the pattern of the Vikings.

I have had an enduring interest in the Vikings because from an early age I was fascinated by their beautiful boats which I came to believe had sought a similar path towards seaworthiness as multihulls, namely lightness of structure and lack of ballast. I took *Starship* to Norway in search of their craft and found the Gokstad and Oseberg ships. The astonishing richness of the craftsmanship of the goods found with the Oseberg ship took me by surprise, but probably the single fact which most affected my thinking was that the fabulously extravagant burial of this ship was in honour of a <u>woman</u>.

I had always held the stereotype view of the Vikings as a load of ignorant thugs dressed in horned helmets, floating around armed to the teeth, plundering, pillaging, and you-know-what-ing, wherever they went. It is very clear that such a bunch of bullies would not have invested the enormous effort required to honour a woman in the manner of the Oseberg ship burial. I suddenly knew that the Vikings were not all the kind of people that popular history portrays; they were too sophisticated for the simple story to be the whole truth. But who were they and where could I find their ghosts to speak to me? Strange to say, I did not find them in the Norway/Sweden/Denmark that I visited.

I found them, to my surprise, in Orkney and Shetland. First there was the historical link in the family tree that I discovered in St Magnus Cathedral in Kirkwall then there was the geographical connection of the names of the islands and places on the charts, followed by craftsmanship and design evolution in the construction of the local Shetland boats. The key which suddenly unravelled the whole mystery of the people was a book, available in Penguin paperback, called the *'Orkneyinga Saga'*. This brilliant work tells the gripping story of men who would grace any Hollywood epic. There is a strong strain of violence, but it is linked to political manoeuvring, not simply aimless bloodshed. The book gives an insight into a powerful culture shaped by alternative Codes of Honour from the ones that we hold today. *Orkneyinga Saga* explained the stereotypes and replaced them with the foundations of understanding. This allowed me to follow the Viking culture through into other written works. The knowledge I gained led me to a more accurate understanding and greater appreciation of English history. By the time we were leaving Orkney I found myself sailing not over anonymous stretches of water but along highways in the sea where battles had been fought, where meetings had been arranged, where heroes had escaped and history had been written. Cruising should be so much more than simply sailing a boat from A to B. Knowing more about the history or geography of a location can enormously enhance the cruising enjoyment as it did in this case.

In the night I had checked the breeze direction to discover it was southerly which wasn't very encouraging for the 45 mile trip to Wick, especially as the forecast was for south-easterly 6-7. When I awoke I casually picked up the compass to check the wind to find that it had gone to the north-west; ideal for the journey, if only it would last. After frantic activity we were away at 06.30 under full sail passing out of Deer Sound heading for Mull Head close hauled at seven knots. It was brisk and clear with patches of sunshine, distant rain showers and crisp, sharp waves that gave us the odd thump and splash as we drove north-east to round the granite headland. The tide was favourable until about 10.30 so the first few hours were vital to our progress. This section of the voyage down the eastern side of Orkney had been done in the opposite direction in thick fog, so it was of particular interest to see, for the first time, where we had sailed before.

As we rounded Mull Head I was most taken by the vivid red colour of the cliffs, cloaked with green vegetation and topped with green fields filled with grazing animals. It was disturbing to see odd off-lying patches of rock, not to mention the islands around Copinsay which was a maze that we had negotiated by 'feel' on the way up. We didn't really have too much time to look, as the fair wind and tide sped us along at an average seven knots running nice and level.

At times, some places ahead were obscured by rain clouds but we seemed to slip between them. We could see far inland across the lower islands to the cloud shadows dappling the hills of Hoy in the clear distance and a long way to the south we could see the Scottish mainland. In fine weather, cruising amongst these islands would come close to perfection if the major danger of the Pentland Firth could be avoided; upon reflection this would only need one vital change to be made to man's work.

The Churchill barriers block any exit from Scapa Flow to the east and create a long and sometimes dangerous voyage to link with the other islands to the north. To make a sluice or gate in the barrier at Holm Sound capable of opening at high and low water would create many more possibilities for all craft. Sheltered harbours on either side of the barrier would generate increased trade and activity at St Mary's. The time for such a project would be now, to take advantage of the oil revenues.

Leaving Holm Sound we picked out Grim Ness, behind which we had sailed in the fog and we also took a careful look at the rocks off Old Head which we had previously viewed from much closer quarters. Our speed allowed us to arrive at and cross the Pentland Firth at slack water, which we did to the west of Muckle Skerry.

We'd made great progress but the wind was dying and the tide soon began to run against us off Duncansby Head where there were some interesting stacks to look at. We used the spinnaker to maintain four knots but progress became slower. We had sunshine, cliff scenery, beaches and some castle ruins to entertain us so we persevered with sails until about 13.30. We'd been just off Noss Head for 30 minutes when we started our motor and went down to Wick to enter the harbour at about 14.15.

It was a big, modern-looking harbour basin which was relatively empty, but the harbour master and his two assistants could not decide where to place our one little yacht in this enormous empty expanse. The problem, it seemed, was that they were expecting a very important visitor and everything would have to be just right when the celebrity arrived in the full glare of Press publicity. After lots of pondering and discussion between themselves they placed us ... blocking the entrance, then decided that wouldn't do. Instead, they sent us to the farthest corner, to go alongside a steel-hulled fishing boat still under construction, but the workmen aboard her said that she'd be moving the next day, so we went alongside the wall close by. The harbourmaster came round to say that we couldn't stay there either and put us against another wall where we blocked the boatyard slipway, saying that we could move later once the Greenpeace ship had entered and tied up.

We expected a mighty ship to enter as half of the vast harbour had been reserved for it, but when it turned up it was just a normal, converted Aberdeen trawler called *Moby Dick* of Hamburg, trendily painted with a white whale, a rainbow and some stripes. After catching up on our sleep we moved across the harbour as instructed, to go behind the Greenpeace which had a noisy diesel generator running, filling the harbour with its racket and fume pollution. Not the best advert for conservation or peace. We walked slowly around the town in the evening but it seemed a dull and dirty little place. Gavin and Carol retrieved their car ready for departure.

Wick Harbour - Greenpeace ship astern of us.

Wednesday August 24.

The weather forecast of south-easterly wasn't too favourable for departure, which was a good thing because as Gavin and Carol had to leave it wouldn't have been very nice to have dragged them out of bed and chucked their bags on the quay as we sailed away. We said our goodbyes properly for we were genuinely sorry to see them go. They were undoubtedly the best crew that we could have wished for. Gavin knew all about boats. Carol was immune from sea sickness and cooked in the most trying of conditions, but their gentle easy-going nature, acceptance of the rigours of cruising and their willingness to do ANY job, singled them out as being exceptional.

We had a lazy day clearing and cleaning then shopping whilst we waited for the westerly winds to arrive, which every forecaster insisted were just around the corner. We needed them in the afternoon when the tide was favourable, but they didn't come. With just over 50 miles to our next stop at Findhorn and only a crew of two, we needed reasonably favourable conditions. We planned to average 5 knots for 10 hours, including a run of foul tide, to arrive off the tricky Findhorn entrance in daylight and this demanded departing after midnight. In the evening we walked around Wick again and discovered that the residential areas are quite pleasant and not as depressing as the town centre. We also explored around the dock where the local craft were of interest.

The local trawlers now fish for scallop; the smaller inshore boats were miniature versions of the bigger craft. They held true to scale so that on the really tiny craft the wheelhouse was virtually too small for a man to enter. They were mainly derived from the Shetland model form but almost all had decked ends to make them more seaworthy.

Thursday 25 August

The alarm dragged me into consciousness at 12.30, feeling so tired, it was as though I had never been asleep. The silent black dock was illuminated with orange street lights making the greasy water look like ink. The shipping forecast emphasised for the third day running that heavy westerlies were blowing, but nobody had told the wind suppliers for our sea area. The wind was still from the south and the tide was adverse. Having invested the effort in getting up I decided to have a try at making some progress under motor. I was soon regretting it.

The waves bumped, banged and crashed all about the boat. Tacking off a headland against a foul run of tide is a completely wasteful exercise and probably we would have lost ground. By holding on with the motor we inched forwards but at the great cost of extreme discomfort. My plans for five knots with the fair west wind were quite irrelevant. I'd actually departed at 02.00 and by 05.00 I made just six miles and was seriously considering returning but I knew that being in the right place at the right time is all-important and even six or seven miles might be critical at the far end of the journey when we tried to cross the dangerously shallow, river bar at Findhorn.

MI issue 295 Episode 75.

<u>Wick - Findhorn.</u>
<u>August 26. Thursday.</u>
Why would anybody in their right mind fight a foul tide under motor alone, crashing to windward for three hours in the middle of the night just to cover six miles? I asked myself but was unable to supply any answer that really convinced me, apart from the immediate fact that I'd become locked into a position of least-discomfort at the wheel and doing anything except just sitting there was going to be harder than what I was enduring. Turning back and returning to Wick would mean losing all the effort of those wave-thumping hours of pain that I'd already endured. Running off is a gamble anyway, for there is always a chance that a more favourable wind change will arrive at the very moment that any small advantage has been discarded and the ground lost has to be made up again. Contemplating giving up was defeatist anyway and a signal to start thinking more positively.

In sailing there are compensations for discomfort, otherwise we would cease to put up with it. On this night the clear starry sky was as good as I have ever seen it, especially as the clarity came right down almost to the horizon so that I was able to admire constellations lower than I thought possible.

Navigation was aided by bright lights twelve miles out at sea from oilrigs on the Beatrice Field. As the tide turned at 05.30, so the wind shifted slightly to the east to allow me to set the main which did a great deal to help steady the boat by adding power. The coming of the daylight was most welcome and soon I could see the mainland shore beginning to move past.

At about 07.30 the force 4 wind went another 10 degrees east and we could mercifully give the motor a rest and make progress with just the sail on about 220°m. This easterly movement began to form mist along the shore which is always a danger along this coast.

At 09.00 the wind freed to south-east and we found ourselves reaching at a speed which allowed us to cover six miles in three-quarters of an hour instead of the three hours earlier.

Initially I had given up hope of reaching Findhorn entrance for the morning tide and was looking for the evening tide, but calculations showed that if I could maintain speed I might make it by 13.00 which would be 2 hours after HW. Would I have sufficient depth to enter? Whilst I was wrestling with this problem the wind slowly died leaving us barely making way again.

Now isn't this typical of cruising? All the plans are carefully laid and one sets out with high hopes, only to have them dashed and then raised and then destroyed again. Dealing with all these ups and downs can be disheartening as one never knows what is going to happen next and all previous efforts spent on planning have been a waste. So it was here. I settled for sailing slowly and arriving on the late tide ... when a fresh north-easterly blew up and away we went again goosewinging.

Direct progress was being made once more and this freed me for some domestic duties during the course of which I dropped an essential plastic lid overboard; fortunately it floated. An incident of this type is annoying but it presents an ideal opportunity to execute a man-overboard drill without having to throw off all those expensive life-rings, lights and Danbuoys which decorate the stern of most craft. As we sailed back it was all too apparent how difficult it would be to see an isolated object in even a small sea. The process of steering, sail handling and keeping a sense of direction filled the brain. Picking up a lid or a brush overboard is a much more relevant experience than a pre-rehearsed harbour exercise. Whilst both are helpful, the former really does begin to convey the seriousness of what a proper man overboard situation might feel like. After we'd retrieved the lid there was a silence for a time whilst we both contemplated what we had realised.

Our destination, Findhorn, was very different from the places that we had recently visited. It is a broad sandy estuary bordered on the western side by a coniferous plantation called Culbin Forest. The sleepy little village is isolated by the estuary on one side and a sea of sand dunes on the other. The entrance was on the southern side of the wide Moray Firth and so it faced north and was obstructed by a complex shifting sandbar. For many cruising sailors the intricacies of entering would have overcome any desire to go in, but having learned to cruise from the River Deben which has a shifting shingle bar I was willing to give it a try. Rather like Blakeney and Wells on the North Norfolk coast, entry had first to be made through a gap offset to one side of the river entrance and then the boat had to be sailed parallel to the shore before making the actual entry. With an onshore wind this meant running down onto a lee shore and sailing amongst the breakers on the parallel part of the entry which can be unnerving and in heavy weather very dangerous.

As we approached I wasn't exactly certain of the time of high water due to conflicting information, but I knew that I would be going in against the ebb. It would have been extremely hazardous if not impossible in a fin keeler of my size. I attempted to contact the boatyard and the Yacht Club on the V.H.F. to confirm my entry information but the Moray Coastguard came on to inform me that neither organisation kept a listening watch, so we were on our own.

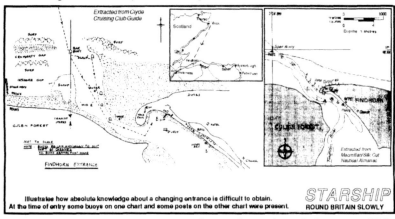

Illustrates how absolute knowledge about a changing entrance is difficult to obtain.
At the time of entry some buoys on one chart and some posts on the other chart were present.

STARSHIP
ROUND BRITAIN SLOWLY

We closed the entrance under main and reefed genoa. This would slow us down, allowing increased thinking time and it would improve tacking speed if swift reactions were required. I deliberately stayed left, knowing that all marks would then be to my right. I constantly scanned the shore and the sea, realising that my greatest danger would be to unknowingly get inside the channel markers. When still quite a long way out I glimpsed a 'stick' well to my right and reached across to find a spar buoy which was the outer mark. Inshore amongst the waves was an orange buoy so we ran in, gybed and then sheeted in close hauled to sail another quarter of a mile inside the breaking surf to the next buoy where we turned inshore again heading for wooden posts which marked the end of a sand spit on our left. The water in which we now sailed was turbulent with the echo sounder on five feet, as the sea met the stream of the running river. The end of the spit had seals lying basking in the sunshine on firm yellow sand. The water around us had a great deal of natural floating debris in the form of branches, grass stems and even small trees being carried past.

Once inside, there was a very sharp left hand turn around a couple of starboard marks and then we were amongst the moored craft. A little further inside there was a clear gap in front of the Yacht Club and then a second group of moorings, so we took one of these and waited for someone to tell us that we couldn't stay there. Nobody came.

It was a beautiful afternoon and we were tired following the twelve hour passage from Wick. Despite the beautiful surroundings: the gentle interest of the village opposite where boys fished, older folks sat on benches, dogs ran for sticks and mothers walked babies, we retired below to catch up on our sleep.
Did you spot our cruising mistake?

Half an hour later we found ourselves beginning to heel over because our mooring was outside the channel, though in line with the other moorings and we took the ground about 1½hrs before low water. We were back with coffee-brown peaty water which didn't allow us to see the bottom at 20 feet to which we had become accustomed. In all our other anchorages we'd sounded our way in and done calculation on the range-of-the-day to ensure that we remained afloat. This time we were lulled into a false sense of security by the warm, soft, gentle atmosphere of the place after such an emotionally trying journey.

We had come to Findhorn because when I had first conceived the idea of cruising all the way around Britain I was overawed with the totality of the undertaking. I knew nothing of the places that I had to go to, except, I had made a couple of contacts through MOCRA with Hugh Davidson who sailed from Findhorn. His cruise account to Orkney and Shetland in his Telstar trimaran *Red 3* was a great help to me. I thought that if the smaller tri could happily sail these waters then my boat should be relatively safe. I made tentative arrangements to visit Hugh and this provided me with a mental target for the outward journey. I wasn't sailing endlessly, aimlessly onwards; I was actually sailing towards a meeting with my friend. Unfortunately, tragically, Hugh died before we reached Findhorn, but we continued to correspond with his wife Phemie who was then about to become the Commodore of the Royal Findhorn Yacht Club.

We went ashore to the club to use the showers and to make telephone calls. We were then waiting for our next crewman Ray Weston to arrive.

<u>Friday August 26</u>
It was nice to lie in bed, not taking the shipping forecast and seeing sunshine streaming in through the window. We met Phemie at the Yacht Club and helped prepare balloons and decorations for the Annual Ball. We went to the Ship Inn for lunch and talked a lot. Went shopping. Returned on board. Decided to check the engine as it had seemed reluctant to start when we'd moved moorings earlier as advised. Checked the usual things and everything was OK. Decided to leave it ... but then thought to do a quick-check start. Turned the key. Loud thump and then nothing. Went below, removed the injector and hand cranked it for one cycle. On the up stroke WATER gushed out of the top of the cylinder. We were in serious trouble.

MI issue 296. Episode 76.

<u>Findhorn - Peterhead.</u>
August 27/28. Saturday/Sunday.
<u>The people.</u>
In cruising you meet some interesting people. In Findhorn we met Peter Shuttleworth who showed us the best mooring to use and advised us about the different ports on the next step of our journey. We talked about Macduff/Banff and Frazerburgh. We also talked multihulls with Peter who was a qualified naval architect. He had the usual preconceptions about multihulls staying the right way up. Some of our answers to his questions came as a surprise to him. Formal training can restrict knowledge instead of opening up avenues. Even though his trade was to design ships he hadn't realised that they were form stable and it was their **shape** was a major factor in keeping them the right way up. Peter had come from Cumbria and knew the Barrow group of multihullers which I had first heard of in Milford Haven. He talked of Ernie Diamond, Bernard Rhodes, and Dick Crowe the builder of the trimaran *Mud Slide Slim*.

Phemie Davidson was very busy at the club following her election as Commodore, but she still found time to entertain us and to drive us around the countryside. We met Derek Munroe owner of *Lulu* a 9M Catalac as he was using his jeep to rescue a Range Rover with a trailered boat in tow, which was stuck in some shingle on the shore. When he heard of our problems he offered to loan us a comprehensive tool kit to tackle the water that we had found in our diesel engine.

<u>The engine</u>.

Why does a cylinder fill with water? Maybe the head gasket had gone? There was no chance of getting a replacement gasket, because this was a Bank Holiday weekend, but I thought I'd better check it out. I disconnected the water supply and turned the engine. The water didn't come from the gasket it seemed to be sucked back from the water-cooled exhaust. This was a major surprise. I drained and checked the exhaust which allowed the engine to run badly, blowing lots of smoke from the air intake almost as though it was running backwards. Further investigations were required.

At each check of the next logical step I had to dismantle and reassemble; taking the rocker cover off, disconnecting fuel and water supplies etc. During the course of these two days we must have taken the engine down and rebuilt it eight or ten times. Nothing seemed to make any difference. I turned the motor by hand meticulously checking its cycle. It all operated perfectly. There was nothing wrong with it. It just didn't work. After two days of doing everything possible including turning it over full of seawater so that it blasted me full in the face and splattered the whole of the cabin, I concluded that I needed more expert advice as I had reached a stalemate position.

Whilst this was going on inside the boat, there was some excitement happening outside too. A gale arrived and gradually increased in severity until in the afternoon with the strength of the tide running against it we had a really rough ride. It was exceptionally bad and at times we wondered whether the mooring would hold us. We even had waves splashing against the windows, something that rarely happens even at sea. It was too good to miss so we took a breather from fumbling in the bilges to watch the windsurfers doing spectacular things close to the shore.

Monday 29 August.

The nearest diesel engineer was in Lossiemouth; expensive and difficult to get hold of. I'd been given the name of a local farmer who was considered to be the resident diesel expert so I cycled over to see him. He was mending a combined harvester as we talked over the problem and he had little further information to offer. It was a mystery to him, but nevertheless, he said he'd come at 11 o'clock to have a look. We waited for him to turn up but he didn't arrive, so we got the message that the harvest was more important than our engine. Quite right.

The dilemma.

Each day as 2 o'clock came around we had itchy feet to be off as it was high water and the optimum time to cross the bar. I was also starting to get a vague feeling of beginning to overstay my welcome. Visiting voyagers are a refreshing and welcome sight when they first arrive but once they had done the social round, seen the sights and related their story, they're supposed to sail away. If they are still around when everybody else has to return to work again and they've got technical problems, they start to become a bit of a liability. Ray my crewman had travelled a very long way to enjoy his annual holiday and all he was seeing was the inside of my engine by torchlight. For these reasons I was feeling under pressure. I'd reached the end of my options. I couldn't get help in reasonable time at reasonable expense and if 2 o'clock went by again I'd be locked in for another 24 hours. Staying was becoming less comfortable, going wasn't realistically possible.

At the time I was trying to check the timing of the cams by reference to Top Dead Centre when I decided upon a final impossible chance. I extracted the follower rods for the tappets and changed them over. I hardly tightened down the head bolts and didn't bother with tappet clearances; I didn't even put the oil cover back on top of the engine as I knew it couldn't work because it appeared that the wrong valve would be open as the piston was firing etc. I pressed the button and it ran perfectly. We just sat and looked at each other in amazement ... then exploded into action.

Departure.

Alison had already said that the tide was turning before the engine burst into life, so there was immediately a race on to catch the tide before it was too late. We had the additional problems of getting our bicycle back from ashore whilst reassembling the engine and returning the borrowed spanners. There was a great deal of frantic activity and the tide was running pretty strongly by the time that we were ready to go at about 16.30.

Due to the rush I was still uncertain about the health of my engine, so I decided not to use it unless I was absolutely forced to. This meant sailing out of the moorings and the harbour with a very strong westerly wind blowing which was the tail of the previous day's gale. We reefed heavily to keep a manageable jib, but we were still very pressed in the gusts.

The tide was under us and helped push us through the wind shadow of the forest out to where the ebb was meeting the incoming

337

waves. As we powered towards this turbulent junction we knew that we needed every bit of thrust to cut through the waves. We were soon into the thick of the surf struggling to sheet in our tiny scraps of sail as we tacked along the surf line to the west staying in the roughest, whitest water working up to the mark, where, with some relief we were able to bear away northwards with a sense of achievement, knowing that our boat had carried us through a rough but exhilarating ride by using her muscle power.

Progress.

No sooner did we ease the sheets than we felt her begin to lift and sing. No squatting on the water to shoulder the waves aside now, she revelled in her element. At the slender spar buoy we turned eastwards and the sails went out to their limit, but the speed didn't falter. We were running with enough wind to keep her going and going. The following waves began to pick her up and make her slide, smooth and rolling with the white bow wave creeping back and joining the float waves in a flurry of foam. We were really moving.

Having sailed *Starship* all the way around Britain to this point, I think that at last, we found the sail that we'd long been looking for in terms of continuous speed with the right sea state to give a wonderfully comfortable ride. Occasionally we'd break into a surf that went on past the first lift and swoop, to feel like accelerating faster and faster. Down in the cabin the sound of the water rushing past created a pattern of noise. Most of the time the rush of the surf would build to a crescendo then subsides before building again, so when the noise began to be sustained and the helmsman whooped in joy as we surfed succeeding waves without interruption, there were smiles of appreciation from down below. This was sailing.

The whole run of the tide was against us as we sailed east towards Kinnaird Head identifying the towns of Buckie and MacDuff as we passed, reminding us with their distinctive names that we were still in Scotland. The wind abated at times, but we arrived due north of Kinnards at 23.30 having averaged seven and a half knots over the ground, which represented some lovely progress - but all good things must come to an end.

Peterhead.

We had been enjoying the westerly component of a south-westerly wind deflected by the coast, so that as we began to turn southwards towards Rattray Head, the wind moved further to south-west and we were close hauled. Gradually we were unable to lay the headland

and as we went further offshore we began to feel the surge of the combined waves and swell coming up from the south. They were big ones which needed climbing and most of the time I was glad that it was too dark to see them. Occasionally a flash of grey-white in the night showed where the tops were breaking. The south-going tide was helpful, but it did nothing to ease the sea state. We maintained six knots as we tacked down towards the lights of the town.

Standing off the harbour were several big ships glowing like blocks of flats with all their lights ablaze. We picked our way through them. Peterhead itself seemed to have big oil installations to the north and south and there were lights absolutely everywhere so it

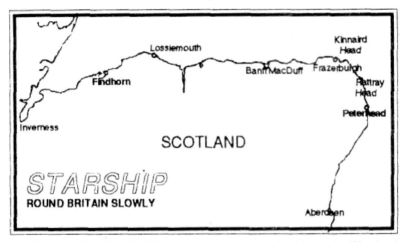

was impossible to decipher what we were looking at. We had expected to see a distinct harbour wall, but there was nothing visible.

I sailed south of the town to get the angle of approach correct and then started to run back, edging inshore. We eventually picked out the lighthouse on the end of the southern breakwater which appeared to be very low in the water. There were brightly blazing ships secured on the inside, behind the lighthouse. As we slipped through into the outer harbour I expected to see a large blank expanse of clear water, but I was amazed to see at anchor, an enormous fleet of fishing boats almost completely filling the place. There was only restricted space between them to manoeuvre and sailing around in the darkness it was difficult to gauge distances whilst keeping a lookout with all the many different lights being multiplied by the reflections from the dark water. It was like a crystal maze.

As we reduced sail to slow ourselves down we spotted a yellow marker which appeared to define an area in which craft were anchored. We made a run and anchored in deep water within the marked area close to the buoy. At last we were able to pull down the sails and get our bearings.

The lights of a fishing boat entered the harbour. He came straight towards us and rounded the yellow marker just to one side of us, then headed up a narrow channel into what must have been the inner harbour. I'd made a mistake. We were positioned at the turning mark in some kind of traffic lane.

The squat shape of ragged little harbour boat bristling with rubber tyres came bustling out of the darkness. I guessed what was coming. Quite a blast of strong Scottish dialect for stopping where we had done close to the workings of the new harbour wall ... getting in everybody's way ... and why hadn't we asked permission before coming in?

Oh dear. I'd got it all wrong ... again.

MI issue 297. Episode 77.

Peterhead - Montrose.
30 August. Tuesday.
It was the early hours of the morning and very dark except for the confusion of harbour lights. I was getting a severe ticking off from the skipper of the harbour tug for entering his port without asking and for then having the nerve to anchor in the wrong place. His words were all the more wounding from being delivered in a dour Scottish accent. "Why did we nay monitor Channel 16?" In the confused tension of watching lights and angles when entering I'd forgotten all about it, but this sounded like a very weak reply to a man who knew his way about the place blindfolded. "Did we nay ha' an engine?" Well... no ... we didn't think that we had. It wasn't really possible to shout across the full explanation that whilst we had one, we actually didn't know if it was safe to use because we'd only just repaired it. His voice was incredulous, "No! Ye ha' nay got an engine? Well hoo di'-ya expect tay manoeuvre?" Then his voice changed. "Get ready and I'll gi'-ye a tow." There was relish in the ominous words. He was going to enjoy this and maybe at the end of it we would have learned a lesson about the proper way to come into his harbour.

There was a throaty roar from his diesels as he surged around and began to creep towards the delicate white seabird that was our yacht with his steel-tyred, rusty bulldozer. We were going to have to pick up our anchor, then pass him a line as he quickly got ahead of us before we drifted or were thrust back by his prop-wash onto the large yellow harbour buoy which was close astern, OR ..."I'll try the engine." I shouted across the black gap at the advancing threat. I did not want my floats to feel even its most gentle caress. If ever I needed the engine it was now. I turned the key and the engine started perfectly. What a relief. "Follow me." he shouted through his little window and he surged off enveloped in the clamour of his mighty exhaust. He threaded us through the anchored fishing fleet and took us into the south-west corner of the harbour. After a couple of tries we got our anchor to hold where he'd indicated. We tumbled into bed at about six in the morning.

I awoke again about eight o'clock and stumbled about the boat in a sleepy condition until I casually looked out of the window. Twenty yards from the boat, ROCKS, sticking up out of the water. I was instantly fully awake. I rushed to the echo sounder. Six feet under us. Fumbled for the almanac to discover with some relief that we were at low water and then I noted with interest that this was about the biggest spring tide of the year. It was another reminder never to be complacent about anchoring once the hassle of entering a new harbour has subsided and the feeling of relief can be mistaken for a sense of security. It was another narrow escape. We returned to bed until dinner time.

It was still very windy and we weren't going anywhere in a sailing sense, so I put Ray and Alison ashore to go shopping whilst I pottered about the boat doing all the many little jobs which had been accumulating whilst attention had been focussed on the engine. When they returned we had a big meal and a quiet, lazy time recovering.

31 August Wednesday.
We'd been having strong southerly winds for some time and there was a succession of depressions waiting out in the Atlantic to follow each other through. This day had yet another strong wind warning.

We whiled away our time watching the German fishing fleet which had taken shelter en mass whilst waiting for the weather to improve. They all had the same brown deckhouses and black rusty hulls. They rolled badly out in the exposed harbour and slowly, one by one they would up anchor and creep down into our corner which had the best shelter. We monitored the VHF which had endless exchanges about ship movements, Russian Klondikers coming in, oil rig tenders going back and forth and local fishing craft returning with their catch. Whatever happened to the strict VHF procedures that only we yachtsmen adhere to, we wondered? The exchanges between the locals were spoken in such a broad dialect that we had to vie with each other to interpret their meaning. We learned a great deal about harbour management.

We were waiting for the shipping forecast at 14.00 and when it came it was the usual depressing message about more heavy wind on the way. We looked like being stuck for at least another couple of days in harbour. Ray wasn't having the kind of sailing holiday that he had enjoyed with us previously. He hadn't anticipated spending days just waiting in some remote corner of a commercial port. He worked in a port himself. It was decided that he should make his way back home and return to work to save his precious holiday days. It was the right thing to do. I helped take him ashore to begin the long journey back.

Alison and I were now faced with the problem of being shorthanded and although we didn't fully realise it at the time, the nature of our journey changed subtly. We were no longer sailing gently from port to port exploring our way round Britain. From this point onwards we were on a delivery trip attempting to return *Starship* to her home port without delay for we had run out of time ourselves. I began to ring up friends who might be able to come and help us sail the boat from Peterhead or even join us in a few days' time, somewhere further south. For a variety of reasons, not least the proximity of the Bank holiday, I drew blanks and we were feeling fairly low when we returned to the boat in the evening. Crossing in the dinghy we both noticed how the weather had settled down and was quieter than it had been for days. I felt that we might make just a little progress down to Aberdeen which although it was only 30 miles might keep up the momentum of our journey which would have an important psychological effect. We had learned that waiting for perfect sailing conditions means getting stuck in one place; any small opportunity must be exploited if progress is to be made.

The forecast said that the wind would go from south-west to south-east and I felt that this could be exploited, so we took the risk and prepared to leave. This time we got clearance from Harbour Control and slipped out under sail at 21.10 into a light wind which allowed us to do about three or four knots on a course of 150°m. Twenty minutes after leaving we could hear Harbour Control asking the harbour tug of our whereabouts, so they must have missed seeing us go. I derived a perverse pleasure that the tug was still puzzling about us as we sailed out of range.

Our course of 150°m turned out to be inadequate for the adverse tidal run on such a big spring tide. We actually just slid away to the east until about 01.15, but I had guessed that this might happen. When the tide turned it was accompanied by a mighty wind shift to the south east which put me well up to windward and allowed us to sheet in on the other tack and sail 220°m almost parallel with the coast. We really began to move south progressing at about six knots.

It was a light night and pleasantly warm, there were fishing boats scattered about which made steering easier as it was simply a matter of picking a distant glow which was close to the course and heading for it. A couple of the lights that we aimed for seemed different from the others. When they materialised they were oil rig platforms like cities on stilts, their lights blazed away as beacons in the night. By four o'clock in the morning we were off Aberdeen but ten miles out to sea, as I had decided to try to push on further to capitalise on the fair wind and tide. Stonehaven was the next port to the south but I knew it not to be very suited to a south-easterly blow and the next port of Montrose appeared to be more attractive from the point of view of size and facilities. If I could reach Montrose it would mean that I had covered 65 miles which was a significant step. To achieve this I was knowingly taking a number of risks.

i) The south-easterly could bring a fog to obscure the entrance.

ii) I could run out of favourable tide and then I would be slowed by the north-going ebb. If I was delayed too long I would be at sea in what was forecast to become a force 7 wind. The strength of the wind was already increasing.

iii) Of Montrose, the almanac advised, *'Entrance to harbour is dangerous with strong on-shore winds during ebb tide as heavy overfalls develop.'* I did several calculations to discover the time when the tide would turn in the entrance and I concluded that with a bit of luck I might just scrape in before the strength of the ebb had built up. Everything was on a bit of a knife edge, but I had struggled hard to get up to windward and I didn't want to throw the extra 30 miles away. Dawn was creeping across the underside of the clouds behind us and ominously, we had a beautiful red sky in the morning.

The powerful light on Todhead point to the south of Stonehaven helped me to fix my position as I closed the land which was grey and misty and looking featureless in the poor visibility. At eight o'clock I had to reef the genoa as the wind was beginning to gust five and I was broad reaching in a mounting sea. The waves were coming up from behind the beam and slewing the boat occasionally whilst

343

sometimes catching her a slap or a thump. I was pretty tired by this time.

Ahead in the mist I glimpsed the white of the lighthouse at Scurdie Ness marking the entrance to Montrose, so I shaped a course to approach it from seaward. The boat felt a little more comfortable close reaching as it cut down on the worst of the stomach churning lurches caused by the bigger steeper seas picking the boat up and throwing her sideways. The wind was getting stronger by the minute and the time had ticked away to the turn of the tide. It was ebbing and getting stronger and things were getting a bit desperate. I'd pinned myself into a corner and I knew that getting out of it wasn't going to be easy. I couldn't stay at sea because the fatigue was catching up on me and conditions could only get worse. I guessed that the entrance was going to be bad so I made a conscious decision before I arrived that come-what-may I was going to go in. I switched on Channel 16 to monitor the harbour traffic, but there was silence. It seemed an age before we arrived off the lighthouse so that I could see the entrance. My worst fears were confirmed. The sight of the sea state in there was horrifying.

MI issue 298. Episode 78.

<u>Montrose.</u>
<u>1 September Thursday</u>.
Tired after sailing all night, cold and queasy, I looked across the mounting waves towards the entrance at Montrose through driven grey drizzle and added fear to my emotions. The sight was terrifying. Some of the biggest, whitest, roughest, smoking overfalls that I have

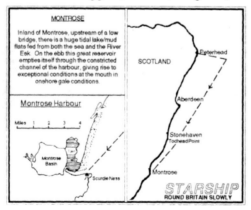

ever seen or ever wish to see. The sea itself was in total confusion as a mighty ebb from the river did battle with the sea, urged on by the force 6 wind blowing directly into the entrance.

I had run out of options. I forced myself not to think, nor to look again; I had to go right ahead with my earlier decision to go straight in. Staying out would only make things worse as the weather conditions were deteriorating rapidly. I turned and headed in, knowing that it was the worst decision that I had ever had to make in my sailing. I was going to rely on my boat being a multihull. Rely on her ability to be taken by the surf; to slip sideways when hit by any weight of water and to ride with her shallow draught in the thinner, aerated surface foam instead of locking a heavy deep keel down into solid water which would slow her or trip her in the conflict to come. I braced myself and trusted her abilities to bring us through as we plunged into the maelstrom. We became a paper boat in a washing machine, totally at the mercy of those overpowering seas crashing all around us.

Our worst moment came when we were picked up and broached so that we headed uncontrollably for the rocks on our left. Only totally releasing the main and sheeting the jib aback induced her to return to her wild run, like shooting turbulent, explosive rapids in a Grand Canyon torrent. I noted even in these desperate moments that sheeting the jib amidships was the best strategy to hold a running course in such extreme conditions. For some time we sailed on the edge of survival, deafened by noise, scoured by salt water, fighting for control, until suddenly the waves ahead looked slightly smaller and we knew that we were going to come through.

Deep inside the river mouth we could see a tough little tug-like craft burying its blunt nose into walls of water. I couldn't believe that anyone would willingly go out into the seas that we had just endured. Feeling a sense of relief that we were now safe I joked with Alison about him going out to check his lobster pots. He was almost disappearing as he crashed into some of the waves. What on earth was he doing? He came out in our direction and it slowly dawned on me that he was possibly coming to assist us in some way.

The coast to the right of the entrance had a broad beach of flat sand and the water on this side ran more smoothly. I side-slipped over onto this sheet of water which rushed towards us like a conveyor belt running at a high rate of knots. We managed to stabilise ourselves to run goosewinged, seeking the edge of the rougher water to ensure that we had sufficient depth. As we got further in, the increasing strength of the funnelled wind ran us close to broaching even though we only carried half our main and one third genoa.

The outcoming craft made a turn ahead of us in a crashing shower of white water. We could read the word PILOT along the side of his upright little wheelhouse above his rubber-tyred gunwale. He led us and we tried to follow, but sometimes we took a bit of a shear in the worst gusts. We were averaging between eight and nine knots and we came into the river at about three, until we passed the point where the buildings began, when the strength of the tide slackened allowing us to stem it more easily.

The harbour turned slightly to the right and presented a big bleak expanse of water surrounded by steel-piled, concrete-lipped quays with cranes, factories, warehouses and lorries, all looking dull and industrial in the falling rain. A small crowd of people stood hunched against the elements close to the place where the pilot indicated that we should berth. We later came to realise that this crowd had gathered from various workplaces to watch us, because it had not been expected by those ashore that we would survive.

The tide ran through the harbour in a visibly turbulent stream, filled with floating rubbish and small trees as this exceptional tide had scoured the river banks inland. The straight walls of the harbour made it impossible to completely escape from the water flow, only a couple of tiny corners in angles between quays caused swirling eddies free from its direct strength. The pilot signalled us to cross the stream at ninety degrees into a blank corner which was only the length of our boat. We needed engine power similar to his in order to cross the flow, then come to a dead stop. Had we gone in we would have crumpled all three bows instantly against the piling. We made a couple of passes to show willing, but we then had to shout across declaring ourselves unable to do it.

We went further into the harbour and rounded up in a place behind two fishing boats. Some men caught and secured our lines up on the quay and a crowd of working men formed a line above us, discussing our situation. They agreed that we couldn't stay there, it was too shallow and another fishing boat wanted the berth ahead, we'd block his approach. In the end we had to agree to go forward of the fishing boats and they helped warp us around. Then the fuss died down and they all drifted back to their work discussing the strange boat, the like of which had never been seen in these parts previously.

A Coastguard and some officials arrived on the quay above and in the nicest possible way they pointed out the folly of our recent performance, entering in those dangerous seas. They were justified and I was feeling chastened for having got myself into such a position. We were slightly at cross purposes over the precise nature of the wrong-doing. Their major concern was that I had entered **under sail** in such extreme conditions. They wished to know why we hadn't used our engine. I was slightly taken aback and had to explain about our comparative speeds under sail and power. They asked a number of questions about the boat's characteristics, because all who had watched couldn't understand why we had not been swamped or rolled over. They listened intently like a jury weighing the evidence.

I think that when they had arrived they were sure that I had behaved with irresponsible disregard and they wished to see their spokesman make this plain to me. Their shared backgrounds were rooted in big, commercial power vessels and chunky fishing boats, with just the occasional glimpse of heavy traditional yachts. As I answered their questions they seemed to become less certain that my actions had demonstrated total incompetence. They seemed to recognise that if what I was saying was true then the boat was somehow the key to our survival, but nobody in their group could confirm or deny its qualities from prior knowledge. Was I just a reckless individual thoughtlessly risking life, or had I taken decisions based upon new and different information from theirs? Could a boat be safer with sails than with an engine? Could this small weird craft run through big surf without being overturned? In the end, in the absence of solid proof, they were thrown back upon the undeniable evidence of their own eyes. It had actually done what they had previously known to be impossible, so maybe the action of entering wasn't totally irresponsible? Or was it just luck? They still felt ill at ease and I felt very unhappy.

For their parting shot they wanted to know why I hadn't called in on the VHF working channel. My explanation about monitoring the silent channel 16 and having my hands rather too full to call did little to impress them.

When they had gone I was most dejected about the whole incident. I had done something that I hadn't really wished to do and I felt that I had let myself and the boat down by taking such a risk. It was the lowest point of the journey.

My misery was made even worse by being left to try to protect my float from being eaten away by the rough, piled sides of the quay. The tide and blustery wind carried us backwards and forwards so that the fenders and planks needed constant adjustment from me standing outside in the cold steady rain. Having been up all night, being physically drained by the sailing and then emotionally drained by getting into harbour, there was now no rest and it looked like I'd be up all day. I had no ladder to get ashore and I was marooned, because I was unable to adjust my warps which had been inexpertly wound around the bollards on the quay leaving me insufficient length for adjustment. I was trapped and had plenty of time to contemplate the dangers of sailing.

Just how dangerous had that entry been? Had I placed myself in greater danger than (say) a singlehander in a storm? Was the degree of danger comparable with what a rock climber or a boxer experiences? I have always taken the position of self-sufficiency and I did not require nor request assistance, but could this attitude be defended in circumstances where 'assisting services' were present and conscious of the situation that I was placing myself in? Should sailors be allowed to endanger themselves and if so, who decides to what degree? In times past this degree of danger was commonplace, daily, in the lives of working fishermen, is it now wrong to experience it? Is it only wrong if others know about it?

Considerably later a head peered over the quay edge and a man asked me if I'd be staying, because it was £5.75 a night. I was being asked to pay for this torture. Unfortunately for him, I unburdened my grievances upon him, but fortunately for me, he turned out to be the equivalent of my fairy godmother. The wind was now slackening and the tide was about to change. He helped us move down into the little corner first indicated to us by the pilot when we came in. This was the only place in the harbour that gave reasonable shelter from the stream. Once we were secured and fendered near a dockside ladder I was finally able to snatch half an hour of sleep midway through the afternoon, after which things slowly began to improve.

Friday 2 September.
A huge ship came in and unloaded its cargo of wood pulp for papermaking. Lorries, forklift trucks and men swarmed all over the quays all morning. We were warned that we would have to move from our berth at some stage because a boat was coming in that wished to use it.

The weather forecast was abysmal with a continuation of bad visibility and heavy winds. Our next sailing leg would be to cross the wide mouth of the Firth of Forth so we needed a reasonable slant in the breeze. We looked like being stuck again for some time.

MI issue 299. Episode 79.
Montrose - Seahouses.
Montrose was not the best place for a yacht to stay. The harbour was industrial and featureless; the tide ripped through its concrete

channel unrestricted and the water was laden with dangerous flotsam, but we were pinned down by inclement weather and had little choice. Our problems went deeper. The next step on our journey was to cross the combined mouths of the River Tay and the Firth of Forth a distance of about sixty miles which constitutes a very real and exposed sea journey. However it was not as simple as that, if we should succeed in the crossing there was no obviously inviting harbour to aim for to recoup lost energies. We would be obliged to continue sailing looking for somewhere to stop and with just two of us aboard, this wasn't desirable. Scanning through all the information it became clear that harbours were an enormous problem on this east coast. Almost all were small with very tight entrances; they were often shallow or drying and had off lying rocks strewn about their approaches. Without exception the almanac described them as dangerous in some respect and all had warnings about attempting entry in onshore conditions.

By going deep into the Firth of Forth we could find harbours with better prospects, but this would add extra days of sailing to the journey. In addition, the Firth was directly upwind into the continuous south-westerly, F6 winds that we were experiencing.

Not having a definite objective is wearying to the mind which endlessly casts backwards and forwards, constantly evaluating potential solutions. Reading and re-reading details of harbours, computing distances, converting them into hours sailed to the different locations, weighing one strategy against another, looking for dangers and attempting to circumvent them, all of which means that the skipper wanders about in a dazed silence not quite hearing conversations, never really seeing what is happening nor appreciating events.

Friday 2 September

We knew that we'd have to move our berth from the only spot in the place which had a modicum of shelter from the endlessly speeding tidal flow, because another boat was coming in to use it. The weather forecast was poor and a harbour official was asking us for our dues. The daily rate was £5.75 and the weekly rate was £15. I decided on a bit of sympathetic magic which I'd last used when trapped in Brighton Marina in similarly trying weather conditions. I paid to stay for the complete week.

No sooner had I paid than the magic began to work. The weather brightened, the sun shone and the wind went around to the west. This is just how fate works, as soon as I was committed to staying, the weather improved. If I took advantage of it to sail away, I would lose my money. We were cautious. We tested the spell by doing our washing and hanging it out on deck to dry ... surely it would now rain? The good weather persisted. We heard that the timber ship which had just unloaded was leaving at three o'clock so I thought that we might risk taking a chance too. I called harbour control to tell them that we'd go immediately after the ship departed. They confirmed.

I completed a few odd jobs and was ready to cast off when the harbour official arrived at the top of the wall bringing me my change of £9.25 as I'd only stayed for one day, instead of the whole week. This was unexpected. I looked at the money in his hand as he extended it towards me. How could I explain that I didn't really want it as it was actually part of a superstitious belief on my part? As the money passed into my hand the sun went in and a cold gust of wind flurried the harbour.

We cast off and motored into midstream to stow our fenders and planks, fastened the float hatches and removed the sail covers. Specks of rain splattered the deck and the wind shifted back to the south. We set off for the harbour mouth; the rain fell, the visibility dropped and suddenly we could hardly see the entrance marks. The wind strengthened. It was no good, my spell had been broken and as my previous gambles had hardly proved successful I decided to play safe. We turned around and motored across to the quay on the western side to secure ourselves away from the commercial movements on the eastern side.

The quay above us was used for assembling anchors and chain for lightships, oil rigs and big ships. Mountains of rusting metal were stacked around us and our ship's compass deviated ninety degrees. The rust dust blew off the quay onto our decks where it adhered with great tenacity to create rust streaks everywhere, permanently staining our paintwork.

3-4 September..Saturday / Sunday.
We explored by shopping in Montrose and we walked out to the lighthouse on the end of Scurdie Ness to watch the majestic lines of waves marching up from the south. By contrast we visited the enormous expanse of sand dunes which protect the town from the sea and discovered there a timeless scene in an area where fishermen dried and mended their nets, draping them over lines of posts driven into the sand in the traditional manner. I rested, checked the boat and filled my mind with the decisions which had to be made.

Serial Starship

Berwick-on-Tweed was a notional target which provided me with the mental hooks upon which, I could try to hang my strategic thoughts.

<u>5 September Monday</u>.
The 05.30 alarm woke me after a reasonably quiet night. The wind was still in the south but the visibility was good. I decided to go. My plan was to do hourly tacks down inside the shelter of Fife Ness and then an extended tack out across the firth to pick up St Abbs Head. As we cleared the lighthouse and began to feel the true weight and direction of the wind I experimented with the course to see how close I could come to it and was pleasantly surprise to find that the southerly tack was very reasonable allowing us to sail 190-200°m proving that the wind had more west in it than could be felt in the harbour. At Force 4 we had the best wind strength for *Starship*; not comfortable, but the best for making progress. This allowed an immediate change of plan. We were able to cut out the tacking and

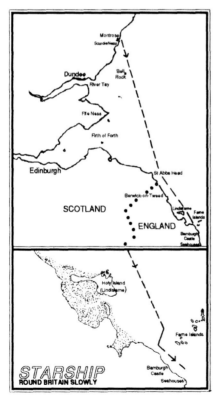

lay right across to St Abbs closehauled. Only sixty miles of bashing to windward, what good luck. The lighthouse on Bell Rock provided a good point to assist with my position fixing. We passed outside it and never lost sight of the distant land behind the rock. From 06.30 to 10.30 we averaged six knots to windward which, when counted, adds up to a whole lot of waves to hit. When we eventually came clear of any land shelter that there might have been from Fife Ness we took the direct force of wind and waves in a steady force five gusting six as we fought our way across the Firth of Forth itself.

The sun shone and despite the discomfort of riding the bucking bronco it was a relief to be out at sea and making definite progress rather than being trapped in port wondering when and where to go. It was clear and fresh and free out there. We could always see sections of the coast and progress was such that by 13.00 we were 10 miles north of St. Abbs Head and we began to notice the blessed relief of having the waves diminish in size. Suddenly the struggle ebbed away and we were speeding across water which actually felt flat compared to the roller coaster crashing banging that we'd been experiencing.

The high green hills ahead rolled like folded velvet, looking lush and prosperous. Far to our right were distinctive conical shaped islands, the most northerly being Bass Rock which gave us convenient position fixes. What had been a south-westerly wind became a westerly as we neared the land. On passing St. Abbs Head it followed the land right around to become north-westerly, falling ever lighter, so that eventually we were ghosting along goosewinged with just a faint breeze. We lazed in the hot sun watching flights of gannets heading past us for their nesting site to the west. The contrast with the morning's sailing was total. This was complete reward for our earlier efforts.

A small open fishing boat ahead suddenly started chasing towards us with its crew waving to us to alter course out to sea. They had set a drifting net right across our track. Their accents were distinctively different from the Scottish voices to which we had become accustomed. We were sailing into a different country. At 15.30 we sailed back into English waters once more, after a couple of years sailing away. At 16.00 we were about six miles off Berwick-on-Tweed having to tack downwind to make sufficient breeze to continue sailing.

As I mentioned earlier it had been my target to reach Berwick as being a port of reasonable size that I could enter without excessive difficulty. Achieving the target by four in the afternoon on such a lovely day with a favourable wind meant that we could push on, so we headed south-east for the corner of Holy Island.

The 'castle' on Lindisfarne grew from the land as though it was in a fairy tale. Someone was burning stubble in a field so that a huge column of grey smoke rose high into the air giving the impression that Viking raiders had attacked again as they did in AD 793, heralding the expansion of their interests to the British Isles.

Passing south in the buoyed channel we found the area between the channel marks littered with lobster pot buoys in the very area designated for craft to pass through. We wondered at the selfish short-sightedness of some fishermen.

Bamburgh Castle dominated the land opposite the Farne Islands which were scattered in isolation well out to sea. We sailed up towards the mighty fortifications in a dying south-westerly breeze, seeking out the starboard mark which indicated the entrance into the inside passage. There was a blazing red sunset astern behind Lindisfarne. The castle and the smoke in the still evening air were reminiscent of a scene from a Hollywood epic. We became becalmed close to the Farne Island itself. Looking out to the Longstone it was difficult not to remember that this was where Grace Darling helped her father the lighthouse keeper, to row his open boat out to an isolated rocky reef to rescue survivors from the packet steamer *Forfarshire* which had been wrecked in a northerly gale on almost exactly this date (actually 7 September) in 1838. On our tranquil evening it was difficult to imagine how horrendous the conditions might have been for the few people who clung without much hope to the slippery rocks for hours, whilst angry waves washed over them.

The tide was against us and there was no wind. We'd been going since six-thirty in the morning and darkness was falling. We had to stop and rest, lest we too should end up like the hapless passengers of the *Forfarshire*. We looked around us for a haven.

MI issue 300. Episode 80.

North Sunderland - Hartlepool
5 September Monday
Becalmed with darkness about to fall we wondered what we should do. The two of us were tired after having sailed 80 miles from Montrose across the Firth of Forth.

Coming in from the sea from all directions were many small fishing boats heading for home as fast as they could go. Their home was the tiny harbour at North Sunderland also called Seahouses. We were close to the entrance and the wisest decision was to go in for the night, but unfortunately we had no idea of the layout inside because this harbour was so small that it rated hardly a mention in any of the pilotage information that we had aboard. The only intelligence that could be gleaned was virtually exactly the same as for every other minor harbour on the coast *'Good shelter except in onshore winds when swell makes outer harbour very uncomfortable and dangerous. Inner harbour has excellent berths but usually full of fishing boats.* Judging by the traffic this last section was probably very accurate.

353

Over the high sea wall I could see a number of yacht's masts to the left of the narrow entrance, so I decided to have-a-go and to follow the next trawler going in. When he turned right into the commercial bit, I would turn left and join the yachts. The plan went well until the moment we passed between the rugged outer walls when I could see that due to this being the time of low tide, all the yachts were actually high out of the water and dry, all secured in their individual wooden cradles standing in a jagged rock strewn basin. The fishing trawlers passed into a northern basin reserved completely for them, which had an entrance so narrow that it could be completely blocked off simply by securing two boats side by side in the opening.

We had to do a quick right turn into an area of the outer harbour which was shallow and exposed, in fact the very section earlier described as *'very uncomfortable and dangerous'* should strong onshore weather develop. For us, on a calm night it was worth the risk and indeed it provided us with a welcome respite.

The quay wall was very high but some local line-fishermen helped secure our warps to bollards amongst the fish boxes on the quay. They were fascinated by our boat, the like of which they had never seen there before. They spoke with very strong Geordie accents and were humorous and outgoing. They soon fell to telling sea stories especially when they heard that we had sailed around Britain to reach this point. One man spun an enthralling yarn about being trapped by a blizzard in the Loch Maddy Hotel on North Uist in the Outer Hebrides where we too had been imprisoned by fog, (see issues 256-258) and how the captain had gotten drunk enough to insist they cast off and sail across to Skye. We laughed and joked and were genuinely warmly welcomed. We answered all the usual questions about the boat, including the most important ones about the size and power of her engines and whether we slept in the floats.

It was now quite dark but the inner basin was brightly illuminated like an amphitheatre. From the high walls we looked down on the bustling, colourful action. The day's fishing catch was being boxed then swung ashore on ropes into the eager hands of the men who loaded the waiting transports to take it inland. Many tourists lined the circular rim of quays to watch. There was a strong impression that much of the movement and activity was as much for the benefit of this audience, as it was to get the catch ashore. Up in Lerwick we had seen this quantity of fish transferred from huge ocean-going trawlers into the Klondiker factory ships in a matter of moments using industrial vacuums and conveyors controlled by a couple of men operating the correct switches at the right moment. Here, the whole male population of the town seemed to be engaged in packing, lifting, calling, directing and just being involved in the wonderful traditional atmosphere created within the bowl of this floodlit theatre.

Their scenic fishing craft were painted with the extravagant detail and infinite care usually reserved for restored steam engines. The main players strode the boards of deck and quay with the self-assurance of characters handed directly from father to son through generations. The dialogue had purity from being refined over many years to short exchanges in the broadest regional dialect, as a confirmation of the technical expertise of the players. There was pride in what they did and a great love of being part of the drama.

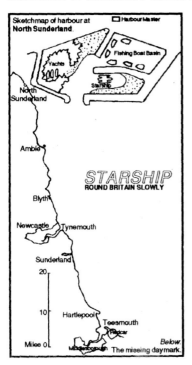

Sketchmap of harbour at North Sunderland.

It was evident that all who took their place derived great self-respect by confirming their daily role in this central act of community. We tourists were watching the final evolution of the fishing village developed over centuries. One wonders if this unique and precious sight has continued to survive the more recent impositions of EEC fish quotas, declining fish stocks and recession.

The sign said £3 a night for us, but no demand was made. The Harbour Master advised us on the boat's precise position and assured us that we wouldn't touch the bottom as the tide fell. The locals confirmed that we wouldn't touch the bottom as they helped secure us. At six the following morning we gently grounded in the soft sand, but we were soon afloat again.

September 6 Tuesday.
We departed this picture postcard place at 09.45 using mainsail and motor, wanting to make good a course of 165°m. I discovered that

progress to windward was only possible with the engine and the tightest courses available were 130° or 200°m. The light breeze was moving from the sea onto the land, which on this coast means fog or thick mist. I had planned to take one long tack out to sea and then one back in again to arrive off the Tyne at the end of the favourable run of tide, but as the land dissolved into the mist behind me I rebelled at the idea of motoring all day and seeing nothing, so I engaged in a series of one hour tacks to follow the scenic route. Such tacks brought us in to determine our position by sights on the castles or factory chimneys ashore, then took us outwards again through the 'inshore lobster pot zone' past the 'rod and line fishing-for-the-day' area of hire boats, back out into the empty sea surrounded by the silent mist with only the hazy sun above.

This was a special day for me personally as I officially ceased my secure employment of the past 23 years to cast myself adrift on the sea of life. If ever I concluded my Round Britain journey I would have to find new ways to earn a living, but that was an adventure to come. On this day the feeling of sailing instead of reporting to work had an extra special element of freedom attached to it.

At about 12.30 the wind freed a little allowing us to proceed under sail alone, down to the distinctive industrial headland of Beacon Point where a mighty chimney makes navigation certain. The offshore tack was headed and the tide stopped helping us at 15.00, so my hopes of reaching Tynemouth were diminishing when the day darkened further and the mist immediately thickened. We headed in towards Blyth for I had a nice big chart devoted solely to this harbour and our position had been so well fixed that I hoped to sail right into the entrance.

The first thing to appear through the murk was the unmistakeable form of a lighthouse, slightly upwind so we did a bit of pinching to get there as it was probably the one on the end of the breakwater. The white shape beckoned to us and I took a series of sights to ensure that I didn't get too close to some rocks just to the north of the entrance. I was looking for a navigation mark to confirm the position of the rocks. We got nearer and nearer, but there was no mark. It was getting very dim as the mist was becoming fine rain, when I suddenly noticed the land alongside the lighthouse becoming clear enough to see buildings. The scale of what I was looking at instantly changed. This wasn't just a little light on the end of a breakwater at all, it was a proper full-sized structure surrounded by buildings. It was standing on a small outlying island linked to the shore by a causeway. I wasn't in the place that I had thought myself to be. There was no harbour, I was sailing ashore. I was momentarily stunned. I searched the chart in a panic. No lighthouse marked. The only lights were at Blyth and Tynemouth. Where was I? Should I turn left or right? Could I hit rocks in an instant? My eyes burned into the chart. Where was it? It MUST be there. It was a huge white lighthouse... NOT on the chart.

I did a crash turn and headed out to sea returning along my incoming track whilst I stared at the disappearing building. It WAS there, I COULD see it. I wasn't dreaming, but I was in a state of disbelief. Once clear, I dived below to look at other charts which might overlap this area. I was using the latest chart, new and fully corrected right up to date, yet there was no lighthouse. I pulled out a five year old chart which fortunately covered the area and there it was. Curry Point with St Mary's Isle lighthouse marked on it a couple of miles to the south of Blyth. Mystery solved. With a sigh of relief we bore away and ran back up the coast to pick up the harbour entrance despite the bad visibility in what was now pouring rain.

I was later told that the lighthouse was no longer in use, but I feel that someone in a cartography department had made a serious error in no longer including it even as a daymark on the chart. Other, much lesser objects WERE included, whilst this enormous white painted object was not. It certainly gave me a fright and dented my previous belief in the total infallibility of the Admiralty chart.

Blyth Harbour was one of those vast silent constructions which sprawl across so great an area that people by comparison become so small they just disappear. A voice over the radio from a remote control tower directed us to the eastern side of the central pier in the south harbour. We secured between two of the pier's enormous, barnacle-encrusted legs, weaving a cat's cradle of fenders, planks and lines to protect us from their abrasive embrace. It was a long climb up the dripping, cold, steel ladder to the pier decking. There was nobody to be seen. The only noise came from the many pigeons roosting under the protective trusses of the wooden pier. The top of the pier was the domain of herring gulls and great black backs which stood silently on one leg, reluctantly opening one eye as we passed trying hard not to slip on their accumulated droppings. We could see ships distantly in other parts of the dock complex but they appeared not to move. Sailing craft belonging to the members of the Royal Northumberland Yacht Club were arranged in two tightly rafted rows secured alongside each other, but there were no visitors to them whilst we were there.

September 7 Wednesday.
The Yacht Club used an old sailing ship hulk for its premises which had angled solid teak decks. We made full use of their showers and read their noticeboard which suggested that Amble, ten miles to the north was a more significant yachting centre with its own marina.

We visited Harbour Control to pay our dues before departing at 11.45 to continue tacking south in similar conditions to the previous day. Our first pair of tacks took us down to Tynemouth at 14.00 and other tacks took us to just north of Hartlepool at about 19.00. Hartlepool was probably going to be my next stopping place. No sooner did we arrive off the land than the wind did a 90 degree shift to the south-east and began to rapidly increase in strength. We suddenly found ourselves having to tack against the foul tide just to make the last mile. Darkness was coming on and the wind was increasing sufficiently to make me reef. I was getting really annoyed with the weather which was making me struggle for every inch of progress. I used the motor and forced my way up to the headland, but by this time it was properly dark. The entrance was by no means clear due to shore lights behind the harbour lights. I was not relishing the thought of running down towards the lee shore to squeeze through a tricky entrance at Hartlepool ... not being certain of the alignments. I was getting an uneasy feeling about this as it was looking like a recipe for an instant, early end to my Round Britain Cruise.

MI issue 301. Episode 81.

<u>Teeside - Whitby</u>
7 September Wednesday.
Struggling in strong winds on a dark night we tried to decide whether to attempt running downwind into the entrance of Hartlepool or to find another option. Looking around I suddenly spotted other moving lights upwind to the south. The lights moved oddly. They were high, atop cone-shaped pillars. They were ... yachts! Sailing. Lots of them. We had sailed for many months, never really seeing more than one other yacht every couple of days usually at a great distance, then suddenly we found ourselves surrounded by a racing fleet; some running down to a mark, some tacking back, all fully crewed, racing around the bay on a very dirty Wednesday night.

Thoughts of going into Hartlepool were momentarily set aside; instead we turned this way and that to avoid the unexpected traffic, picking our course through by interpreting their navigation lights, always working upwind until we found ourselves at the Longscar cardinal mark from where I could distinguish the entrance channel lights to the River Tees even further to windward. Finding a haven to windward was much safer than risking going towards a lee shore, so Hartlepool as an option was forgotten.

We were monitoring the VHF working channel and could hear the many exchanges generated by the huge commercial area of Teesside, so I joined in and obtained permission to enter a quiet backwater area known as Paddy Hole just inside the entrance. The controller said that there was nothing big on its way in or out of the Tees, but as we crossed the channel near to the southern breakwater we were being chased by an incoming ship which seemed pretty big to me. The pilot on board was in contact with Harbour Control who advised him that a yacht was going into Paddy Hole. 'I think I see him.' said the pilot, who was cutting right through the bulk of the racing fleet at that time. We turned smartly out of the main channel and immediately the depth on our echo sounder dropped to a couple of metres for we were entering at low water.

It was a pitch black night but ahead of us on a hillside spreading right across our field of vision was a mighty orange-illuminated industrial area surrounding the Redcar blast furnaces. It was a surrealist, futuristic vision of hell not like anything we'd seen in the rest of Britain. The rising columns of smoke and steam absorbed the colour and writhed like forest-fire flames. The swift moving clouds above reflected back the orange glow from their underside and the water ahead mirrored the thousands of individual lights which lit the whole complex of buildings, roads and compounds. Every object before us appeared only as black silhouettes against this panorama of orange light, making it difficult for us to see where we were going. The black tongue of land to our left offered some shelter from the strong wind, but that same wind blew unpleasant fumes directly from the furnaces down onto us. We could smell the furnace exhaust and we had its nasty acrid taste in our mouths and throats.

We motored slowly ahead peering into the light trying to make out some detail. The land came in from the left. The echo sounder dropped rapidly back around its clock face, 6ft, 5ft, 4ft. We put the engine out of gear and drifted slowly forwards searching for a route towards a small cluster of boats which we could just make out on moorings further in. The fluttering light on the sounder went down to 2ft and held steady. The tide was at its lowest so we were relatively safe, but still there was a feeling of tension as our eyes searched the darkness for clues. Then to the right, about 50 metres away a tall post came into view, with a topmark which couldn't be distinguished. Searching my detailed chart in the Almanac proved only that it wasn't marked. The land came in even further from the left but its distance away was difficult to judge in the dark. Maybe it projected out to the post at this point? We edged gently to the right; still the water was only a few inches deep beneath us. We held our breath. The boat was going very slowly as a nudge was expected. The sounder light dropped right back to zero and the scraping of our keel as we stopped proved its accuracy.

There was no need for panic as we were within a few metres of the post and we floated again almost immediately. The wind carried us round the post leaving it to port as its topmark indicated. Relieved that we'd re-entered the shallow channel we began motoring left again towards the distant craft. The depth never fell below 3ft but when we reached the group of moorings it was still only 5ft and all the boats were considerably smaller than us which indicated that maybe the moorings weren't too heavy. It was still blowing quite strongly. We took several attempts to catch and secure the biggest spare mooring in the group during which time we ran the risk of picking up any unseen warps around our prop.

It was 21.00 and I was pretty tired, but being on the unknown mooring in windy conditions meant that I had to sit observing a couple of transits to establish that we were safe enough as we swung back and forth in the gusts. After a while I took a couple of hours sleep then made a further position check followed by more restless sleep and another check, until the gradual realisation that we were safe finally allowed relaxation. The water was relatively flat except that the wash from commercial vessels passing out in the main channel, crossed the shallows and occasionally, without warning would violently disturb us.

8 September Thursday.
I woke up and looked out of the window. There was a man walking slowly past, only a few metres away from the float. The tide was right out, but we remained afloat. As he walked at the edge of the shallows he was stooping to explore the water just ahead of him. He wore a bright orange jacket and had a bag slung around his shoulder. He bent and picked something up then put it into the bag. To the left and right other people were similarly engaged further up the muddy beach. They were dressed in ordinary clothes which were darker and so more difficult to see as the day was sombrely overcast and cold. They were picking up shell fish.

The dilapidated buildings we could see ashore were a random collection of shanties, wooden planked and patched, surrounded by rusting pick-up trucks and drying improvised fishing gear. Our boat was covered in a film of greasy soot which fell constantly from the grim sky. This was an awful place. The sight of these poor people searching along the shore for food was somehow medieval and seeing their isolated, bleak and poisoned little village made me wonder why they chose to remain in such a place.

The wind was lighter and seemed to have moved back to the south east, which was to be expected for that was the direction we wished to go, down to Whitby on the North Yorkshire coast.

The people disappeared ashore as soon as the tide made and we saw nobody as we cast off the mooring to begin slowly motoring out towards the turning-mark post. We had travelled quite a distance when we heard a distinct shout and looking back we saw two men in a small rowing boat. One of them waved in our direction. Was it to us? We looked back. He beckoned and shouted. What did he want? Come back, he motioned. We discussed this odd turn of events. Does he want to tell us something? Does he want money for the mooring? They'd stopped rowing after us. Should we go back? They went alongside a small open fishing boat and began to climb aboard. Was a chase about to develop if we didn't return? At that moment my boat fleetingly scraped the rocky bottom, so I instantly turned and motored slowly back. Maybe they wanted to advise us after all.

When we neared them they called across that we should not go out towards the turning post as it marked a rocky outcrop dividing this anchorage from the main channel. They indicated that we should follow the contour of the shore and go out directly. We thanked them and explained that in the night we had come in around the post at low water which amazed them. They looked afresh at our incredible craft and asked in their thick Geordie accents how much water we drew? The post's topmark indicated the port edge of the main channel. Our channel was only indicated by the presence of pot markers which were known and understood by the locals.

We motored out to the South Gare breakwater and then sailed closehauled on a course of 080°m taking us away from the shore which disappeared once more into the thick mist. There were numerous big ships anchored in the vicinity and the wind gradually increased to allow us to make about four knots. After about an hour at 12.45 the wind suddenly shifted south-west and we moved onto 130°m parallel to the coast at about six knots. At 13.30 the wind went west and died so I headed south to confirm my position against the land. We went east again for an hour against a fresh south-easterly when the wind became fluky again.

Both progress and navigational accuracy were proving very difficult in these constantly changing conditions. I tacked south-west to check my position with the high cliffs at 15.30 then struggled to make eastwards progress in the shifting wind. Suddenly the wind went completely and in looking southwards the mist lifted to reveal an unreal and ghostly ruin set on top of a high headland. It was a most fitting introduction to the picturesque fishing village of Whitby, where, amongst other things, the famous horror story of Dracula was written.

As the mist lifted slightly and the pale disk of the watery sun appeared I could begin to make out the cleft in the land where the harbour lay. To my amazement, just off the entrance was the unmistakeable shape of a square rigged ship at anchor. Then the mist descended again leaving me with the mental photograph in sepia tint and the worry about which century I might find myself in when I sailed out of my misty never-never land.

Fortunately the next thing to materialise out of the fog was a north cardinal mark and just as I reached it so did a big, modern, powered fishing launch which planed by at about fifteen knots also heading in. The visibility cleared again to reveal about five or six other power craft converging from all over the sea, packed with 'fish for the day' tourists returning after a day's sport. Ahead of us lay the *Sir Winston Churchill* with her tenders ferrying her sail-training crew back from a trip ashore.

Mindful of the tickings-off that I had received in Peterhead and Montrose for not asking permission to enter, I called Harbour Control and was advised to stay outside as a ship was about to leave. I was about 50 metres from the entrance in the middle of a long string of small boats going in. I peeled off to one side and they all continued. Monitoring the radio we waited whilst the ship inside negotiated a lifting bridge and then the lower harbour, an exercise which took three quarters of an hour whilst streams of pleasure craft continued to enter ... except us. I had wanted to go shopping ashore, but instead I sat observing my watch ticking closer and closer to shop-closing time. Eventually the ship cleared and we went in through the narrow entrance to experience the immediate shock of having our senses overwhelmed by the unique qualities of Whitby.

MI issue 302 Episode 82.

<u>Whitby - Dowsing Light</u> 8th September. Thursday

Whitby is a special place. We saw nowhere else in Britain quite like it. We came to it following several days at sea in fog and mist where the colours were faded to shades of grey. Our previous landfalls had been pastel tinted and our anchorages dark with the night. Our ears had accustomed themselves only to the constant sounds of wind and waves and we were in no way prepared for the sensory assault which we received after passing in through the narrow breakwater entrance to the harbour.

The town is close-packed, layer upon layer, climbing up the precipitous hillsides on either side. There is instant, vibrant interest in activity all around and amongst the stacked buildings as they recede into the distance up the narrow valley. There was so much to see that our heads were spinning. Our ears were blasted by the combined noise of the funfair and the marketplace, whilst the colours were so bright and varied that they hurt our eyes. There were people everywhere, shouting, lifting, running, carrying, waving, observing. There were boats in fleets, arriving, moving, departing, unloading, motoring; gulls in chorus, wheeling, diving, calling and fighting. The shear pulsating energy enveloped us, attracting and mesmerising, then overwhelming us. What a place.

We went over to the deep-water quay wall on the right, as directed by one of the pilots and fastened to a steel monohull yacht of about 33ft which in turn was alongside a couple of biggish fishing boats. We need not have worried about missing the chance to go shopping, in a rip-roaring place like this there was almost always somewhere open. In our exploratory walk ashore we quickly discovered a real sailing gem, an ordinary filling station with a pump selling marine diesel, which saved us all the usual trouble of having to arrange to buy the stuff. Having been in a succession of bleak, difficult, or unwelcoming harbours recently it was an enormous relief to arrive in a place where we felt we could easily stay for a rest and explore for three or four days.

The contrast which Whitby made with our last stopping place was particularly marked because we had travelled only 28 miles as the seagull flies from the ghastly, industrially polluted, depressingly bleak collection of hovels at Paddy's Hole on the Tees to this lively place where life appeared so much more full and healthy. We watched the constant comings and goings of the steel fishing boats and the traditional wooden cobles then compared the quality of life of their occupants with those poor souls we'd seen enslaved by the tide to pick shells at low water by wading in the cold mud of the Tees.

In a way this reinforced one of the observations we had noted on our journey around Britain. We had seen the contrast in the lifestyles of people in many different places. For some people life could be one of almost constant toil, for others, living relatively close by, life was undertaken with comparative ease. There appears to be an inertia holding people to the place of their roots and upbringing, which, if only it could be overcome, might in some cases make their existence so much more fulfilling.

Some places seem blessed with special qualities. We noticed on this east coast alone, for example, an outstanding feeling of honesty and personal security when we were in Lerwick, where the people seemed relaxed and unhurried. In Findhorn we noticed the clarity of the weather conditions, the superb sunsets and the outstanding beauty of the area, which has become a spiritual gathering place. North Sunderland and Whitby both had the comradeship and industry of their fishermen as an underlying base upon which the ambience of these places was founded. Some of the locations in between were depressing and lifeless by contrast, yet their occupants remained just as tied to them as those luckier people close by in places blessed with more desirable characteristics. I wondered how much location can enter into a person and what effect it might have. Much, much later I was very interested to see a television programme about the film maker Ridley Scott who was responsible for the films 'Alien' and 'Blade Runner' among others. His son explained that Scott had been raised within sight of the same bleak, blast furnace scenery on the Tees which had made such an adverse impression on us and he felt that this had entered into his father's art as an underlying, darker quality. Art being a creation based upon imagination and memory. Could life be shaped so differently by locations less than thirty miles apart, as they are at Whitby and Teesmouth?

The wind was forecast to come from the north-west which would be favourable. This was something that we'd not experienced for many days now. We needed that wind, for with only the two of us on board we had to make progress in one of two ways. Either we could day-hop along the coast, stopping to rest each night, or we could go out and sail continuously trying to cover distance rapidly, but this really required a favourable slant to the breeze. We had reached a place where day-hopping was about to become more difficult and covering distance would solve our problems.

We had roughly sixty miles to go to the mouth of the Humber, and from the information in the almanac this river was not an inviting prospect. The book listed three likely stopping places, but added that the first was expensive; the second should not be attempted without the very latest chart, whilst the third was for emergency use only. It added that we **would** find a welcome at one place thirty miles upriver and another one eighty miles in.

After the Humber with its swift tides came the shallow sandy expanses of The Wash with the only real prospects being the North Norfolk harbours of Blakeney and Wells. They were a further fifty miles from the Humber and I knew from experience that entering and leaving them was hazardous and tide dependent. A further thirty to forty miles was needed to reach Great Yarmouth or Lowestoft, whereas the direct distance sailing straight across The Wash totalled roughly one hundred miles which was possible for us providing we didn't have to beat to windward – that's hard work for a long time.

As we went to sleep that evening, we were (for once) in a no-lose situation. We were happy to stay at the place we were in until the forecasted wind arrived. If it should come we would be pleased to use it. The only real requirement was to get a good night's sleep to recover from the efforts expended reaching this point.

Friday 8 September
I expected a quiet night but it was not to be. There were craft moving about in the harbour until quite late then at three in the morning there was a very loud engine noise outside accompanied by men talking so close to us that they seemed to be on board. I dragged myself from my bed.

A steel trawler had reversed in, to the quay at 90 degrees across our bows between ourselves and the row of craft ahead of us. They had done this to gain access to a crane on the quay which was used for lifting otter boards from the trawl nets ashore for repairs. Squeezing the trawler in there must have taken great skill and lots of very tight rope as it had been done across a strong tidal flow. One of the crew was positioned with a fender to ensure that the steel side did not come into contact with my bows, but notwithstanding this, I dressed and went forward just to show that I was interested in the situation. They changed their boards and extracted themselves in a masterly manner.

At seven o'clock one of the trawlers inside us was departing and whilst it was technically possible to leave everything to the yacht beside me and between us, I thought it best to show willing and lend a hand. I never managed to get below again because another trawler came in to change otter boards and requested that we slack off our lines to lay further back, but behind us on the quay was the icehouse and the main diesel bunkering point for all the trawlers, so a stream of them began to squeeze in, or move out and the clearances between craft were such, that it required constant vigilance from us and adjustment of warps to stay out of harm's way.

At 08.00 I glanced up from my continuous activity to see the weathervane high on the Abbey on the cliff top. It indicated that the wind had gone to the north and I knew that our easiest option was to get going, to escape all this frantic movement. By 08.45 we were passing through into the lift and scend of the waves in the outer harbour under engine. Out we went into the open sea to find a perfect force 3-4 north-westerly blowing, but what was even more wonderful was the clear visibility. My constant complaint on the east coast was that whilst I didn't mind too much enduring all manner of discomforts in order to complete my sail round Britain, I **did** mind NOT seeing anything, due to the constant fog. One patch of mist looks very much like every other.

The lovely, lovely, green coast and white lighthouses moved past whilst we cross checked our position as we made good progress for once. At 10.30 we were crossing Robin Hood's Bay wondering why it is called that. Did he go there for his holidays? By twelve o'clock we were off Scarborough with its distinctive castle. The next landmark was Filey which brought back a flood of childhood memories for me as we'd often holidayed there. I'd forgotten about the white cliffs of Flamborough Head and was quite impressed with them.

At 14.15 we reached the point when it was time to decide whether we should head for the Humber or go directly for the tip of Norfolk in the Cromer area. I laid off the distances between the lightships on the route. It was 43 miles to Dowsing. From Dowsing to Dudgeon was 23 miles and then a further 21 miles would take us to the Haisborough Light about 10 miles off Cromer. We held onto our course of 130-140°m and watched as Flamborough and Bridlington fell astern at seven knots.

At 16.30 we spotted the gas platform on the Rough Gas Field and we were almost alongside at 17.30. This was good news because reference to the chart showed that the tide flooded into The Wash from both north and south. As it ebbed, the streams moved in reverse. I was carrying the rising tide from the north and if only I could make enough southwards progress I might catch an extra hour or two of help riding the southern ebb as it returned southwards. This dream slowly crumbled as with the onset of evening the wind faded and even the spinnaker could not make up the deficit though it did try its valiant best. By 20.00 we were about 20 miles off Spurn Head where we had to start the motor to stem the tide. To this point we had covered about 70 miles since leaving Whitby.

Motoring into the night can be pretty tedious, but as all the traffic used the same route as us to make the crossing, there were many ship's lights coming and going which needed constant tracking. Ahead, lay the rotating arcs of the Dowsing light growing closer until it strained our eyes to look directly at it. The lightship was a surprisingly small object, a tiny, bright, human oasis on a circle of glistening sea sending spoked beams in constant motion, chasing endlessly round the horizon. This jewel, in the centre of its own black universe passed at about 22.00.

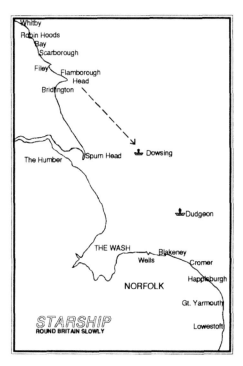

MI issue 303. Episode 83.

Dowsing –
Somewhere in the sands.

September 10 Saturday.
Homeward Bound.
From the Dowsing light to the Dudgeon, small navigation marks confirmed our position at 01.30 and again at 02.00 as we droned onwards under engine at constant speed. Dudgeon was passed at 04.15 and was tracked as it fell astern, to make certain that the boat was holding the course that she was being steered.

We were entering the area of sandbanks off the Norfolk coast which I rate as being the worst navigational maze anywhere around the British coast. The Thames Estuary might have as many submerged banks with attendant buoys, but the scale of that area seems smaller and tighter. Position fixing is more certain in the Thames due to the distinctive beacons, structures and landmarks. The 'Cromer Corner' right down to Lowestoft is more sprawling and the marks are much more widely spread. The tide is ferocious yet gives few obvious, clear indications of its speed and any indistinct landmarks ashore, such as water towers or funfairs are duplicated along the coast so that it is not possible to be certain exactly which water tower one is looking. I didn't wish to become involved with the sandbanks off Yarmouth; I planned to pass outside them, clear of all dangers.

Fifteen miles due north of Cromer at 05.15 as the dawn crept in, we were able to continue under sail once more in very light conditions with the wind back in the south-south-west. We sailed parallel to the coast on 130°m closehauled, initially in fog. Gradually as the sun grew brighter the mist thinned to give us a nice day, but we were still not able to see anything more than a couple of miles distant.

We should have passed within two miles of the Happisburgh (pronounced Haisborough like the sands) light vessel at about 07.00 but we heard nothing. I checked the characteristics in the almanac and we should have heard the ship, but there was only silence. We sailed on keeping a sharp watch as there was little to be seen or heard. I had no other method of confirming my position as I carried no electronic aids. I knew that I was in the vicinity of the Haisborough Sand and at about 08.30 I noticed that the water was swirling brown and disturbed. The echo sounder reading was only fifteen feet which is rather shallow when one is apparently in the middle of the open sea. Clearly we were passing over a bank but it was difficult to determine precisely where. We were in clearer water when I spotted a South Cardinal mark to my right which agreed with my analysis that I had just passed the southern tip of the sand and was two miles west of the S. Haisbro buoy.

Plotting carefully, we sailed down to the NE Cross Sands, East Cardinal picking up the flash and siren of the Newark Lightship even though we were three miles upwind. It was difficult to discern and could only be found by looking along the handbearing compass in the direction of where it should be. The wind was falling very light again and we were being forced gently out to sea until at about 11.15

we were becalmed once more. The tide would become adverse at about 12.00 so we began motoring on 200°m which should take us in towards the coast at a gentle angle.

Just after 13.00 a strongish southerly breeze began to blow so we set main and genoa and fell off on the inshore tack on about 230°m. Half an hour later we came upon a band of turbulent water ahead of us where the tide was tumbling like rapids northwards. Beyond it lay the smooth swirling waters over an offshore sandbank and fairly distantly, as if drawn by a blue pencil in the mist we could make out the land. To the south on our left was a buoy and a mile to our right was another buoy. We sailed in to the edge of the bank where the water shoaled to about fifteen feet and then tacked out again. The tide was ripping against us at such a rate that we could hardly stem it on the offshore tack. On the inshore tack we lost ground rapidly. I wanted to make up to the buoy to the south to give myself a positive identification of my position for I had been travelling in a best-guess situation for quite a long time. We engaged in a couple of pairs of tacks taking quite some time but which resulted in us gaining only about 25 metres.

If I could manage to get right inshore I would be able to enter either Lowestoft or Yarmouth to rest for I had enjoyed little sleep since leaving Whitby in the morning of the previous day. The pressure of this navigational memorising and calculating was beginning to take its toll on me. I felt that I knew my position within two miles, but I had to be much more accurate when I chose a place to cross the sandbanks barring my access to the coast. I had been in direct contact with these very sands previously and I did not wish to repeat the experience on a falling tide. The word 'sand' is deceptive; they are not soft by any stretch of the imagination. As I had made little progress tacking I decided to lose ground and sail back to the port buoy to the north which would confirm exactly where I was. We fell away with wind and tide together and hurtled towards it so fast that I was fearful we would pass it too rapidly to identify it if it should rotate away from us at the last moment.

We rounded up close to the buoy and read its name ... East Holm. I put the boat back onto the offshore tack to stem the tide and went below to check the chart only to find myself with a big problem. The buoy wasn't on the chart.

On a journey such as ours around the coast, one needs a multitude of charts and pilotage books. As I couldn't afford to buy them all, I was obliged to borrow charts and this was the cause of my problem. I had borrowed a whole group of charts for this stretch of coast which were a mixture collected from many sources. Most were reasonably up to date, except for the one which I now found myself on. It turned out to be ten years old. In many places on my journey I have used charts older than this without qualms. In rocky areas chart information remains relevant, but I now learned ruefully that for areas of shifting sand, reasonably current charts were essential. I paid the penalty for my penny pinching, because East Holm wasn't marked. Even more troublesome, it wasn't listed in the almanac which only mentioned selected buoys as waypoints.

I cross referenced all the information that I had and I felt that I could mark the buoy's position onto the chart from my observations and calculations. It made no difference. I could not hazard my boat across the sands without certain knowledge. I returned on deck to take a final back bearing on the disappearing spec of East Holm as it was re-absorbed into the mist. The boat was sailing 178°m at five knots and making good only 090°T. We were going east. With the disappointment of not solving my problems my strength began to ebb

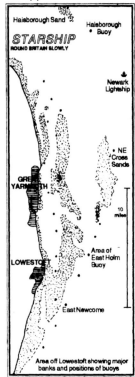

as fatigue grew within me. I needed some rest and I had to make a decision.

I had two main options. I could anchor on the edge of the sands until the tide had dissipated its strength, or I could continue to sail this holding tack. We would jog slowly outwards and then begin to make progress when the tide weakened. I could then return inshore somewhere between Lowestoft and Southwold to re-establish my position where there were no off lying banks. I laid off the track on the chart. Three hours jogging outwards and then three hours returning. I added the tide and I was off Southwold with a clear run home. Going into Lowestoft was a red herring really, it had such a dangerous entrance with the tide sweeping across it ... and nightfall would be coming on. I asked Alison to maintain the course and I collapsed into my bunk.

We followed the pre-planned action and I was woken to tack the boat at 18.45. At 19.30 it was coming prematurely dark. I was roused when Alison said that we were approaching two gas platforms and one of them had just switched on its lights. It took a moment or two for this news to penetrate my dreamland where no gas platform had previously existed. I stumbled up on deck to see in the gathering gloom that one platform was changing into a DFDS ferry heading for Scandinavia or other foreign parts. The second platform was so square and monolithic that I thought for a moment that it looked like Sizewell power station, but it motored away northwards so rapidly that my dream of exceptional progress towards the south went with it. At least the darkness would bring an end to the mystery of where we were, as soon as the big flashers were switched on. I stayed at the helm, so as not to miss them.

We continued the inshore tack and at last there came the first flash of a big light rotating under the low cloud. I also saw a clear north/south traffic lane with ships coming from both directions. Other lights, cardinal marks of one kind or another began to appear. I had my first disappointment when it became clear that the big white flasher wasn't Southwold as I'd hoped it would be. From the smaller marks it was clear that we were coming back in to the coast on the off-lying sandbanks somewhere off Lowestoft and we had not made a great deal of progress. We changed the helm again so that I could concentrate on our position fixing.

Southwold flashed four but my light was flashing three and searching the chart I couldn't find anything flashing three except Smiths Knoll which ought to be well to the north of me by this time, I hoped. The light wasn't a lightship because it had shore lights behind it. The only other light of any size that I could see was a double one with a red and white on the same tower. The almanac listed such a light at Lowestoft. It could be used as a transit on the entrance.

Sunday September 11.
At 01.56 the red and white and the big flashing white came in line to give me a transit of 290° (correctly written 110°). Putting this on the chart ran the line through the East Newcome buoy. EAST Newcome, of course, EAST = 3. They had probably upgraded this mark to assist in finding the channel. Two smaller marks were just passing to seawards so I checked the chart to see if a small danger was indicated. Yes. The bearings crossed with the transit on Lowestoft entrance and we finally knew where we were. It was quite a relief after the long uncertainty of the day.

We headed south looking for Southwold again and after a little while we were clear of all offshore marks. With a couple of dodges to avoid fishing boats we were once again in the open sea. Each time I have rounded that corner from Cromer to Lowestoft I have had the same terrible tangle with the sandbanks. I hated the place, but I was determined that next time I would buy a new chart as it just wasn't the place to play games with old ones.

Whatever happened to Southwold light? I'd passed it previously on three occasions and never yet seen it. It is positioned on a cliff top and its problem was that it had its head in the clouds when there was low visibility such as there was on this night. Maybe we would pick up Orfordness just before dawn if we were lucky? The boat was going well, driving hard to windward, but we needed the speed as the tide was adverse once again.

As day dawned I dug out my old chart of the bay off Harwich and Felixstowe which I hadn't seen for four years. This was going to be the day when my inward track would cross with my outward track and I would finally tie the knot to claim my circumnavigation of Britain. My mind was filled with memories as we pounded along. I longed for the coast to come and for the familiar landmarks of home to appear. Aldeburgh, Orfordness, Sizewell, any of them would signify that we were on the final stretch. I made a mental note not to get Channel fever. Many an accident has happened on the last leg because one relaxes, thinking that it is all cut and dried. I must NOT hit the Cork Sands.

MI issue 304. Episode 84.

Position not quite certain. Maybe off Southwold?
September 11 Sunday.
How long had I been sitting here steering? I tried to calculate, but the answer wouldn't come clearly. What time had I come on watch yesterday evening? I couldn't quite remember. I sat wedged at the wheel watching the oncoming waves as the sky became lighter. We climbed waves and we clipped them, crashed them aside or soared smoothly over. She was going well. But...where was the land? We should have seen something by this time. Was it yesterday or the day before that we had left Whitby? My memory wouldn't give a definite answer. I was in a half-doze, half-awake mental situation. I expected to see land now that it was light enough for a visible horizon. I stirred myself from my cramped discomfort and stood bracing myself against the bucking motion, scanning the horizon to windward; waking myself with the cold wind outside the doghouse striking my face. I **must** see land soon. My starboard tack course

was west of south so even allowing for leeway I'd be coming in on the coast. Maybe the tide was carrying me outwards? What was the tide doing? When did it turn? The answers just weren't coming like they should do. Maybe I should go onto port tack and sail directly in towards the coast. If I did that and the tide was against me I'd be swept north-eastwards at such a rate that I'd lose all which I'd suffered to gain. Was the tidal flow against me? How far down the coast had I come? Could I afford to lose ground? Was I off Sizewell or even Aldeburgh? Surely I must have passed Southwold by now? She was sailing well enough.

I sat wrestling with times and figures and angles and they all just made tangled threads of thoughts inside my head whilst the boat drove hard to windward and my gaze remained on the horizon. It was inevitable that something should appear at some time. It was only a matter of time. Patience.

Beyond a distant ship far ahead came the first grey smudge of something solid. I hardly dared to hope as there had been previous false alarms; darker patches of sea; ship superstructures hull down below the horizon. I looked away and sailed for five minutes before daring to look again. It was still there. Probably Orfordness lighthouse. My eyes drilled the horizon for detail as we punched on, close-hauled into the good force five. I waited. To the left there gradually came a headland; Felixstowe, it must be Felixstowe. It had a town on it. Great, it was Felixstowe. I must be spot on target. Slowly but surely the details emerged. I could make out the hotel blocks. I could see where the land descended on the right towards the low land near the entrance of the River Deben. Oh what a relief. Home at last. It had been a long, long sail from Whitby. So much trial. So much uncertainty amongst the sandbanks. Soon we would be within the shelter of the bay. I looked for Walton-on-the-Naze but it wasn't quite visible; perhaps it was too misty? Maybe it was the angle that I was approaching the coast? I tried to relate my course to the geography of the land features, but my tiredness wouldn't allow it all to make sense to me. My fuddled brain couldn't make the adjustments.

Another yacht came tacking up from the channels down in the Thames Estuary. Perhaps this wasn't Felixstowe? Where were the dock cranes? Does Felixstowe have big tower blocks like that? I didn't think it had? It looked more like Clacton and Frinton as the headland projected in isolation. Yes, it was FRINTON seafront. Stupid! I thought I'd better be careful not to put myself on the Gunfleet Sands ahead and to my left. What a fool. I'd been carried further south than expected and actually gone just off the bottom of my chart. Good job I knew the place. I'd have to beat back northwards as the wind was shifting and easing. I wondered how far I'd have to go to get clear of the top end of the sands. I could fix my position on the lighthouse ... but ... Frinton doesn't have a lighthouse ... does it? Felixstowe certainly doesn't have one. Was it a lighthouse standing white amongst the houses? It was. Where the hell was I? I looked to the right for Walton-on-the-Naze, but it wasn't visible. There were no piers. WHERE was I?

The wind which had been so strong for so long was dying and heading me. It was the effect of the land. Suddenly I was losing the driving power to get nearer to discover my position. At this rate I would go straight by. This time I HAD to confirm. Nothing must stop me. I started the motor to force my way inshore.

I came in to where there were other boats. People were fishing. It was a holiday place. Why didn't I know it? It was an English town, full of people going about their normal business, but somehow transplanted onto my section of coast. It became completely calm in the lee of the land. I motored on, incredulous. What was this place? I was Gulliver arriving at his most fantastic location. Suddenly, with a chill in my spine, I recognised the land. Arches supporting the houses at the water's edge, a strange castle-like building. Its essence flooded over me, washing through me like a wave of fear and realisation, I knew the place but I couldn't bring myself to say the words within my head. There was only knowledge without words.

We approached a huge navigation mark. It said LONGNOSE. I have never been so shocked and mystified in all my previous sailing as when I read this single word which appeared to me to be written in a foreign tongue. All my senses and understanding still placed me close to Felixstowe and this word, this object, had no place there. I looked at the buoy and at the land which was now so close. To avoid facing the reality, I called below to bring Alison up to the cockpit to look at the features of the town. I needed to have another person believe what I could not bring myself to accept was true. She looked. 'Where are we?' she said. I hesitated. I put the engine out of gear. We drifted and the words came. 'We're in Kent. This is Margate ... North Foreland ...in Kent. We have sailed fifty miles too far.' There was a long silence. The boat rocked on the wash of the passing craft. We just stood looking at the land. My brain had ceased functioning.

How could I have sailed fifty miles too far? Fifty miles in one night ... by accident ... beating to windward. Fifty miles of effort when I was desperate to end the journey. Fifty miles. It was impossible. It was a mystery. It was astonishing. It was true. I slumped in my seat, weakened by shock. It was still only 11.00 in the morning. A few more miles and I'd have run into France ... if the Goodwin Sands hadn't got us first.

The tide was just beginning to run north, but I couldn't take it. I was exhausted and I had no chart. Sailing across the estuary without a chart could be dangerous to one's health. I knew. I'd just done it.

We set plain sail and bore away for Ramsgate on the returning breeze which ran south around the headland. It was time to have a rest for it had already been a long day. I had finally tied the circumnavigation knot as I approaching the Longnose buoy when my inward track crossed my outward one. It was not a triumphant occasion.

Ramsgate didn't have its outer harbour when I was last there. It had greatly improved the access. We entered at 13.30 and made fast to a pontoon for which we were charged double the monohull rate, for reasons difficult to explain by the employee of Thanet District Council who collected the due. The huge monohull ahead was almost as beamy as us but he only paid once. We had a good sleep and a long shower then wandered slowly around the town. I was still in a daze about my navigational error and trying to explain it to myself. I bought a chart and looked at the route back. We listened to the forecast which said that the weather was deteriorating and would go from westerly 5/6 to north-westerly 6/7 next day. After beating almost all the way down the east coast we were about to start beating back up again, except the weather would be worse. It was a complete disaster.

The pressures of the continuing journey did not allow me to make a detailed analysis at the time to discover how I managed to make such a catastrophic error. I had to accept the situation and concentrate on extracting myself from it, rather than agonising about how I came to be there. After the journey I became involved in other matters and had to return the crucial borrowed chart of the area around Lowestoft. Only years later have I been able to retrace the critical moments to seek answers, using an ancient chart marked with East Holm. This is what I suspect happened.

The first stage of the error commenced as I sailed away from the East Holm buoy off Lowestoft. I took a back bearing to check the effect of the powerful tide on my course being steered. That bearing showed me being pushed eastwards despite sailing a course of nearly south. I believed the bearing and acted upon it. After the event it became clear that the boat had continued to sail more south than east making good five or six knots against wind and tide whilst I slept. It is possible, but I think unlikely, that I took the back bearing on the wrong buoy. It is more likely that I moved into an area of lower tidal flow or that the flow markedly decreased in the later hours of its run.

I wondered for some time whether when I came on deck to see the 'gas rigs' (which turned out to be ferries?) if one of them had actually been the Sizewell power station which I took it to be at first glance. I now feel sure that it was a ferry, due to my later confirmed position against other very significant lights.

I was looking for a big flashing light and when it came I attempted to identify it on the Lowestoft area charts when I was no longer on them. The second stage of my error was the classic one, making the evidence fit the position that I thought I was in. The 'flashing three' light came into transit with a 'red and white' shore light at two o'clock in the morning. I made them Lowestoft harbour entrance. I now know them to have been the Shipwash lightship and Orfordness light respectively. At that point I was almost home. The sailing distance mental error was then about fifty miles.

In a nutshell, my fundamental basis of belief was a strong mental image that the tide had stopped my progress and I'd remained near to Lowestoft, which was a worst-case supposition, but the boat had in fact achieved an unbelievably best-case progress thanks to Alison's steering, having sailed fifty miles bringing us down to Orfordness. When I was mentally sailing Lowestoft to Felixstowe on a single tack through the night, I was in reality sailing Orfordness to Margate which is roughly fifty miles again. The average speed throughout was about five or six knots against a genuine force five which shifted west only during the last couple of hours.

Had I at any time been able to make a calculation of the hours involved I might have grown suspicious, but that did not happen. The root cause was fatigue and this is the most important lesson to be learned. This type of fatigue, caused by being on watch too long over a period of days, is very difficult to self-diagnose. The most telling warning sign for me was my inability to carry through simple mathematical calculations to produce definite answers. This is a symptom that I had already been aware of from previous occasions, but still I did not respond to that knowledge. I hope that if I should find myself in a similar position again I will be able to recognise my condition and as a result of this incident, react. What I will then DO, knowing that my mind is no longer reliable, remains to be seen.

I have been overtaken by innovative technical progress. The most effective action these days is to buy the current electronic position/location-fixing devices and with them, surely, such a huge error could no longer be made ... except … following power failure.

MI issue 305. Episode 85.

Across the Estuary.
September 12 Monday.
Sure enough the wind was up and had moved to just north of west. I wouldn't normally set out in a forecast 6 or 7, but as usual my hand was being forced by circumstances. The weather was about to set into a steady northerly run and I couldn't afford to linger in the expensive berth on the pontoons in Ramsgate. The longest that the westerly wind could last for, was only this one day and it gave me the chance of sailing a single port tack all the way across the Thames Estuary. Once the wind went north it would be a dead beat in much colder conditions. We weren't looking forward to the sail, but my thoughts weren't exclusively negative.

We had been living aboard and sailing since the end of July during which time we had sailed the north coast of Scotland, Orkney, Shetland and the whole of the East Coast experiencing a wide variety of conditions. I'd come to know that *Starship* was a rugged craft which needed strong weather to extract her best performance, as she'd proved in the trip down to Margate. I felt that she was strong enough to race the weather to get us back home once more. The most important question was whether we, the crew, were strong enough to endure the pounding to come. I hoped that the full night's rest had unscrambled my brain sufficiently for me to keep track of our whereabouts in the sandbanks maze of the Thames Estuary.

The time to leave was 11.00 when the tide would take us up to the North Foreland. We motored out and set a reefed main and half genoa whilst in the shelter of the land. We went away on a fast broad reach which gradually became tighter as we passed Broadstairs. Just off Hope Point we took our first concentrated gust which really dug the boat into the water making her accelerate like a car away from the traffic lights. Approaching the corner we could see that the Longnose buoy was occasionally disappearing behind the waves in contrast to the calm of yesterday. The water beyond was a mass of white crests resembling the rosts of Shetland as the water poured around the headland into the South Channel against the wind. There was nothing for it but to take the medicine. All was prepared below with everything movable placed down on the floor and the companionway hatch was closed. I progressively winched her in until the sheets were bar tight. She came tight on the wind as we drove her at speed into the roaring mass of the sea.

My strategy for the estuary was simple and direct. I had determined to sail closehauled straight across, daring and dodging the sandbanks rather than trying to sail right around the outside. Going round might mean that I'd arrive level with Felixstowe too far offshore and then be vulnerable to a windshift which would make me struggle to get back up to the land. Crossing the banks meant that I might get sheltered water from them as they calmed the sea, and eventually I would benefit from reduced wind due to the shelter of the land.

The tide was setting us into the river as we went across the Queen's Channel and the waves were big and wet. I always forget just how salty the taste of the sea is. My doghouse usually keeps me dry, but this time it was impossible under the conditions. The view through the windows was the same as that seen through the door of a washing machine. In between waves I had to keep snatching a look around the side screen to check all was clear ahead. We were really driving *Starship* hard and smashing water everywhere. Alison was steering and I was tracking the navigation precisely, because I knew that we would be passing over some very shallow water at times. It was essential for me to know exactly where we were at every moment.

It was noticeable how very much smoother the water was as we crossed the tail of the Margate Sands, compared with the heavy water in the channels on either side. This confirmed the decision to cross the sands. The Tongue Sands gun platform lay close to our course and it was a surprise that such a big and well defined structure appeared as an insignificant dot on the chart, whilst the buoys, almost invisible in these conditions, which guarded it were shown so large.

We were making good a straight line course of 330°m which took us close to the Edinburgh Channel. Under most normal circumstances we would have followed the channel, but this meant running off in heavy seas then trying to tack back against wind and tide around the dogleg in the channel. Our alternative was to hold our course and sail straight over the sandbank. This is the essence of sailing the estuary; to have a shallow draught craft which can pass over the banks and then to calculate safe depths and take calculated risks. Getting it wrong, might mean paying the ultimate penalty.

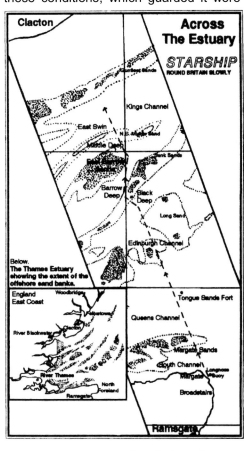

The first bank to be crossed was the test for all the others to follow. We were at high water and as we passed over this bank the shallowest **charted** depth was 1 metre on our track. Our echo sounder showed a minimum depth of 3½ to 4 metres which gave me my margin of safety from which I could calculate the probably depth that I would read as I crossed each succeeding bank. I could then evaluate the risk which would progressively increase as the tide fell and decide whether I could take that risk.

The Black Deep channel was very rough, but we were travelling at about eight knots all the time and each channel is only about a mile wide where the tide runs strongly, before another mile of relatively smooth water is encountered over the next sand. 'Sand' is not the best descriptive word for the texture of the banks. 'poured concrete' gives a more accurate picture. They are not the place to park a boat in such conditions. Some kind souls have erected sundry beacons near likely crossing points and these are of immense help in confirming that the risk is being run in exactly the right spot, because no matter how often you sail over the banks you always get a shudder in your spine and an emptiness inside as you watch the echo sounder descending lower and lower.

After crossing the Barrow Deep we had a nice long sail across the top of the East Barrow Sands. At one stage when the sounder showed 7ft I decided to run off a little to the north as it was getting a bit too close for comfort. On the chart this area was shown as an underlined 1 with a 7 after it which would put my wreckage four feet up in the air at low water if I should touch it.

The Middle Deep and the East Swin together made up the Kings Channel and we continued to power-sail across into what was still a very murky day with blown spume all around, making quite incredible progress. It was 14.15 and we were within five miles of the shore at Clacton yet unable to see it as the weather was so bad. Our position probably meant that we would cross the estuary in only three and a half hours which is excellent as it is usually regarded as a full day's sailing. I was beginning to think we'd make it when I looked to windward into the area where the entrance to the River Blackwater would be if only the stormy day would allow us to see it. To my horror, the whole horizon was covered with the blackest clouds that I have ever seen. It was like night in there and it was coming our way.

Not wanting to create alarm I just mentioned to Alison that I'd be reefing the main (despite its already relatively small size). I clambered on deck and edged forward along the windward side. I had only had time to gain the mast and unlock the through-mast, boom-rolling handle when a squall of intense ferocity struck us, accompanied by driving black rain which instantly reduced the visibility to only a few feet. The noise and force were overpowering, like standing in a tunnel as an express train passes through within only a few feet of you. I lay back on the reefing handle to reduce the main as rapidly as possible, but it refused to turn despite the halliard being released. Looking along the boom I was alarmed to see that the aluminium tube was bending away in the middle with the wind force in the sail. It had taken on such extreme curvature that it could not be made to rotate. The boat was heeling to a steep angle and things were beginning to happen in slow motion. I was isolated in the roaring noise. My flogging oilskin hood blinkered my vision through the restricted tube ahead. Turning my head I looked towards the leeward float watching it being compressed down into the water. The sea reached the level of the gunwhale at the same time along the full length of the float even though it has a complex shape which makes it deeper in some places than in others. I can remember thinking that the design was correct for the design-thinking at the time of her construction, as the deck commenced being submerged. The float had never done this previously and I was watching for reasons of technical interest rather than fear. The boat was heeling to a steep angle. The shock of the enormous wind pressure was sustained, on and on. I was bracing myself against it. I was a detached observer; my brain was photographing the images as the water came up either side of the float and met down the centreline as its hull went beneath the water.

MI issue 306 Episode 85.

September 12 Monday.
Home again.
It was the most ferocious gust of wind that we had taken during our entire trip round Britain and we were only a few miles from home off the entrance to the River Blackwater. There was no danger of the boat going over despite her momentarily submerging a float; there was still a long way for her to go before she entered the danger zone. Nevertheless at a time such as this, one needed to have certain knowledge of the working principles of the multihull and to be comfortable with that knowledge. It would have been excessively stressful not to have been a believer. The stiffest monohull would have suffered a knockdown at least. We were still sailing.

Almost immediately the float was emerging as we drove forward. The sea itself had now disappeared from view to be replaced by a thick froth all being blown down to leeward. It reminded me of an Antarctic blizzard where the snow drives away in lines across a flat plain. The blackness of the squall, the lashing rain and the noise isolated us entirely from everything except the small circle of sea in which we struggled. I had thrown myself onto the top of the inflatable dinghy lashed between the crossbeams on the windward side. I wanted to add my weight to it to stop in from breaking free.

From my position I was shouting to Alison at the wheel to luff the boat into wind, although shouting was a reflex reaction rather than a logical one. Nothing could be heard in that wind tunnel. Frantic motioning was more effective and the boat came round, reducing strain which allowed the arched main boom to straighten. I crawled to the mast and began to roll the sail as the pressure was released. Incredibly the noise now was even greater as the heavy beating of the sails was added to the din. The mast, the rigging,

everything was being shaken. I locked the reefing handle and lay on the windward deck waiting for a few moments to see if the squall would diminish and also because any movement by me was potentially dangerous. To stand up was impossible. I pulled the drawstrings of my hood tighter to protect my face from the stinging rain. I could see the genoa sheets flogging themselves into a solid ball so I slid along the deck and back into the cockpit to attempt to roll the sail using its reefing winch.

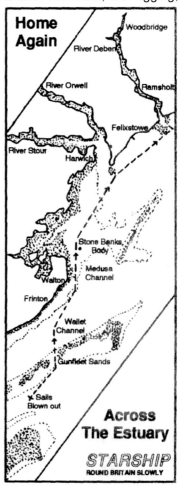

Alison was shouting at me "It's gone. It's gone." and looking forward I saw that the genoa was completely ripped to pieces with only tattered flags waving from the stay. The sail appeared to have exploded backwards because pieces of leech line and strips of cloth were tightly wrapped around all the stays which supported the mast. I was unable to roll the remains of the sail with the winch because the resistance was so great, I left them to flog and turned my attention to my other sail. Taking a securing rope, I went forward again to try to keep the mainsail intact. I clawed the sail down and then wrestled to tame it with the rope. I could see that the middle battens had been driven straight through their pockets and had disappeared astern.

The initial blasts easily exceeded force 10 in my estimation and experience and the squall lasted between five and ten minutes, then the wind slowly returned to the previous strength of about force six, but with much clearer air. Alison was understandably quite shaken, saying 'What do we do now?' as she looked up at the rags aloft where shortly before we'd had sails. We checked that there were no ropes in the water and started the motor to keep us going slowly ahead towards the land which was just becoming visible. This time it *was* Walton and Frinton and there was no lighthouse.

The headsail posed a particular problem for it had been roller reefed prior to disintegrating. The reefing system turned it in one direction around the stay but the many tattered strips of sail had wrapped themselves around the stay in the opposite direction and tied themselves in knots. It steadfastly resisted any effort to roll the remnants which were still big enough to be giving the boat quite a severe shaking. Much of the sail was too high for me to reach and it was not possible to lower it. The noise, vibration and wind resistance of the sail was insistent and I had to do something about it before I could make progress again. Even if I reached land and shelter I still had no idea of how I could tackle the sail.

I took a spare halliard from the mast forward to the sail and wound it round and round the stay. Slowly it calmed the worst of the crackling-flogging and brought it to an acceptable level so that I could think of proceeding once more. I went below and sorted out my storm jib which I set hanked onto the inner forestay. I have rarely used it as it is so small, but in force six or more it generates about the right power to balance the drive of the reefed main. I re-hoisted the main which although damaged was still workable and we began to move again.

By this time we were across the Gunfleet Sands and into the Wallet just off Frinton. The engine was cut and we went off at quite a lick up the Medusa Channel towards Harwich and the Stone Banks buoy. Ahead, we met the only other craft which was daring enough to brave the conditions. It was a cruiser with a funny Chinese name, carrying a reefed junk rig. He was sailing to windward as tightly as he could, but making no progress as he was at the limit of his sail carrying power and constantly being knocked over by the gusts. It was a good illustration of the importance of having a stiff boat if you want windward ability. We went past almost upright and when we looked back later we could see that he was still sailing in roughly the same position as when we'd first spotted him.

We gained the comparative shelter of the land at Felixstowe and freed off for the Haven Buoy marking the entrance to our river. We arrived at the Deben river bar with the tide ebbing in full spate and the wind directly against us. I knew that waiting for low water would mean an entry in darkness so we doused our sails, put the motor on high revs and began the slow process of getting in. When the wind was peaking we stood still, but in any slight lull we went forward a few inches. It was a matter of sitting and waiting whilst keeping a check on the leading marks as we were swirled from side to side by the flow. Eventually we were into the channel and progress became more certain. It was nice to be back in the home river again having been away for so long; it was a surprise to see how crowded it had become.

We picked up a spare mooring above Ramsholt where we spent a night twisting and turning with the wind against the tide, dreaming of the blissful nights of stillness that we had found in the Hebrides and Orkney.

Tuesday 13 September.
We took the tide up to Woodbridge, motoring in the congested channel and found our own mooring to be in a heavily barnacled condition, but still quite serviceable. It was a welcome object to have aboard for it meant that we really had completed the journey. There would now be time to replenish, refurbish and to digest the many lessons learned about cruising.

The most immediate lesson was about that squall which blew out our sails on the very last day of our four year journey. It proved that the elements could be just as dangerous right in our own backyard; we didn't have to sail to exotic locations to find danger. At sea, one needs a slice of luck to succeed. Should I meet such a monster on a future occasion I would think very carefully before releasing my sheets quite so rapidly. The sails took the strain whilst they were being held tightly, but once freed to flog, they were destroyed.

The sail around Britain was the learning experience of a lifetime. I learned to cruise. I learned the diversity and the challenge of the British Isles. I appreciated the help and the friendship of the many different crewmembers that had assisted me in the adventure, but most of all I learned what a trustworthy boat *Starship* is. Initially, I must confess I had my doubts, but she sailed on when both skipper and crew had reached the end of their endurance and she performed magnificently in adversity. She proved if proof was needed, that trimarans are not only for racing but can succeed in the rougher, knockabout world of family cruising.

Finally the question most frequently asked. What next?

Words of appreciation for Jack and Muriel Heming.
A letter to me expressed appreciation for *'the way I look deeper into things... the way I outline the options and the conditions requiring the readers to think along with me'*. I must say that this way of writing was only possible because I was not writing under the usual restrictions that editors impose upon their contributors. Magazines generally only allow contributing writers a very limited space in only a few issues at the most. This has the effect of either condensing an account into lists of courses steered and places visited, which can become tedious. Alternatively the writer may choose to highlight selected sensational incidents. Thanks to Jack Heming of *Multihull*

International I was able not only to furnish my account but also to diverge from the bare story to include my emotions and impressions which resulted in a much truer picture of the totality of cruising.

We didn't sail just to exercise the mechanics of sailing but to expand our experience and discover new and interesting people and places, as well as ourselves. We continue to sail.

385

Writing the book

I was a member of MOCRA, the Multihull Offshore Cruising and Racing Association. I had engaged in some written submissions to their newsletter. As with many sailing organisations the core of their membership was the racing fraternity and as multihull craft deliver speed under sail there were proportionally more racing members than cruisers. I was, therefore, slightly unusual in being a trimaran sailor that wrote about cruising. The overwhelming majority of trimarans were predominantly used for racing. I was appointed the MOCRA Cruising Secretary. Jack Heming the editor of Multihull International a monthly magazine based in Totnes that disseminated news to enthusiasts worldwide contacted me. He asked me, as MOCRA Cruising Secretary to send him some cruising news for inclusion in his publication. I had no news, but I thought that I could possibly find a few words arising from my own cruising activity. I guessed I might get about half a dozen pieces and perhaps something else would turn up to fill the gaps. He asked for no more than 2,000 words per submission.

When sailing goes well there is little to write about. 'Adversity' is what generates the 'words'. On this Round Britain sail we had so much of the first that producing the second was never a problem. The journey was so long, so diverse and the challenges so continuous that we were constantly learning our cruising lessons by the Mark 1, direct method and eventually I wrote 86 monthly episodes plus other material. At times the published account lagged some way behind the actual sailing.

Coastal cruising is probably the most severe test in sailing due to the dangerous proximity of the land, entering and leaving the many different ports, calculating and overcoming the restrictions resulting from the tidal streams and the constant threat imposed by other seaborne traffic. The British Isles has an endless range of situations, circumstances, weather variations, sea states, sights and scenes, history, geography, people and places to experience in sailing, that it offers wonderful adventure beyond our imaginations at the outset. We learned this as we went along and only came to appreciate it slowly. This was and is, the ultimate way to learn to cruise.

As the story unfolded, so, more and more readers began to become involved in reading it. It became a 'sailing soap' story. Episodes had cliff-hanger endings and readers sometimes wrote in with their suggestions about how to escape from the sticky situations we found ourselves in. For some readers the divide between fact and fiction was blurred in their minds. These readers found it hard to wait a whole month before finding out what had happened to us. There was even a fan club and a number of requests to bring all the episodes together into a unified whole, thus producing a book. My sailing friends Nico and Sonja Boon in the Netherlands were the first to suggest this and I gave an undertaking to them that one day I would look at it seriously.

The first ten episodes were written specifically with my role as MOCRA Cruising Secretary in mind and contained references to current multihull topics in the news. I subsequently rewrote these ten paper episodes onto the little Amstrad, from which they have been retrieved for the purpose of their inclusion here. This has saved a great deal of work and some material not relevant to the cruise account has been taken out. I have retained the diagrams as they were originally, because they partly indicate the gradual improvement in the quality of production throughout the span of time covered by the sailing. Many illustrations are scanned from the original magazine pages and printing on the reverse sometimes bleeds through. It is hoped that this will not detract from what they show.

The Boat.
Starship.
To make the boat I had to save my money to be able to afford the materials and managed to make her without any single bill exceeded £200. Making the mast and rig involved having three such bills. I worked as a full time teacher and built her in my spare time after work and during my holiday periods. In the first two years of the build I only worked in the summer period. I could step out of my living room window into the back of the boat (see centre pages). As she was a trimaran I could make the separate parts and assemble them elsewhere. I had never really worked with glass fibre construction before, nor with foam sandwich. The technology was evolved for making such boats by Derek Kelsall and I learnt the techniques directly from him and from his writings. The form of the mainhull up

to the gunwhales, the crossbeam structure and the floats were specified by him and everything else was evolved by me to fit the ideas of what I wanted in the boat.

As a sailing centre, chief instructor I was involved in organising sailing courses for children together with adult courses that produced the instructors to teach those children. It was from these adults that several of my crew came as they sought to further their own sailing experience. I had learnt to sail in dinghies and then to cruise, in two small trimarans (see centre pages). I purchased for myself a 20ft, locally-made, plywood trimaran *Mistral*, based on the Nimble design of Arthur Piver, and taught myself East Coast cruising, helped by my wife. All of our sailing learning was self-taught. I also sailed with a fellow teacher, Sq. Ldr. Raymond Williams in his 25ft plywood *Endeavour*. This was an early-prototype trimaran made by Tony Smith who then went on to construct the foam-sandwich prototype of his *Telstar* trimaran design in his back garden, close to mine. This 26ft/8m design became the longest running, commercially-produced, family trimaran in Britain and the United States at that time. With *Endeavour* I learnt by experience, together with Raymond Williams to cruise cross-Channel to France and Belgium.

When we started our family my little 20ft boat was too small. Prior to our first baby we had used a gallon of water per day, but the baby needed five gallons of water a day, even if we towed the nappies on a line behind the boat to clean them. I decided to build a boat big enough for my family whilst my children were babies, so I sold *Mistral* and delivered her under sail, to the Isle of Wight. I then made *Starship* taking about five years to get the boat to the water.

This is the content of the first three chapters published in Multihull International.

MI issue 206. Episode 1.
<u>Pieces which build a Cruising Dream</u>
I first discovered that I was a cruising sailor when racing an Enterprise dinghy, in those far-off days when to acquire such an object of luxury, you had to build your own. (Remember torturing those bottom plywood panels with a mixture of steaming blankets and swear words?) We had just thrashed our way downstream to the windward mark, fighting a heavy breeze, in a narrow river channel, against the incoming tide. As the crew, I was whacked. My

hands were sore, my shins were bruised, and my stomach muscles were knotted with the effort of sitting out. At last, we bore away with the wind and tide to push us homeward.

'Only two more rounds.' grinned the helmsman, as we slid downhill, simply to have to climb back up it again. My heart sank. My backside was wet and we were running close to a broach. I glanced around the boat at the scenery and the wider expanse of water out here wanting only to sail backwards and forwards, appreciating the freedom from pressure and concentration necessary when sailing as efficiently as possible into the wind. I realised that I couldn't have cared less about coming fourth, tenth or seventeenth in the fleet; I just wanted to sail. Whatever it was that made a sailor into a racer, I didn't seem to have it when it came to wanting to win. Racing has its uses, but fulfilling the urge to beat the other guy wasn't one of them for me.

Years later, reading Robin Knox-Johnson's book 'A world of my own.' about his singlehanded non-stop circumnavigation I was struck with the special ending to the voyage. Having departed from Falmouth at its commencement, upon its conclusion when the Customs Officer jumped aboard to ask the 'time honoured' question 'Where from?' Robin was able to answer 'Falmouth!'

I pondered upon this. Sailing 30,000 miles of ocean simply to arrive back in the same place was in a way, cruising, even though he was in a race. I appreciated what was involved in his incredible effort of course, but I had to admit that it would have not been right for me. I thought that if ever I should sail around the world I would have to stop as frequently as possible to 'nose around' and absorb the spirit of each place that I came to. The only record which would interest me would be the slowest journey with the most stops.

If you construct a biggish boat in your back garden as I did, the passers-by will lean over your fence and ask if you are going to sail around the world someday. That is what back garden boat builders are supposed to do by their passing public; sail away into a palm fringed, grass-skirted sunset.

But why the WORLD? I'd ask. Why did it have to be the ultimate voyage? As a native of the British Isles I thought that maybe there were other places of interest to sail. Like where? I was asked. Well there were islands like the Farne Islands, the Shetlands, The Hebrides and the Orkneys. They were places that I knew little or nothing about, yet in WORLD terms they were right on my doorstep.

I wondered if I lived in Australia or South Africa, might I not be planning to sail to them as remote exotic locations. Their names called to me more strongly than the far Pacific islands, maybe because they were closer and more accessibly realisable targets in this stage of my cruising development.

Where are these meanderings leading to?

Well it's all about Cruising and some of the elements which separately, disjointedly, over the years slowly began to coalesce; odd incidents and ideas which were of little significance at the time, but which crept into my sub-conscious mind and lodged there. They explained to me why I needed to undertake a special voyage. I thought it would be nice to sail around Britain, but not in the way of the racers. In my sailing I didn't need another boat to triumph over; neither did I wish to sail past places of interest just because I had a schedule to keep. I needed scenery and adventure, places to explore, and places to linger if the fancy took me. Sunshine was not high on my list of priorities. 'Round Britain Slowly' would be my cruising dream.

The only snag with Utopian cruising concepts is TIME. Unfortunately I had to earn my keep and my family's too, just like any other working wage slave and at this hurdle I almost fell. How could I ever find the finance or the time required? I decided that I would have to take the journey one small step at a time and at the end of each stage try to overwinter the boat wherever she had reached, so that she would be ready to go on again the following season. If I was to visit the locations on my list it could take years, but they would be years of new and challenging sailing, instead of going up and down the same old river as I had been doing for some time.

The challenging and frightening idea would be for me, the local sailor, to sail down that river one day and instead of turning for home when the tide dictated, I should keep on going. I was going to be the weekend sailor whose wake-track didn't turn back. I was going to remain a weekend sailor still burdened with the responsibilities of western civilisation; not 'dropping out', not leaving it all behind, but rushing back to work on Monday mornings as usual. Now my occasional holiday-time sails would always be from different places to newer ones, so there was a chance that I might get shipwrecked before turning the first corner. There would be trials and tribulations, but there would be sights to see, boats to meet and lessons to learn. Lessons to share with other weekend cruising sailors like myself. Like you?

Trimarans.

Explanation for the readers of this book.

The first part of this next section has been rewritten to explain something about the trimaran for non-trimaran sailors. Most trimarans were and still are, primarily racing craft. As such they were at the forefront of the developing technologies involved in their construction. Composite structures were little known or understood in boatbuilding when I made this boat, but much of the pioneering work with this construction method was done in these craft. They were driven to the point of failure by brave people and this gave them a reputation of being dangerous. More recently trimarans have come to be more accepted though they are still comparatively rare. This short section dealt with some of the fears that sailors of more conventional craft may have had.

I still sail trimarans because no other craft feels like they do. They sail so smoothly and they are very responsive. Whenever I take anybody for a cruising sail they are impressed by the comfort and performance. Extreme speed is not the issue; they are so smooth that there is little sensation of speed. I usually warn new sailors, 'you will <u>not</u> feel real speed' only 'responsive smoothness' which is the nearest description that I have heard to conjuring up the sensation of being effortlessly and silently propelled by the wind.

MI issue 206. Episode 2.

<u>The trimaran.</u>

Starship my boat is a trimaran, and that is different. Sailing people have mixed feelings about these craft.

Let's quickly deal with the qualities of different boat types. Monohulls and trimarans like mine are very similar in the way that they sail. My boat is a monohull stabilised by two buoyant floats on the ends of two beams which go right across the boat, instead of the traditional ballast system of hanging a heavy weight on the bottom of the hull. The advantage is that the boat is considerably lighter, so it has a relatively shallow draught and less boat to drag through the water. Her best feature is that she is stiff and rarely exceeds ten or fifteen degrees of heel. This upright sailing stance has the added benefit of making her easy to steer as water pressure on either side of the hull remains more or less the same and she doesn't develop heavy weather helm. Her speed is not startling by modern standards because she has a relatively small rig and is always heavily loaded, but she is easily driven and responsive to handle. It is truer to say that she has speed 'potential' because under certain, rarely found conditions she is capable of moving quickly.

Catamarans and trimarans are always lumped together as 'Multihulls' but in actual fact cats feel quite different from monohulls and trimarans due to their rigid stability and the huge internal accommodation that cats offer in cruising versions. Another major comparison to make between the three craft types is in their 'Ultimate Safety' so it is best to swiftly deal with that issue now and then move on.

Under extreme conditions it would be possible to 'wave capsize' a trimaran when a properly loaded cat would probably survive. A cat however could be 'wind capsized' unless prudently handled in conditions where a trimaran would probably survive. In both cases there would still be a hull to cling to, a substantial life raft. Monohulls only need a relatively small hole in them and they can sink, often rapidly, and it doesn't have to be something exotic like hitting a killer whale, it's usually quite mundane like corroded seacocks. Once they have gone their occupants final hope is a lightweight, inflatable raft not using permanent ballast, the same principle as a multihull. Such comparisons only serve to prove that there is no such thing as a totally safe craft at sea and so most sailors carry on sailing the craft to which they are accustomed, choosing to enjoy their chosen qualities and rarely dwelling too long on thoughts of ultimate disasters.

Starship is to me just like your boat is to you. She is my holiday cruising home and she just happens to be a trimaran, so here is a brief description of how she came to be as she is.

Starship. External.

Starship measures 35 feet by 22 feet and was made of glassfibre and 'Airex' foam sandwich, by myself, working in my spare time in my back garden. She was based on an extremely successful design by Derek Kelsall which was called *'Three Legs of Mann'* A reference to the symbol of the Isle of Man where her owner/builder Nick Keig was based. When I was looking around for the design of a boat to construct, Nick Keig was dominating the racing world. In the 1975 'Azores and Back' race he covered 328 miles in 24 hours sailing singlehanded. This astonishing record stood for many years and the speed potential that it demonstrated was important to me as a cruiser. My requirement was for an easily driven hull that could do distances effortlessly, thus minimising my sea crossing times. I noted that the design wasn't a 'total' racing concept and I felt that I could modify it by making it a little fatter here and there. I used the broader cross sections of another Kelsall cruising trimaran called *Inkwasi* on a shorter overall length. I thought that if I could reduce the power of the rig I would actually have a 'Sheep in Wolf's clothing'. My success in this has often been proven when people take one look at her on the mooring and say 'Wow! She must be fast.' In fact she's quite docile.

On deck
At the bow there is a large anchor-well with a lid; my two anchors are of the C.Q.R. type. The main one 35 lbs. and the kedge is 19 lbs. They are both on Terylene warps with chain close to the anchor. A deck hatch gives the only access to the forward cabin, which is separated from the main accommodation by a major bulkhead in position as part of the forward crossbeam, which would act as a collision barrier if the boat sustained massive damage at the bow. Fixed cowl ventilators have screw-down mushroom ventilators inside them to give complete control. On the starboard side there is a powered vent for the toilet compartment. A long boathook pole is housed along the cabin top and beside it a long narrow window gives overhead light into the galley area below. The halliard winches are removed from the mast and placed on the cabin side just ahead of the cockpit. Halliards are led aft and can be secured in cleats placed just forward of the winches. The advantage of this system is to make the winches available for use with the spinnaker and to allow the steering person to assist in reefing etc. without leaving the wheel.

The wheel position and the main entrance area are completely protected by the doghouse. An overhead window allows sight of the rig from the steering position. A canopy can be rigged to completely seal off the cockpit area at night or in poor weather. During the day this folds back to create a seat on the forward edge of the aft cabin roof, it is comfortably padded and has pockets to house spinnaker sheets etc. There is a single self-tailing sheet winch just behind the helmsman's seat. Both genoa sheets lead to it. The port side winch controls the Genoa reefing system. The pushpit rails are used to carry horseshoe lifebuoys and man-overboard equipment. There are folding steps and a lifting daggerboard rudder angled forwards for balance, as well as an outboard bracket on the transom.

The rig.
There is a conventional masthead sloop with roller genoa and roller boom with a through-mast handle. A small inner (storm) staysail may be set to make her cutter rigged. The mast has a single diamond spreader; there are steps up it and the cap shrouds go out to the floats to give a broad base for mast support. There is an extra forestay ahead of the genoa whose function is to hold the mast up if/when the genoa roller fails, or requires maintenance involving dismantling. A radar reflector is permanently fixed at the masthead. There are masthead navigation lights and a deck floodlight.

The hull
As it is foam sandwich it has no space-taking internal stringers. It is warm in winter and cool in summer, sound deadened and it is like sailing a boat wearing its own lifejacket as there is a boat hull within another boat hull separated by closed cell foam. The bottom of the mainhull has a small skeg to take grounding abrasions. Although centreboard and daggerboards were originally fitted to the boat they were found not to justify themselves as the performance was perfectly adequate and space and weight saving could be gained by their removal. The boards were removed. At her deepest she floats in two feet of water, but most of her can be in even shallower water than that. The floats just clear the water at rest.

External crossbeams are of hollow box section steel, hot-dipped galvanised after fabrication. They give minimal profile, low drag to both air and water allowing the boat to be dismantled for road transport if this should ever be necessary. They are clipped on top and bottom with one inch stainless steel bolts and are stayed to the hull with stainless rigging wires. The space between the floats and the mainhull is covered in webbing netting to provide an open platform for the storage of the inflatable tender etc. when under way. The nets allow conventional guard rails to be dispensed with.

The floats are of solid glass construction with strengthening stringers. They have three sealed compartments in each with a long central area which is accessible through screw-down deck hatches. They provide excellent storage for fenders, warps, planks, fuel and indeed any grubby smelly objects, remote from the main hull.

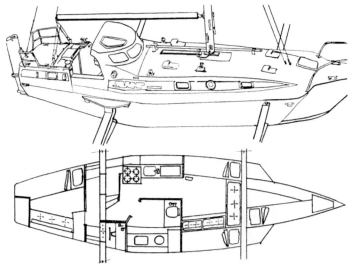

The engine is an Arona (Italian) 13hp diesel with a traditional conventional drive through a stern tube to a folding propeller. Whilst being compact and lightweight it gives good thrust astern or ahead and never cavitates (a potential problem with light, shallow draught craft). A 4HP longshaft outboard is used to power the inflatable tender. When sailing, this motor is housed on the transom of the mainhull as a belt and braces measure, so that it can be used in an emergency to power the mother craft at about four knots in still water. This facility has proved invaluable on several occasions.

Below deck.

<u>Aft cabin.</u>

Just inside the transom is a locker with an internal door as well as a transom door. It stores emergency equipment for use if the boat should be inverted. The locker has internal electrical leads so that a small generator may be operated inside it, quietly, to charge batteries, or provide 240v ship's power etc. The cabins are lined with foam backed vinyl and all major woodwork is teak, or sycamore strips for white ceilings, inside and out. All floors including the steering position are carpeted. The aft cabin has a permanent berth and a convertible seat/berth. All navigational equipment is housed here next to the cockpit. There is a chemical toilet and access to the engine which is beneath the cockpit floor. The engine space is power ventilated and is gained from the aft cabin.

Cockpit.

Beneath inward-facing cockpit seats there are self-draining lockers for gas storage, diesel, outboard fuel etc. The helm-person tucks into a cosy steering position with engine controls and compass just before them, as well as a shelf packed with food 'goodies' to while away the watches. It is possible to sail without wearing oilskins. This protected wheelhouse is rigidly constructed and strong enough to walk on. It allows on-deck crew to walk the full length of the boat from stem to stern without having to drop down into the cockpit. The narrow seating area behind the wheelhouse can be sealed off with a canopy, thus making the whole internal length of the boat accessible as protected accommodation.

Entrance and Bathroom.

Protection for the main companionway entrance means that it doesn't leak. Clipped just inside are the echo sounder and VHF radio. It is wide enough for two people to pass. The galley is immediately below to port, there is a gas oven and sink/drainer with powered water supply from a tank beneath the floor. To starboard the most unusual feature of the boat is the bathroom, which IS a ROOM not a sentry box. It is possible to dress and undress with comfort and privacy and it is greatly appreciated by ladies aboard. There is a marine toilet, sink and a shower well in the floor.

Saloon.

The main saloon has wing berths on either side, a seat across the front of it and down the starboard side. Underneath the port wing berth there is an escape hatch to allow access in or out of the cabin in the event of inversion. A fold-down table can be used to convert the seating area into a double berth. All around there are cupboards and storage beneath seats and floor.

Forward cabin.

The forward cabin is accessed from its own deck hatch. It has a long pipe berth. There is a small opening window giving communication through the bulkhead to the main cabin. This fore cabin is popular as the occupant can choose to be involved with the rest of the crew by opening the window, or can secure privacy by closing it, but most importantly they can't easily be involved in washing-up or cooking. The forward cabin is also used as a dump for spare sails.

Early Planning – an appeal for help – and an invitation for the brave.

The following section is an abbreviated version of a very unusual offer that was made to the readers of Multihull International magazine, when this account was first published.

It is one thing to dream of castles in the air, but it quite a different thing to actually build those castles. If the job is to be done, at some stage one has to pick up the first brick and put it in position. A cruise around Britain is a comfortable dream, but to DO it there has to be a day when one steps aboard and casts off the last rope, knowing that years will pass before that rope can be secured again in the same place, providing fate doesn't first intervene.

The Grand Plan for the first season's sailing was to concentrate on the English South Coast, slowly cruising its length right out to Land's End and beyond to the Scilly Isles, then returning to Cornwall to find a place to leave the boat for the winter. The second season would take the boat up the Irish Sea through Wales to Scotland.

An appeal.

I know my little patch of the East Coast very well and I would be able to advise a visiting cruiser where to go for reasonable mooring fees, how to access public transport, chandlers, shops and yard facilities. This is easy to do for the place where you live. But how do you get started in a new place? To some extent there is an element of luck, which I am not overburdened with and there's an element of finance (with a boat my size, I am destitute). So if you live somewhere along my route and can help me with local advice I will be grateful to receive it. You must surely have some tips about the places that I should visit or the secret anchorages that I might wriggle into. Descriptions in pilot books tend to peter out as soon as the river meanders too much or becomes only tidally accessible, but my boat has the ability to creep further upriver, sliding in on the rising tide and sitting upright when aground providing the river bed isn't too rocky. As an East Coast ditch crawler the head of the creek is often the most fascinating place for me, where prices are more reasonable, the service and the smiles are more forthcoming. The very purpose of this cruise is to stop and see the natural beauty of places, but with so many places to explore, how can I choose? Maybe you can help me?

An Unusual Invitation.

As this story unfolds I hope that it will be an interesting one, but there is a chance that it could be very different from any cruise story that you have ever read, because you can be a part of it. If you contact me, my summer cruise is flexible enough to take you as crew or divert to visit you if you live in my target area.

This is a new concept in yachting journalism, so remember where you saw it first. There are no excuses left for you. We're inviting <u>you</u> to get up, get out and *do* it. Come along and actually get wet, or get suntanned; secluded stream or ocean roar; beach or jagged rock; crowded harbour or silent isolation, you can read about <u>you</u> being there in the pages of this magazine. To transport yourself from your armchair onto my cockpit seat with the wheel in your hands you must first contact me.

I then gave details of how contact could be made and there were readers who took up some of the offers being made...

<u>Starship additional information.</u>

When selling Starship I prepared drawings showing the equipment and layout on board. Here are the drawings with the divisions being on the main bulkheads. They are not necessarily to exact scale in relation to each other.

1. <u>Bow section</u>.

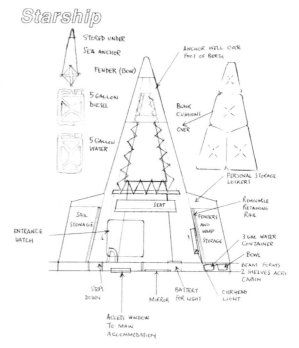

Midship section.

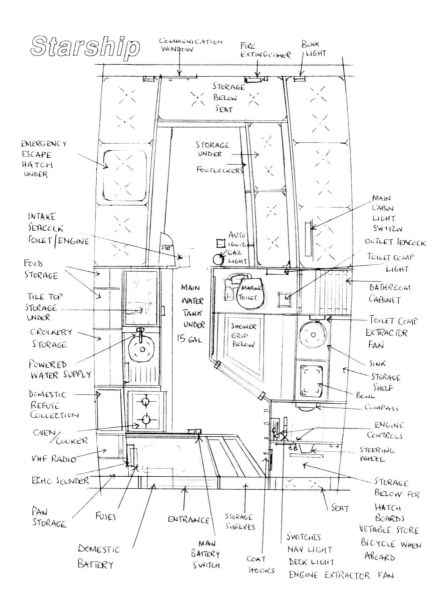

Starship

COMMUNICATION WINDOW
FIRE EXTINGUISHER
BUNK LIGHT

STORAGE BELOW SEAT

EMERGENCY ESCAPE HATCH UNDER

STORAGE UNDER
FOOTLOCKERS

MAIN CABIN LIGHT 8w +12w
OUTLET SEACOCK

INTAKE SEACOCK TOILET/ENGINE

AUTO IGNITION GAZ LIGHT
STEP

MARINE TOILET

TOILET COMP LIGHT

FOOD STORAGE

MAIN WATER TANK UNDER 15 GAL

BATHROOM CABINET

TILE TOP STORAGE UNDER

SHOWER GRID BELOW

TOILET COMP EXTRACTOR FAN

CROCKERY STORAGE

SINK

POWERED WATER SUPPLY

STORAGE SHELF

DOMESTIC REFUSE COLLECTION

BOWL
COMPASS

OVEN/COOKER

ENGINE CONTROLS

VHF RADIO

STEERING WHEEL

ECHO SOUNDER

STORAGE BELOW FOR HATCH BOARDS

PAN STORAGE
FUSES
ENTRANCE
STORAGE SHELVES
SEAT
VETABLE STORE BICYCLE WHEN ABOARD

DOMESTIC BATTERY
MAIN BATTERY SWITCH
COAT HOOKS
SWITCHES NAV LIGHT DECK LIGHT
ENGINE EXTRACTOR FAN

Stern section

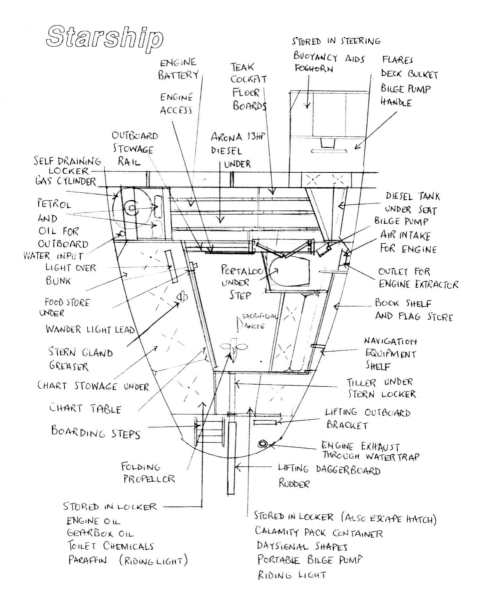

Starship

STORED IN STEERING
BUOYANCY AIDS
FOGHORN

FLARES
DECK BUCKET
BILGE PUMP
HANDLE

ENGINE
BATTERY

ENGINE
ACCESS

TEAK
COCKPIT
FLOOR
BOARDS

OUTBOARD
STOWAGE
RAIL

ARENA 13HP
DIESEL
UNDER

SELF DRAINING
LOCKER
GAS CYLINDER

PETROL
AND
OIL FOR
OUTBOARD
WATER INPUT
LIGHT OVER
BUNK

DIESEL TANK
UNDER SEAT
BILGE PUMP
AIR INTAKE
FOR ENGINE

OUTLET FOR
ENGINE EXTRACTOR

PORTALOO
UNDER
STEP

FOOD STORE
UNDER

SACRIFICIAL
ANODE

BOOK SHELF
AND FLAG STORE

WANDER LIGHT LEAD

STERN GLAND
GREASER

NAVIGATION
EQUIPMENT
SHELF

CHART STOWAGE UNDER

TILLER UNDER
STERN LOCKER

CHART TABLE

LIFTING OUTBOARD
BRACKET

BOARDING STEPS

ENGINE EXHAUST
THROUGH WATER TRAP

FOLDING
PROPELLER

LIFTING DAGGERBOARD
RUDDER

STORED IN LOCKER
ENGINE OIL
GEARBOX OIL
TOILET CHEMICALS
PARAFFIN (RIDING LIGHT)

STORED IN LOCKER (ALSO ESCAPE HATCH)
CALAMITY PACK CONTAINER
DAYSIGNAL SHAPES
PORTABLE BILGE PUMP
RIDING LIGHT

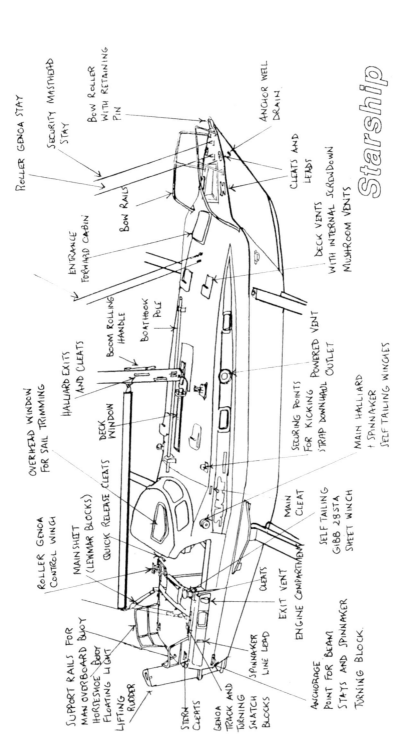

ROLLER GENOA STAY

SECURITY MASTHEAD STAY

BOW ROLLER WITH RETAINING PIN

ANCHOR WELL DRAIN

CLEATS AND LEADS

BOW RAILS

ENTRANCE FORWARD CABIN

DECK VENTS WITH INTERNAL SCREWDOWN

MUSHROOM VENTS

BOOM ROLLING HANDLE

BOATHOOK POLE

HALLIARD EXITS AND CLEATS

SECURING POINTS FOR KICKING STRAP DOWNHAUL

POWERED VENT

OUTLET

MAIN HALLIARD + SPINNAKER

SELF TAILING WINGNES

OVERHEAD WINDOW FOR SAIL TRIMMING

DECK WINDOW

MAIN CLEAT

SELF TAILING GIBB 28 STA SHEET WINCH

ROLLER GENOA CONTROL WINGS

MAINSHEET (LEWMAR BLOCKS)

QUICK RELEASE CLEATS

CLEATS

EXIT VENT

ENGINE COMPARTMENT

SUPPORT RAILS FOR MAN OVERBOARD BUOY

HORSESHOE BOAT FLOATING LIGHT

LIFTING RUDDER

STERN CLEATS

GENOA TRACK AND TURNING SNATCH BLOCKS

SPINNAKER LINE LEAD

ANCHORAGE POINT FOR BEAM STAYS AND SPINNAKER TURNING BLOCK.

Starship

Owners.

Starship was sold to **Malcolm Legg**
1995. Malcolm died in about 1997.
He made many changes to the boat.
These are some.
The whole boat was painted white.
The doghouse cut off and a fabric
structure replaced it.

The beams were remade in aluminium.
The engine was changed
Fins were added to the floats
The trampolines were changed to fabric.
Cockpit remodelled to reduce the aft cabin
There were radical changes internally
including cutting away the forward
watertight bulkhead. This may have been a
modification too far as it greatly removed
her emergency buoyancy at the bow.

She was kept mainly in the South Devon/Plymouth area

Norman Reed bought her and she moved to the Thames estuary. She spent much of her time based at the Greenwich Yacht Club on a mooring close to the London Dome or O2 arena. She remained fundamentally unchanged in his ownership. He cruised in the area and visited the River Deben, her home river. He died about 2004.

Richard Topham bought her and she moved to be mainly in the Bristol Channel and South Devon area. Richard did a great deal of work on her, restoring and updating her. When Richard came to sell *Starship* in 2012 he drew up a specification which showed her to be in very good condition with much of her equipment updated.

　　　　One major change that Richard made was to put a 50ft mast and rig on the boat. She had always been able to carry such a rig, but I had erred very much on the side of caution with my 36ft mast. My small rig meant that she never really began to move until the wind reached about F4; with the new rig she performed much better in lower wind speeds. Richard met the owner of *Three Legs of Mann* at that time and the two boats sailed together. It was very pleasing for me to hear that under all-round sailing conditions *Starship* was the equal and sometimes better than *3 Legs* the very boat that had inspired her.

Kenneth was her last owner who only had her for a short while. He had her re-lined inside and replaced the trampolines.

Prior to her final sale she was in excellent condition as can be seen in this description.

Richard Topham's Specification 2012.

OVERVIEW:
She has a small comfortable double berth forward and an adequate pilot berth to starboard below.
Furnishings were renewed 2006 and are Rubber Backed Marine Grade.
A full size chart table and chart store are located to Starboard.
The aft cabin is a cosy double with 6" medium density foam and 3" memory foam (lush).
Both doubles have anti sweat 1" sprung matting bases. There is ample storage and access to engine water sea-cocks below this berth.
There is a Solar (hang up shower) which we use in the cockpit.
Stainless Gas Hob/Grill with control protector bar + gas Alarm.
A 3-way Chest Fridge to port with a toilet/washroom to starboard of the companion way.

CROSS BEAMS:
These are welded Marine Grade Aluminium box sections with tang supports connected to large internal hoop/u frames making them very stiff extremely strong and relatively light (the rig hardly moves tack to tack). Surveyors note; "These are the best I have seen!"
Starship has the benefit of full (solvent free epoxy) osmosis protection below the water line, and expensive but maintenance free Coppercoat antifouling system, with confirmation of process/receipt from a professional coatings company (10+ years life left as never sanded).

EQUIPMENT:
Starship is equipped with Cobra DSC Radio (2009), Furuno Radar, Nasa Log/Echo, Lowrance Chart Plotter, Fish Finder, Magellan GPS, Programmable Autohelm (older type but superb). Later type 'more efficient' Eberspacher programmable Blown air diesel heating with a

pipe to the helms feet, New water tank/piping with Carbon/Silver filter (all ships water tastes as good as it gets).

MAST & STEERING:
Was replaced in 2007/2010. A 'Z Spars' Mast now stands 50ft from the deck with LED Tri colour and Anchor light. There is a 'Stack Pack' (2008) with integral collar and a Hydraulic Boom Vang (no topping lift required). Jibe preventers fitted.
She has a Full Battened Mainsail. Headsails are older but serviceable and set well (see pictures). An 11m x 9.3m Spinnaker with Snuffer.

RUDDER:
The rise and fall rudder (controlled from the cockpit for shoaling) was replaced with an increase of 20% 2010. This provides a nice balance for the extra power of the rig and she steers beautifully on Hydraulic wheel steering. The bearings were also recut.

GROUND TACKLE:
A Lofrans Anchor Winch was fitted 2006. It lifts the 35lb Delta Anchor 2008 with 15ft 12mm chain to a Stainless heavy duty Swivel then 8mm chain woven to Anchorplait. A Fortress Guardian stern anchor is also carried with an alloy kedge stored below.

BASICS:
The main hull and sponsons were wet bead blasted using the famed 'Farrow System' to bring her back to the substrate. The above waterline areas were then re-coated as follows:
2 coats epoxy primer, 2 coats epoxy high protection, 2 coats 2 pack polyurethane. Coarse kiln dried sand was added to give the decks a final slip resistant finish.
Upgrades as per survey requirements: New switched whale pumps with non-return valves to the outlets and armoured power supply cable were fitted in each sponson.
There is a rope cutter on the prop shaft.

TO DO:
The shore-side mains power would benefit from an upgrade (perhaps re-wire to trip switches). The present owner rarely uses it and has two earth leak protectors available.

The netting is ok for dinghy storage (we use harnesses on the jackstays) but has been repaired and will eventually need replacement. There is also the possibility of a stunningly beautiful and extremely well priced south coast mooring.

From the owner:
Overview. *Starship* was by Paul Constantine who wrote a vast number of articles about his UK circumnavigation and exploits in boating magazines. He has expressed that he wishes to stay in touch with the vessels future owners.
She was designed by Derek Kelsall a legend in Multihull design. Her full evolution and history can be traced with many documents available.

Beginning and End.

These Beginning sections are extracted from the account of the complete building of *Starship*.

Beginning.

A journey of a thousand miles begins with one single step.
An elderly lady visitor to my completed boat could not believe that I had made it myself. She kept asking how I could start on something like this. Where did I begin? Eventually to convince herself she insisted, then demanded that she should be shown, exactly, the very first bit of the boat that I had made, so that she could construct her image from that point. Without such a reference she could not bring herself to understand how it was possible.

How does one start? What is the first step? I felt that the mental planning and preparation were the first stages, but many people engage in these exercises without becoming boat builders. Perhaps the first couple of concrete physical steps towards building were both carried out with a pen. I wrote to designers for study plans enclosing sums of money. The money gave me a feeling of commitment, of embarking upon the project. I had a strong feeling of destiny when I actually picked up my pen to write the big cheque for the designer. Once I had paid this money I could not go back. I was sure that I had taken the first irrevocable step when I slipped that letter with its cheque into the post box. After this I knew without question that I had crossed a boundary. I had started and to start is half the battle.

<u>Launching</u>. Some thoughts.

Think of the mechanics of the launch. Does the mast go up before or after? When will you apply the anti-fouling? How can the steering be tested to see if it will operate correctly. Do we smash the bottle or do we pour it? How easy is it to smash a full bottle? How safe is it? A launching could be the formula for endless sleepless nights, but I couldn't afford to miss my sleep, nor could I afford an elaborate ceremony. Finally, I couldn't afford to miss checking all the bilges the moment she touched the water. This very important job could only be done really well at the moment of contact. If there was to be a launching then I wanted to be head down in the bilge which isn't within the spirit of a traditional launch.

The final deciding factors were finance and time. I could not bring the boat to launch readiness including the mast, rig, sails and steering within the time available, yet some kind of a ceremony was required The traditional launching ceremony was too complex and I am a simple fellow that prefers to tackle my problems one at a time rather than all at once. The **Launch**, meaning putting the boat in the water for the first time was a technical operation and I decided to do it with only a couple of close friends to assist me. If anything went wrong the boat could be withdrawn from the water, whereas if all went well I could proceed with subsequent steps. The craft would then be ready for a separate little ceremony, that of **Naming** the boat which would involve the usual bottle of champagne and perhaps, if the preparation was complete, the boat could be moved under power for the first time. When I finally hit upon this simplified order of events I began to sleep more easily.

From. <u>The Launch</u>.

I launched on Saturday July 21 It wasn't a grand affair. She had been brought round to the top of the slipway on the previous day and I had antifouled her in the evening. She had her floats folded, but when she was halfway down the slipway and all obstructions were finally clear, we pulled out and fixed the stays on her starboard float and edged her down into the water.

From. <u>The Naming</u>.

On the morning of July 26 I went down to the boat very early, for I still had the rudder and the tiller to connect up.

In the early afternoon my parents and my wife and family arrived with snacks and champagne. They had worked so hard in preparation. My children had been involved in making flags to trim the boat and they were thrilled and excited to see their handiwork decorating her.

Friends began to arrive and the atmosphere developed into that of a traditional launching. I was secure in the knowledge that my boat wasn't going to sink.

At the appointed time my wife and I crossed onto the mainhull carrying the champagne bottle. The words were spoken and the champagne emptied onto the bow and then over the name on the side of the deckhouse for the benefit of the assembled cameras.

The engine was started. With my heart in my mouth I asked to be pushed away from the quay and as the last line came aboard we were suddenly free. It was at that precise moment that all those bucketsful of resin, those miles of fibreglass, the tins of paint, sheets of plywood, boxes of bolts, screws, tubes, rope and numerous other inert materials magically transformed into a living object capable of unaided movement.

… And many years later.

The End.

On April 5 2013 I was informed that the relatively new owner of *Starship*, taking her from the Solent to the West Country had engine failure at Portland Harbour and the boat was washed onto the rocks of the breakwater. I understood that the port float was ripped off as was the rudder blade and the fin from starboard float, resulting in it being badly holed. She was towed off and the owner and crew rescued. The holed float supported the lifeboat crew as it had buoyancy tanks in the ends. Effectively she had no floats and she capsized under tow and sank when totally filled with water.

She was not the same boat that I had built. She had been greatly modified. She was fitted with a big rig and 50ft mast. The internal forward bulkhead had been cut away to give direct access from the main cabin into forepeak berth, thus losing a big flotation bubble. She had similarly had her doghouse cut off. Film of the event could be seen by putting: Weymouth lifeboat, then,1st ILB launch 03/04/2013 into a search engine where the event was recorded on YouTube.

When I watched the video I could immediately see that if her port side been fendered, so that she could be towed **alongside** a rescue boat she would have entered harbour and survived. I could also see that if she had sunk in relatively shallow water she could easily be recovered. Her mast and rig could be carefully unfastened and recovered by scuba divers. A couple of flotation bags would lift her neutrally buoyant hull and she could be recovered by pumping out, because there was no fundamental damage to the mainhull. A couple of polystyrene blocks attached to a plank secured to her port cross beams could replace the missing float for her to be returned to shore where she could easily be restored.

It was a woeful, heart-rending loss.

The owner sent me this email.

Very sad about Starship. I talked through the events with the Insurer's surveyor who seemed to agree that there was nothing I could have done to save Starship. The engine had ceased to function (turned out we had picked up rope near the harbour entrance). Having lost way, unfurling the foresail would have resulted in impact bow first, thereby denying the protection that was offered by the outriggers. The main had suffered damage during the journey (broken from the clew and the gybe preventer on the boom had broken so jury rigged a new gybe preventer and stowed the mainsail.

I have no idea where Starship is. She has either sunk to the bottom or has been cast ashore somewhere by the wind and tide.

Kenneth.

The wreck of *Starship* may well be on the seabed in the vicinity of Portland Harbour, but the **spirit** of *Starship* for all those associated with her over the years, lives on in the words of this book.